SAY YES

DISCOVERING PURPOSE, PEACE, AND ABUNDANCE IN YOUR DAILY LIFE

AMDG!
Christina Semmens

CHRISTINA SEMMENS

Cover Design: Debbie O'Bryne

Photograph of author by Rachel Clarke Photography

Paperback ISBN: 978-1-64746-269-7
Hardback ISBN: 978-1-64746-270-3
EBook ISBN: 978-1-64746-271-0

Library of Congress Control Number (LCCN): 2020908510

To All Those Who Have, and Continue
to Inspire, Challenge and Accompany
Me in the Pursuit of Holiness

—This Journey Doesn't Happen Without You

TABLE OF CONTENTS

Foreword. ix

Acknowledgments. xi

Introduction xiii

PARTE 1: DISCOVERING DEEP PURPOSE

Chapter 1   It's a Process, Not A Program 1

Chapter 2   Whose Am I? 5

Chapter 3   The Call To Holiness. 11

Chapter 4   Your Unique and Unrepeatable Mission 18

Chapter 5   Come and See. 29

PARTE 2: ENCOUNTERING AUTHENTIC PEACE

Chapter 6   The Four Steps to Holiness 41

Chapter 7   Step One—Daily Prayer and Meditation. 44

Chapter 8   Answering the Phone 48

Chapter 9   Step Two--Living the Life of Grace 54

Chapter 10   Living the Fullness of the Life of Grace 61

Chapter 11   The Life of Grace Flowing Nonstop 66

Chapter 12   Step Three—Growing Daily in Virtue 72

Chapter 13   Step By Step, Day By Day 78

Chapter 14   Step Four—Abandoning Ourselves to
God's Will. 87

Chapter 15   Hitting God's Will on the "DOT" 92

PARTE 3: EMBRACING ABIDING ABUNDANCE

Chapter 16   The Myth of the Lone Ranger. 105

Chapter 17   The Power of a Soul Friend 112

Chapter 18   Saints Come in Clusters 118

Chapter 19   Friendship Hidden in Plain Sight 125

Chapter 20   The Power of Story 135

Chapter 21   Sharing the Divine Life Within. 142

Chapter 22   The Crown Jewel. 150

Chapter 23   Living the Consecration 158

Chapter 24   "All In" 168

Say Yes Checklist. 179

Next Steps and Resources 181

About the Author 183

Endnotes. 185

FOREWORD

This book is an action plan. In it, you will find all the direction and encouragement you need to live life to the full as a 21st century Catholic Christian.

It is also an exhortation.

So often we fail to find happiness in God, or even to seek for it - as if He were not enough, or were inaccessible to us. What is it that we are missing? Why do we fail to grasp the treasure of grace and of divine intimacy which He places right in front of us? Could it be for lack of encouragement?

Christina Semmens delights in showing us what is possible and how to get there. In my own life, she has proven herself a loyal friend and a trustworthy guide in matters of the heart, mind, and soul. God has given her the mission of serving others through prayer and accompaniment, and this book is a rich compilation of spiritual "best practices" which are the fruit of experience and are shared with love.

The Christian life is never easy, but it is richly rewarding both now and in eternity. Only the Catholic Church offers us all of the tools we need to fully receive the gifts that God has for us. Holiness is within our grasp. God wants to have a relationship with each one of us, and desires for us to live incredible, heroic, meaningful, saintly lives. This truth is beautifully illuminated throughout these pages, which show us that holiness - and adventure - is possible in every time and place.

Amid the many solutions which have been proposed for the spiritual malaise of our time, saying "yes" to holiness is perhaps the simplest and the most necessary. Only by saying "yes" to God can we become saints. The world does not need mediocrity or half-hearted love; it needs your heart to be made new in Christ. This is the greatest gift you can give to the Church and to the world. Yours is an unrepeatable story; your life is an unrepeatable gift.

I hope, dear reader, that you will approach with an open mind and heart the rich treasury of practical wisdom contained in these pages. Be encouraged, that you might freely receive what has been freely given: an opportunity to encounter Jesus Christ in a truly life-altering way. It is the Lord who asks; it is for you to respond. Don't hold back - say yes!

--Father Joshua Altonji, Chaplain
Saint Stephen the Martyr Catholic Church
Diocese of Birmingham, Alabama

ACKNOWLEDGMENTS

I have been blessed with many people coming in and out of my life for various reasons and seasons who have impacted me in profound ways. There are too many to mention, so I will not try to cover them all, but there are a few that I would like to touch on.

First and foremost, I'm thankful to my parents, especially my mom, for raising me to believe in myself, live a life of integrity regardless of cost, and encouraging me to always strive to be the best that I can possibly be. Mom, I'm still working to become half of who you already are—a beautiful, intelligent and capable woman with a heart for others.

For my husband Paul, who has supported me in countless ways, and shown me from the very first day we met what true servant leadership is. Your love has enabled me to reach for my dreams—even when I wasn't sure myself what they were. For the sacrifices you have made to build the life we have, and for all the ways that you continue to strive to become fully the man God created you to be--know that I am in awe and humbled at having been given the gift of you as my husband, partner and friend. I choose to love you today and always.

For my sons--Sean, Rob and Mike. Thank you for your love, support and inspiration. Having each of you as part of my life is precious gift, and know that my efforts here are to try and help create a better world for you and all those you love in the years ahead.

I've had so many incredible coaches, mentors, and colleagues from whom I have learned so much, and I'm eternally grateful to them, particularly my spiritual directors. I can't even begin to describe how each of you has changed the trajectory of my life, so thank you for sharing your time and wisdom. And a special thank you to my athletic coaches—you each taught me what it is to be tough, disciplined, and to never stop fighting for my dreams no matter what.

To all the priests who have played a significant role in my life: my Jesuit "priesty boys" through the years—especially Fr. Michael Zeps, SJ, Fr Gregory Carlson, SJ and Fr Andy Alexander, SJ--for your friendship, inspiration, and the laughter shared through the years; my current and former pastors, especially Fr Phil O'Kennedy, Fr Mark Spruill, and Fr Rick Chenault, Jr.—know of my love, admiration and gratitude for each of you personally, and also for freely sharing of yourselves and showing me how to lovingly shepherd God's people. I am humbled by knowing all of you, and I hope that my efforts here help to make our work in the vineyard a little bit easier.

Finally, to my AVI Family, especially the Brothers and Sisters of the Apostles of Interior Life. Thank you for loving me and giving this child of God an eternal family along with a temporary place to call home on this side of eternity. Know of my hopes and prayers that someday we will be able to celebrate together around the Heavenly Banquet Table.

Ad Maiorem Dei Gloriam!
Christina

INTRODUCTION

"Begin at the beginning. That is the only way to tell a story."

— attributed to William Shakespeare

So, where to begin? As William Shakespeare says, *"Begin at the beginning."* I will, but I want to take a page from Shakespeare himself and set the stage so hopefully everything in this book will make greater sense and resonate more deeply for you.

Let me tell you a quick story about my own journey.

Before I set out on this path, it probably appeared to the world I had it all together.

Going through high school, I was a capable student and athlete. I graduated in the top ten percent of my class of more than 300 students, played three different varsity sports, and was atop my age group in local area triathlons. I was musically talented, singing, and playing instruments. I founded a chapter of a national service club, volunteered in numerous projects, and was named "Senior of the Year." All of this resulted in my being selected to receive a national four-year Army ROTC Scholarship. That accomplishment led to my being able to attend a prestigious private liberal arts college, Marquette University in Milwaukee, Wisconsin.

What all the successes and accolades covered up, though, was a fearful, insecure, and anxious little girl whose biological father had rejected her. I bit my nails and worried constantly I would fail my classes. A complete fake as I pretended that I didn't care about guys noticing me yet trying to prove I was worthy of being loved. Overwhelmed by the demands of trying to manage my life on my own for the first time, and almost despairing I would ever have the happy life I dreamed of.

But then something happened that changed my life forever.

I encountered the great love of my life. Or more accurately, *He* encountered me, right near the end of my freshman year in college.

At the time, I was not practicing any faith tradition. I had been raised Presbyterian but had pretty much walked away from any belief in God by the time I graduated high school. Near the end of the spring of my freshman year, though, God and I had made peace. Or at least I was willing to acknowledge His existence. But my view of Jesus in the grand scheme of things was just that he was a good moral teacher who lived long ago, nothing more.

The weekend leading up to Easter, though, a friend invited me to attend Good Friday service with her, and since I had nothing better to do that night, I said yes.

The service was at Gesu Church, a huge gothic style cathedral located right on Marquette's campus. As I walked in, I saw a life-sized cross set up down in front of the altar which was going to be used for veneration later in the service. But when I saw the cross, I couldn't get past the last row.

I found myself kneeling in the last row, and as I knelt there, Jesus said clear as day, "I love you. And I died for you."

I started crying as I asked Him, "How is that possible? Don't you know I am not worthy of that love? My own father doesn't want anything to do with me, why would you?"

Jesus replied, "I love you so much, Christina, that I would have died for you—even if you were the only person living on the earth."

That was it. I was an emotional wreck. I continued to cry, but as I did, I felt Jesus' love and peace envelop me and completely fill my heart, mind, and soul. In those moments, I experienced authentic love, peace, and fulfillment.

And my life hasn't been the same since.

I don't remember much of the service that night, but from that moment onward, I wanted more of that love, peace, and fulfillment, so I made a promise to Jesus that I would put Him first in my life as I tried to serve Him with every fiber of my being.

The subsequent journey has taken me in many directions. First was my going through RCIA (Rite of Christian Initiation of Adults) and being received into the Roman Catholic Church on March 25, 1989.

But although I now had profoundly encountered Jesus, and could receive Him in the sacraments of His Church, I didn't realize I was still *a long way* from being transformed into His image. But I didn't know what or how to go about trying to draw closer to God or become more like Jesus each day anyway, so I inadvertently reverted back to *my* ways of doing things.

Ways that were still rooted in a disordered mind, heart, and soul.

A mind that went seeking the solutions offered by the world to try and calm my anxieties and worries—self-help books and programs, therapy, and yoga.

A heart still seeking to earn love and prove I was worthy of it by doing all of what I thought would please God. I got a Bachelor, and later Master of Arts degrees in both History and Theology; I poured myself into various ministries of the Church even as I served as an officer in the United States Army; I pursued certifications in the various areas where I ministered—Youth Ministry, Human Sexuality, Theology of the Body, Catholic

Social Teaching, and, most recently, Spiritual Mentorship, to try and serve people better.

A soul that was convinced I should (and could!) do it all on my own. The adage of "God helps those who helps themselves" was paramount in my spiritual life. I wasn't relying upon God or asking Him what HE thought I should be doing. Oh, I would spend time in prayer—but only when I needed something. I was like the kid at college who would only call home if I needed some money to take care of an emergency.

And because of it, I wasn't being transformed into the image of Jesus. I was still living a worldly life, pursuing things other than God that I thought would *really* bring me happiness and fulfillment—prestige, success, wealth, comfort, while thinking I was living a Christian life.

But in reality, I was living on my terms, not God's.

And because of it, I made a lot of mistakes by causing a lot of pain and suffering, especially to those closest to me. I committed grave sin over the years by breaking every single one of the Ten Commandments, not a boast but a reality.

I made other things first in my life other than God. I took His name in vain, I missed Mass and failed to keep the Sabbath holy. I did not honor my father and mother, used contraception, had an affair, and got a divorce. I married outside the Church. I stole, lied, and coveted that which is not my own.

All these things came as a result of my trying to do things *my* way and trying to do everything with only *my* power vs being obedient to God's will and truly relying upon Him and being an instrument of the Holy Spirit.

It is apparent to me *now* that every time I stumble and fall since I encountered Jesus on Good Friday more than three decades ago, it is because I revert back to that fearful, anxious, worried little girl who needed to prove I was worthy of love, rather than living as the beloved daughter in union with her Father's desires for her and who has been given everything necessary to live a life of purpose, peace and abundance.

Over time, He has revealed His plan for me, and taught me how to draw close to Him and rely upon Him in all things. I am no longer fearful, anxious or worried about the events of daily life. I am at peace.

I know beyond a doubt that I am loved beyond measure, beloved daughter of my Heavenly Father. Despite my sins and failures, my Lord has never failed or faltered in His love or mercy for me, and been extraordinarily patient with my weaknesses. In fact, like Saint Paul, God has graciously still used me to help bring about His plan in the lives of those around me in spite of those weaknesses.

He has been my strength, my light, and my salvation, and has given me all the graces I have ever needed—even when I have doubted Him—and He has showered me with even more graces and blessings than I could ever have imagined. The result now is I am living a life full of purpose, rich in peace, and overflowing in abundance.

But the biggest piece of knowledge He has shared as I have walked the Way with Him is the extraordinary life I am leading isn't just for me.

It's what God desires for *everyone*.

For *each and every one* of His sons and daughters.

And that includes you.

Yes, *you*.

And if it is possible for someone like me to do this, I know with, and through God's grace, you can, too.

I am a person who likes to get to the point of things. Give me the bottom line upfront and paint me the vison of why something should be done, and then I'll get to it. And when I say get to it, I mean I tend to go all in—the 110% kind of in.

I have been that way with my spiritual life, too.

My life has been God preparing and helping me develop my particular way to communicate with others in a clear, concise, and straightforward manner what they can do to pursue holiness and become a saint.

During the last three decades, no matter what profession, field, occupation, activity, or sport I have participated in or been involved with, I have encountered serious people of faith desiring to grow closer to God and become holy men and women, too. But, like me, they would find themselves fighting discouragement, worry, and anxiety, and really struggling to experience a life of purpose, peace, and abundance.

Now a lot of folks would say this is just part of the spiritual life. There *is* a cross, so offer it up, and just resign yourself to always struggling with discouragement, worry, and anxiety.

But those statements are only the *partial* truth. Because the *full* truth is Jesus left us His Church, and His Church has the blueprint for the spiritual life.

There are particular thoughts, practices, and habits, that when we incorporate them into our lives: they will allow God to work in our minds, hearts and souls to banish our doubts. It gives us cause to have hope in the midst of any tragedy, and will allow us to live lives so full of love and mercy and generosity, people will stop and ask, "How can I live like that, too?"

This book is intended to show you clearly and concisely. A step-by-step guide to ensure you can build the strong foundation you need to SAY YES to the life God created you for.

That is the blueprint I am going to share.

A *process* that can help us set aside all our fears, worries, and anxieties, and the discouragement which comes when we see and experience the evil running rampant in our world today.

A process that will allow us to live in the faith, hope, and love that we are created for, ensuring our lives are filled with purpose, peace, and abundance of the like we could never dream. It will prepare us to celebrate and enjoy the Heavenly Banquet for all eternity as holy men and women in the Church Triumphant, part of the Communion of Saints.

And it's *His* Way.

His Way is not a secret. Most of what I am going to share with you here is simply wisdom which can be found in Sacred

Scripture and in His Church. It's the same Way of the saints who have walked before us.

But just like the treasure in the field, you have to go looking for it, and in our busy, chaotic and distracting world today, it can be easy to miss. I know I did for a long time.

So this book is designed to make that wisdom a bit more accessible and easier to implement, so like me, you, too, can begin to quickly see results in your life, and then you will be able to sustain them for the long haul.

That is what this book is about, and this introduction is my personal invitation to YOU to come and join me on the journey.

So, if you're ready to set out on a journey of a lifetime, a journey of transformation, a journey that will lead you to living the life God created you for, one of purpose, peace, and abundance, then SAY YES.

SAY YES, and then turn the page and let's begin.

PART 1

DISCOVERING DEEP PURPOSE

CHAPTER 1
IT'S A PROCESS, NOT A PROGRAM

First, let me be VERY clear.

The blueprint I share in this book is a *process*. It's *not* a program.

God help us, but the last thing this world needs is another program.

Programs are what is killing us right now. Why? Because there is a program for everything. Programs are all about doing something to produce a product, while a process is focused upon taking action. Programs are static, while processes are active.

But programs have serious negatives when applied to the spiritual life—three big negatives actually.

The first negative is that a program gives you the impression there is a stop date for what it is you are doing. And there is no such thing in the spiritual life.

The second negative is programs imply that there are one-stop-shop solutions for everybody.

The third negative is programs gives the impression that the program is *the* solution to whatever problem you are trying to solve.

But I love processes.

Why? Here are a few reasons.

1. Processes do not end, but are ongoing, flexible and can be tailored to fit the needs of each individual or community.

2. Processes are not a one-stop-shop but can respond to the *actual* needs and questions of the person vs. responding to the needs and questions I think they have.

3. Processes are not the solution to every problem but allow for an encounter with a person.

4. Processes allow you to care for the individual, and thorough care of the individual, you care for the whole community.

But here's the biggest reason.

Because Jesus started and modeled a process for us, so I think we should strive to emulate the Master, don't you think?

My goal is to give you *everything* you will ever need to grow closer to God, become more like Jesus, and experience purpose, peace, and abundance in your daily life so you can embrace the life you were created for.

Pretty ambitious, right?

But I am a firm believer in the idea of "Go big, or go home", so that's my promise to you.

Now a lot of folks would be afraid to make such a promise. And I totally get it. And I would be absolutely terrified to do that—except this isn't *my* promise, it's God's promise.

God has given us everything we need in this world to become just like Him and live and experience a life of purpose, peace, and abundance.

We just have our priorities mixed up, which goes back to Adam and Eve and original sin, and is the whole reason we need a Savior in the first place.

But it wasn't supposed to be that way. You see, in the beginning, God created, and it was *all good*.

In the Garden, man and woman were in union with God, each other, themselves, and creation. There was no sickness and death. There was no shame or nakedness. There was no hunger or thirst.

Love reigned among God and all His creation.

All was in right order. And Adam and Eve were right ordered, too.

But then original sin came along, and all that perfect love, union, and order was broken.

Man was no longer in union with God, or Eve, or creation, or worst of all, even himself.

Same result for Eve.

The result was sin and concupiscence.

Where we now disobey God and misuse people and creation in disordered ways—ones that are selfish, uncharitable, and prideful.

Our intellects are now darkened, our bodies weakened, and our priorities disordered.

The true goal of the spiritual life is about becoming right ordered again. Where we seek and strive with God's grace to reclaim our original union with Him, others, creation, and ourselves, and become right ordered.

But if we judge by the world around us, it would appear to be downright impossible.

I don't think I need to share here the statistics about how many people fail in their goals to eat more healthy foods or to exercise consistently. Or how many people fail to stop smoking, drinking, or using drugs.

Or how many people vow to read the Bible, but then give up about three weeks in. Or who begin a prayer habit, but then life gets in the way, so they stop. Or who keep meaning to get to confession, but weeks, then months, and then years slip by, and they still haven't gone.

But all is not lost!

It doesn't matter if we are fallen and disordered. It doesn't matter that we are invariably going to fail, mess up, fall short, and give up—or at least be tempted to and praise God; we don't need to be perfect, we simply need to be willing to get up and begin again.

Becoming holy, becoming a saint isn't about never falling. Instead, it's about getting up one more time after we fall, and as you grow, to try to get up a little faster and less discouraged than the last time you fell.

And this is where we come back to the goal of this book and God's promises.

Because the key to becoming right ordered is about learning *the process* through which we can seek and strive to grow closer to God and become more like Jesus.

And it's in using this process we discover purpose, peace and abundance in our daily life.

And God has provided us exactly what that process is, and that's what this book is about.

It really is that simple.

We just SAY YES to the process.

Now, turn the page, and let's keep moving forward...

CHAPTER 2
WHOSE AM I?

The beginning of the process to discovering purpose, peace, and abundance in your daily life must begin with checking whether some vitally important truths are firmly rooted in our minds and hearts. Whether they are rock solid is important because it is upon these basic understandings our spiritual lives will rest as we are working to pursue holiness with God's grace and make a dwelling worthy of our Lord in our minds, hearts, and souls.

The first of these truths is to know the answer to the question "Whose am I?"

You'll notice I didn't start with "Who am I?" but rather with "Whose am I?" I am being intentional here because although "Who am I?" tends to be the question people ask, we can only find the real answer to that question if we first know *whose* we are.

This is because the world is constantly trying to quickly define and categorize everyone, and the usual way this can be done is by asking "Who are you?" Since the world has a very shallow view and understanding of who a person truly is, invariably, the answers people are expected to give to this question is usually about something they *do*, vs. who they actually are. Eventually, this becomes so ingrained in us, we forget who we really are because we have forgotten *whose* we are.

Unlike the world's superficial "Who am I?" that looks to only define and determine our value by what we do, "Whose am I?" focuses upon whom we belong to and what we are becoming.

Because when we know *whose* we are, we inherently know we matter, that our lives have meaning, and we have a deep purpose.

Remembering *whose* we are is even more important when we begin to become intentional about the spiritual life. Because remembering *whose* we are will become the key to opening the lock on the door to a life of purpose, peace, and abundance.

And when we know whose we are, then we have no doubt, even amid all the lies of the world around us, who we truly are.

So, *whose* are we?

Children of God. Children of the King. We are sons and daughters, the princes and princesses of the great High King Himself.

That's right. YOU are royalty, baby. And you don't have to marry into it like Meghan Markle did with Prince Harry. You simply need to acknowledge your heritage, live out this identity of who you really are, and this reality becomes apparent in your life.

Really? That's it? Well, not quite.

My own life is a case in point. I have struggled with believing this truth I am a beloved daughter of a good and loving Father who cares for my every need because my reality growing up seemed to be everything *but* that.

My biological father struggled with alcohol and other issues, so he was absent from my life. Additionally, after my parents divorced, he failed to pay child support regularly, so money was often tight. And then as I got older, and despite reaching out a few times to try and connect, he chose to *not* have a relationship with me. I felt unlovable and unworthy of being loved—until I encountered Jesus on that Good Friday evening.

It was Jesus who revealed the depth, breadth, height, and length of the Father's love for me when He told me *"Even if you were the only one in the world, I still would have died for you."*

Through Jesus' eyes, I began to see my life as God does. I saw God wasn't anything like my biological father, absent, disinterested, and uncaring. Rather, I began to see God's fingerprints of love and care *all* over my life. It was then I really began to be able to embrace the reality I am His beloved daughter, precious in His sight.

Saint Pope John Paul II echoes this truth when he wrote, *"Only in Christ can men and women find answers to the ultimate questions that trouble them. Only in Christ can they fully understand their dignity as persons created and loved by God."*

Now, the world would very much prefer for us to forget this truth of whose we are, and so works hard to distract us. Or, if we do remember, relishes the opportunity to remind us of when we have failed to act like sons and daughters of the King, and tries to convince us that therefore we must have forfeited our birthright. But all that is false.

As Christians, our identity is solidified in baptism. We are "named and claimed" in this profound moment of grace when a person's name is written in the Book of Life, and we are empowered with the gifts of the Holy Spirit to be priests, prophets, and kings in the world.

Through baptism, we are also made brothers and sisters in Christ, our sins are washed away, and we are stamped with an indelible mark upon our minds, hearts, and souls that we are a member of God's family forever—beloved sons and daughters upon whom He looks and delights.

This is why we must know *whose* we are. When we acknowledge our identity as sons and daughters—that we were made in the image and likeness of God and called to participate in the life of our Creator—then we realize our lives and the life of every person we encounter is a unique creation filled with beauty and dignity who is able to know and understand goodness and love.

It is in our capacity to do good and love others that our life then reflects the royal beauty and dignity, and reminds ourselves, as well as others, of not just whose we are, but then helps us always answer correctly the question of "Who am I?"—regardless of who asks, and no matter the number of times we are asked.

We will be able to say without hesitation I am a beloved son or daughter of God, I am made in His image and likeness, and created to be one in union with Him beginning now and for all eternity.

Mother Teresa of Calcutta is a beautiful illustration of someone who knew who she was because she knew *whose* she was. She would frequently describe herself as merely an instrument, "a pencil in the hands of God." Her ministry of caring for the sick and dying in the streets of Calcutta drew involvement and support from thousands of people across the world, Even more amazing was to see the growth of her religious community, the Missionaries of Charity. From only 12 sisters in 1950, there were more than 4500 sisters and 500 brothers by the time of her death in 1997. All as a result of her clearly communicating by her very life how it was possible to live a simple life of love poured out for others.

Why were people drawn to this small Albanian woman who stood just over five feet tall?

Because she knew without a doubt whose she was, and she lived out that reality so well her life became a beacon of love, goodness, and beauty shining brightly in the darkness of the world.

In the Roman Catholic Church, people like Mother Teresa are saints. (Mother Teresa was officially recognized as a saint on September 4, 2016.) But she was not recognized because she was perfect throughout her entire life, far from it.

Since Mother Teresa's death, the world has come to know of her great struggles with discouragement, doubt, and feelings of abandonment, but she persevered. And by the time she got to the end of her journey, people recognized she was extremely close to living a perfectly right ordered, or saintly, life.

Her story is a life rooted in knowing whose she was, and therefore, she knew who she was, and she lived out that reality. The result was the world was made a better place because of her having been in it.

And THAT is what each of us is called to be. Not to do. But to *be*. To be, in our own unique way, a shining example of love, goodness, and beauty.

So what's your story so far? Is it one that will inspire others to be their best selves? Inspire them to live generously and courageously? To live as the person they were created to be—sons and daughters of the High King?

Saint Brendan of Bir observes, *"If you become Christ's, you will stumble upon wonder upon wonder, and every one of them true."*

Those wonders upon wonders are the threads of goodness, love and beauty that are woven into each of our lives through our good intentions or good words, and in the best way, the good deeds done.

So often, people simply chalk up events and circumstances of their life to karma, luck, or coincidence.

But it's none of these things. It's actually a person, and I have had the extraordinary grace and privilege to encounter Him. He is the Great High King of Heaven, Jesus Christ. And the King is very clear on who it is I should be, because of *whose* I am.

I should be like Him—perfect and holy because I am created in His image and likeness. In other words, a saint.

St Peter Julian Eymard writes, *"To sanctify yourself is to form Jesus Christ within you."* Or as I learned from the Sisters and Brother Priests of the Apostles of Interior Life religious community, *"Holiness is transforming union with God."*

With that understanding in mind—then all of what I should be doing, saying, and even thinking should be about allowing Jesus to be formed within me. I should be actively working to identify the habits, circumstances, and sometimes even people, that are either helping, or hindering me from writing a story of love, goodness, and beauty in my life.

And as I do this, my true identity of whose I am, and who I am becomes more apparent, and then my life reflects it as well.

But it's a process. And because the spiritual life is a process of a lifetime, it is why we need to know without a doubt whose we are, so we can always answer properly who we are.

And because we are His, you and I matter.

Our lives mean something.

Even if you can't see how this is possible, it's still true.

This life is about *whose* I am, and who I am in the world because of it.

For each of us is a pencil. A member of royalty, especially created to write a chapter in an unforgettable story, for a particular purpose. And it's that purpose we will focus upon next in the process.

First, though, take a moment and remember *whose* you are. You are a child of God.

SAY YES to your dignity and greatness.

Now, turn the page. Your crown awaits you.

CHAPTER 3
THE CALL TO HOLINESS

Once we know *whose* we are, the next truth we need to have rock-solid in our minds is the answer to the question, "Why was I created?

Unfortunately, in a world increasingly driven by a person needing to prove one's "worth" or "usefulness," this question has been subverted instead into "What purpose do I have?" The answer relates to what I discussed in the previous chapter about the world being focusing upon what you do, rather than whose, and who, you truly are.

Although there have been numerous ways this question has been answered throughout the centuries, the only one we need to focus upon here is the one given to us by Jesus Himself. He taught, "Be perfect, as your heavenly Father is perfect." To be perfect is another word for holy, so, from the beginning, the life of a Christian disciple has been a call to holiness.

This may seem like a tall order, but Jesus did not leave us orphans. He gave us the Holy Spirit to ensure we would have the means to strive for perfection. Through our baptism, we put on Christ and become sons and daughters of God and sharers in the divine nature so through God's grace, we are made holy. We must then try to hold on to this holiness and live it out in our daily lives.

Throughout the last two millennia, the Church has continued to express the call to holiness as *the* fundamental calling of all Christians.

Most famously is Saint Irenaeus' quote in the 2nd century, "*The glory of God is man fully alive.*"

In the United States, the concise answer provided in the Baltimore Catechism from the nineteenth century is often referenced to provide an answer to this critical question of why I was created. It states plainly: "*We were made in the image and likeness of God ... to know him, to love him, and to serve him in this world, and to be happy with him forever in heaven.*"[1]

More recently, the Second Vatican Council which gathered from 1962-1965, focused upon this universal call to holiness extensively in one of its primary documents, *Lumen Gentium (The Dogmatic Constitution of the Church)*. The main message of *Lumen Gentium* is that *all* members of the Church, all of Christ's faithful, whatever their rank or status, are called to the fullness of Christian life and the perfection of charity.

You see, we humans are unique. By being made in the image and likeness of God, we can think and understand and experience love, goodness, and beauty. We have a capacity that is unlike any other creature, for we can reason, therefore, we have the ability to *choose*.

"*It is our choices, Harry, that show what we truly are, far more than our abilities.*"

This quote is made by the character Professor Albus Dumbledore in the *Harry Potter* series by J.K. Rowling. And the essence of this statement is dead-on, for it *is* our choices that determine how we will respond to circumstances and people in our lives, and ultimately, whether we choose to say and do what is good and right and just in our own lives. And whether we are choosing to live our story so it reflects whose we truly are.

We spend our lifetimes choosing whether we will fully embrace this identity and use the gifts we have been given to be ministers of love, stewards of all that has been given us, and "prophets of a future not our own."[2]

So often, however, we get focused upon our sinfulness, or how imperfect we are, and we think we have to *earn* God's love and eternal salvation by doing things.

But *earning* God's love isn't how it works.

Father Bede Jarrett explains this idea of God's love for us beautifully in the book, *Catholic Meditations*:

> "*God cannot cease to love me. That is the most startling fact that our doctrine reveals. Sinner or saint He loves and cannot well help Himself. Magdalen in her sin, Magdalen in her sainthood, was loved by God. The difference between her position made some difference also in the effect of that love on her, but the love was the same, since it was the Holy Spirit who is the love of the Father and the Son. Whatever I do, I am loved. But then, if I sin, am I unworthy of love? Yes, but I am unworthy always. Nor can God love me for what I am, since, in that case, I would compel His love, force His will by something external to Himself. In fact, really if I came to consider, I would find that I was not loved by God because I was good, but that I was good because God loved me. My improvement does not cause God to love me but is the effect of God's having loved me.*"[3]

When we fail to remember we are loved regardless, and fall into the trap of believing we need to earn our Father's love, we become much more susceptible to succumbing to doing what the world tells us we should be doing with our lives—a life where we strive to secure fame, fortune, and power. Or to focus on a life where every "need" is catered to, and where we are able to live a life of ease and comfort, or to practice the philosophy of Epicurus of "eat, drink, and be merry."

Yet we are designed for more; for SO much more.

Jesus and His Church have told us this from the beginning. But in case you still doubt, look to the deepest desires of your heart. We *long* to be more than what the world offers to us. There is a reason statistics show people who supposedly "have it all"—the famous, the powerful and the wealthy, are not any happier or fulfilled than those who are not famous, powerful or wealthy.

It's because we have been designed for much more than what this world has to offer us.

Our destiny is to spend all eternity with our Heavenly Father. He created each of us from the beautiful, loving communion of the life of the Trinity—the Father, Son, and Holy Spirit—and each of us is *personally invited* to share in that life of loving and beautiful communion here on earth and into eternity.

Saint Elizabeth Ann Seton, the first American born saint and founder of the first American religious order, the Sisters of Charity, said, "*We know certainly that our God calls us to a holy life. We know that He gives us every grace, every abundant grace; and though we are so weak of ourselves, this grace is able to carry us through every obstacle and difficulty.*"

But we tend to not want to hear that truth.

We don't want to hear we are called to be holy. Or to know we are called to become saints.

We don't want to acknowledge we are each invited to BE MORE—because we are *masters* at self-deception and excuses.

Or at least I know I am. For the longest time, although I *knew* I needed to prioritize God and His plan for my life, I chose to *not* do this.

I would go to Mass on Sundays, but only when it was convenient for me. My time and talents were focused on work, and my treasure was being used to buy all the supposed material "necessities" one needs in life—things like cars, furniture, entertainment, clothes, etc.

God also was not a part of my decision making when it came to who I should date, activities I pursued, or how I should spend my time and money. I was doing what I wanted to do, when I wanted to do it, and how I wanted to do it. I wasn't living a life that was "right-ordered"—a life where God's plan for my life directed my thoughts, words, and actions.

Not putting God first soon became a pattern in my life. My refusing to live a right-ordered life (mostly because it wasn't popular, easy, or convenient), continued for almost a decade. I looked around and saw despite living what would be considered a fairly comfortable life, I still found I was restless, anxious, and unhappy.

I was pursuing what the world told me I should be—a person of fame, power, and wealth. I had found success and received promotions as an Army officer, won a national fellowship, obtained a Master of Arts degree in history, and successfully wrote and published two children's historical fiction books.

I was living what was supposed to be an "exciting life"—a life full of trips and memorable experiences, but the experiences were fleeting. No sooner would I return home then I would begin looking for the next thing/trip to satisfy me, and then the cycle would repeat itself again.

Although I was living life "my way" and doing what I wanted to do and when I wanted to do it, it left me empty, unhappy, and unfulfilled. I knew something was "off" or missing from my life. I could sense I wasn't fulfilling my true potential.

I realized I wanted to become more than what I was. I wanted to become *who* I was created to be.

That realization helped me finally see through my own deceptions and excuses. I realized the main reason for my discontent and unhappiness was I had rejected God's plan for my life—to become a holy person, a living, breathing, wonder-working saint.

I had *chosen* to say NO to God's invitation to be more, to become holy, and then I spent *years* deceiving myself and making excuses. I resisted by holding on to an improper vision of whose and who I am, and who I should become, by doing all the things I *thought* I liked more.

The bottom-line truth though, is that although I felt this dissatisfaction in my life, I still hesitated because I didn't really want to change. I was too *comfortable*.

Pope Emeritus Benedict XVI once said, *"The world offers you comfort. But you were not made for comfort. You were made for greatness."*

Becoming holy is greatness in the spiritual life. And becoming a saint means getting inducted into the Hall of Fame. God's Hall of Fame. Our names won't be placed on plaques in the halls of heaven, though. Rather, our names are already written on the very hands of the One who created us to become perfect like He is. And we become saints by living lives of greatness.

The Church Fathers of the Second Vatican Council have called *every one of us* to engage in spiritual heroism—the universal call to holiness—and not settle for a second—or a third-rate life. Rather, we need to answer His invitation to become saints. To answer the call to holiness.

So, what is the greatest way to live?

Jesus showed it to us. To live a life of love poured out for others.

Saint Vincent de Paul, whose own life of loving and caring for the poor inspired Frederic Ozanam to found the St Vincent de Paul Society which now has more than 800,000 members working with the poor across the world, once said *"I am sent not only to love God but to make Him loved. It is not enough for me to love God if my neighbor does not love Him."*

This understanding of what it is to live a life poured out for others is echoed by the great 20th century American spiritual master, Fr. Thomas Merton: *"To say that I am made in the image of God is to say that love is the reason for my existence, for God is love. Love is my true identity. Selflessness is my true self. Love is my true character. Love is my name."*

Our world has not only forgotten this, but it also continuously downplays the reality that we tend to make *really* poor choices when we are not living out of love for others. And what is true, authentic love? It is willing the good of the other.

But what we most often forget is we are *not* the creators, but creatures.

And we need to always keep before us *why* we were created and *what* our purpose is.

And our purpose is to become holy. To become a living, breathing, wonder-working saint in this world and into the next.

For you ARE a marvelous creature, and this is what you were created for—to be a saint.

SAY YES and answer your call to holiness.

And then *choose* to turn the page to discover your unique and unrepeatable mission.

CHAPTER 4

YOUR UNIQUE AND UNREPEATABLE MISSION

"Be who God meant you to be, and you will set the world on fire."

— Saint Catherine of Siena

In the two previous chapters, we have answered the questions of whose and who we are—beloved sons and daughters of God; and why we are here—to become saints, holy men and women who pour out their lives loving others.

The third truth we must now seek to ensure is rock solid in our minds is to answer the question, "What is my unique and unrepeatable mission?"

To answer, we must properly understand our vocation.

The Latin root of the word vocation is "vocare," or "to call." In this case, God's call. So, a person's vocation is found in their response to God's call in their life.

Unfortunately, vocation is one of the most misunderstood concepts in our world today, primarily because most people are unaware there are actually three layers to our vocation that need to be integrated within our lives. These three layers are the universal call to holiness, state of life, and personal mission.

The first layer, the universal call to holiness, is the call to "become perfect like our Heavenly Father is perfect" that we discussed in the last chapter. We must always remember each of us was given life from God's abundant and overflowing perfect love. And it is to this perfect love we are invited to return to and to do that, we must become, and be in union with, the perfect and holy love to which we are returning.

The second layer is rooted in the reality we are each designed to portray God's image and likeness in a distinct manner according to the particular gifts and talents with which He has endowed us during our life here on earth.

Father Jacques Philippe, a world-renowned retreat master and author concerning the spiritual life wrote in his book, *In the School of the Holy Spirit*:

> *"God loves everyone with unique love; he wants to lead them all to perfection, but at the same time has very **different paths for different people**. This means that the frequency and characteristics of the inspirations of grace will differ from one person to another. We cannot force the Spirit, God is the master of his gifts. That said, it cannot be doubted that God will grant each person at least the inspirations he needs for his own sanctification."*[4]

These "different paths" Father Philippe refers to are the states of life—consecrated or matrimony. Many people are sometimes confused because there are many forms of consecration in our midst—priestly, religious, and single. However, whatever path God calls a person to follow, God gives us the graces to pursue it. It is this second layer of vocation that most people are referring to when they speak of someone "discerning a vocation."

Finally, every man and woman has a unique and unrepeatable mission which flows from their inherent design. A design placed there by God from the moment of conception to ensure each of us is capable of becoming a holy man or woman in our particular way. And God will give, and continue to provide us whatever characteristics—be it a talent, personality trait, or skill, along with the graces necessary for us to become and fulfill our unique and unrepeatable vocation. This is the third layer, our personal mission.

Each of us must undertake the great task of striving to become who we are created to be, doing what we are created to do, in the place where God has placed each of us to do it. One of my former pastors succinctly expressed the essence of personal mission this way, "Be who you are, what you are, and where you are."

These are the three layers of vocation—the who (a saint), what (state of life), and where (personal mission). All three need to coincide and become an integrated whole so we can fulfill the unique and unrepeatable mission for which God designed us—to be signs and witnesses of His love in the world.

Because the truth is *no one else* in the history of creation can be who you are, or do what only you can do, and do it wherever you are in the world at this particular moment in history.

Now, this idea can be pretty daunting stuff. This reality that I am a unique and unrepeatable creation destined to do what no one else in the world now, or throughout all of history has ever done before?

Whoa! Wait a minute, you might say! I'm no Abraham Lincoln or George Washington! I'm just little ole' me. I don't have any "superpower" to speak of. I just get up and walk the dog, go to work, keep the house in order, drive the kids to soccer practice, and binge watch an occasional Netflix show, or see the latest Marvel movie.

How could I be unique and unrepeatable?

Well, God tells us in Jeremiah 1:5, "*Before I formed you in the womb, I knew you.*"

YOU are important. YOU have a purpose. And YOU have a mission.

The world might view you and your life to be insignificant, but to God, it is the role of a lifetime.

Saint Cardinal John Henry Newman's poem, "Purpose" gives us greater insight into this idea:

I am created to do something or to be something for which no one else is created; I have a place in God's counsels, in God's world, which no one else has; whether I be rich or poor, despised or esteemed by man, God knows me and calls me by name.

God has created me to do Him some definite service; He has committed some work to me which He has not committed to another. I have a mission – I never may know it in this life, but I shall be told it in the next....I have a part in a great work; I am a link in a chain, a bond of connection between persons. He has not created me for naught. I shall do good, I shall do His work; I shall be an angel of peace, a preacher of truth in my own place, while not intending it, if I do but keep His commandments and serve Him in my calling.

Therefore, I will trust Him. Whatever, wherever I am, I can never be thrown away. If I am in sickness, my sickness may serve Him; in perplexity, my perplexity may serve Him; if I am in sorrow, my sorrow may serve Him. My sickness, or perplexity, or sorrow may be necessary causes of some great end, which is quite beyond us. He does nothing in vain; He may prolong my life, He may shorten it; He knows what He is about. He may take away my friends, He may throw me among strangers, He may make me feel desolate, make my spirits sink, hide the future from me – He still knows what He is about. I ask not to see – ask not to know – I ask simply to be used.

Let me say it again, YOU have a purpose. YOU have a mission.

Yet, in our world today, most people hesitate to embrace their purpose and mission.

Why? Because our society is currently experiencing a "crisis of purpose."

Dr. Holly Ordway, a Professor of English and Apologetics at Houston Baptist University, describes this "crisis of purpose" as a direct outgrowth of the culture in which there is continuous distraction. A culture with virtually no silence, no reflection, no sense of "home," and where both history and cultural inheritance have been negated to have little or no consequence in the lives of both men and women.

The result is we now have generations of people who have little to no true knowledge of ourselves, resulting in an inability to live right-ordered lives directed by purpose or filled with meaning. Consequently, despite a preponderance of activities geared towards seeking and obtaining happiness, this "crisis of purpose" virtually guarantees happiness will continually elude us.

This inability to experience true happiness has created an endless cycle in which people now hesitate to make *any* decision or pursue *any* path out of fear they will then irrevocably preclude finding happiness at some point because of prior decisions.

Yet, because we are beloved sons and daughters of God, we need not fear making decisions!

Why? Because God is using everything in our lives to help us accomplish our purpose and mission.

God communicates this to us through Saint Paul in Romans 8:28, "*We know that all things work for good for those who love God, who are called according to his purpose.*"

Yes, *everything*.

"Your work—whether it is a chore around the house, a homework assignment, a sports practice, or a job with an office and a paycheck—isn't just a means to an economic end. Nor is it something you need to 'get over with' in time for the weekend. It is an essential part of your sanctification,

a share in the divine brotherhood of Christ, and a means of discovering your true self."[5]

Christopher Wesley, a parish youth minister and author of several books, including *Rebuilding Confirmation*, shares the idea that each person needs to discover their "GPS." Similar to a GPS (Global Positioning System) that directs us to a particular geographical place, an individual's GPS can do the same for directing them to their particular mission.

An individual's GPS is comprised of their Gifts, Passions, and Self. Gifts are in correlation to talents/skills, Passions are in regards interests/motivations, and Self are in relation to one's personality/temperament/motivations.

Of course, each of us have our own distinctive personalities. For example, some of us are social butterflies and love going to every party in town, while others prefer a quieter life—perhaps spending time walking their dog or meeting up with friends for coffee.

It is also evident each one of us has unique skills, interests, talents, and motivations. But we must strive to put them to use in a right-ordered manner directed by God, so they can lead us to the path we must walk to become the saints God created us to be.

Additionally, we must strive to discover our unique "superpower." Our superpower is the one thing you do better than almost anyone you know. This is the thing you most enjoy doing and love continually learning about. It's also probably something you naturally excel at, but that doesn't necessarily mean that you will not have to work to continue to develop it.

Fortunately, in the world today there are some very easy, practical, and time-tested ways to identify your gifts, skills, and talents. What might motivate and inspire you, and can give you insight into your strengths, weaknesses, and other general characteristics of both your personality, temperament, and motivations?

Some numerous assessments and evaluations can be done to nore accurately identify our gifts, passions, personality, and temperament makeup, and I recommend you use them—things like Myers-Briggs, Clifton StrengthFinders, the Bennett Spiritual Temperament Assessment, and the Siena Institute's Spiritual Gifts (Charisms) Inventory.

But the most accurate assessment I have encountered in the last three decades is the MCORE.

The MCORE (Motivational Core) is different than most assessments as it uses personal achievement stories (things people determine they did well, enjoyed doing, and found deep satisfaction while doing them) as the narrative tool to facilitate self-discovery.

MCORE is derived from SIMA® (System for Identifying Motivated Abilities), which is profoundly powerful at identifying your unique pattern of motivated behavior, and it is backed by more than half a century of empirical research.

In a nutshell, the MCORE reveals the equivalent of your spiritual "thumbprint" by revealing the core motivations that fundamentally motivate you. This then provides you significant insight into what can most naturally bring you great satisfaction, and/or the perspective you may need when engaging in particular activities or circumstances to experience the greatest personal fulfillment when engaged in those activities or circumstances.

What I love most about the MCORE, though, is it can quickly give you a very clear personal mission statement rooted in your three core motivations. For myself, my top three core motivations are: Serve, Explore, and Meet the Challenge. So, my integrated mission statement is: "I am fundamentally motivated to serve others as I explore and meet challenges."

A personal mission statement can help you clarify your priorities and give you focus about your purpose and unique and unrepeatable mission.

The four components to any good mission statement are: 1) it should be something that motivates you; 2) is something you do (or can do); 3) has a target, person or group you are helping; and 4) describes the positive impact you are seeking through your action.

Some personal mission statements by some people you might be familiar are:

"I tell stories to help people grow."—Steven Spielberg

"To serve God and my fellow man by being an example of a life committed to service."—Tony Robbins

"To be a witness to hope."—Saint Pope John Paul II

"To quench Jesus' thirst by serving the poorest of the poor."—Saint Mother Teresa of Calcutta

My MCORE integrated mission statement does the same for me concisely, simply, and directly. It provides clarity and focus about who I am and what and where I do those things that bring me deep satisfaction as I fulfill my personal mission.

Now, a quick note of caution. All assessments and a personal mission statement should only be used as the *tools* they were designed to be to help you increase in self-knowledge.

Any results you receive should be put at the service of gaining insight into what your unique gifts, talents, charisms, personality, temperament, and motivations are so as to discover, develop, and integrate the three layers of your vocation. It helps you to more accurately realize who, what, and where *God* wants you to be as you fulfill your unique and unrepeatable personal mission.

This entire undertaking of discovering your true self needs to be done in light of God's plan for you. Only when we are seeking God's will throughout this process can we discover what is truly in harmony with the deepest essence of our being, and this is what creates true clarity and purpose.

When this clarity and purpose orients all aspects of our lives, it translates into an authentic simplicity and directness about life that embodies one's entire existence, and this tends to draw others to them like moths to a flame.

Look at any great leader throughout history—Alexander the Great, Julius Caesar, Napoleon, George Washington, Abraham Lincoln, Mahatma Gandhi, Winston Churchill, Nelson Mandela, and even Adolph Hitler, inspired others to follow them because of their clarity and purpose.

But how to find that clarity and purpose in your life? How might you discover your unique and unrepeatable mission?

Father Jude Winkler, O.F.M gives us an excellent place to start.:

> *"It is essential to discern what the Spirit wants when we are making important choices in our lives. Through prayer, fasting, spiritual reading, spiritual advice, discernment of signs, sorting out our hidden motivations, etc., we develop a sense of what God wants of us."*[6]

God is continuously revealing His will for us either through His own Word, through His Church, and through others.

This is why immersing ourselves in Scripture as we ask God to reveal our unique and unrepeatable mission for which He created us is so powerful. Saint Augustine, Anthony of Egypt, and many other saints have come to know of God's will for them through meditation on Sacred Scripture.

Still others have gained insight through the study of the teachings of the Church, or by immersing themselves in corporal and spiritual works of mercy like Saints Francis of Assisi or Mother Teresa of Calcutta did.

Insight into our personal mission also comes through asking of ourselves and others different questions. What am I good at? Whom would I do anything to help? Who do I wish I could do more for? Who does my heart break for? Who has God placed in my path who needs my help right now? What makes me come most alive? Or when have I felt most alive helping someone else? What can I start doing today? What can I learn today? Who can I reach out to who is already helping in a way that intrigues me?

As you ask these questions and others like them, clarity will begin to emerge about your purpose, and then as you take steps to pursue that purpose, you will gain even more insight into your personal mission.

We need to take the time, every day, to pursue our purpose and strive to fulfill our personal mission. Because your purpose, mission, and happiness are all interrelated. They are all tied to you knowing who you are (a son or daughter of God); why you were created (the call to holiness and your eternal destiny to become a saint); and what you were created for (your personal mission of loving God and others in the unique and unrepeatable way in the place where God has placed you); *if* you are to have any chance at finding fulfillment (happiness).

The only way for this to be possible is to orient oneself towards God, strive to become holy by becoming "right-ordered," and continuously seeking what *He* desires for you and your life.

Continuously seeking His will is the process of discernment, and entire books have been written about how to go about it. But discernment can be an especially daunting word in Catholic circles where most people believe it only tends to happen when there is some momentous decision before us.

But we have to change this mindset. Discernment is not only for "big decisions." Rather, it should be done continuously. It's not a one, or two, or even three, and we are done with discernment. Rather, discernment is about learning how to *perceive*, about being able to see or hear something. Probably one of the most beautiful definitions I heard to describe discernment was shared by a religious sister of the Apostles of Interior Life who said, *"Discernment is God unveiling for you His will for your life."*

And that's the most beautiful part of the fact each of us has been created out of love; for real, authentic, covenantal love; and destined to live in love with Christ for all eternity. The same Jesus Christ in whom we live and move and have our being.

Our God is not some harsh taskmaster who gives us a checklist of things we have to do that is going to make our lives miserable and unenjoyable. That is not the purpose or the mission for which He created us.

No, God invites us instead to accept His invitation to open our hearts to Him, so then HE can do the work of transformation within us.

This transformation doesn't happen overnight. It is a slow, hard slog. Sometimes it's with cement boots on as we try to go up a muddy hillside, and we end up sliding backwards more than we move forward. So, at times, it can be painful, discouraging, and exhausting.

But through all of it, God loves us beyond measure. We are His children who He has created to love Him and others as we fulfill our unique and unrepeatable mission.

As we pour ourselves out as signs of God's love in the world in the unique and unrepeatable way only we are, and in the way only we can do, and in the place where God has placed us, we fulfill our personal mission. And like Jesus, we will then be able to bear witness to the magnificent and marvelous love God has for each and every person in the world.

Remember the words of Saint Catherine of Siena, *"Be who God meant you to be, and you will set the world on fire."*

It's high time to strike the match and start burning.

SAY YES to your unique and unrepeatable mission.

Now, turn that page to come and see.

CHAPTER 5
COME AND SEE

Up to this point, we have focused upon making sure we are clear about the answers to the fundamental questions of our lives.

Who are we? Why we are here? What is the purpose of our lives?

The answers to these questions are the foundation blocks upon which we discover our deep purpose, and help prepare us to begin our spiritual journey in earnest. We must decide whether we will accept the invitation offered by God for us to begin to participate in the life of the Trinity here and now, so as to prepare to live in union with Him for all eternity.

This is the key decision Jesus places before each of His disciples. We see Him do this in the Gospels, and we can see how each person Jesus encounters responds differently.

In John, Chapter 1, verses 35-51, we see Jesus gathering His first disciples:

> *The next day John was there again with two of his disciples, and as he watched Jesus walk by, he said, "Behold, the Lamb of God." The two disciples heard what he said and followed Jesus. Jesus turned and saw them following him and said to them, "What are you looking for?" They said to him, "Rabbi" (which translated means Teacher),*

"where are you staying?" He said to them, "Come, and you will see." So, they went and saw where he was staying, and they stayed with him that day. It was about four in the afternoon. Andrew, the brother of Simon Peter, was one of the two who heard John and followed Jesus. He first found his own brother Simon and told him, "We have found the Messiah" (which is translated Anointed). Then he brought him to Jesus. Jesus looked at him and said, "You are Simon the son of John; you will be called Cephas" (which is translated Peter).

The next day he decided to go to Galilee, and he found Philip. And Jesus said to him, "Follow me." Now Philip was from Bethsaida, the town of Andrew and Peter. Philip found Nathanael and told him, "We have found the one about whom Moses wrote in the law, and also the prophets, Jesus son of Joseph, from Nazareth." But Nathanael said to him, "Can anything good come from Nazareth?" Philip said to him, "Come and see." Jesus saw Nathanael coming toward him and said of him, "Here is a true Israelite. There is no duplicity in him." Nathanael said to him, "How do you know me?" Jesus answered and said to him, "Before Philip called you, I saw you under the fig tree." Nathanael answered him, "Rabbi, you are the Son of God; you are the King of Israel." Jesus answered and said to him, "Do you believe because I told you that I saw you under the fig tree? You will see greater things than this." And he said to him, "Amen, amen, I say to you, you will see the sky opened and the angels of God ascending and descending on the Son of Man."[7]

In these sixteen verses, we see the various ways in which disciples came to Jesus. First, Andrew and John, the Beloved Disciple, went seeking Him, and when Jesus asked what they were seeking, He responded with an invitation for them to *"Come and See."*

Andrew then went and brought his brother, Simon, who would become Peter, to Jesus. In this instance, we see Peter being introduced by another to Jesus. However, when Peter himself came before Jesus, he had to decide whether to accept his new name, and if he was going to stay with Jesus alongside his brother and John.

Jesus then goes seeking a disciple the next day. This is Philip. Philip not only decides to follow Jesus, but he also goes and gets his friend, Nathaniel. When Nathaniel expresses doubt about the truth of who Jesus might be, Jesus reveals to Nathaniel how He has already seen him standing beneath the fig tree. In short, Jesus reveals He already knew Nathaniel, and it is this revelation that convinces Nathaniel to profess Jesus is the Son of God and King of Israel.

In the gathering of the initial disciples, we see many of the different ways people can come to be followers of Jesus. Some are seeking—like Andrew and John, while others are brought to Jesus by a family member, like Peter. Others are sought out by Jesus—Philip, and then others not only need to be introduced by a friend, but they also require a revelation of truth about the reality of who Jesus is before being willing to follow—Nathaniel.

This wasn't just the case in Palestine more than two thousand years ago, but continues to be the way of God throughout the centuries since, and nothing has changed all the way up into the present day.

Each of us is given a similar invitation because Jesus will not cease encountering each and every person in the world in whatever place, way, or manner they may need in order to come to know Him.

Regardless of the way in which we do come to encounter, and then stand before Jesus, we each have a choice to make.

Will we follow?

Will we SAY YES and accept the invitation to *"come and see"* the great love He has for each one of his sons and daughters?

Will we experience the reality of how He has known us since *"Before I formed you in womb I knew you."*[8]

Will we trust His promise *"For I know well the plans I have in mind for you, plans for your welfare and not for woe, so as to give you a future of hope."*[9]

Will we SAY YES?

Unfortunately, most people in our Church today don't even realize there *is* a choice.

Thoughts tend to run along these, or very similar, lines (at least they did for me) ... "I've been a Catholic all my life, and I'm doing what I'm supposed to do. I come to Mass when I can. I receive communion and go to confession if I have done something really serious. I give to the parish. I'm a pretty good wife and mother. I'm not perfect, but I do pretty well most of the time. God is merciful, so He'll understand. It's not like I've killed anyone, so I should be good to get into purgatory at least."

Yet the reality is the spiritual journey is so much more than just getting by.

Because if we do truly answer Jesus' invitation to "come and see," then we set out on the greatest journey of our lives. And the Church teaches during that journey, we move through the Purgative, Illuminative, and Unitive Ways. Each of these "ways" representing a stage through which we progress as we grow in intimacy with God.

Using Saint Francis de Sales' descriptions, the Purgative Way is the stage on the spiritual journey when we begin to "purge" ourselves of our selfishness through a serious commitment to grow in our relationship with God through regular prayer and turn away from all serious sin.

The Illuminative Way is a time to continue deepening our prayer life while growing in humility, virtue, obedience, and an increasing love of neighbor.

The Unitive Way is a time when we are ruled by love, when our wills are in perfect union with God, we are following the inspirations and counsels of the Holy Spirit, and Jesus is living in and through us.

This is the full essence of what it means to set out and follow the Master. But most people barely make it to the starting line of the Purgative Way.

But then, even if we do get to the starting line, and realize there is a serious choice to make before us, we still normally need to overcome some internal or external conflicts, or not fall prey to some very common mental mistakes.

Those internal conflicts tend to be things like believing we are not loveable, or we are too big a sinner, or we are not worthy of God's love. External obstacles include thoughts such as my family will be upset, I don't have time, I have too many responsibilities, or I am not willing to take a chance I might lose whatever it is that is most important to me.

Invariably, almost all these conflicts are rooted in a faulty understanding of what saying yes to Jesus will mean for our lives, and this is where we tend to fall prey to common mental mistakes.

These mental mistakes are called survivorship bias, loss aversion, availability heuristic, and confirmation bias, but if you bear with me a minute, I'll give you examples so you will be able to see if they are at work in your life.

Survivorship bias is the idea we focus only on people who are successful and whatever they did to be successful, and we presume (here's the mental mistake) anyone who uses a similar strategy will also find success.

So, when we are considering whether to SAY YES and follow Jesus, we will focus upon the many examples of people who are successful, fulfilled, and happy people who are *not* people of faith. Our survivorship bias has us focus on those examples, and then we conclude that to be successful, fulfilled or happy doesn't necessitate being a follower of Christ.

Loss aversion refers to our tendency to want to avoid any kind of loss in our lives. This seems to make total logical sense because who wants to lose anything or anyone? Until you accept the reality we are very protective of the things we have, and we will often do *ridiculous* things to keep what we already have.

I am sure all of us can think of an example of when we have done something illogical, just so we didn't have to take a chance in possibly losing someone or something—like perhaps remaining friends with someone who was a bad influence on us, or maybe keeping too many jackets (or whatever it might be) "just in case" we might need it.

When we are choosing whether to follow Christ, this idea of loss aversion is exemplified by the rich, young man who comes and asks Jesus what he must do to find eternal life. Jesus told the young man he needed to keep the commandments, and when the young man told them he had done this since he was a boy, Jesus responded with the invitation, *"If you wish to be complete, go and sell your possessions and give to the poor, and you will have treasure in heaven; and come follow Me."* The young man responded by going away sad for he has many possessions.[10]

The common mental mistake of loss aversion is to think if we follow Jesus, then we might lose someone important to us, or we might need to give up everything good—like having fun or owning beautiful things, or going on nice vacations, but this is not the case at all. Loss aversion makes us hesitate by making us think that is the case.

The availability heuristic is when we assume whatever information comes to mind most easily must mean they are the most important things to remember. This mental mistake causes us to overvalue the impact of things we can remember, while underestimating the things we do not hear about.

An example of this is that because we don't hear about, or can't remember numerous instances of people actually becoming saints, we think either a lot of people are not becoming saints, or think it's not possible to become a saint, and we make this a "truth" we then apply to our lives.

Matthew Kelly, labels this idea that you, myself, or anyone else in the world is incapable of becoming a saint, as *"the biggest lie ever told in the history of Christianity."*[11] But it's all just a result of a common mental error.

Finally, there is confirmation bias. This is when we unconsciously are searching for information that will confirm our preexisting beliefs while we ignore or devalue any information which contradicts what we already believe.

When this is applied to whether we choose to follow and put Christ first in our lives, it means we tend to only find information that supports what we already believe to be true for NOT making a change. Like "I don't have the time," or "It's not possible," or "It's too difficult." So, we justify our "decision" to not make a decision. To not make a change.

So, are we condemned to never be able to make a decision that isn't faulty in some way?

Not at all.

But the key is to recognize when these mental mistakes might be at play, and to compensate for them through self-awareness. But self-awareness must be rooted in a rock-solid understanding of the three questions we previously discussed—who we are, why am I here, and what am I called to do?

This is why we must start with those questions and the three fundamental truths of the answers to those questions *first*. Because our understandings of these questions and the answers to them will influence whether we are even able or willing to *consider* responding to God's invitation.

If I don't have those answers rock-solid in my mind, then I probably am going to not even see the point of responding with a yes OR a no. Because I am still far too caught up in everything the world says is important.

But once you are aware of the answers, and then the reality of God's invitation, and then move through all whatever internal or external "stuff" you may have—we still are left facing the REAL elephant in the room.

Our fear.

Now, what most people don't realize is that our fear is intrinsically tied to whatever we really love.

Saint Thomas writes in his *Summa Theologica*, *"Fear is born of love."* [12]

So, whatever we fear losing the most, that is the very thing (or person) that we love most, and that tends to be what we hold on to tightest, and resist anything we think might threaten what we love.

So, as we consider the great invitation before us, we *have* to control our fear.

But then after we control our fear, we must respond with courage.

But what exactly is courage?

Brene Brown, author of *Daring Greatly*, defines courage as "acting in the presence of vulnerability." And vulnerability is "any time that there is uncertainty, risk and emotional exposure."

So, courage is the willingness to be vulnerable.

In my children's historical fiction book, *March to Canada*, Abraham Hollister, tells his eleven-year-old son, Matthew, *"Doing the right thing when you are scared is what courage is about."*[13]

But doing the right thing when you are frightened of losing something (or someone) you love is downright difficult—if you don't love *enough*.

And that's usually how fear paralyzes us when we are choosing whether to follow Jesus.

We love the things in our possession and are afraid of losing them more than we love God, so we find that we lack the courage to set aside those things and do what is necessary to grow closer to God.

In particular, we find that we rarely have the courage to answer God's invitation to participate in the fullness of the life of the Trinity in the here and now.

Because we believe that *our* plans, *our* thinking, and *our* comfortable ways of living, are all more important, and we fail to find the courage to respond to God's marvelous invitation.

We don't answer the invitation to *"come and see"* how Jesus can transform us and help us live lives of purpose and meaning. Simply because we aren't willing to act with courage in the presence of vulnerability.

Or to embrace the uncertainty as to what may happen if we put God first in our lives. Or to be willing to risk failing as we struggle to develop the habits necessary to allow God to truly transform us. Or to emotionally expose ourselves to others by admitting that we need a Savior.

For me, this prayer by Saint Mother Teresa of Calcutta encapsulates my response to Jesus' invitation:

"He is the Life that I want to live.
He is the Light that I want to radiate.
He is the Way to the Father.
He is the Love with which I want to love.
He is the Joy that I want to share.
He is the Peace that I want to sow.
Jesus is Everything to me.
Without Him, I can do nothing."

But first, each of us must decide—will I follow? Or will I turn away like the rich young man?

It's time for you to answer with courage.

It's time for you to set aside all of your fears and to come and see the great plans God has in store for you—plans of hope, and purpose, and peace, and abundance.

But He needs YOU to trust His promises.

He needs YOU to open the door and step through.

He needs you to set out with Him on the journey and *"Be not afraid."*

SAY YES and *"Come and see."*

Now turn the page. Your Beloved is awaiting you.

PART 2

Encountering Authentic Peace

CHAPTER 6
THE FOUR STEPS TO HOLINESS

O ur journey thus far has focused upon the truths that must be rock-solid in our minds so we can discover and live out our deep purpose.

The foundation upon which we build is the absolute clarity and focus of who we are. We know without a doubt our lives have dignity, and we are called to holiness. We understand our lives have meaning because we have an unique and unrepeatable mission only we can do in the world. Finally, we must SAY YES to the journey and so prepare ourselves to embrace and pursue our life's purpose through which we will find our ultimate happiness and fulfillment.

Only after we have embraced the answers to these questions of our life will we have in place a foundation strong enough to attempt the journey to become fully whom we have been created to be—unique signs of the Father's love and mercy in the world.

But *what* and *how* might we go about fully becoming those unique and unrepeatable signs of love and mercy in the world?

I spent decades searching for the answers.

But Saint Gerard Majella crystallizes the essence of what is the key to what and how we need become who we are created to be when he wrote, "*Who except God can give you peace? Has the world ever been able to satisfy the heart?*"

It is vital to know and understand that it is our spiritual core, our interior life, that sparks our imaginations, inspires our hearts, gives life its beauty, and helps us shape the world in which we live. As disciples of Christ, the spiritual reality we profess is what is to shape our thoughts, words, and actions, for it is "from Him in whom we live and move and have our being."[14]

All the self-help books and programs in the world contain a common theme. The idea is that it is from the thoughts and beliefs about oneself that the physical realities around us are impacted, and this not only determine our capabilities but also whether we will be successful in exercising those capabilities.

Within the interior life, this means we must immerse ourselves in developing a relationship with the One who is to shape our minds, inspire our hearts, and ultimately, transform us into images of Himself in the world—living, breathing, wonder-working saints.

But what exactly motivates us to make any change in our lives? People debate this, but most often, truly *lasting* change is rooted in love.

Saint Clare of Assisi said, "*We become what we love,*" and this is absolutely true. But the *entirety* of her observation gives us insight into why it is so vitally important to choose what we love with care:

> "*We become what we love and who we love shapes what we become.*
> *If we love things, we become a thing.*
> *If we love nothing, we become nothing.*
> *Imitation is not a literal mimicking of Christ, rather it means becoming the image of the Beloved, an image disclosed through transformation.*
> *This means we are to become vessels of God's compassionate love for others.*

So how do we do this? How do we become a saint? How do we become holy, or to "become perfect as our Heavenly father is perfect"?

By undertaking four practices or steps.

These "Four Steps to Holiness" are: daily prayer and meditation, living a life of grace by frequenting the sacraments, growing daily in a life of virtue, and abandoning yourself to the Will of God.

These seem to be very simple steps, and they are. But just because they are simple doesn't mean they are easy, and this is where having our foundation firm is key.

Because everything we do needs to be motivated out of our love for Jesus. Our focus needs to be upon making whatever changes may be necessary so as to be transformed by the One we love.

Thomas Merton observed about his own life that once he came to understand he was not supposed to be about getting his ideas straight, but rather about getting his life straight, then he was set free to really pursue an intimate relationship with God. A good friend of mine, John Granger, calls this process of getting our lives straight, as becoming "right-ordered."

And that's really what we're about here. We're striving to put God first in our lives so we can become right-ordered and become fully transformed into His image in the world.

The Catholic Church has taught these fundamental practices for more than two millennia, and the lives of all the countless saints instruct us as well. *Every* spiritually fruitful practice of the interior life falls into one or another of these four steps. And without one or another of the steps, you will inevitably stall or even stop altogether, on your spiritual journey.

All of what we are to do, and all of how we are to go about these practices in our interior life is so we may become the creation God made us to be—holy men and women.

SAY YES to the Four Steps of Holiness.

Now, turn the page. It's time to start.

CHAPTER 7
STEP ONE—DAILY PRAYER AND MEDITATION

*"Of all human activities, man's listening to God is
the supreme act of his reasoning and will."*

— Saint Pope Paul VI

As I just discussed in the previous chapter, all of what we are to become, and how we are to go about doing it in our spiritual life fall into practicing the 4 Steps.

It is the first one, Daily Prayer and Meditation, that I will address now.

For me, prayer is how I recharge and refocus every morning. To use a technology analogy, it's how I am "plugging in to recharge and reboot." All of us need to recharge, and very often, due to the responsibilities we have in our daily lives, it is vital we take a break and reboot so we gain perspective on why we are doing all of what it is we care about. But it's impossible to recharge or reboot without us plugging in.

Ok. I know there are wireless charging platforms out there. However, you still have to place your device on that wireless charger for recharging to happen, and rebooting is only possible if, according to Apple, "Your device is plugged in and connected to a wireless network!"

So, any of us have your device miss a key update because you didn't do one or the other of those two things with your device? I know I have, and the results were catastrophic—at least technologically!

In spiritual parlance, the process of plugging in and connecting to the wireless network is called prayer. The fact is we need to be present to God—to pray—every day because it is through prayer that we are "recharged," and God has an opportunity to give us a "reboot"—His perspective on all the issues and events going on in our lives.

"Prayer is not a question of what you say or feel, but of love. And you love when you try to say something to the Lord, even though you might not actually say anything."[15]

Saint Therese of Lisieux echoed this understanding of simply being present when she wrote, *"For me, prayer is a surge of the heart; it is a simple look turned toward heaven, it is a cry of recognition and of love, embracing both trial and joy."*[16]

And there will be trials and joys in your prayer, but of all the spiritual practices you need to fight for, it's this one. It's worth every minute. It's worth every struggle and challenge to form the habit of daily prayer and meditation.

Now, there are three different types of prayer the Church instructs us about: these are vocal prayer, meditation, and contemplation. The first two types of prayer are on us as we have to set about doing most of the work. We have to show up.

Most of us tend to be very familiar with vocal prayers—examples are the Our Father, the Hail Mary, novena prayers, chaplets, etc. There are many, many, different vocal prayers--the words of someone else. Therefore, the name vocal prayer.

Meditation is where you immerse yourself in the Word of God and spend time in quiet reflection, talking with God. The most common way to enter into meditation is to use Sacred Scripture, especially the Gospels.

The reason for this is that Scripture is the *Living Word*.

The Church teaches how this is experienced by discussing the four senses of Scripture.

Biblical scholars refer to four distinct senses of Scripture: the literal, the allegorical, the anagogical, and the moral. A Latin poem from the Middle Ages sums up what each sense is about quite well.[17] In English, it reads this way:

The literal sense teaches what happened,
The allegorical what you should believe,
The moral what you should do,
The anagogical where you are going.

And the Catechism beautifully teaches "The profound concordance of the four senses guarantees all its richness to the living reading of Scripture in the Church."[18]

It is in this richness that we immerse ourselves in daily meditation. It is why the same Scripture passage will never speak to us quite the same way it did to us before. (And if we are finding this to be the case, then we probably need to go back and listen to God's voice a bit harder!).

This is why meditation is *immersive*. We immerse ourselves in the richness and beauty of the living voice of God that comes to us in His Word, and we need to be *quiet* and spend time in silence with the Word to hear His whispers. For God is *always* whispering to us.

Now all of our meditation prepares us for the third type of prayer—contemplation.

But only *if* God wills it.

Because contemplation is all according to God's grace. We do the work, we prepare our hearts and our minds and show up to have that conversation with God, and then if He desires it, we will enter into times of contemplation. Times when we are truly in union with God. But again, contemplation is not something *we* do, rather, this is God's grace working in us.

And that's the thing for us to always keep in mind. To be friends with God just means to have a conversation with him. St Teresa of Avila, who is the Doctor of the Church of Prayer, tells us exactly that, prayer is simply a conversation with God. So instead of getting all caught up in, so how do I pray? Just remember it's really pretty simple. It's just about sitting down and having a conversation.

So, open yourself up to encountering the embodiment of peace in the person of Jesus.

Commit to having intimate, loving conversations with the Person who is your best friend.

Enter into *the* loving friendship that will transform you and your life now and for all eternity.

SAY YES to daily prayer and meditation.

And it's time to turn the page. Your phone is ringing.

CHAPTER 8
ANSWERING THE PHONE

S o, you want to practice the step of daily prayer and meditation. You are all in for having conversations with God and growing in friendship with Him.

But exactly *how* do you go about it?

As I mentioned briefly in the last chapter, the Church teaches there are three types of prayer—vocal, meditation, and contemplation.

Vocal prayers are just that, anything we say aloud by ourselves or with others. There are many prayers and novenas to the Holy Spirit, angels, and each of the saints, or for a particular intention, etc. You name it; and there is a prayer for it.

There is no lack of vocal prayers one can offer, and it can quickly become overwhelming.

I get the struggle because it's hard to choose which ones to focus upon. But what's important is not that we do every prayer, but rather we strive to offer prayers that have meaning to us.

For example, if we or someone we know is fighting cancer, perhaps we pray a novena to Saint Peregrine, the patron saint of those struggling with cancer. Or if we are seeking mercy or comfort for someone who is dying, we may offer a Divine Mercy Chaplet. Or if we are offering prayers for the protection of someone spiritually, we can offer a Saint Michael or Guardian Angel prayer, or maybe the Chaplet of Saint Michael.

The options are just about innumerable. Be attentive to how the Holy Spirit is calling upon you to intercede on your behalf, but especially for others God has had cross your path, and tailor your vocal prayers in response to the needs you encounter in your own life and the lives of others.

Now one of the great challenges in maintaining and persevering in daily prayer is it can be challenging, or just downright difficult because it seems like the other person in the conversation isn't talking back. Maybe God hasn't picked up the phone on His end?

But that's not true. God is *always* whispering to us.

God is always on the line. He is always speaking. But we have to learn how to listen.

And this is the purpose of meditation, the second type of prayer. We must work hard so we can learn how to listen and how to identify God's voice more easily. To do that, we have to be spending time having a conversation to begin with, because if we're not showing up, then it's pretty difficult to have a conversation at all.

It's the same concept as if you don't answer a phone call. It's impossible to talk to someone else if you are not on the line. And that's the purpose of daily prayer and meditation. It's about us answering the phone.

And one of the best ways to answer the phone and have a conversation with God is by opening the Scriptures and encountering and immersing ourselves in the Word Himself.

LECTIO DIVINA AND THE FOUR R'S

The most common way this is done is through a practice known in the Church as Lectio Divina. Lectio Divina is an ancient prayer form of opening up the Word of God and then prayerfully immersing ourselves, and meditating upon it. I am not going to go into detail about Lectio Divina here, but rather I'm going to give you a little different, simpler kind of acronym to keep in mind if you are just beginning meditation.

Because there are a TON of different ones out there. But I want to share this one with you that was shared with me by the Apostles of Interior Life, a religious community of consecrated brothers and sisters. I have had the benefit and privilege of knowing and being in community with them as I am a promised Family Member of the Apostles. Part of my promises as a Family member is to live out this practice of daily prayer and meditation, and the Apostles acronym for how to engage in meditative prayer is through using the "four R's."

The four "R's" are: Read, Reflect, Relate, and Resolution.

So, you begin with *Read*. Whenever you come before our Lord in prayer, you ask the Holy Spirit to help open you up to becoming immersed in His Word, and then you read.

Next is *Reflect*. So, as you read, you seek to use all of your senses and engage your mind by directing your thoughts to Him, who is the Living Word. This is similar to a form of imaginative prayer, called Ignatian prayer. This involves seeking to use all of your senses to place yourself alongside the Lord during a Gospel scene.

And then you *Relate*. This means you relate what is in your heart to God. You share what you are feeling, seeing, hearing, and tasting, and perhaps even smelling as you go deep into Scripture. The most important piece of relating is to remember it's a conversation. So, as you are relating to our Lord all of what you are thinking and feeling, you need to allow Him to speak to you about whatever it is He desires to share with you. This means we need to practice silence.

It takes time and practice. And then sometimes you are sitting there, and you're thinking, "I got nothing." But if you persevere, eventually, you will begin to hear the whisper of His voice. And once you hear His whisper, the timbre of it, the rhythm and cadence of it, then you will become better at hearing His voice more easily. The more you practice, the better you get. This is why it is SO important for you to fight as hard as you can to carve out time to spend in meditation *each and every day*.

And the final R is *Resolution*. A resolution is a small, concrete action you do during the day that helps you take whatever it is our Lord has spoken to you during your meditation, and make it a part of your life throughout your day. This is where the rubber meets the road, for it is through your resolution that the power of God's Word can truly reveal itself and be present in your life. It is through a resolution that you will be more open to allowing His word to take root in your heart and to prompt you to see yourself as He sees you and to be able to identify those times when you are not in good relations with Him. You will be able to ask yourself, "How am I not holy?" and then hear His response. Or "How am I going to try and respond to what you've shared with me today, Lord?" Your resolution emerges from answering these questions.

So those are the four R's. They are one of the easiest ways you can begin to practice meditative prayer using Scripture.

THE ROSARY

One of the most beautiful prayers you can use for meditation is the Rosary. Many people think it is simply a repetitive vocal prayer, but this is not entirely accurate. The Rosary can be of great value, because although it has elements of vocal prayer, it can easily lead you into meditation. This is due to the opportunity to meditate on the mysteries of the faith. This is most commonly done using the different Mysteries of the Rosary, which are scenes from the life of Jesus and Mary. But one can also use other excerpts from Scripture, or any teaching of the Church, or writings of a saint. Anything that causes you to read, reflect, relate, and resolve to ponder more deeply about the truth, goodness, and beauty of the Good News.

Saint John Paul the Second commended the fruitfulness of the practice of praying the Rosary for believers when he said, "To pray the Rosary is to sit at the foot of Mary. And when we sit in the school of Mary, you learn at her feet about the life of her Son."[19]

The Rosary is so effective that it can serve as the perfect instrument to help prepare us for entering into the third type of prayer, contemplation. By showing up and doing the work within our hearts, minds, and souls through vocal prayers and meditation, God can more easily share the graces necessary for someone to enter into contemplation. And contemplation is when you come before Him and enter into a truly transforming conversation with Him in which no words are necessary. Where you just look at Him, and He looks at you, and it is perfect union.

CONSISTENCY

Although there are many different ways you can choose to pray, don't get hung up on which prayer to do, or about whether you are doing it correctly. Rather, make sure to choose a time and a place, and then PRAY. Block out the time, even if it's only ten minutes, but make sure you choose it and commit to it. That's how you begin to cultivate the habit of daily prayer and meditation.

Consistency is the key, though.

For the longest time, although I *knew* the key to growing closer to Jesus was by spending time with Him in prayer, I struggled to establish a daily prayer life. First, it was the whole "I don't have time to pray, I am busy doing other things" excuse. Then, it was, "I'll pray when I get time during the day."

I went through a whole assortment of different excuses for years. Still, it wasn't until I finally admitted to myself I didn't *want* to take the time to sit down and pray that I began to really make any serious headway in faithfully spending time every day in prayer.

And it was simply about faithfully showing up and answering the phone.

Jesus wants to be our refuge. He wants to help us not become distracted by the million things going on around us, but rather focus upon Him who is peace amid the storms of life. He knows it is only in Him that the infinite longings in our hearts will find an infinite response, and it's only in Him that we will find true and lasting peace.

Dr Allen Hunt, in his book, *Dreams for Your Grandchild*, writes, "Ten minutes a day can make all the difference in the world. The more time you spend in the classroom of silence, the more clearly you will hear the voice of God in your life. A daily routine of prayer is the ultimate game-changer. As you begin to pray consistently, you will notice other parts of your life opening up in healthy ways you never anticipated."[20]

All of prayer is a communication of love for the other. How, where, and when we pray is not as important as the fact that *we do it*. Not out of obligation, but out of love. Born from our desire to spend time with our best friend, our lover, our Beloved—the One in whom we discover our purpose, meaning, and destiny. Or, "The One in whom we live and move and have our being."

But to actually spend time with Jesus in prayer and meditation *every day* is the key.

It is the primary conduit through which our relationship with God is established and maintained throughout our lives— minute by minute, hour by hour, day by day, week by week, month by month, year by year—and into eternity.

And it will become the means through which God will transform you into the unique sign of His love and mercy in the world He created you to be.

SAY YES to taking the time each and every day to entering into conversation, so you will ensure that you have *God's* love and vision for your life.

Ask, and you *will* receive.

God's on the line.

SAY YES and answer the phone.

Now, turn the page to take the next step and live the life of grace.

CHAPTER 9
STEP TWO--LIVING THE LIFE OF GRACE

*"Few souls understand what God would accomplish in them
if they were to abandon themselves unreservedly to him and
if they were to allow his grace to mold them accordingly."*

— St Ignatius of Loyola[21]

Step Two—Living the Life of Grace, is a critical component in our journey towards holiness. Because of its importance, we must ensure we are receiving the graces of God that are available to us and to allow those graces to mold us accordingly.

To accomplish this, we must be attentive to three different aspects to living the life of grace. These aspects are: 1) ensuring we are living the life of grace in accordance with the Church's teaching; 2) seeking to increase the flow of grace; and 3) doing the work necessary to keep the life of grace flowing nonstop.

The life of grace begins with an encounter in the sacraments of the Church. And I say *encounter* intentionally because it is through the sacraments that we can personally encounter the person of Jesus Christ in real and tangible ways.

The Catechism of the Catholic Church, paragraph 1131 states:

> "*The sacraments are efficacious signs of grace, instituted by Christ and entrusted to the Church, by which divine life is dispensed to us. The visible rites by which the sacraments are celebrated signify and make present the graces proper to each sacrament. **They bear fruit in those who receive them with the required dispositions.**"22 (bold emphases mine)*

The purpose of this chapter is not to go into a discussion about what sacraments *are*, but rather how we can ensure they can be most effective within our interior lives.

In the last two chapters, we focused upon the first step of holiness—spending time in daily prayer and meditation.

The first step is *the key* to ensuring you will be open to receiving God's love and vision for your life. And this is why it is necessary to commit to making prayer a *daily* practice.

Next on the journey is living the life of grace. Living the life of grace is accomplished primarily by frequenting the sacraments of Holy Eucharist and Reconciliation. "Frequenting" simply means we are seeking to receive God's graces in both of these repeatable sacraments more often than what the Church mandates in its Precepts.

If you are unaware, the Precepts are the Church's guidance as to the responsibilities of the faithful as to what are the bare minimums necessary for living out the faith.

The seven Precepts are:

1. To attend Mass on all Sundays and Holy Days of Obligation.

2. To confess our sins at least once a year.

3. To receive Holy Communion at least once a year, during the Easter Season.

4. To observe the prescribed days of fasting and abstinence from meat.

5. To provide for the material needs of the Church, each according to his or her abilities.

6. To observe the marriage laws of the Church.

7. To participate in the Church's mission of Evangelization of Souls.

So, if you are fulfilling the Precepts, then you will be attending Mass on all Sundays and Holy Day of Obligation, and most likely receiving Holy Eucharist more than once a year.

However, to live the life of grace and truly *frequent* the sacraments, you will need to commit to go to Mass on more than just Sundays and Holy Days. For Reconciliation, this means to receive the sacrament more than just once a year.

Why? Fr Jacques Philippe tells us in his book, *In the School of the Holy Spirit*:

> "*However great our efforts, we cannot change ourselves. Only God can get to the bottom of our defects, and our limitations in the field of love; only He has sufficient mastery over our hearts for that. If we realize that we will save ourselves a great deal of discouragement and fruitless struggle. We do not have to become saints by our own power; we have to learn how to let God make us into saints. That does not mean, of course, that we don't have to make any effort . . . We should fight, not to attain holiness as a result of our own efforts, but to let God act in us without our putting up any resistance against Him;* **we should fight to open ourselves as fully as possible to His grace,** *which sanctifies us.*"[23] **(bold emphases mine)**

To strive to open ourselves as fully as possible to God's grace, we have to be working to make sure we are actually receiving them in the first place. This means we must be attentive to living out our faith—living the life of grace—in accordance with the laws of the Church.

Fr Joseph Langford, in his book, *I Thirst:40 Days with Mother Teresa,* explains this:

> "*This means that it is not enough that we receive the Eucharist daily or reflect on God's word daily. The problem is that our own weak faith can have the effect of quenching the Spirit. Though it is true that the sacraments are sources of infinite power and holiness, we sound their depths only according to the degree of our faith. The exercise of faith changes us in 2 ways. First, it awakens and intensifies our awareness of Jesus' presence and thirst in our lives. And secondly, it increases our readiness to receive Him...To benefit fully from our daily contact with the Lord, we need to be sure that we are touching Jesus in faith.*"[24]

As I have learned on my own journey, we are absolutely blessed by the reality that as Catholics we have access to *all* of what it is that Jesus wants to give us in order to help us become holy in this life. He has given us His Word in the Scriptures, His very self in the sacraments of the Church, and His Spirit present in His Church to guide, encourage, and support us.

This is because Jesus knew from experience life could be difficult and full of challenges—many ups and downs and joys and sorrows. And Jesus knew without Him, we weren't going to be able to make it. He knew we wouldn't be able to do what He asks us to do—which is to follow Him and to become "perfect as our Heavenly Father is perfect."

Without Jesus, we aren't able to truly become the saints God created us to be. Jesus knew we wouldn't be able to share the love and mercy God wishes to shower upon the world if we weren't being filled up with His love and mercy.

So, when we begin to consider the question of "How do I live a life of grace?" our answer is straight forward. In addition to daily prayer, we must come and receive Jesus in His sacraments. To do this, we come to Mass, receive Holy Eucharist, and we go to frequent Reconciliation.

But the reality is that we need to first begin by making sure we're being faithful about attending Mass. Father Roman Guardini instructs us *everything* we do at Mass should have but one intention—to serve God.

> *"We do not come to church to attend the service as a spectator, but in order, along with the priest, to serve God. Everything we do—our entering, being present, our kneeling and sitting and standing, our reception of the sacred nourishment—should be divine service. This is so only when all we do overflows from the awareness of a collected heart and the mind's attentiveness."[25]*

So, how well are we serving? How present are we as we enter God's presence? When we kneel, when we sit, when we stand? But how attentive are we when we receive our sacred nourishment?

And are we coming to Mass as frequently as we should? *Every* Sunday (or Saturday evening) *and* on all the holy days of obligation?

Obligation can be a difficult word in our society today. We think, oh gosh, I have to do something, so therefore we don't want to do it. It's just like any two-year old who is told he has to do something and of course the first word is no!

Even though we might be older, we're the same way. Part of the reason for a habit of daily prayer and meditation is so that we are taught and learn how to be childlike—humble and trusting, so then we can trust in the Church that Jesus founded through the coming of His Holy Spirit more than 2000 years ago. For it is in His Church, that His most abundant graces come to us, particularly in the sacraments.

At our Baptism, each of us is baptized into the life of the Trinity. It's from our Baptism we are called to be priests, prophets, and kings and are called to enter into the work God is giving each of us to be able to help him bring about the redemption of the world.

Yet Jesus knew we would tire. He knew we would struggle and. That we would be hungry. That we would need Him to be able to fulfill our obligations. To be able to respond in love to all He calls us to. And this brings us back to the habit of frequenting the sacraments, of living the life of grace.

The two sacraments that are going to give us the grace we need consistently are the Holy Eucharist and Reconciliation.

Now, *all* of the sacraments are encounters with Christ and the opportunity to receive His grace for the journey. But the Eucharist is the source and summit of our faith. Saint Thomas Aquinas sums it up beautifully, *"The Eucharist is the Sacrament of Love. It signifies Love. It produces love. The Eucharist is the consummation of the whole spiritual life."*[26]

We need to grow in God's love and grace. To do that, we need to be following the precepts of the Church and fulfilling our obligations. We need to observe the prescribed days of fasting and abstinence from meat, provide for the material needs of the Church as we are capable, observing the marriage laws of the Church, and participating in the Church's mission of evangelization.

But most importantly, we must be coming to Mass *every* Sunday and *every* Holy day of obligation and to be receiving the sacraments of Holy Eucharist and Reconciliation more than the bare minimum of once a year.

This is the first aspect of living the life of grace. To ensure we are living it in accordance with Church teaching.

So put God first in your life and make it a priority to go and receive the graces God desires to give you in accordance with Church teaching.

SAY YES to living the life of grace.

Now, turn the page to begin receiving the fullness of His graces.

CHAPTER 10

LIVING THE FULLNESS OF THE LIFE OF GRACE

The second aspect of living the life of grace is in seeking to establish habits that increase the amount of grace present in our life.

Why?

Isn't doing what the Church teaches in the Precepts enough to live out our faith?

No, it's not.

Living our faith in accordance with the Precepts is the *bare minimum* to ensure that our spiritual life does not die. The Precepts are the equivalent of being on life support. Our souls are barely breathing if we are attempting to live our faith merely at the level of the Precepts.

If we are serious about striving for holiness, about finding the purpose, peace, and abundance God desires for us, then we need to be doing all we can to get a hold of every bit of grace we can get our hands on, and then some so it becomes possible for us to live in the fullness of the life of grace.

This means we need to be seeking to receive the sacraments frequently.

Now, what is beautiful about our faith is there are many ways in which we can immerse ourselves more deeply into the life of grace, especially regarding the mystery that is the Eucharist. We can easily utilize numerous methods to increase our devotion and continue to grow in the right dispositions necessary to receive the fullness of graces present in the Eucharist.

However, the three I am about to share with you here though, are not only very simple and easy to implement but have also proven to be *extremely* effective for growing quickly in the life of grace.

FIRST, COME TO MASS MORE THAN JUST ONCE A WEEK.

Think about it. If we're only eating food once a week, our physical bodies would decline pretty quickly. Our interior soul needs nourishment, too, and coming to Mass more than once a week enables us to receive more nourishment for our spiritual life.

The Church gives us an obligation of coming at least once a week primarily because we need our spiritual food, the Eucharist at least once a week, but the more frequently we can receive the Eucharist, the more we are filled with God's grace.

We come to Mass to be reminded of Jesus' love for us, and how loveable we are. SO loveable that not only did Jesus die for us, but He becomes food for us. So, when we receive the Eucharist, we get to come into contact with GOD—Body, Blood, Soul, and Divinity.

Saint John Vianney tells us, "*Upon receiving Holy Communion, the Adorable Blood of Jesus Christ really flows in our veins, and His Flesh is really blended with ours.*"[27]

Because the Holy Eucharist is no ordinary meal. Blessed Pier Giorgio Frassati said, "*I urge you with all the strength of my soul to approach the Eucharistic Table as often as possible. Feed on this Bread of the Angels from which you will draw the strength to fight inner struggles.*"[28]

How could we say no to that?

THE SECOND PRACTICE IS TO COME BEFORE OUR LORD IN ADORATION.

This is our opportunity to just "hang out" and spend quiet time with Him. Where we continue to be transformed simply by being in His presence.

Many people question, or even doubt the value of this practice because it can be difficult to see how spending time doing what the world considers to be, "nothing" could have such a profound impact upon us. To illustrate, let me share the analogy of how Adoration is like going to the beach to get a suntan.

Tons of people love going to the beach and just laying out in the sunshine. The warmth as you literally "bake" in the sun, and the peace they experience as they do nothing but lay on their beach towel. Now, if you use sunscreen and do this several days, you end up with a suntan (vs. if you forget to use sunscreen, and then you get burned pretty quickly!).

But this is a beautiful way to think about the time you spend before our Lord in Adoration. For when you bask in the glow of His love for you, you rest in His presence. And, as we spend time in Adoration, we end up getting a suntan, too. But this one is a "Son-tan," where instead of our skin getting darker, Jesus gradually transforms us interiorly so we look more and more like Him to any person who encounters us.

Even the simple practice of coming before Jesus when the Blessed Sacrament rests in the Tabernacle can have a positive impact. So even if there is no Adoration available in your local area, developing the practice of stopping by the church for a "short visit" to say hello will also have a long ranging impact on your spiritual life.

THE THIRD PRACTICE IS SPENDING TIME IN THANKSGIVING AFTER HOLY COMMUNION.

In many parishes there is a time of quiet, or soft music that is playing as we receive Holy Communion. This is designed to help us reflect upon the fact we have just received the Lord of Lords, and to remind us that when we receive the Holy Eucharist, this is the closest we're ever going to be to Jesus in this world.

But part of the reason for intentionally spending time in Thanksgiving is to increase the time we can give thanks. This is to ensure that regardless of what different parishes may do or not do, we will still be able to keep gratitude at the forefront of our receiving Jesus in Holy Eucharist.

So instead of turning around and talking to your neighbors in the pew after the final blessing, or hurrying to get to the parking lot, take a moment and kneel or sit down quietly and spend a short amount of time giving thanks to our Lord for the great grace you've just been given. Try to spend at least three to five minutes, immersing yourself in Jesus' love for you.

Now, as you look to incorporate this practice into your own spiritual life, you might be wondering what or how it is you should pray. I suggest a better way to spend this time is not to pray using any particular words, but simply share what is in your heart, and try to remain as close to Jesus as you can.

However, if you still are finding this to be difficult, a wonderful image to use is from the Last Supper. To envision how the Beloved Disciple, John, laid his head on the breast of Jesus after the first Eucharist during the Last Supper. And for us to be mindful of this image as we strive to be close to Jesus in a similar way.

I know if we are taking the opportunity to grow in awareness and thanksgiving for this great gift, and striving to stay as intimately connected with Jesus as possible during the time we give thanks, then we truly open ourselves to growing in our appreciation of the Holy Eucharist.

Father Jacques Philippe writes:

"What prevents us from receiving more abundant graces from God may be quite simply our not being sufficiently grateful and not thanking him for the graces he has already

given us. There is no doubt that if we thank God with all our heart for each grace received, especially for the inspirations [of the Holy Spirit], He will grant us more.[29]

So, by practicing Thanksgiving after Communion, we allow Jesus to transform us and help increase within us the "right dispositions" mentioned in the Catechism so we can truly open ourselves to receiving the *fullness* of grace from the sacraments.

Saint Pope John Paul II reminds us *"From the Eucharist comes the strength to live out the Christian life, and the zeal to be able to live life with others."*[30] This is absolutely true, which is why we need to strive to grow in our capacity to receive and incorporate practices into our daily lives that help us grow in appreciation of the Holy Eucharist.

Seek to live the life of grace as fully as possible so God can mold you into the perfect, unrepeatable image of Himself He created you to be. Because if we do, we will be transformed in ways we cannot even begin to imagine.

And how could we possibly say no to that?

SAY YES to living the fullness of life of grace.

Now, turn the page to keep the life of grace flowing nonstop.

CHAPTER 11
THE LIFE OF GRACE
FLOWING NONSTOP

So why do we say no to living the life of grace in its fullness? Because we love our sin more than Jesus.

Ouch.

Harsh, but true, isn't it? Because the truth is that if we are not willing to do *whatever* is necessary in order to receive Jesus more frequently in His sacraments—especially His Body, Blood, Soul, and Divinity in the Most Holy Eucharist—then we are *lying* when we say we want Jesus to be Lord of our lives.

Why am I so direct? Because again, we are masters at self-deception, especially when it comes to our sinfulness.

> *"Many Christians regard Confession in the light of an unimportant act of piety, if not mere ceremony . . . many go even frequently to Confession, but so few amend, and consequently derive little or no benefit from the Sacrament. ... Be, then, most thoroughly convinced of the immense importance of this Sacrament, and be filled with an earnest desire of approaching it worthily, bestowing the utmost care and attention upon your preparation for this great duty, if you desire to obtain eternal salvation.*

Confession is one of the seven Sacraments instituted by Christ; it is called the Sacrament of Penance, and by its means alone can he who has committed mortal sin after Baptism hope to save his soul; therefore it is called by the holy Council of Trent: the second plank after shipwreck. In this Sacrament, Jesus Christ has deposited His Precious Blood, that it may be to our souls as a salutary bath wherein they may be cleansed from all the stains of sin, their wounds closed, their maladies cured, their weakness strengthened, and grace unto salvation imported to them. This Divine Blood is dispensed to us by the priest in the holy absolution, and is **abundantly poured forth upon all souls approaching the tribunal of confession with proper dispositions."[31]** *(bold emphases mine)*

This is why we need to frequently receive the sacrament of Reconciliation (also known as Confession or Penance). It's about cultivating those "right dispositions" in the midst of this most beautiful sacrament of our Lord's forgiveness and healing, the one we tend to neglect and forget about.

And why might that be? As I stated before, perhaps it's because we love our sin more than Jesus? It can be a difficult reality to face, but if we are not willing to adjust our schedules, make time with our Lord in Adoration a priority, or make sure to come and encounter Him in confession regularly, then how can we truly claim to actually love God "with our whole heart, our whole strength, and our whole soul?"[32]

The Catechism explains this dichotomy beautifully:

"Through the sacraments of Christian initiation, man receives the new life of Christ. Now we carry this life 'in earthen vessels,' and it remains 'hidden with Christ in God'. We are still in our 'earthly tent,' subject to suffering, illness, and death. This new life as a child of God can be weakened and even lost by sin. The Lord Jesus Christ,

*physician of our souls and bodies, who forgave the sins of the
paralytic and restored him to bodily health, has willed that
his Church continue, in the power of the Holy Spirit, his
work of healing and salvation, even among her own members. This is the purpose of the two sacraments of healing:
the sacrament of Penance and the sacrament of Anointing
of the Sick."[33]*

Because each time we come to Confession, we are not just
being forgiven for our sinfulness. We are also being *healed.*

Confession is about encountering God's beautiful mercy
and allowing Him to give us the graces we need to be able to
fight against the very thing that we're confessing. That's the *true*
purpose of reconciliation. To heal us not only of our sinfulness,
but to heal us of those very sins we are confessing. As our Lord
explained to St Paul, *"My grace is sufficient for you, for My strength
is made perfect in weakness."[34]*

The sacrament of Reconciliation can also help us grow in
our awareness of what exactly are the things I might need to
confess. I know one of the things that I struggled with early
on when I was beginning to try and come to the sacrament of
Reconciliation more frequently was, well, what do I confess? I
haven't done any mortal sins I know of, so what is it I should be
confessing?

Venerable Archbishop Fulton Sheen gives us beautiful insight into how we should look at our lives in regard to sin. He
says:

*"No one who thinks it is just the breaking of a law really
grasps the evil of sin. When we have the Spirit of Christ, we
understand that sin is doing harm to one we love...Nothing
but the Holy Spirit can really convince us of sin...our conscience is smothered by repeated evil. We rationalize our
evil deeds. Public opinion sometimes even approves of sin."[35]*

So in a world that often approves of our sin, and even numbs our conscience to that sin, how can we develop the awareness we need so the Holy Spirit can assist us in identifying those times when we intentionally, or unintentionally, harm the very One whom we claim to love above all things?

THE DAILY EXAMEN

Integrated into a habit of daily prayer and meditation, the practice of a daily Examen can be a beautiful tool. It helps us allow the Holy Spirit to guide us and transform our conscience into one that is sensitive about how and when we are harming God and others.

The Examen is a tool given to us by Saint Ignatius of Loyola. St Ignatius was the founder of the Society of Jesus, the Jesuits, and he encouraged his brother Jesuit priests to perform an Examen at least once a day. Just as it helped them, it can help us too.

The Examen is designed to be *brief,* and asks us to focus upon the blessings of God first. This is starting with what we hear in some circles today as "an attitude of gratitude." From there, we then look to try and see the movement of the Holy Spirit in the midst of our day's events, people, and activities and identify the times where we have failed to love and serve God as He has called us to. Once we see how we have failed, we ask for God's forgiveness, and then ask for His grace to begin again. Through the practice of the Examen, we gradually grow in our awareness of, as well as our capacity to identify our sins. Finally, it also helps us begin to identify whatever our predominant sin might be.

What is a predominant sin? Simply, a predominant sin is the one sin that we tend to *always* be confessing. You probably know what I am talking about. It's that one that when we do get to confession, it's the sin we seem to be confessing—*again*.

For myself, my predominant sins are pride and anger. I have struggled with those continuously throughout my life, and although I have gotten better, (and I can see some growth in these areas of my life), I still struggle. It can be extremely frustrating and discouraging to be confronted over and over with what seems to be the same sin, especially if we are striving to deepen our interior lives and come more frequently to the sacrament of Reconciliation.

But that's exactly *why* we need to go more frequently to the sacrament of Reconciliation.

Because as I said before, confession is not just about the fact we are forgiven: it is also the opportunity to be healed of our wounds. Those very wounds we tend to see as weaknesses, but which can actually become places of strength our Lord can work through—if we let Him. And *if* we but frequent the sacrament of Reconciliation.

It All Comes Together

It is in this way that Jesus can make us vessels of His grace, love, and mercy for all the people who encounter us in the midst of our daily lives. Because then, people will not just encounter us, but they will also encounter Jesus, especially if we are being frequently filled with His graces in the sacraments of Holy Eucharist and Reconciliation.

It's only then we are capable of being His presence of love and mercy to others. And this is what the life of grace is all about. Where we allow ourselves to be filled with God's grace, and then we go out into the world as unrepeatable signs of His love and mercy.

> *"As a man must be born before he can begin to lead his physical life, so he must be born to lead a Divine Life. That birth occurs in the Sacrament of Baptism. To survive, he must be*

nourished by Divine Life; that is done in the Sacrament of the Holy Eucharist."[36]

There is no other authentic way to strive for perfection.

"Everything in the religious order—sacraments, devotions, teaching, scripture, moral discipline, preaching, etc.—is meant to bring us to this deeper state of being, to this Divine Connection. Jesus calls it "abiding" (Jn 15:4). The Latin for this is maneo which means "to remain" or "to stay" or "to endure" (or like the Marine Corps' Semper Fi). This Divine Connection, this conformity to love, this participation in the Divine Life of God is the very power of the Holy Spirit and is referred to as being in a state of grace."[37]

This is why frequent reception of both Holy Eucharist and Reconciliation are such phenomenally effective instruments to bring about holiness. Because it just is NOT possible to frequently receive our Lord—Body, Blood, Soul, and Divinity, and remain the same.

So, set aside those things that close off your heart, mind, and soul to receiving the very graces you need in order to be sustained in the pursuit of holiness. Because living the life of grace is all about how we allow God's grace to transform us into the saints He created us to be.

For through, with, and in His grace all things ARE possible.

SAY YES to the graces of God flowing in your life nonstop.

Turn that page. It's time to take your next step on the journey towards holiness.

CHAPTER 12

STEP THREE—GROWING DAILY IN VIRTUE

"Think well. Speak well. Do well. These three things, through the mercy of God, will make a man go to Heaven."

— St. Camillus

Although we may be spending time with God each day in prayer and striving to frequently receive His graces, we still need to do our part to lay the foundation upon which we can build a life directed towards the pursuit of holiness. This is what the third step—daily growth in virtue is all about.

So, what is virtue exactly? Simply, virtue is the habitual disposition to do the good with ease, promptness, and joy. When someone is virtuous, they don't have to think about it. They just do it. And this is why this is an activity that must be practiced daily so we will be capable of doing the good easily, promptly, and joyfully.

It is impossible to stress enough how important it is to attempt each and every day to grow in virtue as our Lord is calling us to do. But many times we hesitate to do this because we think daily growth in virtue is some theoretical thing that is going on "out there," rather than something that is intrinsically a part of each and every event going on within our lives.

Daily growth in virtue is, at its essence, our ability to recognize and see that God is working in, through, and with everything—all the people, things, and events of our life, to help us become more like Him.

Mother Angelica, deceased founder of the community of the Poor Clares of Perpetual Adoration in Irondale, Alabama, but who is more well-known as the founder of Eternal Word Television Network (EWTN), once said, *"All of life is a school of holiness. Everything that happens to you, the bad weather to an ingrown toenail, is an opportunity for us to become like Jesus."*

If we keep this in mind, then we realize that growing in virtue each day is not some ethereal thing "out there," but rather is a normal, natural part of our lives. This reality is evident by how the Church begins its determination for whether someone should be declared a saint. The canonization process begins by examining whether that person lived a life of heroic virtue. In other words, whether they lived holy lives. So, lived virtue *is* holiness.

But like anything in life, virtue has to be practiced. We don't just happen to be virtuous. We have to work at it. This is why many practices and devotions to assist us with growing in virtue have developed throughout the centuries. These methods are all focused upon helping us invite God into whatever it is we are doing throughout the course of the day, regardless of our state of life, occupation, or location.

Now, none of these practices or devotions are about another "thing to do." Rather, these devotions are about providing opportunities for us to become more fully aware of God's presence, and then for us to intentionally allow Him to become more fully present into every aspect of our lives—down to every thought, every word, and every action.

This is the primary reason why the first step we must take on the journey to holiness is daily prayer and meditation. For it is only in the midst of immersing ourselves in conversations with the Living Word, that we can be transformed. Saint Paul writes in Romans 12:2, *"And do not be conformed to this world, but be transformed by the renewing of your mind, that you may prove what the will of God is, that which is good and acceptable and perfect."*

As our thoughts are transformed, then so will be our words and actions. It really is just as Jesus tells us in Mark 7:15, *"It is not what goes into a man that defiles him, but what things proceed out of a man that defiles him."*

Then as we are slowly transformed, we are then better able to fight against our disordered tendencies and sinfulness. We become ever more rightly aligned and pointed towards "what is good and acceptable and perfect." We become what is known as "right-ordered."

When people ask me what it is to be "right-ordered," I love to use an analogy by a good friend of mine, John Granger. It's an "upside down snowman."

Simply think of a snowman. You have the largest ball at the bottom, a medium ball in the middle, and a smaller ball on the top. Everything is in proportion and balanced, so the snowman stands upright with no problem.

Now, in the classical world, it was thought a person was comprised of three parts—Body, Mind, and Soul. Now, correlate each part of the classical person with a ball of the snowman—the Body is the large ball on the bottom, the Mind is the medium ball in the middle, and the Soul is the small ball on top. A "right-ordered" person is one in which the mind, or will, directs the body, and then the soul, or the heart of the person, directs both the mind and body towards a higher goal or purpose.

Now, think about our world today. Almost everything is about bodily needs first. What feels good and tastes good takes precedence over anything else. Sometimes you'll hear about using "mind over matter" or "willpower" in order to make our bodies do and act as we desire them to as we impose training programs, or self-discipline, to achieve a "beach body" or lose unwanted weight, or to eat healthier foods so we avoid illness or disease. Or perhaps we desire a particular job, or want a promotion, so we are willing to sacrifice sleep and other recreational activities to receive the training or take the courses necessary to get a particular degree and so be able to apply for a different job.

But for someone to strive for a greater purpose outside of things than those associated with the Body or Mind? Extremely rare.

So, if you take this and apply it to the snowman analogy, you'll see in our world today, the tiny ball of the Soul is at the bottom, the middle ball of the Mind is in the middle, and the large ball of the Body is on top. This makes us "upside-down snowmen."

And as a result of being "upside-down snowmen," few of us are "right-ordered" in our spiritual lives because we are being distracted by all the lesser goods associated with our bodies and minds.

To become "right-ordered" is the great struggle and goal of the spiritual life. Where we struggle and strive to the best of our abilities along with God's grace, to transform every thought, word, and action to reflect what is good, acceptable, and perfect.

When we become completely right-ordered, by putting first things first in our life, then our every thought, word and action proves to be what is good, and acceptable and perfect, and we have become "perfect like our Heavenly Father is perfect." We will be living virtuously, choosing to do what is good easily, promptly, and with joy.

We will have been transformed into saints.

To reiterate, this is why the first step towards holiness is to practice daily prayer and meditation. The conversation with God must be happening, to allow the transformation to begin. Then, through the second step, by living the life of grace and frequenting the sacraments, we receive God's assistance in the struggle, along with the grace to persevere on the journey.

But our efforts are needed in this battle.

God can do whatever He desires, so if He wishes for us to become a saint, He can do it—with or without our help. But that isn't how God usually works. God desires for us to *choose* Him.

But not only that. God also desires for us to SAY YES and assist Him in bringing about not just the sanctification of ourselves, but also everyone and everything in the world.

God does this by making it possible for every word and action to *have meaning*.

In His infinite love and grace, God has created each of His creations. Particularly those who have been baptized in the name of the Father, the Son, and the Holy Spirit, to become His adopted sons and daughters. And it's these sons and daughters who have the opportunity to help sanctify the world in which they live through their thoughts, words and actions.

But only if those thoughts, words and actions are offered through, with, and in union with Him.

This is how our lives have purpose and meaning. There are no accidents as to who we are, what we are, or where we are. God has uniquely made us to be and do exactly what He created us to be, exactly where we are, in order to do exactly what only we can do.

Why? To help sanctify and "make holy," everything around us through our thoughts, words, and actions.

But we have to *choose it*.

There is a relationship between our daily prayer, the life of grace, and our growing daily in virtue. For when we spend time in conversation with God and allow Him to transform our minds and hearts, then His Sacraments will give us the grace and direction we need so we can grow in virtue *in the particular way that God is asking us to do in our life at that particular moment*.

This is NOT a self-help improvement program. No, this is God, our loving Creator and Father, who is inviting us to enter into the work of our own redemption. Not as slaves, but as *friends* alongside Him.

And as we continue to grow in our relationship with Him while continuing to receive His graces, what happens is we increase our capacity to perceive His Hand at work in all things, and to persevere in our daily life whatever may come—be it bad weather or an ingrown toenail.

And this enables us to help fight the good fight. The good fight to become right-ordered and overcome sin with God's help, and to become who God originally created us to be. This is how daily growth in virtue becomes a vital piece for making progress in the spiritual life.

Because when we fight the good fight, and struggle to overcome sin in our lives with God's help, we become a little more of whom God created us to be. We either begin, or we continue to perfect the virtues in our life.

What's that look like? We become a little more patient. We become a little kinder. We become a bit more peaceful and less anxious as we respond to the events occurring in our life. We're filled with joy, even when difficult and challenging things happen.

And people start to see that. That's the difference. It's a slow and gradual transformation of our thoughts, words, and actions becoming right-ordered by being directed towards only what is good, true, and beautiful. This transformation eventually becomes perfected virtue, or "heroic virtue," when it is seen expressed in the lives and examples of the saints.

Heroic virtue is a clear sign God is present and working in the life of a person, particularly when they respond quickly to challenges and situations in their lives with a love or mercy or kindness that cannot be rationally explained—except it must be the grace of God.

This is what we must strive for every day.

SAY YES to growing daily in virtue.

Now turn the page to keep moving forward, step by step, and day by day.

CHAPTER 13
STEP BY STEP, DAY BY DAY

We have said yes to growing daily in virtue, but exactly how might we go about it?

There is a plethora of activities within the Tradition of the Church that can help in our pursuit. Things like: a Morning Offering: asking the assistance of our Guardian Angel; making a "Heroic Minute," whereupon waking, you immediately arise from bed and begin your day; praying the Angelus; fasting: and offering up sacrifice of anything we do not like, did not choose, cannot change or cannot understand.

Honestly, there are as many ways to grow in our awareness of God's presence and how to invite Him into active involvement in our lives as there are people in the world.

This is not to avoid answering the question of how one can go about growing daily in virtue. Rather, it is to stress the point that there are a *multitude* of practices, methods, and activities one can undertake to help bring about the growth of virtue in one's life, therefore, there is not *one* way to go about doing it.

What do I mean? Simply, what works for your life and the habits you need to cultivate for growing in virtue are going to be different from what someone else's life and habits for growing in virtue will be.

So, does that mean we have to stumble around in the dark until we find the best ones that work for us?

Not at all. The lives of the saints are our greatest resource for helping determine what practices are most effective. In the last two millennia, some commonalities have emerged, and it is apparent there are some practices which should be a part of *everyone's* journey towards holiness.

But to use in this step of growing daily in virtue, let's focus on four: Daily Resolution, Spiritual Reading, Works of Mercy, and the Name of Jesus.

DAILY RESOLUTION

The key to growing and continuing to grow in virtue is to attempt to do *something* every day. It doesn't have to be some major accomplishment. Rather, a daily resolution should be something small. Something concrete. Something *doable*.

Very often, the question people will ask me is, "How do I come up with a resolution?"

First, I jokingly point out that it's not about how do *we* come up with a resolution, but rather, how do we discern more accurately what *God* wants us to do today? And this takes us back to our first step—the practice of daily prayer and meditation.

What did God share with you during your conversation with Him that day? What message from His Living Word in Scripture spoke to you or stirred your heart? Or what particular thing did God point out to you about a particular attitude, or behavior, or habit you should be attentive to adjusting? All of these become sources for a daily resolution.

For example, from Scripture, Jesus' telling us "…unless a grain of wheat falls to the ground and dies, it remains just a grain of wheat; but if it dies, it produces much fruit. Whoever loves his life loses it, and whoever hates his life in this world will preserve it for eternal life."[38] From this Scripture, my reflection and subsequent conversation with my Lord might lead me to recognize how I am holding on to life as *I* envision it, rather than being accepting of the life before me. Perhaps further conversation and reflection reveals I am lacking in gratitude for the many blessings God has given me, and I should work at cultivating a greater attitude of gratitude. A good daily resolution for me that day might be to look for blessings in my life throughout the day, and each time I recognize one, to intentionally stop and say, "Thank you, Lord."

So, during the day, I strive to implement that resolution. At the end of the day, I can use a Daily Examen to see how I did, or didn't do, in responding to God's grace that day. I do this by focusing upon how well (or poorly) I did for implementing my resolution for that day.

Some days as I look back, I do well in responding to God's grace and implementing my daily resolution. Other days though, I completely and totally suck at it!

But more often than not, I do ok. I find I respond some of the time to God's grace, and at other times, I don't. This can get discouraging, especially if we are trying to change a habit—like refraining from having the last word in a conversation, and I see during the course of the day I only refrained from this habit two out of the 20 conversations I had. Still, in the life of growing in virtue, I can't stress how important it is to try and be a glass is half-full kind of person. This is because we are looking for *progress*. (This is a process, not a program, remember!)

We need to focus on the fact we were able to do *something* a little better. We refrained from an uncharitable action. Or we stopped ourselves before we spoke judgmentally about the performance of someone at work. Or we thought about a person who hurt us with mercy. These seem to be small and insignificant occurrences, but in the spiritual life, *everything matters.*

For God's grace can take even the smallest of things and make them great. We just have to do what we can, and God will do the rest. Saint Francis de Sales brilliantly illuminates the process of implementing daily resolutions: *"…what can you do to strengthen your resolutions and make them succeed? There is no better means than to put them into practice."*[39]

So, regardless of what you might deem to be the "success" of your daily resolutions, if you simply put them into practice, you *will* grow in virtue.

SPIRITUAL READING

In our world of videos and image dominated media, the idea of reading can seem a bit "old-fashioned," but the power of the written word cannot be overestimated.

In the business and leadership world, it is a given that if a person wants to become a top performer and be successful, then they need to read. And I'm not talking about the occasional book here and there, but a habit in which a person reads constantly and consistently.

Recent studies show 85 percent of successful people read two or more self-improvement or educational books per month, so the lesson here is if we want to be successful in the spiritual life, then we need to be reading, too.[40]

When we read, we are actively engaging ourselves in the process. We cannot "sit back" and watch the ideas be presented. We have to actively encounter and engage with them, and then those same ideas accompany us as we wrestle with what we think about them until we determine if we are going to accept or set aside what has been proposed, and then decide how it is going to impact our thoughts, words, or actions. The end result is reading, especially spiritual reading, is fundamentally *transformative*. (Should we be surprised by this considering our Lord is *the* Logos? The Living Word come down from Heaven? But I digress.)

So, if we should be reading, what should we read? In a world in which more than a million books a year are being published, finding a book to read isn't too difficult, but finding books that can serve as good, deep, rich, and faithful spiritual reading can be, so we need to be a bit judicious in our choices.

The best place to start is to begin by reading something you love or think you'll love, and then keep going. The list of good Catholic authors is growing exponentially by the day, so check out publishers like Ignatius Press, Augustine Institute, Dynamic Catholic, Ascension Press, St Mary's Press, and Sophia Press—to name just a few. Or read the "classics." St Francis de Sales' *An Introduction to the Devout Life*, St Teresa of Avila's *The Interior Castle*, or St Augustine's *Confessions* are all excellent (although I have a personal penchant for Augustine's *City of God*).

Or another way to approach the process is by considering the question, "How do we desire to be transformed?" Do we desire to become more merciful? Then read St Faustina Kowalska's, *Diary of Divine Mercy*. Do we wish to develop a devotion to Mary? Then check out St Louis de Montfort's *True Devotion to Mary*. Or how about growing in trust? Then read Jean-Pierre De Caussade's *Abandonment to Divine Providence*. Whatever it is, there is a person, but more often than not, a saint, who has written already about it and can assist you on your journey.

But the final point we must remember as we are searching for good spiritual reading, is to bear in mind a truly good book also serves as a guide, and there are no better guides for the spiritual life than the saints. So, read about their lives. Read about their struggles and challenges. Their successes and joys. Their temptations and failures. Let those who have walked the path of holiness before you help guide you all the way to heaven.

Now, once you have a book, you have got to read it. A book doesn't do you any good sitting on your shelf or your bedside table. You need to open it and read it. Each day if possible.

But this is where spiritual reading differs *vastly* from other kinds of reading. Spiritual reading should be done for a set period of time during a day versus trying to read a set number of pages (or even paragraphs). This is to allow ourselves to read as quickly (or as slowly) as the Holy Spirit desires for us.

This means as we read, we should pause and ruminate as ideas "hit us." In this way, we should mirror our daily prayer and meditation time, where we are stopping to reflect before moving on. Our spiritual reading doesn't necessarily lead to relating, having an in-depth conversation with God, but it might. But that's not the primary goal of spiritual reading.

Although we are hopefully reading with the assistance of the Holy Spirit, especially that we might have "eyes that see and ears that hear," the goal during spiritual reading is to provide good, true and beautiful food for our minds. Through spiritual reading, we are intentionally seeking to transform our minds, and that will assist us in transforming our thoughts, words and actions. This is why and how spiritual reading is such an effective means to grow in virtue in our daily life.

WORKS OF MERCY

Works of mercy are the easiest way for us to grow daily in virtue. This is because whenever we do a work of mercy, we are thinking or doing for the good of others. And more often than not, we are thinking or doing for others out of love, so works of mercy make us more loving, more like Christ.

The Catholic Church has two categories of mercy—corporal and spiritual. The corporal works—feed the hungry, give drink to the thirsty, clothe the naked, shelter the homeless, visit the imprisoned, care for the sick, and bury the dead—all the corporal works focus upon the physical needs of a person. The spiritual works—instruct the ignorant, counsel the doubtful, admonish the sinner, comfort the sorrowful, bear wrongs patiently, forgive offenses or injuries, and pray for the living and dead—all pertain to the spiritual life of a person.

It is easy to see how performing any of the works of mercy can bring about an increase in virtue, and Saint Faustina illustrates how mercy can be expressed in our words, actions, and thoughts:

For there are three ways of performing an act of mercy: the merciful word, by forgiving and by comforting; secondly, if you can offer no word, then pray—that too is mercy; and thirdly, deeds of mercy."

St Faustina is the saint of Divine Mercy, and her entire diary is a recounting of the visitations and subsequent conversations Jesus had with her during her lifetime about His Divine Mercy for souls. Yet this excerpt gives us a succinct insight into why the Catholic Church has stressed the need for Christians to strive to perform works of mercy in the midst of their daily life. Mercy is an expression of God's love, so to do, say, or pray any act of mercy will bring God's love to others, and that is the essence of the evangelization.

But exactly how can I live mercy in my daily life when I might not have time to go feed the hungry, or to go out and comfort someone who is sorrowful?

"Miss no single opportunity of making some small sacrifice, here by a smiling look, there by a kindly word; always doing the smallest act right and doing it all for love."

This advice is from Saint Therese of Lisieux, also called the "Little Flower." She gives us the key to not only living a life of mercy and love but also about growing daily in virtue. St Therese's "Little Way" guides us about growing in virtue by telling us to make use of everything—the smallest of actions, words and thoughts—and to do all of them in, with, and for love.

Just like practicing a daily resolution and doing consistent and continuous spiritual reading, performing works of mercy can help us grow in virtue and ensure the gradual transformation of our minds, hearts, and souls until each of us becomes a brilliant light of God's love and mercy in the world.

THE NAME OF JESUS

The idea of using the name of Jesus to grow in virtue was one I was only recently introduced to, but I have found it to be especially effective with my most pernicious and stubborn of habits. (Should I be surprised considering the power of Jesus' name?!)

Anyway, the practice is to name whatever spirit of temptation you are facing during your day—like loneliness, anger, bitterness, resentment, unforgiveness, lust, greed, pride, laziness, sadness, envy, intemperance, low self-esteem, doubt, despair, etc., and then to confront it by asking Jesus to give you the virtue or grace—spirit of patience, kindness, joy, trust, courage, perseverance, generosity, purity, humility, temperance, divine sonship or daughtership, faith, hope, love etc.—that combats the temptation you are facing.

So, it would look like this:

SPIRIT OF (name the temptation), IN JESUS' NAME, I RENOUNCE AND REJECT YOU.

SPIRIT OF (name the opposite virtue), IN JESUS' NAME, COME INTO MY HEART.

PERSEVERE

As we conclude our discussion about the third step to holiness, just a brief word about perseverance. Because daily growth in virtue is almost entirely about perseverance.

Yes, it is about offering our best efforts, but it's more about *consistently and continuously* offering our best efforts. Saint Teresa of Avila addresses this well:

"…let us strive to make constant progress: we ought to feel great alarm if we do not find ourselves advancing, for without doubt, the evil one must be planning to injure us in some way; it is impossible for a soul that has come to this state not to go still farther, for love is never idle. Therefore, it is a very bad sign when one comes to a standstill in virtue."[41]

So, to recognize that we must never come to a standstill in growing in virtue is extremely important.

Patience is another aspect of perseverance. St Francis de Sales tell us:

"Have patience with all things, but chiefly have patience with yourself. Do not lose courage in considering your own imperfections, but instantly set about remedying them, every day begin the task anew."

We must be patient on this journey. It is a marathon, not a sprint, so be patient and persevere.

Lastly though, we must remember that it's a battle. Thomas a' Kempis writes:

"A man must go through a long and great conflict in himself before he can learn fully to overcome himself, and to draw his whole affection towards God. When a man stands upon himself, he is easily drawn aside after human comforts. But a true lover of Christ, and a diligent pursuer of virtue, does not hunt after comforts, nor seek such sensible sweetnesses, but is rather willing to bear strong trials and hard labors for Christ."[42]

And we choose to do this at the beginning of every day. We have to rely on God and begin over and over again. Every day as if nothing's been done as we remember it's only through His power and grace that we're able to do any of this, but He will give us the graces we need to do exactly what He desires for us—to become saints.

Make and strive to be faithful to a daily resolution. Do spiritual reading that will strengthen your mind and your heart for the battle against our own disordered natures and against the Evil One.

Do works of mercy in accordance with your personal vocation, state of life, and the promptings of the Holy Spirit in your moveable square meter. Use the power of the name of Jesus to conquer all temptations.

SAY YES to grow daily in virtue—step by step, and day by day.

Now, turn the page and abandon yourself to God's will.

CHAPTER 14

STEP FOUR—ABANDONING OURSELVES TO GOD'S WILL

"Life becomes full of joy and peace as the result of our complete abandonment to the Will of God, to be tested on a daily basis."

— Fr Francis Fernandez[43]

Now we turn our attention to completing the foundation necessary for our spiritual journey. This is done by focusing upon step four—abandoning ourselves to God's will.

The practice of abandoning ourselves to God's will is where we really integrate the first three steps—daily prayer and meditation, frequenting the sacraments, and growing daily in virtue. It is in this fourth step that we become more obedient and detached from how it is that we desire for our lives to progress, and become more and more open to how *God* desires our lives to progress.

We do this by simply accepting the ordinary circumstances and daily experiences of our life as God's hand moving and shaping our lives. Not that when something bad happens that we then think that this is God punishing us, but rather in seeing even in those difficult and painful circumstances and experiences God is still at work. Believing He truly will use all things for "the good of those who love Him."[44]

And that's why if we truly desire to grow in the spiritual life, we *must* begin with daily prayer and meditation. Because it is there—during our time alone with the Creator of the universe who loves us beyond measure--that we grow in our love of Him and are encouraged and inspired to truly believe in His promises.

And as we continue to be infused with God's graces of love, faith, and hope, our hearts become more receptive to *all* of the graces He wishes to give us through His sacraments. And then, with His love and grace, we have the strength and courage to attempt to try and grow in virtue as we walk alongside Him each day.

If we abandon ourselves to God's will, if we accept little bit by little bit without complaint the ordinary circumstances and experiences of our daily life, what happens is we are able to die to ourselves, and then we are able to die to our own will little bit by little bit, too.

As we are entrusting ourselves to God more and more, we then begin to embody what Saint John the Baptist spoke of when he said, "*He must increase, and I must decrease*"[45] and also when Saint Paul who wrote in his letter to the Galatians, "*It is no longer I who live, but Christ who lives in me.*"[46]

This is the goal of Christian life! To become like the One who loves us. This is holiness.

It is truly that simple.

So why don't we do this? Well, like all things in life, it's not a black and white answer, but a bunch of greys.

Because the reality is that in order for us to effectively enter into living out this fourth step in our daily life, we are going to need to wrestle and come to terms with some of the greatest philosophical and theological questions of human existence—primarily, the reality of evil, human suffering, and the goodness and providence of God.

Because one of the greatest challenges to the spiritual life is the world proposes to you all sorts of things that *appear* to be very logical reasons regarding why we shouldn't even begin attempting this journey at all—and that is the existence of evil and human suffering.

The questions normally go something like, "How can God be truly good if innocent children suffer and die from cancer?" or "My friend's little brother died in a car accident, how can that be part of a loving God's plan?" or "If God truly loved the world, then why are there so many wars, or so much pain and suffering?"

On the face of it, these seem like logical and rational objections to belief in God's goodness and providence. But God is all good and infinite. And the Catechism of the Catholic Church tells us God is not in any way, directly or indirectly, the cause of evil. Rather, evil was unleashed by the abuse of angelic and human free will, and this is what brought evil into the world with Original Sin which caused disharmony within creation.[47]

But why does God allow evil to remain?

God allows evil because of our free will.

Free will is the power to choose to act for good or evil. And it is our free will that makes true love possible.

Unfortunately, free will also make sin and evil possible. Therefore, if God was to prevent all sin and evil, He would have to take away our free will, but this would mean we would be unable to truly love. So, to ensure we are free to love and do good, we also are free to do evil.

But another reason God allows evil to remain is because He is capable of drawing forth greater goods from it. What are some of those goods? Saint Pope John Paul II tells us there are several: formation and/or correction, an increase in love, drawing closer to God, and unleashing greater love on the behalf of others, like the Good Samaritan.[48]

St Augustine superbly described the providential nature of God's goodness when he wrote: "*For almighty God, because he is* *supremely good, would never allow any evil whatsoever to exist in his works if he were not so all-powerful and good as **to cause good to emerge from evil itself.***" **(bold emphases mine)**

Just think about that for a moment.

For me, that just stops me in my tracks, and causes me to drop to me knees in wonder and awe!

Although I have actually *seen* this type of miracle, (one that comes to mind is the mother of one of the Sandy Hook school shooting victims who publicly forgave the shooter), and although acts of merciful love like this can result in a complete about-face and transformation of the forgiven person so they no longer resemble their former self; I tend to disregard these miracles, or I forget about the reality of what God's power can truly do.

Our biggest failure in this area (at least for me), is constantly forgetting God has taken the greatest evil and suffering *ever*—the death of His Son—and made the greatest good imaginable emerge from it—the salvation of the entire world.[49]

God works similarly in our own lives when He allows our lives to be touched by evil or suffering, but we rebel against it. We tend to forget the wisdom of St. Catherine of Siena who told us, "Everything comes from love; all is ordained for the salvation of man, God does nothing without this goal in mind."

And that, I think is the crux. The underlying issue we may have with evil, pain, and suffering in the world is *actually* more a reflection, or a question *we have* about God's goodness and providence than it is about the presence of evil and suffering.

Because in the face of evil, we struggle to trust God is all-powerful and all-good. That He is our Savior and He is working though all events and circumstances for our eternal salvation (versus our earthly bliss).

Now, don't misunderstand me. It's not that the realities of evil, pain, suffering, sickness and death aren't important issues to address. However, these questions are important only in how our answers inform our *response* to the presence of these things in the world, within our lives and the lives of those around us.

And what should our response be? The same as the disciples, "Lord, increase our faith!"[50]

Most often, our doubts arise because of a lack of sufficient faith in God's goodness and providence when we are faced with evil, pain, or suffering.

And what *is* faith but to have complete trust or confidence in someone or something?[51]

Now, let me be clear. Having faith and trust in God is not as simple as *saying* I have faith, or I trust God. It's about *living* it.

It's about having faith and trusting in the will of our Loving Heavenly Father and allowing Him to fill you with His peace in the midst of whatever storms are present in your life.

And this is why abandoning ourselves to God's will is the fourth step on the path to holiness. It is the integrating agent for steps one through three.

Abandoning ourselves to God's will integrates and strengthens our daily prayer, God's graces received in His sacraments, and our struggles to grow in virtue all together into the habits necessary to strive for holiness in our lives.

SAY YES to abandoning yourself to God's will.

Turn the page, and let's see how we can hit God's will on the dot.

CHAPTER 15
HITTING GOD'S WILL ON THE "DOT"

*"God gives each one of us sufficient grace ever to
know his holy will, and to do it fully."*

— St Ignatius de Loyola

Once we SAY YES to Step Four—Abandoning ourselves to God's will, we need to answer the question of how do we live out this idea? How do we get so good at it that we live out *His* will for us each day?

We do this by attempting to hit it on the "DOT" through the practices of Detachment, Obedience, and Trust.

DETACHMENT

Saint Ignatius of Loyola tells us *"God gives each one of us sufficient grace ever to know his holy will, and to do it fully."* This is absolutely true, but to live out God's holy will and do it fully, we need to practice detachment.

The primary idea of detachment is to accept suffering in whatever form it may come along. Additionally, we must also be simultaneously "detaching" ourselves from anything that might get in the way of knowing, and then doing His will.

For more than twenty centuries, the Church has emphasized the concept of setting aside the "things of the world" in order to pursue Christ and the path of discipleship. However, it was Saint Ignatius, during the eleven months he spent in a cave outside the town of Manresa, Spain in 1522, had it revealed to him—through the grace of God and the Holy Spirit—the fundamental truth that it is our *attachments* to created goods—things like money, power, honor, pleasure—that stand in the way of our being able to respond fully to God's will in our lives.

But you might be asking, how can something like pleasure get in the way of doing God's will?

Here is a simple example. Say you like to cheer on your favorite sports team. You really enjoy watching the game, particularly because you also get to hang out with your family and friends as you do so. And maybe you even have some food and a few drinks as you cheer your team on to victory. All of these things bring you a lot of pleasure.

Now, in this example, there is nothing *bad* going on. Being a sports fan is not a bad thing. Nor is spending time with family or friends. And having some food and a few drinks is not a bad thing either. In fact, these are all *good* things in and of themselves.

So how is it possible that pleasure can get in the way of doing God's will?

Well, depending upon how big a fan you are, your pleasurable activities could very likely conflict with being able to attend Mass on the weekend. So, to get to Sunday Mass (God's revealed will for each one of us), you are going to have to choose between enjoying good, pleasurable activities or doing God's will.

Hopefully, we will have our priorities properly in order, and we will be virtuous, so we will do God's will easily, promptly, and with joy before choosing pleasurable activities. If we don't choose God's will, then we have an attachment that is hindering us from doing His will.

This is why we must practice detachment to truly abandon ourselves to God's will.

But how do we practice it? Again, it begins with step one—daily prayer and meditation.

Why? Because it is only in the light of God's love for us that we can come to know and see ourselves more clearly. And the more clearly we see ourselves, the more we are capable of identifying attachments—those very things that are preventing us from knowing and doing God's will—and seek to set them aside through the practice of detachment.

But detachment is not simply about things of the world. Detachment is also about our interior dispositions, things like our pride and desire for control. Detachment is also about letting go of our ideas about what our lives should look or be like. Father Jacques Philippe, in his book, *In the School of the Holy Spirit*, writes:

> *"To become holy, to become saints, we must of course try as hard as we can to do God's will as it comes to us in a general way that is valid for everyone: through Scripture, the Commandments, and so on. It is also indispensable, as has just been said, to go further: to aspire to know not only what God demands of everyone in general, but also **what he wants more specifically of us individually.**"*[52] (**bold emphases mine**)

I've had people tell me if God would just be clearer about what He wanted them to do—like if He put a message up on a roadside billboard—then they would do it.

Well, the fact is, God *does* tell us what His will is.

God reveals His will to us through both His Absolute and Permissive Will. The absolute will of God is revealed in numerous ways: by doing what is good and avoiding evil; by following the moral law evident and knowable through common sense; by the use of reason and the teachings of Christ that come through the Church; through the duties and responsibilities of our state in life—married, single, or vowed religious; through our commitments to love, honor, care for, and be faithful to our spouse; taking care of our kids, doing our work as if working for God, fulfilling our responsibilities; and through the inspirations God gives. Bottom line, God's Absolute Will is revealed when you are doing what it is you know you are supposed to be doing.

God's Permissive Will is revealed through the events and circumstances God permits or allows to happen in our lives. Simply stated, the will of God is found in those things that we cannot change.[53]

Now, I can hear you saying, what? God *allows* me to lose my job? Or for me to be in accident where I lose the use of my right eye? Or for my spouse to abandon his family? Or for me to have an illness that makes it impossible for me to get through a day without taking frequent breaks during any physical activity?

How can any of these things possibly be God's will?

"Even when God's will does not correspond to your own desires, it is always beneficial for you."[54]

This understanding and level of trusting acceptance expressed in this quote by Saint Arnold Janssen is the epitome of detachment. Why? Because it shows us the attitude we must be striving for. An attitude of accepting, trusting, and living the reality God is a loving Father who cares for each and every one of His children—*even when it doesn't look like it to the rest of the world.*

You see, we are striving to even be detached from our own ideas and expectations of what our life should be like. It is only when we let go of our own ideas and expectations about what life should be about, and SAY YES to God's ideas, that God is then free to mold us into who He knows we can be. Because He's the One who created us to be that way in the first place.

So why is detachment so difficult? Fear.

Father Jacques Philippe describes this reality and the consequences of fear perfectly:

> *"What really hurts is not so much suffering as the fear of suffering. If welcomed trustingly and peacefully, suffering makes us grow. It matures and trains us, purifies us, teaches us to love unselfishly, makes us poor in heart, humble, gentle, and compassionate toward our neighbor. Fear of suffering, on the other hand, hardens us in self-protective, defensive attitudes, and often leads us to make irrational choices with disastrous consequences."*[55]

So how might we overcome our attachments and our self-protective, defensive, and hardened attitudes?

We do it through prayer and immersing ourselves in the power of the Word—the same Word that speaks to us over and over again about setting aside our fear and trusting in Him. Like in Psalm 27:1 *"The LORD is my light and my salvation; whom shall I fear? The LORD is the strength of my life; of whom shall I be afraid?"*

Or in 2 Timothy 1:7, *"For God has not given us a spirit of fear and timidity, but of power, love, and self-discipline."*

And in 1 John 4:18, *"There is no fear in love. But perfect love drives out fear, because fear has to do with punishment. The one who fears is not made perfect in love."*

But especially in Romans 8:28, *"For all things work for good for those who love God."*

Immerse yourself in the Word and spend time in prayer and meditation with Him, and detachment from the things of this world and our ability to know and do God's will can increase with each passing day.

OBEDIENCE

The second practice is obedience. The essence of obedience is found in the Latin phrase, *"In verbo autem tuo,"* which means, *"At your word."* To be obedient, is to be ready "at your word" to do whatever you command me.

This is why Saint Catherine of Bologna said, *"Without a doubt, obedience is more meritorious than any other penance. And what greater penance can there be than keeping one's will continually submissive and obedient?"*

I can only speak for myself, but being continually submissive and obedient is most *definitely* penitential for me!

However, any time we struggle to be obedient, we can look to the life of Christ and His example.

> *"What was the first rule of our dear Savior's life? You know it was to do His Father's will. Well, then, the first end I propose in our daily work is to do the will of God; secondly to do it in the manner He wills; and thirdly, to do it because it is His will."*[56]

Jesus tells his disciples (us!) that genuine discipleship—following Him—involves suffering and even death. He shares this message with His disciples in the Gospels over and over again.

For example, in Matthew Chapter 16:21, *"From that time on, Jesus began to explain to His disciples that He must go to Jerusalem and suffer many things at the hands of the elders, the chief priests, and teachers of the law and that he must be killed and on the third day be raised to life."*

In the Gospel of Mark alone, Jesus predicts His death three different times. The most memorable instance being Mark 8:31-33 when Jesus makes his pronouncement about His upcoming suffering and death, and then Peter tries to argue, but Jesus rebukes him by saying, *"Get behind me Satan! You do not have in mind the things of God, but the things of men!"*

And then in Luke 9:43, *"Pay attention to what I am telling you. The Son of Man is to be handed over to men."*

Why suffering, death, and the cross? Because the Resurrection is *only* accomplished by the Cross.

Scripture is not the only source of this teaching. The Church and all her saints throughout the centuries echo Christ's mandate that true life can only come about through suffering and death.

In Catechism paragraph 2015, *"The way of perfection passes by way of the Cross. There is no holiness without renunciation and spiritual battle. Spiritual progress entails the ascesis and mortification that gradually lead to living in the peace and joy of the Beatitudes."*

Saint Maria de Mattias exhorts us to *"...love the cross very much, for it is there that we discover our life, our true love, and our strength in our greatest difficulties."* and then Saint Katherine Drexel tells us, *"The patient and humble endurance of the cross—whatever nature it may be—is the highest work we have to do."*

But how can we achieve this kind of obedience? We can't. At least not on our own.

This is where the second step—living the life of grace—is critical.

Prior to healing people, Jesus would always ask the person whether they believed He could do it. And then when they expressed faith in His power, Jesus would use physical signs—laying of hands, spit, mud, etc.—to bring about the healing. Jesus continues to do this today through His sacraments.

Just like those whom Jesus healed in Palestine when we express our faith in His power found in the sacraments, Jesus can then use them to touch and heal us of our sin, suffering, and death. Christ is able to ever more fully conform us into being obedient and willing instruments. This is because the power of the sacraments themselves flow from Jesus' suffering and death through which Jesus gave new meaning to suffering and made it possible for each one of us to assist in bringing about the redemption of the world.[57]

But the final reason to strive for obedience is directly tied to a teaching of Saint John of the Cross in which he stated, *"... the way of suffering is safer, and also more profitable, than that of rejoicing and of action. In suffering, God gives strength, but in action and in joy, the soul does but show its own weakness and imperfections. And in suffering, the soul practices and acquires virtue, and becomes pure, wiser, and more cautious."*

Bottom line, emptying ourselves and being obedient, especially while suffering, is how we practice and acquire virtue and become more holy. Need I say more?

TRUST

The final practice we must cultivate to hit the DOT and abandon ourselves to God's will in our lives is Trust.

Trust is the act of following the path, even when it doesn't make sense—as long as it doesn't lead us into sin. And it's about finding the strength and the courage to believe and trust in God's promises to us. His promises that He *is* a good and loving Father, that all things *do* work for those who love Him, and that He is truly capable of bringing good out of *anything*.

St Francis de Sales assures us, *"We shall steer safely through every storm, so long as our heart is right, our intention fervent, our courage steadfast, and our trust fixed on God."*

Padre Pio says it even more simply, *"Pray, hope, and don't worry."*

This is the kind of trust we must cultivate in our hearts and minds so we can experience what St Paul was speaking about when he wrote, *"May the God of hope fill you with all joy and peace as you trust in him, so that you may overflow with hope by the power of the Holy Spirit."*[58]

Often though, we hesitate to trust His promises or follow the path He had laid before us. Or at least I know I do.

Yet here is a great analogy that gives perspective to what we are doing when we fail to trust God:

"We trust ourselves to a doctor because we suppose he knows his business. He orders an operation which involves cutting away part of our body and we accept it. We are grateful to him and pay him a large fee because we judge he would not act as he does unless the remedy were necessary, and we must rely on his skill. Yet we are unwilling to treat God in the same way! It looks as if we do not trust His wisdom and are afraid He cannot do His job properly. We allow ourselves to be operated on by a man who may easily make a mistake—a mistake which may cost us our life—and protest when God sets to work on us. If we could see all He sees, we would unhesitatingly wish all He wishes."[59]

Our fear, our lack of trust, is preventing God, the Divine Physician Himself, from operating on us in the way that He thinks is best! How prideful and arrogant is that?

Because the truth is there is *nothing* God does that is in vain. It *all* has a purpose—all the suffering, the pain, the heartaches, the frustrations, the discouragements, the failures. Everything has purpose and meaning—even if we can't see or understand.

But does abandoning yourself to God's will seem like too big a stretch?

Maybe you are afraid? Afraid the pain and suffering would be too much?

Or maybe it just seems like a downright impossibility?

I used to think all those things, too. Until I read this:

"I realize as never before that the Lord is gentle and merciful; He did not send me this heavy cross until I could bear it. If He had sent it before, I am certain that it would have discouraged me . . . I desire nothing at all now except to love until I die of love. I am free, I am not afraid of anything, not even of what I used to dread most of all . . . a long illness which would make me a burden to the community. I am perfectly content to go on suffering in body and soul for

years, if that would please God. I am not in the least afraid
of living for a long time; I am ready to go on fighting."[60]

That was written by Saint Therese of Lisieux. A simple
French peasant girl who became a Carmelite nun who is now
recognized as a saint and was named a Doctor of the Church
because of her "Little Way."

Therese was afraid, too, but she overcame that fear little by
little through God's love and grace, and by abandoning herself to
God's will. She showed us that we can do it, too—if we but trust.

CONCLUSION

Yet to trust, we must learn to love and be loved.

And this is how we find ourselves having circled back to step
one—spending time in daily prayer and meditation.

For we only trust those who truly know us and love us. It's
why a breakdown of any relationship happens when trust is broken. So, to grow in trust, we must strive to grow in love. And the
only way to grow in love is to spend time with the One whom
we are seeking to love!

Saint Mother Teresa of Calcutta once shared: *"The fruit of*
silence is prayer, the fruit of prayer is faith, the fruit of faith is love,
the fruit of love is service, the fruit of service is peace."

This is why we persevere in prayer and meditation—even
when we might not feel that devotion or love. We *trust* that God
is working within our hearts and minds to give us His peace—
but we have to show up.

And then when we show up, we must make an act of faith,
and surrender ourselves to God. When we SAY YES, God uses
our YES, and makes something good come out of it.

Simply, He makes us into the saints that He created us to be.

For when we SAY YES to abandoning ourselves to God's
will, we open ourselves fully to the possibility of transforming
union with God.

This is holiness. It is what being a saint is all about.

It's about…

…striving for detachment and bringing your life into conformity with God's will for your life, rather than your own.

…striving for obedience and taking up your cross in the knowledge that our Lord's yoke is easy, and His burden light.

…trusting that all things do matter, and in the promise God shared in His Word "*that all things work for good for those who love Him.*"[61]

SAY YES to hitting God's will on the "DOT."

Let us express our fervent desire to abandon ourselves to God's will by praying:

O Jesus, I surrender myself to you, take care of everything![62]

Now, turn the page and let us begin living a life of abundance.

PART 3

EMBRACING
ABIDING
ABUNDANCE

CHAPTER 16
THE MYTH OF THE LONE RANGER

For those of you of a certain age, you probably remember watching, or at least hearing about, the adventures of the Lone Ranger. For those of you who may be unfamiliar with the Western TV series, the basic premise was the Lone Ranger would go to different towns and other lawless situations at the request of innocent people who were either in danger, or who were being taken advantage of. The Lone Ranger would work to find out who the bad guys were, and then would fight to bring about justice, before riding away on his great white horse, Silver.

At the end of each episode, there would be a scene where one of the people who had been helped by the Lone Ranger would discover a silver bullet (the symbol of the Lone Ranger). As they realized who had just helped them, they would look up and would see the Lone Ranger on Silver, rearing up on his hinds legs in victory before he would ride off to his next adventure and seek to bring about justice for someone else.

This idea encapsulates the mindset of many people when it comes to the spiritual journey. We think that just like the Lone Ranger, we have to go into tempting situations and fight for justice and help others, and then we ride off to do it all again—all on our own.

The whole problem with this, of course, is the fact it's all a myth.

Because the Lone Ranger DID have help.

He had Tonto, his loyal Native American friend, to accompany and help him overcome the bad guys and the lawless situations and bring about justice.

So, the Lone Ranger wasn't *really* alone. And neither should we be on the spiritual journey.

Once we SAY YES to God's desire to shower His abundant blessings upon us, we can begin to recognize and fully utilize these many blessings that are present in our daily life. We can truly experience a life of abiding abundance.

One of the first keys to this life of abundance that is present in our daily life is illustrated by the Lone Ranger. He needed an advisor and friend to accompany him, and we, too, have advisors and friends all around us.

Accompaniment is a fundamental NEED we have in life. We were created for relationship in general, but we are *specially* designed for accompaniment during the spiritual journey. Pope Francis has spoken repeatedly about the need for encountering and accompanying our brothers and sisters in Christ, especially those who are on the peripheries.

Unfortunately, in many Western cultures, but particularly in the United States, we have this pervading sense of individualism, the idea individuals are only as good as they are strong, assertive, self-reliant, and independent people who "go it alone." This translates into the additional cultural idea it shows weakness to even ask for help, or that you are defective if you *need* friends and to be in lived relationship with others.

In the spiritual journey, this is anathema. It literally is death to our spiritual selves if we deny our need for relationship. But this cultural imperative is *extremely* hard to overcome, so many people who attempt to strive for holiness on their own. Sadly, since they have either accepted the idea it shows weakness to ask for help, or that they should go it alone, they are perpetuating "the myth of the Lone Ranger."

But God has given us the entire Deposit of Faith—Sacred Scripture, Sacred Tradition, and the teaching authority of the Church, the Magisterium, to ensure we are accompanied on our individual journeys towards holiness.

Sacred Scripture and Sacred Tradition, all the wisdom and knowledge that is safeguarded and shared through the Magisterium of the very Church Jesus founded upon His Apostles, are God's most common supernatural means of communication.

Why supernatural? I mean, aren't the Scriptures and the teachings of the Church just human fabrications of what God is telling us about Himself and telling us how to live?

In a word, no.

Why? Because the Holy Spirit is the source of both.

Yes, human beings wrote the Scriptures, but it was *through* the inspiration of the Holy Spirit that they were written to ensure the Scriptures would always be true and without error—when, as a former pastor of mine liked to say, "they are talking about what they are talking about."

And what are the Scriptures talking about? God and His love for His people. His passionate desire and thirst for each one of us, His sons and daughters. And when the Scriptures are speaking of these things, there is *no doubt* they are true and without error.

But does this apply to Sacred Tradition, too? Is this true for all the wisdom contained within the teachings of the Church and shared by the Church's Magisterium?

In one word again, yes.

Through the inspirations of the Holy Spirit, Sacred Tradition now contains all of the knowledge of all of the greatest minds from throughout the last two millennia.

Bishop Robert Barron uses a wonderful analogy to show the work of the Holy Spirit as he explains the development of Catholic teaching:

"In one very real sense, the Father speaks all he can possibly speak in His Son, rightly called the Logos. There is no more to be revealed, no more to be said than what is expressed in Jesus. Nevertheless, the fullness of that revelation unfolds only over space and time, much the way that a seed unfolds very gradually into a mighty oak."

A lively mind takes an idea, turns it over, considers it, looks at it from various viewpoints, questions it. Then, in lively conversation, that mind throws the idea to another mind, who performs a similar set of operations.

This "play of lively minds" has gone on throughout the centuries. St. John threw the idea of the Incarnation to St. Polycarp, who threw it to St. Irenaeus, who threw it to Origen, who threw it to Augustine, who passed it on to Thomas Aquinas, who shared it with Robert Bellarmine, who spoke it to John Henry Newman and others, who have then given it to us.

Now, who guarantees that this process moves forward? The answer is the Holy Spirit, whom Jesus promised to the Church."

Venerable Archbishop Fulton Sheen echoes the reality of how the Church is an extension of Christ's presence in the world when he said:

"... the Holy Spirit as it was important in the physical body of Christ, is also important in His ecclesial body. The Church, is the historical manifestation of the suprahistorical Christ,

thanks to His Spirit...That is why we obey the Church: she is Christ, and the Spirit is in her." [63]

So, when the Magisterium teaches and shares the truths of the faith, it is Christ speaking, it is the Holy Spirit being made visible in our midst.

Yet, despite knowing this, why do so many people discount the Church and try to go it alone in the world?

Because many times, we tend to get caught up on what we can see before us. Unfortunately, more often than not, tends to involve flawed human beings who misuse their power, are limited by their own prejudices and preconceptions and vices and fears rather than the awesome majesty of souls filled with the Holy Spirit and on fire with love of God and His people.

On my journey to the Church, this idea of the Church being an extension of Christ's presence in the world was actually one of the greatest reasons for my becoming Catholic. As I studied history, it became apparent to me that there is no other way to explain the survival of the Church throughout the centuries with all of the flawed, broken people who have been at her helm periodically, *except* that the Church's origin and the source of power flows from the Holy Spirit.

It's what we celebrate at Pentecost. The birth of the Church through the coming of the Holy Spirit down upon Jesus' Apostles. And then from the Apostles came the preaching, conversions, and baptisms all the way to our own time and place.

So, if not the human failings of those who are striving to serve as Christ's instruments on earth, what is the *real* reason we decide to perpetuate the myth of the Lone Ranger and discount the reality of the presence of the Holy Spirit in His Church now?

Obedience.

Obedience comes from the Latin word, "obedere," "to listen."

Unfortunately, in our world today, people don't listen very much anymore. But on the spiritual journey, obedience is necessary to prepare our hearts for a conversation, for an internal dialogue with God as we listen deeply for His Truth.

And I capitalized truth for a reason because Jesus IS Truth. He is the Way, the Truth, and the Life we are seeking. And He is the One to whom we are seeking to listen. Not to myself, but to Him, who knows what is best for me, and desires to share that with me, but only if I listen.

But we don't want to listen, or we ignore, or modify what we hear. Yet God *knew* this, and it is why He not only gave us Sacred Scripture and Sacred Tradition, but also His Magisterium within the Church to guide and accompany us throughout the journey, too.

God desires us to avail ourselves of all three of these means on the journey home to Him. Yet, more often than not, most people only use one or two of these, and this leads to more struggles in the spiritual journey than our Lord ever had in mind for us.

What do I mean? Well, our Lord *knew* how hard life is. He *lived* it with us. He experienced the good, the bad, and the ugly. I mean, what could be uglier than being betrayed by a friend, abandoned by everyone but His mother and a few disciples as He experiences a cruel and torturous death?

Or the reality of living in exile when he was a young boy; the death of His foster father, Joseph; being misunderstood and persecuted by religious and secular leaders; and even surviving an assassination attempt by His own neighbors in His hometown when He began His ministry?

I'd say Jesus knew quite a bit about the challenges and sorrows of human life. And knowing this, He gave us the very tools we need to ensure we can find our way home to Him.

But our Lord is not a God of bare necessities. He is a God of *abundance*.

Because He didn't just leave us the bare minimum of what He knew we would need to journey through this human life, rather, He gave us an *abundance* of the graces and assistance. He has given us His creation and other human beings; His Word in Sacred Scripture; Himself and the Holy Spirit in the Sacraments; the wisdom of the Holy Spirit found in His Church through the Magisterium and Sacred Tradition; and then to top it all off, He makes Himself available to us anytime we seek to have conversation with Him in prayer!

When someone only uses one or two of the tools He has provided (like using Scripture alone, or only receiving the sacraments), they can (and sometimes do) grow closer to Him and can grow in holiness, but the journey is not as easy for them as our Lord desires for it to be.

We know this because it becomes evident whenever we encounter a person who is making full use of *all* the means given to us by God for the spiritual journey. It is possible then to see the limits imposed by a normal human life cast off, and we see a person living with purpose, peace, joy, and abundance in their lives, and they naturally will share that reality with others.

THIS is what we are called to become and do on the spiritual journey. Jesus told His disciples to leave everything behind for the journey, but Jesus did not send them out with nothing. He sent His Spirit with them, so when the disciples returned and He asked, *"When I sent you out without purse or bag or sandals, did you lack anything?"* And they answered, *"Nothing."* (Luke 22:35)

Our problems in this life tend to stem simply from a lack of *listening* to what Jesus told us we need, and from trying to do this journey on our own.

We must set aside the myth of the Lone Ranger.

SAY YES to being obedient to what God has revealed through His Magisterium.

Now, turn the page to discover the power of a soul friend.

CHAPTER 17
THE POWER OF A SOUL FRIEND

"How many souls might reach a high degree of sanctity if properly directed from the first. I know God can sanctify souls without help, but just as He gives the gardener the skill to tend rare and delicate plants while fertilizing them Himself, so He wishes to use others in His cultivation of souls." [64]

— St Therese of Lisieux

The concept of having a spiritual mentor or director is an idea that has been present in the Tradition of the Church since the beginning. Jesus modeled it for His disciples, and He sent His disciples out in pairs to ensure they would be encouraged and sustained in the work He sent them to do. Jesus continues to encourage us to do this through His Church, who teaches that to progress on the spiritual journey, we should seek to find and entrust our souls to the care of another who has skill in accompaniment.

St Therese likens this skill of accompaniment to that of a gardener. But this type of gardener is one who actively seeks to be an instrument of the Holy Spirit in the process of helping bring forth a beautiful garden within the souls of those to whom have been entrusted to them. These "gardeners of souls" have also been called spiritual masters, guides, mages, directors, mentors, and soul friends. But regardless of the name, their importance for the spiritual journey cannot be underestimated.

St. Brigid of Ireland was quoted as saying, *"Go forth and eat nothing until you get a soul friend, for anyone without a soul friend is like a body without a head; is like the water of a polluted lake, neither good for drinking nor for washing."*

The Celtic tradition was such that *everyone*, whether lay or clergy, man or woman, was *expected* to have a spiritual mentor and companion on the soul's journey. A person in whom they could confide all of their inner struggles, who would help them find their path and who could assist them in discernment. A genuine warmth and intimacy in this relationship and deep respect for the other's wisdom were seen as a source of blessing, and age nor gender differences mattered.[65]

A soul friend, a spiritual mentor, or a spiritual guide is one of the keys to our continued spiritual growth. This is because they can assist us in seeing what we tend not to see, simply because we are too close to accurately see what is going on within our own interior lives.

As human beings we have an infinite capacity for self-delusion because we very easily become blinded by our ideas, feelings, fears, and vices. This shows itself whenever we assess ourselves, for we tend to assess ourselves according to what we aspire to vs. the reality of where we actually are. We also tend to not judge ourselves harshly, but give ourselves credit for our good intentions. All of this points towards our need for someone to accompany us who is outside of our struggle and can give us perspective.

The providing of this perspective can be likened to a person on your belay rope. A person serving on your belay is the person who secures your rope and keeps you safely attached to the mountain. For anyone who has climbed a mountain, or rappelled down a steep cliff knows, having a person on your belay is a fundamental necessity for safety. Your belay can see what you are unable to see, assist you in helping you look for your next handhold, and to avoid dangerous spots on the mountain. But the most fundamental characteristic in this relationship is one of trust. You need to have trust that your belay will not let you fall, while also having faith they are guiding you in the proper direction.

In the same way, a spiritual mentor or director is there on the mountain with you, accompanying, assisting, and guiding. However, just like in climbing a mountain, YOU still have to do the work of climbing. A mentor walks WITH, not FOR you in the interior life.

The benefits and power of having a mentor for the soul are priceless. It is common knowledge if you want to become great at something, you get a coach. So, if you are going to become great in the spiritual life, you find a coach, too. As a mentor and coach, your spiritual director can challenge, encourage, and accompany you as you are striving to climb God's mountain.

But one of the biggest benefits of having a coach is accountability.

Study after study shows that it is only when we are held accountable that we truly make any progress in any endeavor, and the spiritual life if no different. For example, simply knowing someone is going to inquire into how my daily prayer life is going is a motivation for me to actually be praying daily!

In addition to accountability, the benefits of a spiritual mentor are to have a person who will deeply listen and serve as a sounding board for growing in holiness in daily life; can provide encouragement and support when facing challenges and as you engage in continuous discernment as to your personal mission within your state of life; be a resource for guidance in why, what and how to continue to grow in your interior life; and finally, someone you can look up to as a role model for living out the faith.

Much more has been written about the benefits of a spiritual mentor, but the most fundamental thing we need to do on the spiritual journey is *to find one.*

Now, believe me, when I tell you, I know the challenges of finding a spiritual director or mentor. For several years, I drove every six weeks for more than three and a half hours ONE WAY to meet with my spiritual director for an hour before then going through drive-thru to have lunch in my car as I made the drive back in time to pick up my son as he was getting out from school.

Was this difficult? Absolutely. Was it worth it? Yes.

Have I always had a spiritual director or mentor? No, but even during those times, I *never* stopped looking or searching for a person who was open to accompanying me on the spiritual journey. And in time, God would reveal those people to me through prayer and circumstance. Some worked out, while some did not, but *all* of those men and women who have accompanied me through the years have provided me both wisdom and insight that has helped me continue my journey to grow closer to God and become more like Jesus.

So, the key is to always persevere in the search. God desires for you to have a spiritual mentor or director. He doesn't want you to go it alone. He wants you to have someone on your belay who can point out the next handhold for you to consider reaching for as you attempt to scale His holy mountain.

So, don't *ever* give up in the search, and do whatever it takes to be able to allow yourself to participate in what could potentially be an extremely grace-filled relationship.

And that prompts me to make a brief comment about the difficulties of the interior life. Things like spiritual dryness, discouragement, or temptations. Because we WILL encounter them on the spiritual journey.

But why? Most often, it is simply because of some sort of improper alignment, or disorderedness, in our lives in relation to what it is that God created us for and desires for us. This disorderedness will reveal itself in our human tendencies. Like when we are completely focused upon doing what we want, when we want, and how we want, and this usually can result in our not being in complete union with God's will for our lives, and then we run into challenges.

Ralph Martin, in his book, *The Fulfillment of All Desire*, writes:

> *"We may have become careless in being faithful to our spiritual commitments such as attendance at daily Mass, our daily time of prayer, spiritual reading, and so on. Or we may have become careless in valuing the gifts God gives us, or in rejecting or dallying with temptation. Or we may have begun to allow distractions, entertainments, and engagement in worldly activities to deaden our hunger for God . . . Dryness experienced as a result of negligence, lukewarmness, and infidelity—and whatever stage of the downward spiral it may have led to—have only one solution: repentance. This dryness is self-induced; the solution to it is to return to fidelity in our spiritual practices."[66]*

But what about those times in our lives when it's not about our failings, or about our disorderedness? What about when we are simply experiencing life with its sorrows, struggles, and tragedies?

It is especially during those times that we need to persevere and turn ever more firmly to the tools that our loving and faithful Heavenly Father has provided to assist us—His Word, His Church and those people He has placed in our lives, while always remembering WHY we are doing this—to become saints in heaven.

For as Saint Catherine of Sienna once commented, *"Nothing great is ever achieved without much enduring."*

So, just as we have to be willing to keep searching for a trusted person who can serve as our spiritual mentor or director, we must persevere in the midst of the trials, sorrows, and tragedies.

For our Lord has not left us to endure and struggle alone.

He loves us far too much to do that, and it's why He left us the tools we need to help us persevere during this lifelong journey. But we must be willing to utilize the guidance God provides to us through others, and to seek to put the guidance we receive at the service of growing in holiness.

Start searching for your soul friend today.

SAY YES to being accompanied on the journey.

Time to turn the page to discover how saints come in clusters.

CHAPTER 18
SAINTS COME IN CLUSTERS

*"We need a community to help us reach our goal. Faith
is not an individual journey; it's a team sport. We
need each other. We are on the journey together."*

— Matthew Kelly

The second tool, the next hidden gem for our eventual crown of glory in heaven God has given us to be encouraged, inspired, and capable of persevering in the spiritual life is friendship.

Now you may be saying to yourself right now, wait a minute, I have plenty of friends, why do I need to spend time reading a chapter that focuses on friendship? Because I would contend although many of us have "friends," most of us probably don't have true, authentic *friendships*.

I differentiate here because in our world today, especially in social media, we have an extremely strange understanding of who is a "friend." "Friend" status is bestowed upon anyone who likes, shares, or engages with our posts and pictures, and although there is a level of engagement, this is not true authentic friendship.

Why? Because authentic friendship consists, as Scott Galloway writes, *"of making a visible investment in someone else with your most precious resource, you."*[67]

If we are not investing all of ourselves—time, talent, treasure—into a relationship with another, then it's not truly authentic. And since our time is limited, who (and what) we invest ourselves in is what becomes real. It becomes authentic. This is why true and authentic friendships are few and far between, and why, if you have found one, then you truly have found a priceless treasure.

For it states in Sirach 6:14-17

"A faithful friend is a sturdy shelter; he who finds one finds a treasure. A faithful friend is beyond price, no sum can balance his worth. A faithful friend is a life-saving remedy, such as he who fears God finds; For he who fears God behaves accordingly, and his friend will be like himself."

When people speak of what friendship should be, these verses from the book of Sirach in Scripture are often referenced as a "how-to" manual for determining who a true friend is, but particularly the importance of one's friend helping to determine how God-like we shall eventually become.

The old adages of *"Show me your friends, and I will show you who you are,"* and *"You become like the five people you spend the most time with. Choose carefully,"* are both rooted in the idea St Paul expresses in 1 Corinthians 15:33, "*Bad company corrupts good character.*"

So, if we are *truly* seeking heaven and pursuing holiness, why are we going to spend time with those who are not assisting us in that pursuit? If our number one goal is to become holy, and since life is short (and uncertain), then all the more reason we should be seeking out true, authentic friends who fear God and behave accordingly, because this will only help to ensure the possibility we will do the same.

James Clear, author of the book, *Atomic Habits*, and foremost authority on how to bring about the fostering of any type of change in one's life, emphasizes this point when he discussed the value of others during the pursuit to change your habits. He wrote, *"One of the most effective things you can do to build better habits is to join a culture where your desired behavior is the normal behavior."*

This is one of the *key* reasons why friendship is so vital in the pursuit to holiness as we seek to become whom God created us to be.

But an equally important benefit of good, authentic friendship is there is truly nothing more empowering, encouraging, and inspiring than being among like-minded people who are striving to achieve a goal that is larger than themselves.

I am sure we all have heard at least one story of how a war was won, a team won a championship, a business achieved unbelievable profits or results, how a community rebuilt in the aftermath of a disaster or tragedy, or how a group of individuals were able to overcome unbelievable adversity by the simple process of choosing to come together, believed in and support one another as they went about relentlessly pursuing their shared goal and then ended up achieving greatness together.

It is these kinds of endeavors we were designed for from the beginning. We have been made for love. We have been made for relationship. We have been made for community. And the spiritual life is no different.

And that's why saints tend to come in clusters.

Every great saint during the last twenty centuries—Benedict, Francis of Assisi, Dominic, Ignatius of Loyola, Teresa of Avila, Mother Teresa of Calcutta, and on and on—started by pursuing their particular path towards sanctity, and then their clarity about what needed to be done to draw closer to God and become more like Jesus drew other like-minded people to them, and then together, they strove for holiness.

But no family or set of friends better exemplifies this reality of love and intertwined relationships focused upon pursuing holiness than the one headed by Basil and Elder Emmelia in a small community in Cappadocia in the early fourth century. From among the nine children, four—Macrina, Gregory, Basil and Peter—are all canonized saints, as well as two friends of the family—Gregory of Nazianzus and Eustathius of Sebaste.

This cluster of saints did more to advance the spread of Christianity and ensure its orthodoxy than any other group of men and women in the entire fourth century. Their writings influenced, in their own century alone, the great saints of Jerome, Ambrose, and Augustine, but they continue to be turned to for guidance even within the Church today.

God worked mightily and miraculously through all of them. And there are many more saints who are eternally intertwined with the name of their friends—like Saints Ignatius and Polycarp, Felicity and Perpetua, Basil and Gregory, Ambrose and Augustine, Benedict and Scholastica, Gregory and Martin of Tours, Francis and Clare of Assisi, Teresa of Avila and John of the Cross, Mother Teresa and Pope John Paul II.

The list could go on and on, but the point I want to make is this, to become the saints God has created us to be, we *need* good, authentic friendships to challenge, inspire, encourage, and sustain us.

So how do we go about finding such friendships?

Well, first, we need to know what we are actually looking for. We need to understand the nature of friendship itself. And besides love, there is probably nothing more misunderstood in our world today than what friendship actually is, or what it looks like.

Many in our world today speak about different "types" of friends, or the characteristics we should look for in a friend. This understanding of having "types" of friends is rooted in the ancient Greek understanding of the three "kinds" of friendship taught by Aristotle. Those three kinds were pleasant friendship, useful friendship, and virtuous friendship.

Pleasant friendship can be described most easily as someone who you would enjoy hanging out with, grabbing a beer with, going to see a movie with, or maybe watching a sporting event. Simply put, pleasant friendship is where each person enjoys themselves and has a good time hanging out together, but there is nothing more to the relationship other than the pleasurable time spent.

Useful friendship emerges when we pursue a common goal together. These tend to be people we work with, are part of an organization or group we are a part of, or maybe people that we go hiking, cycling, or running with. We each gain value from the presence of the other because we have something to share— be it expertise, skills, support, or encouragement, but there is still a lack of depth in the relationship as it is not necessary to really know the other person to pursue the common goal. When the common goal is removed, the relationship will tend to go by the wayside, too, because the goal is the unifier, not the relationship between persons. These are "friends by circumstance."

Now virtuous friendship is where we want the best for the other. It is a friendship rooted in love because I know, accept, and cherish the *real* you, just how you are with no motive other than to seek your happiness. And if true happiness only comes about from transforming union with God, then a virtuous friend will naturally seek to help another friend discover this purpose, find this peace, and invite them into ever deeper relationship with the One who gives life in its abundance.

St Francis de Sales writes of virtuous Christian friendship, as one focused upon seeking the best for the other, *"If the bond of your mutual liking be charity, devotion, and Christian perfection, God knows how very precious a friendship it is! Precious because it comes from God, because it tends to God, because God is the link that binds you, because it will last forever in him."*

We can see this is the highest and most perfect form of friendship. It is the kind of friendship Jesus modeled for His disciples and the same kind of friendship He invites us into with His Heavenly Father and the Holy Spirit. And this is the kind of friendship we need to strive to surround ourselves with here on earth.

The Cappadocian saints exemplify this idea of virtuous Christian friendship. Therefore, we must study their ways. We must ask: How did they remain so well connected, in such strong friendship with God, so His river of supernatural grace could flow so freely through them? What can they teach us about the ideal spiritual disciplines, the ultimate daily regimen of prayer, of growing in virtue each day, and abandoning ourselves to God's will?

These are the questions we must be seeking to answer as we work to create a cluster of friends in our lives. Friends who are all striving for, and encouraging, inspiring, and supporting others on the journey to holiness. When we can become like the saints of Cappadocia ourselves, and be surrounded by others who are similarly striving for holiness, who knows what plans God has in mind for us and His Church when we are faithful in utilizing this great gift of God's abundance in our lives?

Now there is nothing "wrong' with the other kinds of friendship, or with having different "types" of friends. Like those we confide in, or people who mentor us, or others who understand and accept us, or others who are fun to be around, or those who challenge us, or others who are loyal and faithful presences in our lives no matter what.[68]

But my question to you is this—if the reality is we become like those we spend the most time with, and you truly understand who you are, and are clear about what you want to focus upon. You have said yes to pursuing it, combined with the fact that time is short, why are you not doing *everything* in your power to become, and also demand of all those around you, the goal of being true and authentic friends to one another?

Bishop Robert Barron once said, "*You don't mess around with friendship; you don't turn it into something abstract; you don't compromise with it. You enter into it fully.*"

This is the only way we can become, and the only way we can find authentic friendship in our life is by entering into it fully. But we tend to hold back. Of course, we must exercise prudence and not simply trust anyone completely from day one. But we still want to "hedge our bets" just in case we are wrong about whom we have decided to enter into friendship. But "holding back" guarantees the relationship will never become truly authentic.

For where there is no risk, there is a lack of love. And where there is a lack of love, there is a lack of authenticity. And this is truly sad because "*Friendship is the source of the greatest pleasures, and without friends, even the most agreeable pursuits become tedious.*"[69]

So, we need to be determined to seek out each one of the true, authentic friends God has placed in our lives. And we must be willing to settle for nothing less than surrounding ourselves as much as possible with the *fullness* of loving authentic friendship.

Don't sell yourself short when it comes to friendship.

Not only do we need to seek to be a source of encouragement, inspiration and support to those around us as an authentic and loving friend, but we need to ensure that we, too, are receiving the encouragement, inspiration, and support necessary to strive for holiness each and every day.

It's time for a new cluster of saints to arise in the Church today.

SAY YES to true and authentic friendship.

Now, turn the page to discover the friendship hidden in plain sight.

CHAPTER 19

FRIENDSHIP HIDDEN
IN PLAIN SIGHT

One of the most common problems about friendship in our world today I spoke of briefly in the last chapter is that of finding authentic friendship. Often, our failure to find friends with whom to share the journey to holiness brings about a hesitancy in ourselves to enter fully into a relationship for fear of being rejected or hurt.

So how might we learn to overcome this hesitancy? How can we overcome this fear of being authentic with one another as we strive for holiness?

Turn with intentionality to the Communion of Saints.

THE COMMUNION OF SAINTS

As part of the Body of Christ, we are in union with all God's holy people—living and dead. The Communion of Saints is comprised of three parts—the Church Militant, the Church Suffering, and the Church Triumphant. The Church Militant are those who are alive on earth, the Church Suffering are those souls in purgatory, and the Church Triumphant are all those who are saints in Heaven.

The Communion of Saints is an idea that many people either misunderstand or don't fully embrace, and because of it, many people do not utilize the friendships that are hidden in plain sight.

CHURCH MILITANT

The Church Militant, in particular, is about actively striving for holiness through our every thought, word, and action because our salvation and holiness is *intrinsically* tied to the good of one another. Therefore, everything in life matters, and can have value for assisting someone to grow closer to God and become more like Jesus.

This is especially important to remember as we live in a Christian community. This idea is illustrated in this reflection about relying upon one another's gifts in a community:

> *"The apostles were a close group (actually the whole body of disciples were). Certainly, they had their arguments, but they had some very deep friendships. We can gather this from the Gospels, and see it explicitly in the Acts of the Apostles.*

> *The friendship of Peter and John is a particularly great one. They are main characters in the Gospels, and their relationship is revealed in particular, here, at the end of the Gospel of John and in the Book of Acts. Acts even speaks of specific time they spent together. Neither of them possessed all the necessary Christian gifts. But combined, they must have been an amazing team. Peter had great passion, boldness, and leadership. John had great depth, faithfulness, and love.*

> *Similarly, none of us has everything we need in the Christian life. We need to rely upon others for strengths and for gifts that we don't possess. And others need to rely on us for gifts that they lack. Marriages and families are like this too. We are all necessary parts of the one Body of Christ. We should*

develop our unique qualities, interests, and talents. Also, we should encourage these in others."[70]

C.S. Lewis, one of the greatest Christian writers and apologists of the twentieth century, explains it this way:

"It is a serious thing to live in a society of possible gods and goddesses, to remember that the dullest and most uninteresting person you talk to may one day be a creature which, if you saw it now, you would be strongly tempted to worship. Or else a horror and a corruption such as you now meet, if at all, in a nightmare. All-day long, we are, in some degree, helping each other to one or other of these destinations. It is in the light of these overwhelming possibilities, it is with the awe and the circumspection proper to them, that we should conduct all our dealings with one another, all friendships, all loves, all play, all politics. There are no ordinary people. You have never talked to a mere mortal...But it is immortals whom we joke with, work with, marry, snub, and exploit—immortal horrors or everlasting splendors."

Yet in a world where people are discarded, unloved, and seemingly replaceable, where are we to experience being cherished?

Within our families and with our friends. The Christian family is supposed to be a place of love, both human and divine, with intertwined relationships among friends, the poor, the sick, and other Christians, all united in the worship of God. And our friendships should be striving for the same.

As I shared in the last chapter, the Cappadocian saints arose in the fourth century in and around the home of Basil and Elder Emmelia, and are the model we are seeking to emulate. Families and friends who are gathering together around the shared purpose of striving for holiness in an atmosphere of loving acceptance.

Of all the lessons of the Cappadocian saints, the most important lesson they have for us is love. For it was only out of love for his sister, Macrina, in the wake of her passing, Gregory of Nyssa wrote her biography entitled the "Vita Macrinae Junioris," and is why we have an awareness of this family and their interconnected group of friends.

Such is the power of love in the Church Militant within the Communion of Saints.

Now I know many of us might not have the blessing of experiencing this kind of love within our families or friends. In fact, in a recent article, Charles McKinney made the following observation:

> *"Many have lost their faith in God, because they have lost, through faithlessness, their faith in man. Doubt of the reality of love becomes doubt of the reality of the spiritual life. To be unable to see the divine in man is to have the eyes blinded to the divine anywhere. Deception in the sphere of love shakes the foundation of religion. Its result is atheism, not perhaps as a conscious speculative system of thought, but as a subtle practical influence on conduct. It corrupts the fountain of life and taints the whole stream. Despair of love, if final and complete, would be despair of God, for God is love. Thus, the wreck of friendship often means a temporary wreck of faith. It ought not to be so, but that there is a danger of it should impress us with a deeper sense of the responsibility attached to our friendships. Our life follows the fortunes of our love."[71]*

And this is where the Body of Christ in the form of our parish churches is supposed to fill in the gap. Pope Francis tells us a parish should be *"a family among families, open to bearing witness in today's world...open to faith, hope, and love for the Lord and for those whom He has a preferential love. A home with open doors."*

What might that look like?

It would be a community where each person helps another come to deeper and deeper conversion through many ways—a smile, or a willingness to forgive, or by striving to understand and be present to each other through the charitable use of gifts and talents for the benefit of each person we encounter as we share the burdens of life together with love and rejoicing.

It is in a place such as this that the Church Militant resides. A place where those here on earth are striving to grow in holiness while helping others do the same. Where we teach and help others to see how God sees so we may all be able to look and feel the way Jesus looks and feels and experience and learn how to let our hearts beat with love just like Jesus' does.

But if our churches are not such places, what then?

This is where the Communion of Saints can sustain us all the way to eternity.

Because the Communion of Saints is not just about here and now, it's also about all those who have come before, and all those who are already in Heaven. And just because our friends may have departed from this life, they are never gone or forgotten, nor does their influence cease.

Saint Elizabeth Ann Seton wrote, "*The accidents of life separate us from our dearest friends but let us not despair. God is like a looking glass in which souls see each other. The more we are united to Him by love, the nearer we are to those who belong to Him.*"

THE CHURCH SUFFERING,
THOSE IN PURGATORY

Our brothers and sisters in purgatory experience great joy and great sorrow. Great joy in that they know with certainty that someday they will be with God in Heaven, but great sorrow because they have been given a clear vision of themselves, and they now realize how far away they still are from that eternal moment of transforming union with God.

This is why the Church asks us to pray for the souls in purgatory. Because the bonds of Christian community do not cease at death, but rather these bonds can be perfected through the power of the Holy Spirit when we are in union with Christ in prayer.

Mr. Schmaus, in his book, *Dogmatic Theology*, explains:

> *"The love and fidelity of the Church on earth wins joy and relief for those souls who long to enter into eternal bliss. This stream of charity rises up to benefit of the souls in Purgatory even when we are distracted. Yet when we make sure to direct these prayers for this intention, we can work an even greater good."*[72]

Pope Benedict XVI describes the result of this "stream of charity" beautifully:

> *"We should recall that no man is an island, entire of itself. Our lives are involved with one another, through innumerable interactions, they are linked together. No one lives alone. No one sins alone. No one is saved alone. The lives of others continually spill over into mine: in what I think, say, and do, and achieve. And conversely, my life spills over into that of others: for better or for worse. So, my prayer for another is not something extraneous to that person, something external, not even after death."*

So true, authentic friendship never dies. It is just transformed. We can still will the good of the other by lovingly offering prayer and sacrifice for our dearly departed family members and friends. Each day, we are given the opportunity to continue to love through the many works of mercy; or by receiving the sacraments; or by offering up our physical suffering or the challenges we face in our daily life.

And as we love, we continue to be transformed and purified ourselves, which makes us even more capable of being a true and authentic friend but also prepares us ever more fully for the love relationship with Jesus for all eternity in Heaven.

THE CHURCH TRIUMPHANT

To become saints simply means completely fulfill what we already are as God's adopted sons and daughters. *"Nothing can bring us into close contact with the beauty of Christ himself other than the world of beauty created by faith and light that shines out from the faces of the saints, through whom his own light becomes visible."*[73]

St Anthony of Padua tells us *"Each saint in heaven rejoices over the glorification of the other, and his love overflows to him... the same joy will fill all the blessed, for I shall rejoice over your well-being as though it were my own, and you will rejoice over mine as though it were yours...So shall it be in eternal life: My glory shall be your consolation and exultation, and yours shall be mine."*

To be part of the Church Triumphant of the Communion of Saints is to experience exactly that. But even those in Heaven are called upon to still love.

"The saints teach us, encourage us, challenge us, and inspire us...God is constantly trying to open our eyes to the amazing possibilities that He has enfolded in our being. The saints continue this work, encouraging us to explore all our God-given potential, not with speeches, but with the example of their lives."[74]

Heaven isn't retirement. No, Heaven is where we will have the fullest of opportunities to love through intercession and praying for others, particularly those who are struggling for holiness as part of the Church Militant.

This is why patron saints are so important.

Although the same holds true for all the saints, our patron saints are *particularly* interested in helping and assisting us. There is a patron saint for every profession and hobby you can think of, and we invoke their patronage when we choose and take their name at Confirmation.

For me, my official patron saint is St Michael the Archangel. He was my Confirmation saint, and being a former military officer, I can attest I called upon his aid and protection a LOT!

In addition to our patron saints, any saint inspires us through their writings or by the example of their life has a connection with us and actually desires for us to call upon them for assistance at any time, day or night

I have a whole *pantheon* of saints I regularly call upon. Over the years, what has emerged for me in my spiritual life is having a saint for each day of the week. Saints like John Vianney, patron of parish priests, who I ask for his intercession as I offer prayers for current priests, and for future priestly and religious vocations.

Or Francis Xavier who inspires me to evangelize and share the Good News. Or my "other" Francis—Francis de Sales who is the patron of writers. Maximillian Kolbe inspires me to live out my Marian consecration more fully each day. Mother Teresa of Calcutta and Therese of Lisieux and Faustina teach me what it is to lead a life of merciful love. And then my precious Ignatius of Loyola, who like me, set aside a military profession to pursue being a better disciple of Jesus, and who inspires me to grow closer to God and become more like Jesus every day.

If, for some reason, you haven't really gotten to know the saints yet, I encourage you to start. At a minimum, seek out the patron saint for your profession, or perhaps rediscover your Confirmation saint. But get to know the saints who are already present in your life—regardless of whether you have been aware of them or not.

Now, these are just a few examples of how the saints can aid, inspire, and intercede for us.

But the most important thing to do is to ask for and invoke their help. Make sure to ask for their assistance! For they *will* come to your aid. They *will* intercede for you. They *will* help you.

Angelic Assistance

Saint Francis de Sales wrote, "*Make friends with the angels, who though invisible are always with you. Often invoke them, constantly praise them, and make good use of their help and assistance in all your temporal and spiritual affairs.*"

I already made mention of Saint Michael as he is my Confirmation Saint, but Saint Michael and the other Archangels whom we know about from Scripture—Raphael and Gabriel, totally rock.

And yet, God has given us an even more precious gift—our own personal guardian angel.

Too often, we forget there is an angelic helper who is there to protect us, guide us, and help us through every moment of every day. We are reminded of this any time we pray the Guardian Angel prayer: "*Angel of God, my guardian dear, to whom God's love commits me here. Ever this day, be at my side, to light, to guard, to rule, and to guide.*"

What a blessing! An angel who is present every minute of every day solely to help and intercede for us!

But even more than that, we should look to imitate our guardian angel. Like how we should reverently come before the presence of the God in the Tabernacle; of how we should recollect and desire to be in union with God in all the activities of our day—from our first waking breath to our last thoughts prior to falling asleep; of how to engage with temptations and battle against the devil; but especially in how to exemplify and practice the virtues, especially the virtues of charity, patience, gentleness, generosity, purity, and uprightness of heart.

Talk about the perfect friend!

Now, every one of us has a guardian angel. So even if our family or parish is lacking, even if you are having a difficult time finding true and authentic friends around you, even if you are unaware of the pantheon of saints ready to intercede for you, God *still* has given each and every one of us access to a true and authentic friend.

But only if we are willing to reach out to them for assistance and invoke their aid.

In the same way, we must be willing to seek out all the sources of friendship hidden in plain sight. To seek friendships among the entire Communion of Saints, those living, those who have gone before us, and those who are already awaiting us in Heaven.

Be sustained in friendship here on earth and all the way unto eternity.

SAY YES to friendship hidden in plain sight.

And now, turn the page and discover the power of story.

CHAPTER 20
THE POWER OF STORY

"We become the stories we listen to."

— Matthew Kelly[75]

Another tool and the third hidden gem for our eventual crown of glory in Heaven is story.

God designed us from the beginning in how He formed and shaped us so we are uniquely encouraged, inspired, and supported in our lives through the power of story—for stories are the language which humanity uses to communicate.

Yet numerous studies show after graduation from school, the majority of people no longer read anything other than what might be necessary for some practical purpose, like their work. This is truly sad because stories can be the door through which we can embark upon the journey of transformation. Statistics bear out this reality, again and again, showing how individuals who immerse themselves in story are more imaginative and curious, more empathetic, experience reduced stress, and have an increased capacity for communication and social skills.

For me, stories have always been a huge part of my life. I was blessed with a love of reading, and that has never faded as I am still an avid reader, as well as love movies and television. Over the years, however, I have noticed I tend to gravitate towards those books, movies, and TV shows that tell a phenomenal story. They do this either through the plot itself or by having characters who have great depth and complexity. If one or the other of those things aren't present, then I tend to lose interest quickly.

One of my favorites is J.R.R. Tolkien's *Lord of the Rings* trilogy. Because of Peter Jackson's magnificent film adaptation of the trilogy, most people are now familiar with the story of Frodo the Hobbit, one of the smallest creatures that resides in the Middle Earth. He is given the great task of bearing the great Ring of Power to Mount Doom for it to be destroyed, and in so doing, save all of Middle Earth from the great evil of Sauron. Another favorite of mine is the character of George Bailey in the classic *It's a Wonderful Life* Christmas movie where the angel, Clarence, shows George how profoundly important his life has been—even if George himself is unable to see it.

One that is not as well-known is the character of Lewis Gillies in the *Song of Albion* trilogy by Stephen Lawhead. Lewis, a scrawny graduate student from a family of no importance in our world, is transported to the land of Albion. And as he battles to defend the essence of what is good, true, and beautiful during the Paradise War, Lewis finds himself transformed through his many battles and trials and eventually becomes the great High King, Llew Silver Hand. As Llew, he is not only the defender of the realm of Albion but also serves as the protector of all that is good, true, and beautiful in all the realms of all the worlds, including our own.

More recently, the stories in the *Avengers:End Game* movie and in the *Game of Thrones (GOT)* television series have been inspiring in their portrayal of love and sacrifice. In both stories, which took *years* to share, all of the characters had to turn to, and rely upon one another to try and defeat the greatest threat any of them have ever faced. In the end, it is only through *sacrifice and love* there is even a possibility to win the day. But it was the *stories* of redemption amid the sacrifices being made and the love being shown that subsequently inspired, moved to tears, and gave the other characters the courage necessary for them to continue on their own journey.

And it's the same for us.

The reason these, and other great stories, are so phenomenally popular is because we *long* to be inspired by stories of others who sacrifice out of love for another, for then we are inspired and given the courage to try and do the same in our own lives.

Edward C. Sellner, author of the book, *Stories of Celtic Soul Friends*, points out that all the great spiritual traditions, including Judaism, Islam, Buddhism, and Hinduism, relate their understanding of God and the destiny of humankind through the stories they tell of their founders, heroes, and saints. This is a result of humanity's primal urge to give expression to what people have seen, heard, and experienced has evoked questions, wonder and awe.[76]

Another author, Russell W. Dalton, explains humankind has constructed myths and legends throughout history in an attempt to provide explanations for nature and, like Sellner, similarly states stories are meant to be a means for exploring the ultimate questions of life.

This contention by both authors is firmly evident if one takes the time to look at myths and legends from across the world. For despite the many different places and cultures, they all share similar themes and motifs. But the primary motif is the idea of the Hero's Journey.

The Hero's Journey begins with "the hero" being called to an adventure by a mysterious stranger, who then ensures the hero receives special gifts for his quest. Additionally, the hero either meets or gathers, a group of companions who become his friends. Then together, they must find a way through some type of a dark forest or cave where the hero must descend into the depths to face a great evil, and then finally, after making a great sacrifice, the hero eventually emerges victorious.[77]

Dalton contends these themes and motifs appear because they express deeply understood truths about the human experience, along with human visions of what is divine. Therefore, since all humans share a yearning to find purpose and meaning in their lives and to know God, these spiritual "yearnings" lie behind the similarities in ancient myths and legends.[78]

Powerful stories are evident in the very way they can communicate several different meanings within the same story. These different meanings, or the four senses of literature, are: literal, moral, allegorical, and anagogical.

The literal is the actually story itself; the moral is the lesson the story communicates; the allegorical is how the story represents and points to something else (this is most often done through foreshadowing); and the anagogical (often called the eschatological) reveals the significance of this story in regards to life and death itself.

You can get a quick idea for how the different senses can be at work in the aftermath of a Mass, when people are discussing the homily. Some share what fact impacted them, while others share about the lesson they learned, while still others talk about what is motivating them to action.

Taking this a step further, Fr. Thomas Dubay, in his book, *The Fire Within,* uses this illustration to describe what is occurring:

> *"In the same manner, five hundred people in a parish church all hear the same sound waves during the homily, but they profit from it exactly as they are, or are not, disposed for the message. Jesus taught the same truth in His parable of the sower: from the word of God some hearers yield nothing at all, while others yield thirty or sixty or a hundredfold."*[79]

We honestly shouldn't be surprised by this since there are plenty of examples of this occurrence on a natural level all the time—where people go to hear a motivational speaker, and everyone "hears" something different inspires them to action. Or when people go and see a movie, and someone cries during one scene, but then another person cries during another, and another person doesn't cry at all. This is the power of story and its various meanings at work in the hearts, souls, and minds of people.

But it's not just story that has power, it's also the *words* themselves.

This was most recently illustrated by an experiment done by the furniture company, IKEA.

They took two plants, built containers around each one, and then had people record both positive and negative messages. They then piped into the plant containers the messages. All positive for one, and all negative for the other. Within a month, it was physically evident the power of the words on each of the plants as the plant that has heard nothing but negative was dying—its leaves were shriveled up, its growth was stunted, and it had a lot of brown and yellow amongst its growth; while the plant that had received positive messages was vibrant, lush, full of green leaves and fresh growth—it was thriving.[80]

There are numerous other studies done with other physical items, like rice, or one with water. Each experiment reveals the power of words upon our physical environments and points to the reality that words themselves have great meaning and power.

This fact is evidenced in Scripture at the beginning of Genesis with the use of the motif of "And God said" and "then it was" being used throughout the entire creation story. In fact, the word, "abracadabra" literally means in Hebrew, "I create as I speak."

Even on a natural level, we can recognize the power of names, for it is a special thing when someone calls us by our name. If we hear someone says our name, it stops us in our tracks, and we feel a desire to respond. When we hear our name, we are jerked to attention. This is the power that resides in our name.

And this is reminiscent of God giving new names to those with whom He enters into relationship with, like Abram becoming Abraham, or later the words of Jesus when He proclaims, *"Whatever you ask in my name, I will do it."*[81]

In the Gospel of John, we are given insight into exactly who the Second Person of the Trinity is when we are told *"In the beginning was the Word; and the Word was with God; and the Word was God."*[82] And later on in that same Gospel, we hear how the Word became flesh and dwelt among us, and then that very Word, Jesus, spoke to us; *"I am the Way, and the Truth, and the Life."*

Jesus is the definitive "Word" spoken by God and all of Divine Revelation is summed up in Him.

The Word IS Life itself.

So, what does this have to do with the power of story in our spiritual life?

Everything.

The key to understanding the power of story in our spiritual lives is in realizing history is actually His-Story and *all* of our stories are a part of His-Story. When we see our stories as intricately connected and integral to *the* Story, then we are capable of seeing how all stories, especially our own, are echoes of *the* Story.

The Story of the loving sacrifice of Jesus. A story rooted in His *complete, total, and never- ending* love for each of us. This *is* the Good News, and why men and women for more than two millennia have been inspired to sacrifice and love just like Jesus.

And we now call these men and women saints.

Throughout Sacred Scripture and the story of salvation history, we can see *everyone's* story matters because God always uses the most unlikely of people time and again to bring about His plan for all of humanity's salvation.

The more we immerse ourselves in great stories, the more we can fulfill our three-fold vocation. The more we listen to and share one another's stories, the more we will become inspired and encouraged to pursue the call to holiness and to live out our personal mission of who we are, what we are, and where we are in our particular state of life and so write our respective chapters in His-Story.

Immerse yourself in great stories. Stories that inspire and encourage you to do the good, search for truth, and embrace the beautiful.

Stories that give you the courage to do battle each day of your life as you are transformed into the hero God has created you to be within your own life and the lives of others.

Become an emboldened warrior of Christ.

SAY YES to the power of Story.

Now, turn the page to begin sharing the divine life within today,

CHAPTER 21
SHARING THE DIVINE LIFE WITHIN

"What happens is of little significance compared with the stories we tell ourselves about what happens. Events matter little, only stories of events affect us."

— Rabih Alameddine, The Hakawati

A nother aspect of story is the need to *share* our story with others. It is only through the sharing of our stories about our relationship with God, and how that relationship has made all the difference in the world within our lives, that others are moved to even consider the possibility for themselves, and are also encouraged in their own relationship with Him.

Yet we hesitate to speak. We convince ourselves that "my story doesn't matter," or "Who am I to speak of such things? I am no one important."

But these are lies told to us by the world. *Everyone's* story matters.

Case in point. Oftentimes when we hear the genealogy of Jesus, or any of the genealogies in Scripture, we can "tune out" or get distracted into thinking that these are just a bunch of names that have no meaning. But seek to think about them a bit differently.

Those names are actually *us*.

Enos, Thara, Esrom, Menan, Addi, Joanna, and Melchi all had an integral part to play (these people are all ancestors of Jesus), and tells us that we, too, have a "part" to play in THE great story. But again, we think we are not important, and that our lives don't matter, and therefore, our stories don't matter either.

But our stories do matter. Desperately.

Because there is an even more vital aspect to the importance of sharing our story with others, and it took me years before I truly gained clarity on this point. What I have learned is that *if we fail to share our story, we are killing the divine life that resides within us.*

It is only by sharing our story (evangelizing) that we ourselves are evangelized.

"...*we find salvation for ourselves precisely in the measure that we bring God's life to others,"*[83] so, therefore, "*Each of us ought to ask himself or herself: Have I done all I could in the course of this year for the Immaculata, for the salvation and sanctification of my souls and my neighbor's? Or am I being reproached by my conscience for my laziness, listlessness, my poor zeal ... or my want of self-sacrifice?"*[84]

And just as it is true that someone who teaches comes to know their material more deeply in the process of preparing to present it to another, the same holds true for us in the process of our sharing our story with others.

For when we fail to share how God is working in our lives, then our own faith is weakened. We deny the very essence of who we are—our story—when we fail to share our story.

This is why God has made story the most fundamental way that we communicate with one another.

Why do I say this? Because it is EXACTLY how God in human form—Jesus—did it.

Jesus shared *stories* with those around Him in ancient Palestine, and He continues to share His story with each one of us every day, as He writes out the very details of our lives by entrusting dreams to us, so then they can be brought to life with Him, in Him, and through Him for others.

Once we realize that our *stories* matter, it becomes abundantly clear that we *must* share our story as well as listen to one another's stories if we are to ensure the divine life residing within us burns brightly and can spark and encourage and sustain the divine life of others.

THE NEED

Jean-Baptiste Chautard recounts in his book *The Soul of the Apostolate*, Pope St. Pius X was conversing with a group of his cardinals one day. The pope asked them:

"What is the thing we most need, today, to save society?"

"Build Catholic schools," said one.

"No."

"More churches," said another.

"Still no."

"Speed up the recruiting of priests," said a third.

"No, no," said the pope, "the most necessary thing of all, at this time, is for every parish to possess a group of laymen who will be at the same time virtuous, enlightened, resolute, and truly apostolic."

Chautard continues, "Further details enable us to assert that this holy pope at the end of his life saw no hope for the salvation of the world unless the clergy could use their zeal to form faithful Christians full of apostolic ardor, preaching by word and example, but especially by example. In the diocese where he served before being elevated to the papacy, he attached less importance to the (count) of parishioners than to the list of *Christians capable of radiating an apostolate.*" (*emphases mine*)

If we look at the witness of all the saints throughout the last two millennia, being capable of "radiating an apostolate" means we must be obedient to doing God's will as we fulfill the Great Commission to "go forth and proclaim the Good News and baptize all the nations."

And how do we each proclaim the Good News? By sharing our stories.

We share our story of how the Good News has transformed our lives and has made all the difference in living. Of how, because we no longer are prisoners of sin and death, we can live lives full of purpose, peace, and abundance.

This is *why* it is "Good News!"

Yet, in our scientific world, we tend to deny story has any power to help us. We tend to think stories are only for children, that if we are mature adults, then we will have set aside anything that smacks of "bedtime fairytales" and embrace "real" things we can see, hear, smell, taste, and touch. But when we set aside story, we set aside mystery, and when we do that, we begin to suffocate and kill off our truest self, our spiritual soul.

Dr. Tod Warner beautifully describes what I am talking about in his article, "Mystery, Manner, and the Rediscovery of Great Literature":

> *"Science can explain, but never in total. How will we ever plumb the depths of love? With a paper on neurotransmitters? How will we ever fully comprehend the comforts of loyalty and the heartbreak of betrayal? With colorful PET scans of our brains? During the Enlightenment, certain thinkers assured us that morality would soon be fully defined and predicted using mathematical equations. To borrow from an ill-sourced but brilliant quote, "Some ideas are so absurd than only an intellectual would believe them."*
>
> *We must read and experience. We must open ourselves to mystery that will not be fully explained this side of the*

*grave. We must welcome the contributions of science with-
out being limited by them. After all, we are not simply
material beings; **we are souls of ineffable depth greater
than our constituent parts.**[85] (**Bold emphases mine**)*

We *are* souls of ineffable depth that are greater than our constituent parts. None of us is simply defined by what we can do
or have done. Nor are we merely a conglomerate of our emotions
and ideas. We are *so* much more.

Our story is the divine life intricately woven together and
residing within each one of us. But that reality only becomes
evident in the context of sharing our stories with one another.

Saint Rose of Lima observed, *"Know that the greatest service
that man can offer to God is to help convert souls."* Therefore, no
one is insignificant, and we are all interconnected to bring about
the "happy ending"—when the King will return, and all will
be made well again. When pain, suffering, and death will be
no more.

And yet, we are afraid to share our story. Why?

Often, it is simply because we are fearful of how we may
look or dread the awkwardness of a particular situation. But
we can't let our pride and fear get in the way of doing whatever
is necessary to help the other person come closer to God. As a
Christian, we have a duty to live like Christ, and that means to
love the best we can—even if it means we fail or are rejected.

*"Everyone fails at being who they are supposed to be. A hero is
determined by how well they are who they are meant to be, rather
than being who they are supposed to be."*[86]

And seeking who we were meant to be is the essence of the
call to holiness. It is through our efforts to cooperate with God's
grace to become saints that we truly become the "characters" in
the Great Story that we were meant to be.

But "What story am I currently telling with my life?"[87]
Is your story a story that will inspire and encourage others to
greatness?

Because not only is our story part of *the* Story, our story is the exact vehicle God wants us to use to share Him with others.

And He created you *specifically* to do exactly that.

So, *"consider one's environment, family members, acquaintances, fellow workers, and places of residence, as the place for your mission, in order to win over these people..."* [88]

This is the essence of evangelizing. To simply engage in the act of sharing your story with another.

We do this because *"We have been called to heal wounds, to unite what has fallen apart, and to bring home those who have lost their way."*[89] And we must *"Dismiss all anger and look into yourself a little. Remember that he of whom you are speaking is your brother, and as he is in the way of salvation, God can make him a saint, in spite of his present weakness."*[90]

This is why sharing our story is so important. By being vulnerable, we invite others to do the same, and then we can truly fulfill the mandate Christ gave us to "go make disciples."

And if we truly love Jesus, then we will be willing to be "inconvenienced" by other people who are thirsting to hear our (God's) story. We must be willing to let go of our comfort and embrace our greatness.

We do this by loving others in small ways so they, too, will be inspired to do the same, and then together, we will be able to help defeat an army even more powerful than any army led by a fictional villain, or an army of the undead. By making sacrifices, loving others, and sharing our stories, we can help win the victory in the great spiritual battle for the world, and for those who choose it, *eternal and everlasting life!*

But we must begin by calling one another by name in a culture languishing for connection and relationship. Jesus calls each of us by name, and we must model that to others.

Saint Thomas Aquinas once instructed if we desire *"To convert somebody, go and take them by the hand and guide them."* For *"...there's no direct path to being truly known if we don't allow ourselves to be fully seen—for better or worse. But this kind of living will always require vulnerability."*[91]

And vulnerability is absolutely necessary if we desire to build a bridge of trust with another person. Brene Brown, a world-renowned researcher on what is necessary for deep and abiding relationships, said, "*Trust is earned through paying attention, listening, and gestures of genuine caring.*"

Brown's observation is integrally tied to the adage, "No one cares how much you know, until they know how much you care."

This means we must seek to enter into trusting relationships with one another, so it's possible for our stories to be life-giving. That's precisely why God made us exactly who we are, what we are, and where we are.

"*Talent comes everywhere. Everybody's talented...But having something to say, and a way to say it so people will listen to it, that's a whole other bag. Unless you get out there and try to do it, you'll never know...If there's one reason we're supposed to be here, it's to say something, so people want to hear it...*"[92]

And it's inherent on us to overcome our fear. As I shared in the last chapter, the practice of immersing ourselves in great stories can help us be encouraged and inspired to overcome our fear.

And when we share ourselves with another, they, in turn, will share their story with us, and then we become life for one another because words give life.

For the Word IS life.

And the Word Himself is Love Incarnate.

It is through our words of life to one another that the divine life within is strengthened to help transform us with, in, and through Love Himself into life and love for one another.

But are you paying attention? Are you listening? Are you writing your story down? Are you sharing words of life with another person amid your conversations?

Strive to radiate an apostolate and share the Good News that God loves each and every person and desires to spend eternity with them.

Seek to overcome your fear and share the divine life within you and share your story with others.

Your story *does* matter.

SAY YES to sharing your story today.

Now, turn the page and discover the crown jewel for your heavenly crown.

CHAPTER 22
THE CROWN JEWEL

*"Never be afraid of loving the Blessed Virgin too much.
You can never love her more than Jesus did."*

— St. Maximilian Kolbe

I t was April 2008. Almost two decades after I had been received into the Church. It was then that I encountered what has subsequently completely transformed my spiritual journey.

It was learning the fact that Mary is *the* crown jewel in our heavenly crown that we are fashioning here on earth through God's grace as we are living out our life of faith.

FIRST SATURDAYS AND THE LEGION OF MARY

At that time, I was working in parish ministry, and our pastor was faithful to ensuring there were opportunities for the parish to experience First Saturday Masses and Holy Hours. Up to that time, despite all of my theological studies, I had never encountered Devotion to the Immaculate Heart (First Saturdays), so I found myself intrigued to hear and learn about Mary's messages to the faithful throughout the centuries, particularly at Fatima.

As I learned and entered more deeply into the practice of both First Fridays[93] and First Saturdays in my own spiritual life, I encountered the apostolate of the Legion of Mary for the first time as well. In our parish, the Legion was devoted to visiting the sick and homebound, but one of the primary intentions of the founder, Frank Duff, was to inspire laypeople to live out a Marian spirituality in the midst of evangelizing others, and the apostolate was organized using military terminology from ancient Rome. [94]

Because of my own military background, this language was comfortable for me, but even more so was the term I heard used in reference to Mary—that of "Our Lady." The idea of becoming a legionnaire, a knight, on behalf of a heavenly Queen in the fight against evil resonated deeply in my heart, and I found myself desiring to know more.

Members of the Legion, particularly their Spiritual Advisor at the time, Deacon Skip Graffagnini, were always present at First Saturday Mass since they met immediately afterwards. This resulted in my entering into numerous conversations with Deacon Skip about Mary and her role in the spiritual life. Our conversations were far-ranging and very illuminating, but I will always be eternally grateful to him for introducing me to the idea of Marian consecration as well as the writings of St Louis de Montfort.

St Louis de Montfort

When Deacon Skip first mentioned Marian Consecration, I was a bit baffled, but instead of trying to explain it to me himself, he simply pointed me to the premier proponent of Marian Consecration, St Louis de Montfort.

Me, being the overachiever I am, went looking for the best book there was about St Louis de Montfort, Mary, and

Marian Consecration, and I ended up with a book by Father Helmuts Libietis entitled, *St Louis de Montfort's True Devotion Consecration to Mary*. It was described on the back cover as a "short, easy, and perfect way to make that Consecration."

Little did I know this book contained excerpts from all *ten* of the books St Louis recommended to be a part of the 33 Day consecration preparation! And it also contained excerpts from *all* the major writings of St Louis de Monfort to include *The Love of Eternal Wisdom*, *The Secret of the Rosary*, *The Secret of Mary*, and *Letter to the Friends of the Cross*. Needless to say, I dove into the deep end of what Marian consecration and Marian spirituality was all about. At the end of my consecration preparation time, I was in one word—*amazed*.

What amazed me?

First, St. Louis de Montfort was adamant in his contention consecration to Mary is "the easy, sure, and perfect way to attain heaven." He also introduced me for the first time to the idea that Mary is the "New Eve" just as Jesus is the "New Adam." In other words, God freely wills Mary as uniquely necessary in the present order of salvation because of the original sin of Adam and Eve. To bring about the plan for the salvation of humanity, God determines to invite Mary to become His Mother and subsequently, of His entire Church.

This means that by Mary's acceptance of God's invitation of Divine Maternity, a permanent relationship has resulted between Mary and the Persons of the Trinity. In other words, she is *always* the Spouse of the Holy Spirit, for she consents in faith to the Incarnation of Eternal Wisdom within her.

St Louis de Montfort summarizes this idea brilliantly, "*It is through the most Holy Virgin Mary that Jesus came into the world and it is also through her that He has to reign in the world.*"[95]

All of these ideas, amazed and humbled me. St Louis' writings showed me how utterly lacking I was in my understanding of what the spiritual life was, or the mission for which I, and every baptized person, is called. The mission that to truly become like Christ, we must also become children of Mary, so just like Jesus, we can be formed through the power of the Holy Spirit into profound and powerful representatives of God's love and mercy in the world.

Now, I know some people have been graced with the insight and understanding of Mary's importance early on in their spiritual lives, along with the knowledge that Mary is an integral part of their journey to grow closer to God and become more like Jesus. But these ideas were almost foreign to me.

And as I have subsequently shared these truths with others, I have encountered more folks who were like I was who might not necessarily have any issue with Mary, but who invariably kept her at arm's length in one way or another. By doing so, we had been denying ourselves the very graces we needed to become the saints God created us to be.

Now, up to this point, my experience of Mary had been all head knowledge. I knew *about* her, and I honestly had no problem with any of the dogmas associated with her—the realities of her Immaculate Conception and Assumption, as well as her being the Mother of God and ever-Virgin. These dogmas honestly just made logical sense to me from the very beginning when I was coming to the Catholic faith, especially when combined with my experience of who God is, and through my reading of the writings of the early Church Fathers, especially from the Councils of Nicaea and Ephesus.

But my *experience* of Mary was something different. The idea of needing a mother who could take me to her Son was not something I thought I needed (how little I knew!) because I thought I was already fairly tight with Jesus. So, my question always was "Why do I need Mary to bring me to Jesus?" This attitude was probably a vestige of my Protestant upbringing, as well as the fact that I always had a loving mom in my life, so never really felt like I needed another mother in my life.

But even more, a part of it was probably because I had never been a huge fan of praying the rosary. Looking back, I can see that my experience came more from my exposure to a rote recitation, non-meditative method of praying the rosary, combined with the ignorance of why, what, and how the rosary should be prayed.

Praise God though that in His infinite wisdom, He will always open our eyes and reveal the truths of His ways—if we have but eyes to see and ears to hear. For me, this unveiling of Mary's ever-present role in the spiritual life, and for helping me become a saint was a transformative moment. But what really hammered this home was in discovering *all* the saints have had a special relationship with Mary.

I discovered this as I was preparing for my Marian Consecration, during which I also discovered the writings of Saints Maximilian Kolbe and Pope John Paul II.

Both Kolbe and Pope John Paul built upon the teachings of Montfort. While Montfort urged Marian consecration because it "is the sure means, the direct and immaculate way to Jesus and the perfect guide to him." Kolbe emphasizes how turning to Mary makes our acts more efficacious, while John Paul adds that consecration to Mary is expressly the will of Christ.

In their own ways, both Kolbe and John Paul II emphasize the necessary role of Mary in one's spiritual life to truly open oneself to the workings of the Holy Spirit. And all three contend it is *only through a spirituality rooted in Mary* that we can be more perfectly in union with God's will for us. This is because Mary is the one who did exactly that throughout her entire existence.

St Maximilian Kolbe writes:

> "*The Immaculata: here is our ideal. To approach her, become like her, permit her to take possession of our heart and all our self, that she may live and act in and through us, that she may love God with our heart, that we may belong to her without any restriction: this is our ideal.*"[96]

Additionally, if we truly want to be followers of Christ, then we must imitate Christ. And what did Jesus do? From His first moment of becoming the Word made flesh in the Incarnation, Jesus entrusted Himself to the care of Mary. He belonged entirely to her and was fully dependent upon her, so if we truly desire to be like Jesus, we need to imitate Him by entrusting ourselves to Mary, too.

MARIAN CONSECRATION

When preparing for your Marian consecration, one of the first things you do is select the Marian feast upon which to make your consecration as this then determines the date upon which you begin your preparation. And this is when I discovered something of which I had been unaware of concerning the date of my reception into the Catholic Church.

When I was getting ready to become Catholic, I was completely focused upon Easter Sunday, March 26, 1989. Little did I know at the time, though, that because the Church celebrates the Sacred Triduum, I was going to be baptized and received into the Church on Holy Saturday at the Easter Vigil on March 25th.

Now traditionally, March 25th is celebrated as the Feast of the Annunciation. It is considered by many as the greatest Marian feast of the liturgical year because it is the celebration of the moment of Mary's "yes" and from which humanity's salvation is assured because this is the moment of the Incarnation.

However, when this feast falls during the Sacred Triduum, it is transferred and celebrated on another date. And that's what happened the year I was received into the Church.

But imagine my shock when I realized the date on which Mary had said her yes, and the date on which I said my own yes and was received into the Church, were exactly the same! Unbeknownst to me, Mary had been present and alongside me all along.

I hadn't realized that Mary, in her beautiful and quiet way, had been already at work completing my "yes" and helping me on the journey to continue to work at perfecting my belief, desire and will to become a saint. All so that I could become more like her Son.

But she doesn't do this just for me. Just like her Son, Mary shares these graces she has been entrusted with by her Son with *everyone*. In union with the Holy Spirit, Mary helps each of us in striving to perfect our beliefs, desires, and wills so we can draw ever closer to God and become more like her son, Jesus.

This is how Mary is *the* crown jewel among the hidden gems of assistance God gives us for the spiritual journey.

Saint Maximilian summarized it well when he wrote:

"When we thoroughly examine our soul, we see how extensive the action of the Immaculata has been in it ever since the beginning of the life of each of us up to the present moment. We see how large her pledge is for the benefits that she has in store for the future. Suffice it to recall that any grace we receive every day, every hour, and every moment of our existence is her grace, which flows from her maternal heart that loves us so much."[97]

Now I know that all of what I have described so far, especially about Consecration, can be a bit off putting to many people. You might be thinking as I used to, aren't I decreasing my love and obedience to Jesus who is my Lord and Savior by consecrating myself to Mary?

St. Bernard of Clairvaux answered this objection beautifully when he wrote, *"We must not imagine that we obscure the glory of the Son by the great praise we lavish on the mother; for the more she is honored, the greater is the glory of her Son."*

Or perhaps you are saying, "Wait a minute! I don't have a month to do a bunch of reading and meditation. Now, I can see how it might be a really great thing and all, but I don't have time for that!"

But let me assure you. Marian Consecration is quite simple. You can simply ask her to be your spiritual mother and then begin to live as one of her children.

St Louis de Montfort's consecration prayer is, *"I renounce myself and give myself entirely to you, Mary."*

So, what is stopping you from claiming the crown jewel for the eternal crown that awaits you in Heaven?

SAY YES to consecrating yourself to Mary.

Now, turn the page to start living out that consecration.

CHAPTER 23
LIVING THE CONSECRATION

"All our perfection consists in being conformed, united, and consecrated to Jesus Christ; and therefore the most perfect of all devotions is, without any doubt, that which the most perfectly conforms, unites and consecrates us to Jesus Christ. Now, Mary being the most conformed of all creatures to Jesus Christ, it follows that, of all devotions, that which most consecrates and conforms the soul to Our Lord is devotion to His holy Mother, and that the more a soul is consecrated to Mary, the more it is consecrated to Jesus."

— St. Louis De Montfort[98]

Since making my first Marian Consecration in January of 2009, I have made it a practice to undergo the preparation for a renewal of my Consecration at least once a year. Additionally, I have walked with others as they prepare for their own consecration, and I can attest each time I open myself up to the power of the consecration, another level of gratitude for the graces Mary shares through the consecration on behalf of her Son, Jesus, and her Spouse, the Holy Spirit, has resulted in my heart, mind, and soul.

But the *really* important part of Marian consecration is to live out your consecration by living as one of her children.

So where to begin doing that?

Begin by praying the rosary.

Why? Because it is through praying the rosary that we become more effectively those little children sitting in what Saint Pope John Paul II calls, the "school of Mary."

THE SCHOOL OF MARY

Now, the idea of praying the rosary for me was a huge stretch. I am a visual and kinetic learner to begin with, and although you have some kinetic activity going on with rosary beads, the visuals definitely seemed lacking to me. But this goes back to my not knowing or understanding the why, what, and how praying the rosary is so important for the spiritual life.

First though, let me quickly get a couple of misconceptions out of the way.

Praying the rosary, is NOT about reciting a bunch of prayers as fast as possible to "get through it" or to pray all the prayers as perfectly as possible to make sure those prayers are "acceptable."

Both of these attitudes reflect a misunderstanding of what the rosary is. At its fundamental core, the rosary is about meditating upon the life of Jesus alongside Mary.

This idea made a lot more sense to me once I was married and my mother-in-law and I began to share stories about my husband when he was growing up. Through the eyes of my mother-in-law, I was able to see my husband in an entirely different light, and then was able to appreciate him, and who he is, a new way.

And Mary does the same for us with Jesus. Through meditating on the life of her Son through the mysteries, we are given a new perspective or a different understanding and can more deeply appreciate Jesus for who and what He is—the Way, the Truth, and the Life.

Father Reginald Garrigou-Lagrange, O.P., a Dominican theologian who served as theology doctoral advisor for Saint Pope John Paul II, wrote this about the Rosary:

> *"After Holy Mass the Rosary is one of the most beautiful and efficacious forms of prayer. …The mysteries recall the whole life of Jesus and Mary in their glory in heaven. The mysteries of the Rosary thus divided into groups are but different aspects of the great mysteries of our Salvation : the Incarnation, the Redemption, Eternal life…Thus, the Rosary is a Credo; not an abstract one, but one concretized in the life of Jesus… it is the whole of Christian dogma in all its splendor and elevation, brought to us that we may fill our minds with it, that we may relish it and nourish our souls with it. This makes the rosary a true school of contemplation. It raises us gradually above vocal prayer and even above reasoned out or discursive meditation…The Rosary well understood is, therefore, a very elevated form of prayer which makes the whole of dogma accessible to all."*

So when we pray the rosary, it's about taking enough time to allow Mary to show us an aspect of her Son we may not have noticed before, or to deepen our appreciation of something we haven't necessarily taken the time to truly appreciate.

On the other hand, praying the rosary isn't about doing it "just right" either. There are many, many beautiful prayers associated with the rosary out there, and all of them have a little different emphasis. But the Church teaches that in order to pray a decade of the rosary, you really only need to pray an Our Father, ten Hail Marys, and a Glory Be.

Nothing else is necessary.

Now, Mary asked us in her appearances at Fatima to add the prayer, *"O my Jesus, forgive us our sins, save us from the fires of hell, lead all souls to Heaven, especially those in most need of your mercy,*" so we should try to add that. Otherwise, we shouldn't make praying the rosary complicated. Keep it simple.

But the most important part about praying the rosary is to actually *pray* the rosary.

This can be difficult in our time-obsessed world, but I often challenge people who are having trouble in finding time to pray the rosary to just start by praying a Hail Mary every time they find themselves waiting somewhere—be it at a stoplight or at the doctor's office or at the grocery store.

And when you find yourself in these situations, just pray however many Hail Marys you have time for, and then see how quickly you get up to five Our Fathers, fifty Hail Marys, and five Glory Bes. Like them, you might be surprised by how easy it is, but not only that, you will then have working on your behalf the strongest and mightiest weapon God has given to us in all of history—His Mother.

For there is no denying the efficacy of Mary's intercession throughout history. There are numerous examples of Mary's aid being enlisted, and how her appearance has brought about the conversion of entire peoples. From events like the Battles of Lepanto, Vienna, and Warsaw, to the Miracle of the Sun at Fatima, to her miraculous image on the tilma of Juan Diego as Our Lady of Guadalupe, and how that brought about the subsequent downfall of the Aztec empire, to the healing waters in Lourdes, France. There were also many, many miracles attributed to the Miraculous Medal, a medal created and distributed at Mary's direction to Saint Catherine Laboure in which Mary has interceded and responded to the fervent prayers of believers and non-believers alike.

Saint Maximilian Kolbe wrote about Mary's intercession:

"[The Immaculata] wants the best for me, more than I could possibly wish, and is able to help me, because the Creator can refuse her nothing. It is better therefore to entrust to her

*my worries and my troubles, she will put them right faster
and more easily than I can.*[99]

This is how we are able to live as Mary's children. We pray
the rosary and trust her intercession on our behalf.

So, when we SAY YES and consecrate ourselves to Mary, we
give permission to Mary and the Holy Spirit to actively transform us by forming Jesus in our minds, hearts, and souls.

But even more important than allowing ourselves to be
transformed, is our enlisting the aid of Mary in the conversion
of others.

Saint Maximilian Kolbe again writes:

*"Each conversion and every step on the way to sanctification
are the work of grace, and the dispenser of all graces that
flow from the Most Sacred Heart of Jesus is none other than
His Mother, the Immaculata. Thus, the closer a soul gets to
her, the more abundantly it can draw on these graces. As a
result, our key mission is to bring souls closer to her, to lead
her to souls."*[100]

Mary draws us closer to Jesus because she continues to fulfill
the will of God and be our Mother, the Mother of the Church.

At the foot of the Cross, we are told in the Gospel of John
that Jesus says, *"Seeing His mother and the disciple He loved standing near her, Jesus said to his mother, 'Woman, behold your son.'
Then to the disciple He said, 'Behold your mother.' And from that
moment, the disciple took her into his home."*[101]

It was at this moment that Mary, in union with God's will,
accepted her role as spiritual mother of the Church, and she has
continued to serve as Mother to the entire Church throughout
the centuries.

Saint Pope John Paul II beautifully describes how Mary
fulfills the role as Mother of the Church:

"After the events of the Resurrection and Ascension, Mary entered the Upper Room together with the Apostles to await Pentecost, and was present there as the Mother of the glorified Lord ... Thus, there began to develop a special bond between this Mother and the Church. For the infant Church was the fruit of the Cross and Resurrection of her Son. Mary, who from the beginning had given herself without reserve to the person and work of her Son, could not but pour out upon the Church, from the very beginning, her maternal self-giving. After her Son's departure, her motherhood remains in the Church as maternal mediation: interceding for all her children, the Mother cooperates in the saving work of her Son, the Redeemer of the world. In fact, the Council teaches that the 'motherhood of Mary in the order of grace . . . will last without interruption until the eternal fulfillment of all the elect'. With the redeeming death of her Son, the maternal mediation of the handmaid of the Lord took on a universal dimension, for the work of redemption embraces the whole of humanity."[102]

Mary, overshadowed by the Holy Spirit, conceived and gave birth to Jesus, and then fed, protected and educated Him alongside Saint Joseph, helped initiate and support His public ministry, remained by His side throughout His Passion and Death, and then was present for His Resurrection before she continued to give herself to the work of her Son by becoming Mother to His Church.

This is where the phrase, "To Jesus Through Mary" rings abidingly true. For through Mary, we are transformed into the apostles we are each created to become and are empowered by the Holy Spirit to fulfill and embody our baptismal vows to go carry our cross and inspire us in all we do in this life until we enter into life with her Son in the next.

Living Out Your Consecration

So, what do faithful sons and daughters of Mary look like? Saint Anthony Mary Claret tells us they look like this:

> *"For a Son of the Immaculate Heart of Mary is a man on fire with love, who spreads its flames wherever he goes. He desires mightily and strives by all means, possible to set the whole world on fire with God's love. Nothing daunts him; he delights in privations, welcomes work, embraces sacrifices, smiles at slander, and rejoices in suffering. His only concern is how he can best follow Jesus Christ and imitate Him in working, suffering, and striving constantly and single-mindedly for the greater glory of God and the salvation of souls."*

Saint Louis de Montfort describes faithful sons and daughters of Mary in this way:

> *"True devotion to Our Lady is constant. It confirms the soul in good and does not let it easily abandon its spiritual exercises. It makes it courageous in opposing the world in its fashions and maxims, the flesh in its weariness and passions, and the devil in his temptations; so that a person truly devout to our Blessed Lady is neither changeable, irritable, scrupulous nor timid. It is not that such a person does not fall or change sometimes in the sensible feeling of devotion. But when he falls, he rises again by stretching out his hand to his good Mother. When he loses the taste and relish of devotions, he does not become disturbed because of that; for the just and faithful client of Mary lives by the faith (Heb. 10:38) of Jesus and Mary, and not by natural sentiment."*[103]

But in more practical terms, what would living one's consecration to Mary look like in your daily life?

There are five principles:

1. You renounce your own will. You accept things you do not like, did not choose, cannot change, and do not understand.

2. You entrust yourself to Mary daily. Begin each morning with a Morning Offering and pray the rosary.

3. You do all things with Mary and Jesus, and you look for reminders of Mary throughout the day, so you have many opportunities to entrust yourself to her.

4. You allow Mary to direct any transition, sickness, or loss in your life by asking her to intercede for you, especially that you may be given the courage to bear it in union with God's will.

5. You lead others to Mary so she can help you lead them to Jesus.

All five of these principles are also consistent with the messages Mary has shared in her apparitions across the world throughout the centuries. Therefore, by doing these things, you not only live out your consecration to Mary, but you also allow her to help you draw others closer to her Son, Jesus.

This is because Mary is our greatest model of discipleship, as her will has always been in union with God. It is also because Mary is our Mother, and the Mother of the Church, and through her, the Church continues to draw others to her son, Jesus. In addition, Mary is our greatest intercessor, as she brings before our Lord all our needs, while making every offering and sacrifice we make even more efficacious. Finally, as the spouse of the Holy Spirit, Mary can help the image of her Son, Jesus, become present within our hearts and minds more and more each day.

For just as Saint Pope John Paul II tells us, *"It is from Mary that we learn to surrender to God's will in all things. It's from Mary that we learn to trust even when all hope seems to be gone. And it's from Mary that we learn to love Christ."*

So, don't worry, and turn to Mary. By consecrating ourselves and living out our consecration, Mary will see us safely home to Heaven.

So, you remember the power of Story and the importance of our role in it? Bishop Robert Barron reminds us of this when he shared this about Mary's role in God's story:

> *"The theo-drama is the great story being told by God, the great play being directed by God. What makes life thrilling is to discover your role in it. This is precisely what has happened to Mary. She has found her role—indeed a climactic role—in the theo-drama, and she wants to conspire with Elizabeth, who has also discovered her role in the same drama. Like Mary, we have to find our place in God's story."*

This is the final way that Mary assists us in the spiritual journey.

Mary has been there. She knows of the struggles we face because she was completely human. But the difference between Mary and us is that Mary said YES—to every moment and instance of God's grace in her life.

She *lived* the phrase, *Fiat Voluntas Tua*—Thy Will Be Done.

Mary never said no, regardless of the many challenges, trials, and tribulations and sacrifices she experienced throughout her life here on earth, and this is the pre-eminent way Mary models for us the path of discipleship. She shows us that we, too, can SAY YES to God's grace and be transformed into the saints He created us to be.

So, commit to consecrate yourself to Mary and allow the Holy Spirit to more actively form Jesus in you, just as the Holy Spirit did within Mary.

Embrace Mary as your mother and let her intercede for you in every aspect of your life while helping you make every prayer and sacrifice more efficacious.

Allow yourself to become a soldier in Mary's army and help as many souls as possible to come to know, love, and serve her son, our Lord and Savior, Jesus.

SAY YES to living out your Marian consecration.

Now, turn the page and become all in for God and His plan for you.

CHAPTER 24

"ALL IN"

In 2010, Auburn University won the NCAA Division 1 college football national championship. Although the team had gifted athletes like Heisman Trophy winner, quarterback Cam Newton, the true essence of their success was summed up in the team's motto for that year, "All In."

The Auburn head coach at the time, Gene Chizik, explained that "All In" became the criterion for judging excellence. It meant that every member of the team was completely and fully committed to doing everything necessary to become better, both on and off the field throughout the season, and the result of that "All In" attitude was a national championship.

What many people do not know, however, is that the phrase "All In" came from a discussion amongst the Auburn coaches and team members about the verse from Colossians 3:23, "Work willingly at whatever you do, as though you were working for the Lord rather than for people." What emerged from that discussion was what was necessary to do that kind of work and what it meant to be "All In."

That discussion resulted in the focus and clarity needed about the why, what, and how each team member needed to be engaged in the process eventually led to the Auburn Tigers football team becoming the 2010 National Champions.

And this is EXACTLY the same kind of attitude we must have if we are to become the saints we are created to be.

God is calling us to go "All In" on becoming right-ordered by putting first things first and living the life He has designed us to live—a life filled with purpose, peace, and abundance.

Let's review.

CALLED TO A LIFE OF PURPOSE

Saint Bonaventure wrote, *"If you learn everything except Christ, you learn nothing. If you learn nothing except Christ, you learn everything."*

This is the foundation of living a life of purpose. Because living a life of purpose begins with knowing *whose we are*—sons and daughters of God. From this knowledge, we also come to know we are called to be more than what the world tells us we are—that we are destined for a life with God throughout eternity, and we are called for transforming union with God, to become saints.

But not cookie-cutter saints where everyone is like everyone else.

No, God has uniquely made us to be a particular kind of saint that only we can become, because there never has been, is, or will be anyone else like us in the world.

But we have to *choose* to live this life of purpose to become who we are, what we are, where we are.

We have to SAY YES to the great invitation God gives us to enter into His divine life right here and now and to live a life of deep purpose.

CALLED TO A LIFE OF PEACE

To enter into, and participate in, God's divine life, we must strive to put first things first and become right-ordered. This happens by following the four steps to holiness—daily prayer and meditation, living the life of grace, growing daily in virtue, and abandoning ourselves to God's will.

But the key to *all* of our efforts to become right-ordered is daily prayer and meditation.

Why?

We are called to passionately fall in love with God to embark upon the most magnificent and marvelous adventure of our lives.

Saint Augustine tells us, "*To fall in love with God is the greatest romance; to seek Him the greatest adventure; to find Him, the greatest human achievement.*"

For it is *only* out of love that we will be willing (and able) to try to do whatever is necessary to change our very thoughts, words, and actions, and to open our minds, hearts, and souls to the peace and wisdom God desires to give us through intimate friendship with Himself.

And from this intimate friendship, we become filled with His Word and find ourselves thirsting for more. This is why we must actively live the life of grace by frequenting the sacraments. We must actively seek out and make space in our lives to regularly receive God's divine life through reception of Jesus in the Sacraments, particularly Holy Eucharist and Reconciliation.

As we spend time in prayer and are filled with the Divine Life through the Sacraments, we are then increasingly given the wisdom and strength for growing in virtue each day and abandoning ourselves to God's will more fully.

How?

Most often, through our daily resolution. The daily resolution is where the rubber meets the road in the spiritual life. Because the daily resolution takes the wisdom and insight given to you by God in your conversations with Him, and you can apply it in small, concrete ways in your daily life.

This is how we begin to see, and then sustain, growth in virtue. The process during which our thoughts, words, and actions are transformed, so we more perfectly reflect the Divine

Life which resides within us. And seeing this progress is what encourages us to continue the struggle when the going gets difficult—which it will!

But these signs of growth also encourage us to trust and abandon ourselves to God's will more fully. For as we see small changes, we learn to trust God's plans for us, and then we grow in trust, and we learn to abandon ourselves more and more to His will in *all* the events of our lives.

Our trust then feeds, invigorates, and sustains our prayer and meditation, which in turn, opens us to God's direction for our lives through our daily resolutions. This then causes small changes in our thoughts, words, and actions, and this creates a cycle of ever-deepening trust and abandonment which feeds into our prayer and meditation, and so on and so on. This is why we have to strive to hit God's will for us "on the dot" through our detachment, obedience, and trust.

We have to SAY YES to striving to faithfully follow these four steps each day to the best of our ability while relying upon God's grace to do the rest.

The Catechism tells us,

> *"Spiritual progress tends toward ever more intimate union with Christ. This union is called "mystical" because it participates in the mystery of Christ through the sacraments, - "the holy mysteries," and, in him, in the mystery of the Holy Trinity. God calls us all to this intimate union with him."*[104]

Intimate union with Him! This union leads us directly into the life of abundance.

Called to a Life of Abundance

Saint Gianna Molla said, "*The secret of happiness is to live moment by moment and to thank God for what He is sending us every day in His goodness.*"

And this is spot on.

The more we are focused on the present moment, the more we find happiness, not just in ourselves, but especially in our relationship with others.

For as we live with an attitude of gratitude, we become more and more aware of all God is sending our way in His goodness, and this makes us more open to not merely everything, but *everyone* around us.

A life of abundance is rooted in the reality that my becoming right-ordered and living the divine life is not simply about myself and my choices and my actions.

This is because in the life of abundance, there is no such thing as the idea that a choice or action is fine as long as it's doesn't affect anyone else.

For the true reality is that *everything* affects *everyone*.

Every word, every action, yes, even every thought, has an impact on those around us.

Because we are all interconnected. We might not see it, but we are.

This is why prayer is so powerful. Knowing that someone else is thinking of me, interceding for me, is actively willing my good, in other words, is *loving* me affects me. And because it affects me, this knowledge affects everyone.

We were *designed* for relationship. We were made to be in relationship with one another, and living a life of abundance is about us rejecting what the world tells us to do—to isolate, rely on yourself, and trust no one—and instead to enter deeply into relationships with others, abandon our self-reliance, and to embrace with trust all that God has provided for us to be able to thrive in this world as we prepare to spend eternity with Him in the next.

This is why we must immerse ourselves in the teachings of the Magisterium of the Church and seek out a spiritual mentor or director to help guide us on the journey. It's why we must seek out a cluster of friends (like Jesus did) to walk alongside us amid all the joys and sorrows of life as we encourage and challenge one another to strive for holiness. It's why you must share *your* story of how Jesus transforms you, allowing the Divine Life dwelling within you to breathe and grow within you. And finally, it's why we must willingly entrust ourselves to Mary, our Mother, so she can care for us like she did Jesus, but also so we can be a reminder and inspiration to those around us that all things *are* possible for those who love God.

By embracing relationship, we find we are not alone. Nor have we ever been.

But we have to SAY YES to live life abundantly.

"FURTHER UP, FURTHER IN"

The entire process of striving for holiness, of becoming right ordered, is designed to prepare us for our homecoming in the Eternal Kingdom.

In the final book in the Chronicles of Narnia series, *The Last Battle*, author C.S. Lewis describes the experience had by all the people and creatures of Narnia at the end of time, and their entering into eternal life. Each of the people and animals has the experience of things being more real, true, and more beautiful in this "new" Narnia versus what they had experienced before in "old" Narnia, and this occurred as they moved "further up and further in."

In fact, "Further up, further in" became the cry of all those in the "new" Narnia as they streamed towards what was revealed to be a great walled Garden at the center where each person and creature who had been an integral part of the story of Narnia was gathered together in a realer, and even more beautiful, Narnia.

And this real Narnia was connected to the other real countries, including places from our own world, and all of these places were only spurs off the great mountains of Aslan, the High King.

These scenes all portray a beautiful and magnificent vision of what Heaven will be like for us. Of a great gathering of all the people and creatures, where we are our best selves—young, healthy, and vigorous, where we experience no fear or sadness, but simply love and joy.

HOLINESS IS POSSIBLE

This life of eternal love and joy is what God desires for *every* one of us. Not just a chosen few.

The Catechism assures us of this fact, *"All Christians in any state or walk of life are called to the fullness of Christian life and to the perfection of charity."* All are called to holiness: *"Be perfect, as your heavenly Father is perfect."* [105]

Becoming a saint is for *everyone*.

If we do not become the saint God created us to be, then Heaven will be less than what God had desired it to be—because we are not there.

Hopefully, through what I have shared in this book, you can see that holiness *is* possible. Each of us can become the saint God designed us to be from the beginning of the world so we can radiate His love and mercy to others in the unique and unrepeatable way that only we can do.

That's why *"Holiness consists simply in doing God's will, and being just what God wants us to be."* [106]

So never give into despair. Holiness *is* possible.

But you have to choose to pursue it.

And choosing to pursue it *is* a life and death decision.

Choose Life and Persevere

"Be one of the small number who find the way to life, and enter by the narrow gate into Heaven. Take care not to follow the majority and the common herd, so many of whom are lost. Do not be deceived; there are only two roads: one that leads to life and is narrow; the other that leads to death and is wide. There is no middle way."

St Louis de Montfort did not write these words to frighten people. And I am not sharing them now to berate you for not seriously pursuing holiness, or saying bad things are going to happen to you if you don't strive for and live a right ordered life. That's not how God works.

However, the truth is we do have a choice to make. And like any choice, it has consequences.

Even the choice to follow the Way of Life and pursue holiness is going to be difficult. There are still going to be tears and heartbreak and tragedy in your life even if you choose to pursue the Way.

In fact, the Catechism tells us, *"The way of perfection passes by way of the Cross. There is no holiness without renunciation and spiritual battle. Spiritual progress entails the ascesis and mortification that gradually lead to living in the peace and joy of the Beatitudes."* [107]

This is what we must remember. By simply choosing the Way of Life it doesn't absolve you or mean you get a pass on having to experience any struggles, failures, sickness, sorrows, disappointments, betrayals, or death. But choosing to pursue the Way of Life does make it possible for you to know there is purpose and meaning in all of your struggles, failures, sicknesses, sorrows, disappointments, betrayals, and even death—even if you don't understand what that purpose or meaning might be.

THE WAY OF LIFE IS A PROCESS

Throughout this book, what I have shared is *a process*, not a program. There is no start or stop. There's no first class or last session. There's no graduation.

It's an ongoing process that continues every day of our lives.

The process through which we open ourselves to being transformed through God's grace into the very people He created us to be in the first place. Before original sin and concupiscence got in the way, and we found ourselves in need of a Savior, and in need of being shown a Way to become right ordered again.

This process of discovering purpose, peace and abundance in your daily life is designed specifically to help you take the steps necessary *right now* to re-order your life so through God's grace, the relationships that were originally ruptured in the Garden of Eden—with oneself, God and others—can be healed and made new again.

Because when we are in right relationship with ourselves, then we discover our true purpose, and live as our truest selves. And when we are in right relationship with God, where we are putting first things first in our life, then we discover and encounter authentic peace. And when we are in right relationship with others, we discover and experience a life of abundance we could never imagine.

SO WHAT ARE YOU WAITING FOR?

Now, the only person who can stop you from living a life of purpose, peace, and abundance is YOU.

It's why you must SAY YES.

But you have to CHOOSE it.

Because God isn't going to force you.

Why?

Because He loves you too much.

He loves you enough to wait on you to choose life and not death.

He loves you enough to wait until you discover and understand your true purpose and to come to believe how radically, and profoundly, and deeply you are loved beyond measure.

He loves you enough to wait for you to try every single way the world offers—pleasure, power, fame, alcohol, drugs, possessions to either distract, decrease, or assuage your worries and anxiety before you finally are willing to turn in trusting abandonment to Him to provide you with the peace and wisdom you are truly longing for.

He loves you enough to wait for you to fail over and over again as you try to rely upon yourself and your own resources before you finally turn to availing yourself of the tools He has already provided you so you can persevere and thrive in this world as you journey home to Him.

SAY YES to being "All In."

Your true life awaits you.

He awaits you.

SAY YES.

SAY YES CHECKLIST

Introduction	SAY YES to setting out on the journey to be transformed.
Chapter 1	SAY YES to the process.
Chapter 2	SAY YES to your dignity and greatness.
Chapter 3	SAY YES to the call to holiness.
Chapter 4	SAY YES to your unique and unrepeatable mission.
Chapter 5	SAY YES and "*Come and see.*"
Chapter 6	SAY YES to the Four Steps of Holiness.
Chapter 7	SAY YES to daily prayer and meditation.
Chapter 8	SAY YES and answer the phone.
Chapter 9	SAY YES to living the life of grace.
Chapter 10	SAY YES to living the fullness of life of grace.
Chapter 11	SAY YES to the graces of God flowing in your life nonstop.
Chapter 12	SAY YES to growing daily in virtue.
Chapter 13	SAY YES to grow daily in virtue. Step by step, and day by day.
Chapter 14	SAY YES to abandoning yourself to God's will.
Chapter 15	SAY YES to hitting God's will on the "DOT."

Chapter 16   SAY YES to being obedient to what God has revealed through His Magisterium.

Chapter 17   SAY YES to being accompanied on the journey.

Chapter 18   SAY YES to true and authentic friendship.

Chapter 19   SAY YES to friendship hidden in plain sight.

Chapter 20   SAY YES to the power of Story.

Chapter 21   SAY YES to sharing your story today.

Chapter 22   SAY YES to consecrating yourself to Mary.

Chapter 23   SAY YES to living out your Marian consecration.

Chapter 24   SAY YES to being "All In"

NEXT STEPS AND RESOURCES

DOWNLOAD THE FREE GUIDE

There are a bunch of resources that can help you take this information and these strategies and implement them into your own life.

To help you do that, I put together a free book guide with discussion questions and additional exercises that you can use to help you SAY YES.

Take Step 1, and download those free resources by visiting:

www.sayyestoholiness.com

JOIN THE SAY YES TO HOLINESS MOVEMENT

Do you desire to learn more? Or are you yearning to be part of a community of like-minded people who are on fire to save souls and with whom you can journey with while in the pursuit of holiness? Or both?

Then take Step 2, and check out the opportunities for how you can join the Say Yes to Holiness Movement by visiting:

www.sayyestoholiness.com

ONE LAST THING

May I ask you a favor?

If you got anything out of this book, whether it inspired you or taught you anything at all, I would be forever grateful if you did something small for me...

Will you please give a copy of this book to a friend, family member or colleague?

Ask them to read it.

Let them know what is possible for them if they start to pursue holiness and go about doing the work necessary to embrace the life that God created them for.

Let them know they can SAY YES.

We need them.

We need you.

Please spread the word.

Thank you again,
Christina Semmens

ABOUT THE AUTHOR

Christina Semmens is a Roman Catholic author, speaker, coach and Host of the Say Yes to Holiness Podcast. She holds two Master of Arts degrees—one in History and the other in Theology and also has certification as a Catholic Spiritual Mentor and Motivational Core (MCORE) Facilitator. She is a former military officer, classroom teacher, and a Promised Family Member of the Apostles of Interior Life.

Christina has been involved in ministry within the Roman Catholic Church, especially on a small group and one-on-one basis for more than 25 years. She integrates her knowledge, experience, and education to provide straight-forward, practical and insightful guidance, encouragement and inspiration to those desiring to be fully transformed into the saints whom God created each person to be--holy men and women on fire for love of the Lord in the world.

Christina currently lives in Fort Payne, Alabama with her husband, Paul, where she strives to live out a life of authentic discipleship in the pursuit of holiness while empowering, teaching and accompanying individuals and organizations to SAY YES to holiness by doing whatever it takes to embrace the life God created them for—lives of purpose, peace and abundance.

You can find out more and connect with Christina through her Say Yes to Holiness podcast, through social media on both Facebook and Instagram @sayyestoholiness and at the website, www.sayyestoholiness.com. Her blog resides at www.christi-nasemmens.com. To join her email list and receive the weekly *Say Yes to Holiness Newsletter*, text SAYYESTOHOLINESS to 66866.

ENDNOTES

1   Baltimore Catechism no.3, Question 6.

2   From the prayer "Prophets of a Future Not Our Own" written by Bishop Ken Untener. It was first presented by Cardinal Dearden in 1979 and quoted by Pope Francis in 2015. The poem was part of a homily written for Cardinal Dearden by then-Fr. Ken Untener on the occasion of the Mass for Deceased Priests, October 25, 1979. Pope Francis quoted Cardinal Dearden in his remarks to the Roman Curia on December 21, 2015. Fr. Untener was named bishop of Saginaw, Michigan, in 1980.

3   Father Bede Jarrett, *Catholic Meditations*, p. 51.

4   Fr. Jacques Philippe, *In the School of the Holy Spirit*, p. 26.

5   Father Augustine Wetta, OSB, *Humility Rules*.

6   Rev. Jude Winkler, O.F.M., *Daily Meditations with the Holy Spirit*, p.13.

7   John 1:35-51, New American Bible.

8   Jeremiah 1:4.

9   Jeremiah 29:11.

10   Matthew 19:16-22.

11   Matthew Kelly, *The Biggest Lie in the History of Christianity*.

12   Thomas Aquinas, *Summa Theologica,* II-II, q. 126, a.1.

13   Christina Semmens, *March to Canada*, p. 50.

14   Acts 17:28.

15   Josemaria Escriva, *The Way*, 368.

16   https://www.goodreads.com/quotes/166474-for-me-prayer-is-a-surge-of-the-heart-it

17   The Latin is: "Littera gesta docet, Quod credas allegoria. Moralia quod agas,Quo tendas anagogia."

18   Catechism of the Catholic Church 1706

19   http://www.vatican.va/content/john-paul-ii/en/apost_letters/2002/documents/hf_jp-ii_apl_20021016_rosarium-virginis-mariae.html

20   https://images.app.goo.gl/mgb14oVWoAFZNSgK7

21 https://steubenvillefuel.com/2017/09/13/abandon-allow-grace-quote/
22 Catechism of the Catholic Church, paragraph 1131.
23 Fr. Jacques Philippe, *In the School of the Holy Spirit,* pp.14-15
24 Fr Joseph Langford, M.C., *I Thirst:40 Days with Mother Teresa,* pp.28-29.
25 Fr. Romano Guardini, *Meditations Before Mass,* p. 28.
26 https://www.knightsoftheholyeucharist.com/the-eucharist-is-th e-sacrament-of-love/
27 https://www.azquotes.com/quote/1334078
28 https://www.frassatiusa.org/his-eucharistic-devotion
29 Fr. Jacques Philippe, *In the School of the Holy Spirit,* p. 28.
30 https://quotefancy.com/quote/891322/Pope-John-Paul-II-From-the-E ucharist-comes-strength-to-live-the-Christian-life-and-zeal
31 Fr. Ignatius of the Side of Jesus, *The School of Jesus Crucified,* pp.284-5.
32 Matthew 22:38.
33 Catechism of the Catholic Church, 1420-21.
34 2 Corinthians 12:10.
35 Daily Reflections with Fulton Sheen, p.103.
36 https://www.looktohimandberadiant.com/2013/05/ sheen-and-sacraments.html
37 Church Militant Field Manual.
38 John 12:24-25.
39 Saint Francis de Sales, *The Art of Loving God,* p. 97.
40 Sandy Clarke, "How the Power of Reading Holds the Key to Success", https://leaderonomics.com/personal/power-of-reading-and-success
41 Teresa of Avila, *The Interior Castle,* p. 99.
42 Thomas a' Kempis, *Imitation of Christ,* p. 64.
43 Fr Francis Fernandez, *In Conversation with God,* Vol. 4, p. 419.
44 Romans 8:28
45 John 3:30
46 Galatians 2:20
47 Catechism of the Catholic Church, paragraph 311.
48 Pope John Paul II, *Salvifici Dolores.*
49 Catechism of the Catholic Church, paragraph 312.
50 Luke 17:5
51 Oxford Dictionary online.
52 Fr. Jacques Philippe, *In the School of the Holy Spirit,* p. 19.
53 Dr. Michael Scherschight, School of Faith Daily Rosary Reflection.
54 St. Arnold Janssen.
55 Fr. Jacques Philippe, *Interior Freedom,* p. 47.
56 St. Elizabeth Ann Seton
57 CCC, 1504-5.

58 Romans 15:13

59 Fr. Jean Baptiste Saint-Jure, *Trustful Surrender to God's Providence*, p. 90.

60 St. Therese of Lisieux, *The Story is a Soul*, p. 122.

61 Romans 8:28

62 Father Don Dulindo Ruotolo, *Novena of Surrender to the Will of God*, 1882-1970.

63 Henry Dieterich, ed., *Through the Year with Fulton Sheen*, Ignatius Press, p. 108)

64 St. Therese of Lisieux, *The Story of a Soul*, p. 64.

65 Christine Valters Paintner, "12 Celtic Spiritual Practices that celebrate God in our world," *US Catholic*.

66 Ralph Martin, *The Fulfillment of All Desire*, p. 166.

67 Scott Galloway, "Humans Cannot Survive Alone" Medium, April 19, 2019.

68 Matthew Kelly, "The Six Kinds of Friends You Should Have in Your Life," dynamicctholic.com, November 27, 2018.

69 St Thomas Aquinas.

70 School of Love Daily Reflection.

71 Charles McKinney, "Faithlessness Is The Great Destroyer of Friendship," Feb 20, 2019

72 Cf M. Schmaus, *Dogmatic Theology*, II, p.503.

73 Pope Benedict XVI.

74 Matthew Kelly, *Rediscover the Saints*.

75 Matthew Kelly, *The Rhythm of Life*.

76 Edward C. Sellner, *Stories of the Celtic Soul Friends: Their Meaning for Today* (New York: Paulist Press, 2004), 4.

77 Russell W. Dalton, *Faith Journey Through Fantasy Lands: A Christian Dialogue with Harry Potter, Star Wars and the Lord of the Rings.* (Minneapolis: Augsburg Books, 2003), 8.

78 Ibid, 8.

79 Fr. Thomas Dubay, *The Fire Within*, p. 114.

80 If you want to see this experiment, simply Google, "IKEA Bullying Experiment."

81 John 14:13

82 John 1:1.

83 Bishop Robert Barron

84 Maximillian Kolbe, *Kolbe Writings,* 1079.

85 Dr Tod Warner, "Mystery, Manners, and the Rediscovery of Great Literature" May 20, 2019.

86 Frigga to Thor in *Avengers: End Game* movie

87 Matthew Kelly, *Building Better Families.*

88   Maximillian Kolbe, *Kolbe Writings*, 1127.

89   Saint Francis of Assisi.

90   Saint Thomas of Villanova.

· 91   Chip Gaines, "The Chip Chronicles" *Magnolia Journal*, p. 108.

92   Dialogue from Jack to Ally, *A Star is Born* movie, 2017.

93   The practice of First Fridays is focused upon Devotion to the Sacred Heart of Jesus.

94   Excerpt from the Legion of Mary Handbook: *"The Legion of Mary is an Association of Catholics who, with the sanction of the Church and under the powerful leadership of Mary Immaculate, Mediatrix of all Graces (who is fair as the moon, bright as the sun, and — to Satan and his legionaries — terrible as an army set in battle array), have formed themselves into a Legion for service in the warfare which is perpetually waged by the Church against the world and its evil powers. "The whole life of men, both individual and social, shows itself to be a struggle, and a dramatic one, between good and evil, between light and darkness." (Gaudium et Spes 13) The legionaries hope to render themselves worthy of their great heavenly Queen by their loyalty, their virtues, and their courage. The Legion of Mary is therefore organised on the model of an army, principally on that of the army of ancient Rome, the terminology of which is adopted also. But the army and the arms of legionaries of Mary are not of this world."*

95   St Louis de Montfort, *True Devotion to Mary*, p.1.

96   Maximilian Kolbe, *Kolbe Writings*, 1210.

97   Maximilian Kolbe, *Kolbe Writings*, 1322.

98   St. Louis De Montfort, *True Devotion to Mary*, p. 65

99   Maximilian Kolbe, *Kolbe Writings*, 1102.

100   Maximilian Kolbe, *Kolbe Writings*, 1277.

101   John, Chapter 19: 26-27

102   Pope St. John Paul II, *Mary: God's Yes to Man*, pp. 129-30.

103   St. Louis De Montfort, *True Devotion to Mary*, p.55.

104   Catholic Catechism of the Catholic Church, 2014.

105   CCC 2013.

106   St Therese of Lisieux

107   Catechism of the Catholic Church, paragraph 2015.

DIGA SÍ

Descubriendo el propósito,
la paz y la abundancia
en su vida diaria

Christina Semmens

Cover Design: Debbie O'Byrne

Photograph of author by Rachel Clarke Photography

Paperback ISBN: 978-1-64746-269-7
Hardback ISBN: 978-1-64746-270-3
EBook ISBN: 978-1-64746-271-0

Library of Congress Control Number (LCCN): 2020908510

A todos los que tienen, y siguen inspirando, desafía
y acompañame en la búsqueda de la santidad

—Este viaje no sucede sin ti

TABLA DE CONTENIDO

Prefacio ix

Expresiones de gratitud xi

Introducción xiii

PARTE 1: DESCUBRIR EL PROPÓSITO PROFUNDO

Chapter 1   Es un proceso, no un programa 1

Chapter 2   ¿De quién soy? 5

Chapter 3   La llamada a la santidad 11

Chapter 4   Su Única e Irrepetible Misión 18

Chapter 5   Ven a Ver 30

PARTE 2: ENCONTRANDO LA PAZ AUTÉNTICA

Chapter 6   Los cuatro pasos hacia la santidad 43

Chapter 7   Paso uno: oración diaria y meditación 47

Chapter 8   Contestando el teléfono 51

Chapter 9   Paso dos: Vivir la Vida de Gracia 58

Chapter 10 Viviendo la Plenitud de la Vida de Gracia 65

Chapter 11 La vida de gracia que fluye sin parar 70

Chapter 12 Paso tres: crecer diariamente en virtud. 76

Chapter 13 Paso a paso, día a día. 83

Chapter 14 Paso cuatro: abandonarnos a la voluntad
            de Dios 93

Chapter 15 Acertar la voluntad de Dios en el "BLANCO" 98

PARTE 3: ABRAZAR LA ABUNDANCIA PERMANENTE

Chapter 16 El Mito del Llanero Solitario. 113

Chapter 17 El poder de un Amigo del Alma 120

Chapter 18 Los santos vienen en racimos. 126

Chapter 19 Amistad oculta a simple vista 134

Chapter 20 El poder de la historia 144

Chapter 21 Compartiendo la vida divina. 151

Chapter 22 La joya de la Corona 159

Chapter 23 Viviendo la Consagración 167

Chapter 24 "En equipo". 177

Diga Sí Lista de verificación 187

Próximos pasos y recursos 189

Notas finales 191

PREFACIO

Este libro es un plan de acción. En él, encontrarás toda la dirección y el aliento que necesitas para vivir la vida como cristiano católico del siglo XXI.

También es una exhortación.

Muy a menudo fallamos en encontrar la felicidad en Dios, o incluso en buscarla, como si Él no fuera suficiente o fuera inaccesible para nosotros. ¿Qué es lo que nos falta? ¿Por qué fallamos en captar el tesoro de la gracia y de la intimidad divina que Él coloca justo frente a nosotros? ¿Podría ser por falta de aliento?

Christina Semmens se deleita en mostrarnos lo que es posible y cómo llegar allí. En mi propia vida, ella ha demostrado ser una amiga leal y una guía confiable en asuntos del corazón, la mente y el alma. Dios le ha dado la misión de servir a otros a través de la oración y el acompañamiento, y este libro es una rica recopilación de "mejores prácticas" espirituales que son el fruto de la experiencia y se comparten con amor.

La vida cristiana nunca es fácil, pero es muy gratificante tanto ahora como en la eternidad. Solo la Iglesia Católica nos ofrece todas las herramientas que necesitamos para recibir completamente los dones que Dios tiene para nosotros. La santidad está a nuestro alcance. Dios quiere tener una relación con cada uno de nosotros y desea que vivamos vidas increíbles, heroicas, significativas y santas. Esta verdad está bellamente iluminada a lo largo de estas páginas, que nos muestran que la santidad, y la aventura, es posible en todo momento y lugar.

En medio de las muchas soluciones que se han propuesto para el malestar espiritual de nuestro tiempo, decir "sí" a la santidad es quizás la más simple y la más necesaria. Solo al decir "sí" a Dios podemos llegar a ser santos. El mundo no necesita mediocridad o amor a medias; necesita que tu corazón se haga nuevo en Cristo. Este es el mejor regalo que puedes dar a la Iglesia y al mundo. La tuya es una historia irrepetible; Tu vida es un regalo irrepetible.

Espero, querido lector, que aborde con una mente y un corazón abiertos el rico tesoro de sabiduría práctica contenido en estas páginas. Anímate, para que puedas recibir libremente lo que se te ha dado gratuitamente: una oportunidad de encontrar a Jesucristo de una manera que realmente cambie tu vida. Es el Señor quien pregunta; es para que respondas. No te detengas, ¡di que sí!

—Padre Joshua Altonji, Capellán
Iglesia Católica San Esteban Mártir
Diócesis de Birmingham, Alabama

EXPRESIONES DE GRATITUD

He sido bendecido con muchas personas que entran y salen de mi vida por varias razones y estaciones que me han impactado de manera profunda. Hay demasiados para mencionar, así que no intentaré cubrirlos a todos, pero hay algunos que me gustaría mencionar.

En primer lugar, estoy agradecido con mis padres, especialmente con mi madre, por criarme para creer en mí mismo, vivir una vida de integridad sin importar el costo y alentarme a esforzarme siempre por ser lo mejor que pueda ser. Mamá, todavía estoy trabajando para convertirme en la mitad de lo que ya eres: una mujer hermosa, inteligente y capaz con un corazón para los demás.

Para mi esposo Paul, que me ha apoyado de innumerables maneras, y me mostró desde el primer día que conocimos lo que es el verdadero liderazgo de servicio. Tu amor me ha permitido alcanzar mis sueños, incluso cuando no estaba segura de cuáles eran. Por los sacrificios que ha realizado para construir la vida que tenemos, y por todas las formas en que continúa esforzándose por convertirse plenamente en el hombre que Dios lo creó para ser, sepa que estoy asombrado y humillado por haber recibido el don de usted como mi esposo, compañero y amigo. Elijo amarte hoy y siempre.

Para mis hijos: Sean, Rob y Mike. Gracias por tu amor, apoyo e inspiración. Tener a cada uno de ustedes como parte de mi vida es un regalo precioso, y sé que mis esfuerzos aquí son

tratar de ayudar a crear un mundo mejor para ustedes y todos aquellos que aman en los próximos años.

He tenido tantos entrenadores, mentores y colegas increíbles de quienes he aprendido mucho, y estoy eternamente agradecido con ellos, particularmente con mis directores espirituales. Ni siquiera puedo comenzar a describir cómo cada uno de ustedes ha cambiado la trayectoria de mi vida, así que gracias por compartir su tiempo y sabiduría. Y un agradecimiento especial a mis entrenadores atléticos: cada uno de ustedes me enseñó lo que es ser duro, disciplinado y nunca dejar de luchar por mis sueños sin importar lo que pase.

A todos los sacerdotes que han desempeñado un papel importante en mi vida: mis "muchachos sacerdotales" jesuitas a través de los años, especialmente el Padre. Michael Zeps, SJ, P. Gregory Carlson, SJ y P. Andy Alexander, SJ, por su amistad, inspiración y la risa compartida a través de los años; mis pastores actuales y anteriores, especialmente el P. Phil O'Kennedy, el P. Mark Spruill y el P. Rick Chenault, Jr., conocen mi amor, admiración y gratitud por cada uno de ustedes personalmente, y también por compartir libremente y mostrarme cómo para pastorear amorosamente al pueblo de Dios. Me siento honrado de conocerlos a todos, y espero que mis esfuerzos aquí ayuden a que nuestro trabajo en la viña sea un poco más fácil.

Finalmente, a mi familia AVI, especialmente a los hermanos y hermanas de los apóstoles de la vida interior. Gracias por amarme y darle a este hijo de Dios una familia eterna junto con un lugar temporal para llamar hogar a este lado de la eternidad. Conozco mis esperanzas y oraciones de que algún día podamos celebrar juntos alrededor de la mesa del banquete celestial.

INTRODUCCIÓN

"Empezar por el principio. Esa es la única manera de contar una historia".

— atribuido a William Shakespeare

Entonces, ¿por dónde empiezo? Como dice William Shakespeare, *"Empieza por el principio"*. Lo haré, pero quiero tomar una página del propio Shakespeare y preparar el escenario para que, con suerte, todo en este libro tenga más sentido y resuene más profundamente para usted.

Voy a contarle una historia rápida sobre mi propio viaje...

Antes de emprender este camino, probablemente le pareció al mundo que lo tenía todo junto.

Al pasar por la secundaria, era un estudiante y atleta capaz. Me gradué en el diez por ciento más alto de mi clase de más de 300 estudiantes, jugué tres deportes universitarios diferentes y superé mi grupo de edad en los triatlones del área local. Tenía talento musical, cantaba y tocaba instrumentos; fundé una división de un club de servicio nacional, fui voluntaria en numerosos proyectos y fui nombrada "Senior del año". Todo esto resultó en que fuera seleccionada para recibir una beca nacional ROTC del Ejército de cuatro años, y ese logro me llevó a poder asistir a una

prestigiosa universidad privada de artes liberales, la Universidad Marquette en Milwaukee, Wisconsin.

Sin embargo, lo que encubrieron todos los éxitos y elogios fue una niña temerosa, insegura y ansiosa cuyo padre biológico la había rechazado; alguien que se mordía las uñas y se preocupaba constantemente de que reprobara mis clases; una falsificación completa mientras fingía que no me importaba que los chicos me vieran, pero intentaban demostrar simultáneamente que era digna de ser amada; abrumada por las demandas de tratar de manejar mi vida por mi cuenta por primera vez, y casi desesperada por tener la vida feliz que siempre soñé.

Pero entonces, sucedió algo que cambió mi vida para siempre.

Me encontré con el gran amor de mi vida. O más exactamente, *Él* me encontró. Justo cerca del final de mi primer año en la universidad.

En ese momento, no estaba practicando ninguna tradición de fe. Había sido criada presbiteriana, pero me había alejado de cualquier creencia en Dios cuando me gradué de la escuela secundaria. Sin embargo, cerca del final de la primavera de mi primer año, Dios y yo habíamos hecho las paces. O al menos, estaba dispuesta a reconocer su existencia. Pero mi visión de Jesús, en el gran esquema de las cosas, se reducía a que él era un buen maestro moral que vivió hace mucho tiempo, nada más.

Sin embargo, el fin de semana previo a la Pascua, una amiga me invitó a asistir al servicio del Viernes Santo con ella, y como no tenía nada mejor que hacer esa noche, dije que sí.

El servicio fue en la Iglesia Gesu, una gran catedral de estilo gótico que se encuentra justo en el campus de Marquette. Cuando entré, vi una cruz de tamaño natural colocada frente al altar que se usaría para venerar más adelante en el servicio.

Pero cuando vi esa cruz, no pude pasar la última fila.

Me encontraba de rodillas en la última fila, y cuando me arrodillé allí, Jesús dijo claro como el día, "yo te amo. Y yo morí por ti".

Comencé a llorar cuando le pregunté: "¿Cómo es eso posible? ¿No sabes que no soy digna de ese amor? Mi propio padre no quiere tener nada que ver conmigo, ¿por qué lo harías?" Jesús respondió: "Te amo tanto, Christina, que habría muerto por ti, incluso si fueras la única persona viva en la tierra".

Eso fue todo. Estaba destrozada. Seguí llorando, pero mientras lo hacía, sentí que el amor y la paz de Jesús me envolvieron y llenaron por completo mi corazón, mente y alma. En esos momentos, realmente experimenté amor auténtico, paz y satisfacción.

Y mi vida no ha sido la misma desde entonces.

No recuerdo mucho del servicio de esa noche, pero desde ese momento en adelante, quería más de ese amor, paz y satisfacción, así que le prometí a Jesús que lo pondría primero en mi vida mientras intentaba servirle con cada fibra de mi ser.

El viaje posterior me ha llevado en muchas direcciones. Primero fue pasar por el RICA (Rito de Iniciación Cristiana de Adultos) y ser recibida en la Iglesia Católica Romana el 25 de marzo de 1989.

Pero, aunque ahora me había encontrado con Jesús de una manera profunda y podía recibirlo en los sacramentos de su Iglesia, no me di cuenta de que todavía estaba *muy lejos* de ser transformada a su imagen. Pero no sabía qué o cómo tratar de acercarme a Dios o llegar a ser más como Jesús todos los días de todos modos, así que involuntariamente volví a *mis formas* de hacer las cosas.

Formas que todavía estaban enraizadas en una mente, corazón y alma desordenados.

Una mente que buscaba las soluciones ofrecidas por el mundo para tratar de calmar mis ansiedades y preocupaciones: libros y programas de autoayuda, terapia y yoga.

Un corazón que todavía busca ganarse el amor y demostrar que lo merecía haciendo todo lo que pensé que agradaría a Dios. Obtuve una licenciatura, y luego una maestría en artes, en historia y teología; me metí en varios ministerios de la Iglesia incluso

mientras servía como oficial en el ejército de los Estados Unidos; busqué certificaciones en las diversas áreas donde ministraba: ministerio juvenil, sexualidad humana, teología del cuerpo, enseñanza social católica y, más recientemente, mentoría espiritual, para tratar de servir mejor a las personas.

Un alma que estaba convencida de que debería (¡y podría!) hacerlo todo por mi cuenta. El adagio de "Dios ayuda a los que se ayudan a sí mismos" fue primordial en mi vida espiritual. No confiaba en Dios ni le preguntaba qué pensaba que debía hacer. Oh, pasaría tiempo en oración, pero solo cuando necesitaba algo. Era como el chico de la universidad que solo llamaba a casa si necesitaba algo de dinero para atender una emergencia.

Y por eso, no estaba siendo transformada a la imagen de Jesús. Todavía estaba viviendo una vida mundana, persiguiendo otras cosas además de Dios que pensé que *realmente* me traerían felicidad y satisfacción: prestigio, éxito, riqueza, comodidad, mientras pensaba que estaba viviendo una vida cristiana.

Pero, en realidad, yo estaba viviendo en mis términos, no en los de Dios.

Y debido a eso, cometí muchos errores al causar mucho dolor y sufrimiento, especialmente a las personas más cercanas a mí. Cometí graves pecados a lo largo de los años al romper cada uno de los Diez Mandamientos. Esto no es una jactancia, sino una realidad.

Primero hice otras cosas en mi vida además de Dios. Tomé su nombre en vano, me perdí la misa y no pude santificar el sábado. No honré a mi padre y a mi madre. Usé anticoncepción. Tuve una aventura. Me divorcié. Me casé fuera de la Iglesia. Robé, mentí y codicié lo que no es mío.

Todas estas cosas vinieron como resultado de intentar hacer las cosas a *mi* manera y tratar de hacer todo solo con *mi* poder en contra de ser obediente a la voluntad de Dios y realmente confiar en Él y ser un instrumento del Espíritu Santo.

Es evidente para mí *ahora* que cada vez que tropiezo y caigo desde que me encontré con Jesús en ese Viernes Santo hace más

de tres décadas, es porque vuelvo a esa niña temerosa, ansiosa y preocupada que necesitaba demostrar que era digna de amor, en lugar de vivir como la hija amada en unión con los deseos de su Padre por ella y a quien se le ha dado todo lo necesario para vivir una vida de propósito, paz y abundancia.

Con el tiempo, Él reveló su plan para mí y me enseñó cómo acercarme a Él y confiar en Él en todas las cosas. Ya no tengo miedo, ansiedad o preocupación por los acontecimientos de la vida diaria. Estoy en paz.

Sé sin lugar a dudas que soy amada sin medida, una hija amada de mi Padre Celestial. Porque a pesar de mis pecados y fracasos, mi Señor nunca ha fallado o vacilado en su amor o misericordia por mí, y ha sido extraordinariamente paciente con mis debilidades. De hecho, al igual que San Pablo, Dios me ha usado gentilmente para ayudarme a lograr su plan en la vida de quienes me rodean a pesar de esas debilidades.

Él ha sido mi fortaleza, mi luz y mi salvación, y me ha dado todas las gracias que siempre he necesitado, incluso cuando lo he dudado, y me ha colmado de más gracias y bendiciones de las que podría haber imaginado. El resultado ahora es que estoy viviendo una vida llena de propósitos, rica en paz y desbordante de abundancia.

Pero el mayor conocimiento que ha compartido mientras he recorrido el camino con Él es que la vida extraordinaria que llevo no es solo para mí.

Es lo que Dios desea *para todos*.

Por *todos y cada uno* de sus hijos e hijas.

Y eso le incluye a usted.

Sí *usted*.

Y si es posible que alguien como yo haga esto, lo sé con y por la gracia de Dios, que tú también puedes hacerlo.

Soy una persona a la que le gusta llegar al punto de las cosas. Dame la línea de fondo por adelantado y píntame la visión de por qué se debe hacer algo, y luego lo abordaré. Y cuando digo

que lo abordaré, quiero decir que tiendo a dar todo de mí, dando el 110%.

También he sido así con mi vida espiritual.

Mi vida ha sido Dios preparándome y ayudándome a desarrollar mi forma particular de comunicarme con los demás de una manera clara, concisa y directa, lo que se debe hacer para buscar la santidad y convertirme en un santo.

Durante las últimas tres décadas, no importa en qué profesión, campo, ocupación, actividad o deporte en el que haya participado o haya estado involucrada, me he encontrado con personas serias de fe que desean acercarse a Dios y convertirse en hombres y mujeres santos. Pero, como yo, se encontrarían luchando contra el desánimo, la preocupación y la ansiedad, y realmente luchando por experimentar una vida de propósito, paz y abundancia.

Ahora mucha gente diría que esto es solo parte de la vida espiritual. Hay *una* cruz, así que ofrézcala, y simplemente resignarse a luchar siempre con el desánimo, la preocupación y la ansiedad.

Pero esas declaraciones son solo la verdad *parcial*. Porque la *total* verdad es que Jesús nos dejó a nosotros y a su Iglesia el modelo para la vida espiritual.

Hay pensamientos, prácticas y hábitos particulares que, cuando los incorporamos a nuestras vidas, permitirán que Dios trabaje en nuestras mentes, corazones y almas para desterrar nuestras dudas, darnos motivos para tener esperanza en medio de cualquier tragedia, y lo hará. permítanos vivir vidas tan llenas de amor, misericordia y generosidad, que la gente se detenga y pregunte: "¿Cómo puedo vivir así también?"

Este libro tiene la intención de mostrarle de manera clara y concisa. Una guía paso a paso para garantizar que pueda construir la base sólida que necesita para decir SÍ a la vida para la que Dios lo creó.

Ese es el modelo que voy a compartir.

Un *proceso* que puede ayudarnos a dejar de lado todos nuestros miedos, preocupaciones y ansiedades, y el desánimo que surge cuando vemos y experimentamos el mal que se está desenfrenando en nuestro mundo de hoy.

Un proceso que nos permitirá vivir en la fe, la esperanza y el amor para el que fuimos creados, que garantizará que nuestras vidas estén llenas de propósito, paz y abundancia de lo que nunca podríamos soñar, que nos preparará para celebrar y disfrutar El Banquete Celestial para toda la eternidad como hombres y mujeres santos en la Iglesia Triunfante, parte de la Comunión de los Santos.

Y es *Su* Camino.

Su camino no es un secreto. La mayor parte de lo que voy a compartir con ustedes aquí es simplemente sabiduría que se puede encontrar en la Sagrada Escritura y en Su Iglesia. Es el mismo Camino de los santos que han caminado antes que nosotros.

Pero al igual que el tesoro en el campo, tiene que ir a buscarlo, y en nuestro mundo ocupado, caótico y distractor de hoy, puede ser fácil pasarlo por alto. Sé que lo hice por mucho tiempo.

Por lo tanto, este libro está diseñado para hacer que esa sabiduría sea un poco más accesible y fácil de implementar para que, como yo, usted también pueda comenzar a ver rápidamente los resultados en su vida, y luego podrá mantenerlos a largo plazo.

De eso se trata este libro, y esta introducción es mi invitación personal para que USTED venga y se una a mí en el viaje.

Entonces, si está listo para emprender el viaje de su vida, un viaje de transformación, un viaje que le llevará a vivir la vida para la que Dios lo creó, una de propósito, paz y abundancia, DIGA SÍ.

DIGA SÍ, y luego pase la página y comencemos...

PARTE 1

DESCUBRIR EL PROPÓSITO PROFUNDO

Capítulo 1
ES UN PROCESO, NO UN PROGRAMA

Primero, déjeme ser MUY clara.

El plan que comparto en este libro es un *proceso*. *No* es un programa.

Dios nos ayude, pero lo último que necesita este mundo es otro programa.

Los programas son lo que nos están matando en este momento. ¿Por qué? Porque hay un programa para todo, y los programas tienen que ver con hacer algo para producir un producto, mientras que un proceso se centra en tomar medidas. Los programas son estáticos, mientras que los procesos están activos.

Pero la verdadera razón es porque los programas tienen serios negativos cuando se aplican a la vida espiritual. Tres grandes puntos negativos, en realidad.

Lo primero negativo es que un programa le da la impresión de que hay una fecha de finalización para lo que está haciendo. Y no hay tal cosa en la vida espiritual.

El segundo aspecto negativo es que los programas implican que existen soluciones integrales para todos.

El tercer aspecto negativo es que los programas dan la impresión de que el programa es la solución a cualquier problema que intente resolver.

Pero amo los procesos.

¿Por qué? Aquí hay algunas razones.

1. Los procesos no terminan, pero son continuos, flexibles y se pueden adaptar a las necesidades de cada individuo o comunidad.

2. Los procesos no son una ventanilla única, pero pueden responder a las necesidades y preguntas *reales* de la persona en lugar de responder a las necesidades y preguntas que creo que tienen.

3. Los procesos no son la solución a todos los problemas, pero permiten un encuentro con una persona.

4. Los procesos le permiten cuidar al individuo y, a través del cuidado del individuo, usted cuida a toda la comunidad.

Pero aquí está la razón más grande.

Debido a que Jesús comenzó y modeló un proceso para nosotros, creo que debemos esforzarnos por emular al Maestro, ¿no cree?

Mi objetivo es darle *todo* lo que necesitará para acercarse a Dios, ser más como Jesús y experimentar el propósito, la paz y la abundancia en su vida diaria para que pueda abrazar la vida para la que fue creado.

Bastante ambicioso, ¿verdad?

Pero creo firmemente en la idea de "Ve a lo grande o vete a casa", así que esa es mi promesa.

Ahora mucha gente tendría miedo de hacer tal promesa. Y lo entiendo totalmente. Y estaría absolutamente aterrada de hacer eso también, excepto ...

Como puede ver, esta no es *mi* promesa, es la promesa de Dios.

Dios nos ha dado todo lo que necesitamos en este mundo para llegar a ser como Él y vivir y experimentar una vida de propósito, paz y abundancia.

Simplemente tenemos nuestras prioridades mezcladas.

Esto se remonta a Adán y Eva y al pecado original, y es la razón por la que necesitamos un Salvador en primer lugar.

Pero no se suponía que fuera así. Como puede ver, en el principio, Dios creó, y *todo fue bueno*.

En el jardín, el hombre y la mujer estaban en unión con Dios, entre sí, con ellos mismos y con la creación. No hubo enfermedad ni muerte. No había vergüenza ni desnudez. No había hambre ni sed.

El amor reinaba entre Dios y toda su creación.

Todo estaba en el orden correcto. Y Adán y Eva también estaban en lo cierto.

Pero entonces apareció el pecado original, y todo ese perfecto amor, unión y orden se rompió.

El hombre ya no estaba en unión con Dios, Eva o la creación, o lo peor de todo, incluso él mismo.

El mismo resultado para Eva.

El resultado final fue pecado y concupiscencia.

Donde desobedecemos a Dios y abusamos de las personas y la creación de manera desordenada, egoísta, poco caritativa y orgullosa.

Nuestros intelectos ahora están oscurecidos, nuestros cuerpos debilitados y nuestras prioridades desordenadas.

El verdadero objetivo de la vida espiritual se trata de volver a ser ordenado correctamente. Donde buscamos y luchamos con la gracia de Dios para reclamar esa unión original con Él, los demás, la creación y nosotros mismos, y llegar a estar en el orden correcto.

Pero si juzgamos por el mundo que nos rodea, parecería totalmente imposible.

No creo que necesite compartir aquí las estadísticas sobre cuántas personas fracasan en sus objetivos de comer alimentos más saludables o hacer ejercicio de manera constante. O cuántas personas no dejan de fumar, beber o usar drogas.

O cuántas personas prometen leer la Biblia, pero luego se rinden en unas tres semanas. O quienes comienzan un hábito de

oración, pero luego la vida se interpone, así que se detienen. O quién tiene la intención de llegar a la confesión, pero semanas, luego meses y luego años pasan y todavía no se han ido.

¡Pero no todo está perdido!

No importa si estamos caídos y desordenados. No importa que invariablemente vamos a fallar, equivocarnos, quedarnos cortos y rendirnos, o al menos estar tentados a hacerlo. Alabado sea Dios, no necesitamos ser perfectos, simplemente debemos estar dispuestos a levantarnos y comenzar de nuevo.

Hacerse santo, convertirse en santo no se trata de nunca caer. Más bien, es levantarse una vez más que caemos y, a medida que crece, trate de levantarse un poco más rápido y menos desanimado que la última vez que se cayó.

Y aquí es donde volvemos a la meta de este libro y las promesas de Dios.

Porque la clave para ser ordenado correctamente es aprender *el proceso* a través del cual podemos buscar y esforzarnos por acercarnos a Dios y llegar a ser más vida Jesús.

Y es al usar este proceso que descubrimos el propósito, la paz y la abundancia en nuestra vida diaria.

Y Dios nos ha proporcionado exactamente qué es ese proceso, y de eso se trata este libro.

Es realmente así de simple.

Solo decimos SÍ al proceso.

Ahora, pase la página y sigamos avanzando...

CAPÍTULO 2
¿DE QUIÉN SOY?

El comienzo del proceso para descubrir el propósito, la paz y la abundancia en su vida diaria debe comenzar por verificar si algunas verdades de vital importancia están firmemente arraigadas en nuestras mentes y corazones. Si son sólidas como una roca es importante porque es sobre estos entendimientos básicos donde descansará nuestra vida espiritual mientras trabajamos para buscar la santidad con la gracia de Dios y hacer una vivienda digna de nuestro Señor en nuestras mentes, corazones y almas.

La primera de estas verdades es saber la respuesta a la pregunta "¿De quién soy?"

Notará que no comencé con "¿Quién soy yo?" sino más bien con "¿De quién soy?" Estoy siendo intencional aquí porque, aunque "¿Quién soy yo?" tiende a ser la pregunta que la gente hace, la verdadera respuesta a esa pregunta solo se puede encontrar si primero sabemos de *quién* somos.

Esto se debe a que el mundo está constantemente tratando de definir y clasificar rápidamente a todos, y la forma habitual de hacerlo es preguntando "¿Quién es usted?" Dado que el mundo tiene una visión y comprensión muy superficial de quién es realmente una persona, invariablemente, las respuestas que se espera que las personas den a esta pregunta generalmente se refieren a algo que *hacen*, frente a quiénes son en realidad. Eventualmente,

5

esto se vuelve tan arraigado en nosotros, que olvidamos quiénes somos realmente, porque hemos olvidado de *quién* somos.

A diferencia del superficial "¿Quién soy yo?" que solo busca definir y determinar nuestro valor por lo que hacemos, "¿De quién soy?" se centra en a quién pertenecemos y en qué nos estamos convirtiendo.

Porque cuando sabemos de *quién* somos, inherentemente sabemos que importamos, que nuestras vidas tienen un significado y que tenemos un propósito profundo.

Recordar de *quién* somos es aún más importante cuando comenzamos a ser intencionales sobre la vida espiritual. Porque recordar de *quién* somos se convertirá en la clave para abrir la cerradura de la puerta a una vida de propósito, paz y abundancia.

Y cuando sabemos de quién somos, no tenemos ninguna duda, incluso en medio de todas las mentiras del mundo que nos rodea, quiénes somos realmente.

Entonces, *¿de quién somos?*

Hijos de Dios. Hijos del rey. Somos hijos e hijas, los príncipes y princesas del Gran Rey mismo.

Así es. Es de la realeza, bebé. Y no tiene que casarse con ella como lo hizo Meghan Markle con el Príncipe Harry. Simplemente necesita reconocer su herencia, vivir esta identidad de quién es realmente y esta realidad se hace evidente en su vida.

¿De Verdad? ¿Eso es? Bueno, no del todo.

Mi propia vida es un caso puntual. He luchado con creer esta verdad de que soy una hija amada de un Padre bueno y amoroso que se preocupa por todas mis necesidades porque mi realidad al crecer parecía ser todo *menos* eso.

Mi padre biológico tuvo problemas con el alcohol y otros problemas, por lo que estuvo ausente de mi vida. Además, después de que mis padres se divorciaron, no pudo pagar la manutención de los hijos regularmente, por lo que el dinero a menudo era escaso. Y luego, a medida que crecía, y a pesar de haber contactado varias veces para tratar de conectarme, decidió

no tener una relación conmigo. Me sentí desagradable e indigna de ser amada.

Hasta que me encontré con Jesús ese Viernes Santo por la noche.

Fue Jesús quien reveló la profundidad, la amplitud, la altura y la longitud del amor del Padre por mí cuando me dijo: *"Incluso si fueras el único ser en el mundo, todavía habría muerto por ti"*.

A través de los ojos de Jesús, comencé a ver mi vida como lo hace Dios. Vi que Dios no era como mi padre biológico, ausente, desinteresado e indiferente. Más bien, comencé a ver las huellas digitales de amor y cuidado de Dios en *toda* mi vida. Fue entonces cuando realmente comencé a ser capaz de aceptar la realidad de que soy su hija amada, preciosa a sus ojos.

El Papa Juan Pablo II se hace eco de esta verdad cuando escribió: *"Solo en Cristo pueden los hombres y las mujeres encontrar respuestas a las últimas preguntas que les preocupan. Solo en Cristo pueden comprender plenamente su dignidad como personas creadas y amadas por Dios"*.

Ahora, el mundo preferiría que olvidemos esta verdad de quién somos, y por eso trabaja duro para distraernos. O si lo recordamos, disfruta la oportunidad de recordarnos cuando no hemos actuado como hijos e hijas del Rey, y trata de convencernos de que, por lo tanto, debemos haber perdido nuestro derecho de nacimiento. Pero todo eso es falso.

Como cristianos, nuestra identidad se solidifica en el bautismo. Somos "nombrados y reclamados" en este profundo momento de gracia cuando el nombre de una persona está escrito en el Libro de la Vida, y estamos capacitados con los dones del Espíritu Santo para ser sacerdotes, profetas y reyes en el mundo.

A través del bautismo, también somos hechos hermanos y hermanas en Cristo, nuestros pecados son lavados, y tenemos una marca indeleble en nuestras mentes, corazones y almas de que somos un miembro de la familia de Dios para siempre: amados hijos e hijas sobre quienes Él mira y se deleita.

Por eso debemos saber de quién somos. Cuando reconocemos nuestra identidad como hijos e hijas, que fuimos creados a imagen y semejanza de Dios y llamados a participar en la vida de nuestro Creador, nos damos cuenta de que nuestras vidas y la vida de cada persona que encontramos, son una creación única llena de belleza y dignidad capaz de conocer y comprender la bondad y el amor.[12]

En nuestra capacidad de hacer el bien y amar a los demás, nuestra vida refleja la belleza y dignidad reales, y nos recuerda a nosotros mismos, así como a los demás, no solo de quién somos, sino que nos ayuda a responder siempre correctamente la pregunta de "¿Quién soy yo?", independientemente de quién pregunte y no importa la cantidad de veces que se nos pregunte.

Podremos decir sin dudar que soy un hijo o hija amado de Dios, que estoy hecho a su imagen y semejanza, y fui creada para ser uno en unión con Él a partir de ahora y por toda la eternidad.

La Madre Teresa de Calcuta es una hermosa ilustración de alguien que sabía quién era porque sabía *de quién era*. Con frecuencia se describía a sí misma como un simple instrumento, "un lápiz en las manos de Dios". Su ministerio de cuidar a los enfermos y moribundos en las calles de Calcuta atrajo la participación y el apoyo de miles de personas en todo el mundo, pero aún más sorprendente fue ver el crecimiento de su comunidad religiosa, las Misioneras de la Caridad. De solo 12 hermanas en 1950, había más de 4500 hermanas y 500 hermanos en el momento de su muerte en 1997. Todo como resultado de su clara comunicación por su propia vida de cómo era posible vivir una vida simple de amor derramada para otros.

¿Por qué la gente se sintió atraída por esta pequeña mujer albanesa que medía poco más de metro y medio?

Porque sabía sin lugar a dudas de quién era, y vivió esa realidad tan bien que su vida se convirtió en un faro de amor, bondad y belleza brillando en la oscuridad del mundo.

En la Iglesia Católica Romana, a las personas les gusta la santa Madre Teresa. (La Madre Teresa fue reconocida oficialmente

como santa el 4 de septiembre de 2016). Pero no fue reconocida porque fue perfecta durante toda su vida. Lejos de ahí.

Desde la muerte de la Madre Teresa, el mundo ha llegado a conocer sus grandes luchas con el desánimo y la duda y los sentimientos de abandono, pero ella perseveró. Y cuando llegó al final de su viaje, la gente reconoció que estaba extremadamente cerca de vivir una vida perfectamente ordenada o santa.

Su historia es una vida enraizada en saber de quién era y, por lo tanto, sabía quién era y vivió esa realidad. El resultado fue que el mundo se hizo un lugar mejor debido a que ella había estado en él.

Y ESO es lo que cada uno de nosotros está llamado a *ser*. No hacer. Pero para ser. Ser, a nuestro modo particular y único, un brillante ejemplo de amor, bondad y belleza.

Entonces, ¿cuál es su historia hasta ahora? ¿Es una que inspire a otros a ser lo mejor de sí mismos? ¿Vivir generosa y valientemente? ¿Para vivir como la persona para la que fueron creados: hijos e hijas del Gran Rey?

San Brendan de Bir observa: *"Si se convierte en Cristo, tropezará con maravilla tras maravilla, y cada una de ellas es verdadera"*.

Esas maravillas sobre maravillas son los hilos de bondad, amor y belleza que se tejen en cada una de nuestras vidas a través de nuestras buenas intenciones o buenas palabras, y de la mejor manera, las buenas obras realizadas.

Muy a menudo, las personas simplemente atribuyen eventos y circunstancias de su vida al karma, la suerte o una simple coincidencia.

Pero no es ninguna de estas cosas. En realidad, es una persona, y he tenido la gracia y el privilegio extraordinarios de encontrarlo. Él es el Gran Rey del Cielo, Jesucristo. Y el Rey es muy claro sobre quién debería ser, por quién soy.

Debería ser como Él, perfecto y santo porque soy creado a su imagen y semejanza. En otras palabras, un santo.

Sobre San Pedro, Julián Eymard escribe: *"Santificarse es formar a Jesucristo dentro de ustedes"*. O, como aprendí de la comunidad religiosa de las Hermanas y Hermanos Sacerdotes de los Apóstoles de la Vida Interior, *"la santidad está transformando la unión con Dios"*.

Con esa comprensión en mente, entonces todo lo que debería estar haciendo, diciendo e incluso pensando debería ser permitir que Jesús se forme dentro de mí. Debería trabajar activamente para identificar los hábitos, las circunstancias y, a veces, incluso las personas, que me ayudan o me impiden escribir una historia de amor, bondad y belleza en mi vida.

Y mientras hago esto, mi verdadera identidad de quién soy y quién soy se hace más evidente, y luego mi vida también lo refleja.

Pero es un proceso. Y debido a que la vida espiritual es un proceso de toda una vida, es por eso que necesitamos saber sin duda de quién somos, para que siempre podamos responder adecuadamente quiénes somos.

Y como somos suyos, usted y yo somos importantes.

Nuestras vidas significan algo.

Incluso si no puede ver cómo esto es posible, sigue siendo cierto.

Esta vida se trata *de quién soy* y quién soy en el mundo por eso.

Para cada uno de nosotros es un lápiz. Un miembro de la realeza, especialmente creado para escribir un capítulo en una historia inolvidable, para un propósito particular. Y ese es el propósito en el que nos enfocaremos a continuación en el proceso.

Primero, tómese un momento y recuerde de *quién* es. Es un hijo de Dios

DIGA SÍ a su dignidad y grandeza.

Ahora, pase esta página. Su corona le espera.

CAPÍTULO 3
LA LLAMADA A LA SANTIDAD

Una vez que sabemos *de quién somos*, la siguiente verdad que necesitamos para tener una roca sólida en nuestras mentes es la respuesta a la pregunta: "¿Por qué fui creado?"

Desafortunadamente, en un mundo cada vez más impulsado por una persona que necesita demostrar su "valor" o "utilidad", esta pregunta se ha subvertido en "¿Qué propósito tengo?" Esto está relacionado con lo que discutí en el capítulo anterior sobre el mundo centrado en lo que usted hace, en lugar de quién y quién es usted realmente.

Aunque ha habido numerosas formas en que esta pregunta ha sido respondida a lo largo de los siglos, la única en la que debemos centrarnos aquí es la que nos dio Jesús mismo. Él enseñó: "Sé perfecto, como tu Padre celestial es perfecto". Ser perfecto es otra palabra para santo, entonces, desde el principio, la vida de un discípulo cristiano ha sido un llamado a la santidad.

Esto puede parecer una tarea difícil, pero Jesús no nos dejó huérfanos. Nos dio el Espíritu Santo para asegurarnos de que tuviéramos los medios para luchar por la perfección. A través de nuestro bautismo, nos vestimos de Cristo y nos convertimos en hijos e hijas de Dios y compartimos la naturaleza divina para que por la gracia de Dios seamos hechos santos. Entonces

debemos tratar de aferrarnos a esta santidad y vivirla en nuestra vida diaria.

Durante los últimos dos milenios, la Iglesia ha continuado expresando el llamado a la santidad como *el* llamado fundamental de todos los cristianos.

La más famosa es la cita de San Ireneo en el siglo II, *"La gloria de Dios es el hombre completamente vivo"*.

En los Estados Unidos, a menudo se hace referencia a la respuesta sucinta proporcionada en el Catecismo de Baltimore del siglo XIX para proporcionar una respuesta a esta pregunta crítica de por qué fui creado. Establece claramente: *"Fuimos creados a imagen y semejanza de Dios ... para conocerlo, amarlo y servirlo en este mundo, y ser felices con él para siempre en el cielo"*.[3]

Más recientemente, el Concilio Vaticano II, que se reunió de 1962 a 1965, se centró en este llamado universal a la santidad ampliamente en uno de sus documentos principales, *Lumen Gentium (La Constitución dogmática de la Iglesia)*. El mensaje principal de *Lumen Gentium* es que *todos* los miembros de la Iglesia, todos los fieles de Cristo, cualquiera sea su rango o estatus, están llamados a la plenitud de la vida cristiana y a la perfección de la caridad.

Como puede ver, los humanos somos definitivamente únicos. Al ser creados a imagen y semejanza de Dios, podemos pensar, comprender y experimentar el amor, la bondad y la belleza. Tenemos una capacidad que es diferente a cualquier otra criatura, porque tenemos la capacidad de razonar, por lo tanto, tenemos la capacidad de *elegir*.

"Son nuestras elecciones, Harry, las que muestran lo que realmente somos, mucho más que nuestras habilidades".

Esta cita está hecha por el personaje del profesor Albus Dumbledore en la serie *Harry Potter* de J.K. Rowling Y la esencia de esta declaración está en evidencia, ya que son nuestras elecciones las que determinan cómo responderemos a las circunstancias y a las personas en nuestras vidas y, en última instancia, si elegimos decir y hacer lo que es bueno, correcto y justo en

nuestras propias vidas. Y si estamos eligiendo vivir nuestra historia para que refleje de quién somos realmente.

Pasamos nuestras vidas eligiendo si adoptaremos plenamente esta identidad y usaremos los dones que se nos han dado para ser ministros de amor, administradores de todo lo que se nos ha dado y "profetas de un futuro que no es el nuestro".[4]

Muy a menudo, sin embargo, nos enfocamos en nuestra pecaminosidad, o cuán imperfectos somos, y creemos que tenemos que *ganar* el amor de Dios y la salvación eterna haciendo cosas.

Pero *ganarse* el amor de Dios no es así como funciona.

El padre Bede Jarrett explica esta idea del amor de Dios por nosotros maravillosamente en el libro, *Catholic Meditations*:

"Dios no puede dejar de amarme. Ese es el hecho más sorprendente que revela nuestra doctrina. Pecador o santo Él ama y no puede ayudarse a sí mismo. Magdalena en su pecado, Magdalena en su santidad, fue amada por Dios. La diferencia entre su posición también hizo alguna diferencia en el efecto de ese amor sobre ella, pero el amor era el mismo, ya que era el Espíritu Santo quien es el amor del Padre y del Hijo. Hagas lo que haga, soy amado. Pero entonces, si yo he pecado, ¿no soy digno de amor? Sí, pero soy indigno siempre. Dios tampoco puede amarme por lo que soy, ya que, en ese caso, obligaría a Su amor, forzaría Su voluntad por algo externo a Él. De hecho, realmente si llegara a considerar, encontraría que Dios no me amaba porque era bueno, sino que era bueno porque Dios me amaba. Mi mejora no hace que Dios me ame, sino que es el efecto de que Dios me haya amado".[5]

Cuando no recordamos que somos amados independientemente, y caemos en la trampa que necesitamos para ganarnos el amor de nuestro Padre, nos volvemos mucho más susceptibles a sucumbir a hacer lo que el mundo nos dice que deberíamos hacer con nuestras vidas: una vida donde nos esforzamos por asegurar

la fama, la fortuna y el poder. O para enfocarse en una vida donde se atiende a cada "necesidad", y donde podemos vivir una vida de tranquilidad y comodidad, o para practicar la filosofía de Epicuro de "comer, beber y ser feliz".

Sin embargo, estamos diseñados para más. Para MUCHO más.

Jesús y su Iglesia nos han dicho esto desde el principio. Pero en caso de que aún dude, mire los deseos más profundos de su corazón. Anhelamos ser *más* de lo que el mundo nos ofrece.

Hay una razón por la cual las estadísticas muestran que las personas que supuestamente "lo tienen todo", los famosos, los poderosos y los ricos, no son más felices o satisfechos que aquellos que no son famosos, poderosos o ricos.

Es porque hemos sido diseñados para mucho más de lo que este mundo tiene para ofrecernos.

Nuestro destino es pasar toda la eternidad con nuestro Padre Celestial que nos creó a todos a partir de la hermosa y amorosa comunión de la vida de la Trinidad: el Padre, el Hijo y el Espíritu Santo, y cada uno de nosotros está *personalmente* invitado a compartir esa vida de comunión amorosa y hermosa aquí en la tierra y en la eternidad.

Santa Elizabeth Ann Seton, la primera santa nacida en los Estados Unidos y fundadora de la primera orden religiosa estadounidense, las Hermanas de la Caridad, dijo: *"Sabemos ciertamente que nuestro Dios nos llama a una vida santa. Sabemos que Él nos da toda gracia, toda gracia abundante; y aunque somos tan débiles de nosotros mismos, esta gracia es capaz de llevarnos a través de todos los obstáculos y dificultades".*

Pero tendemos a no querer escuchar esa verdad.

No queremos escuchar que estamos llamados a ser santos. O saber que estamos llamados a convertirnos en santos.

No queremos reconocer que cada uno de nosotros está invitado a SER MÁS.

Porque somos *maestros* en el autoengaño y las excusas.

O al menos sé que lo soy. Durante mucho tiempo, aunque *sabía* que necesitaba priorizar a Dios y su plan para mi vida, decidí *no* hacerlo.

Iba a misa los domingos, pero solo cuando era conveniente para mí. Mi tiempo y talento se centraron en el trabajo, y mi tesoro se estaba utilizando para comprar todas las supuestas "necesidades" materiales que uno necesita en la vida: cosas como automóviles, muebles, entretenimiento, ropa, etc.

Dios tampoco fue parte de mi toma de decisiones cuando se trataba de con quién debía salir, actividades que realizaba o cómo debía gastar mi tiempo y dinero. Estaba haciendo lo que quería hacer, cuándo quería hacerlo y cómo quería hacerlo. No estaba viviendo una vida "ordenada", una vida en la que el plan de Dios para mi vida dirigiera mis pensamientos, palabras y acciones.

No poner a Dios primero pronto se convirtió en un patrón en mi vida, y mi negativa a vivir una vida ordenada correctamente (principalmente porque no era popular, fácil o conveniente), continuó durante casi una década. Esto fue hasta que miré a mi alrededor y vi que, a pesar de vivir lo que se consideraría una vida bastante cómoda, todavía me encontraba inquieta, ansiosa e infeliz.

Estaba persiguiendo lo que el mundo me dijo que debía ser: una persona de fama, poder y riqueza. Encontré éxito y recibí ascensos como oficial del ejército, obtuve una beca nacional, obtuve una maestría en historia y escribí y publiqué con éxito dos libros de ficción histórica para niños.

Aunque estaba viviendo la vida "a mi manera" y haciendo lo que quería hacer, y cuando quería hacerlo, me dejaba vacía, infeliz e insatisfecha. Sabía que algo estaba "apagado" o faltaba en mi vida. Pude sentir que no estaba logrando mi verdadero potencial.

Me di cuenta de que quería ser más de lo que era. Quería convertirme en *quien* fui creada para ser.

Esa comprensión me ayudó finalmente a ver a través de mis propios engaños y excusas. Me di cuenta de que la razón principal de mi descontento e infelicidad era que había rechazado el

plan de Dios para mi vida: convertirme en una persona santa, una santa viva, que respira y hace maravillas.

Había *elegido* decir NO a la invitación de Dios para ser más, para ser santa, y luego pasé años engañándome a mí misma y poniéndome excusas. Resistí aferrándome a una visión inadecuada de quién y quién soy, y en quién debería convertirme, haciendo todas las cosas que *pensé* que me gustaban más.

Sin embargo, la verdad fundamental es que, aunque sentí esta insatisfacción en mi vida, todavía dudaba porque realmente no quería cambiar. Estaba *muy a gusto*.

El papa emérito Benedicto XVI dijo una vez: *"El mundo te ofrece consuelo. Pero no fuiste hecho para la comodidad. Fuiste hecho para la grandeza"*.

Hacerse santo es grandeza en la vida espiritual. Y convertirse en un santo significa ser incluido en el Salón de la Fama. El Salón de la Fama de Dios. Sin embargo, nuestros nombres no se colocarán en placas en los pasillos del cielo. Más bien, nuestros nombres ya están escritos en las mismas manos de Aquel que nos creó para ser perfectos como Él. Y nos convertimos en santos al vivir vidas de grandeza.

Los Padres de la Iglesia del Concilio Vaticano II nos han llamado *a todos* a participar en el heroísmo espiritual, el llamado universal a la santidad, y no conformarnos con una segunda o tercera vida. Por el contrario, debemos responder a su invitación a ser santos. Para responder al llamado a la santidad.

Entonces, ¿cuál es la mejor manera de vivir?

Jesús nos lo mostró. Vivir una vida de amor derramada por los demás.

San Vicente de Paúl, cuya propia vida de amor y cuidado por los pobres inspiró a Frederic Ozanam a fundar la Sociedad de San Vicente de Paúl, que ahora cuenta con más de 800,000 miembros que trabajan con los pobres en todo el mundo, dijo una vez: *"No solo soy enviado a amar a Dios, pero para hacerlo amar. No es suficiente para mí amar a Dios si mi prójimo no lo ama"*.

Esta comprensión de lo que es vivir una vida derramada por los demás se hace eco del gran maestro espiritual estadounidense del siglo XX, el Padre Thomas Merton: *"Decir que estoy hecho a imagen de Dios es decir que el amor es la razón de mi existencia, porque Dios es amor. El amor es mi verdadera identidad. El desinterés es mi verdadero yo. El amor es mi verdadero carácter. El amor es mi nombre"*.

Nuestro mundo no solo ha olvidado esto, sino que también minimiza continuamente la realidad de que tendemos a tomar decisiones *realmente* pobres cuando no estamos viviendo por amor a los demás. ¿Y qué es el amor verdadero y auténtico? Dispuesto al bien del otro.

Pero lo que más olvidamos es que *no* somos los creadores, sino las criaturas.

Y debemos tener siempre presente ante nosotros *por qué* fuimos creados y *cuál* es nuestro propósito.

Y nuestro propósito es ser santos. Convertirse en un santo vivo, que respira y hace maravillas en este mundo y en el próximo.

Para usted que ES una criatura maravillosa. Y para esto fue creado. Para ser un santo.

DIGA SÍ y responda su llamado a la santidad.

Y luego elija pasar esa página para descubrir su misión única e irrepetible.

CAPÍTULO 4
SU ÚNICA E IRREPETIBLE MISIÓN

"Sé quien Dios quiso que fueras y prenderás fuego al mundo".

— Santa Catalina de Siena

En los dos capítulos anteriores, hemos respondido a las preguntas de quién somos y quiénes somos: amados hijos e hijas de Dios; y por qué estamos aquí: para convertirnos en santos, hombres y mujeres santos que derraman sus vidas amando a los demás.

La tercera verdad que ahora debemos tratar de asegurar es sólida en nuestras mentes es responder la pregunta "¿Cuál es mi misión única e irrepetible?"

Para responder eso, debemos entender adecuadamente nuestra vocación.

La raíz latina de la palabra vocación es "vocare" o "llamar". En este caso, el llamado de Dios. Entonces, la vocación de una persona se encuentra en su respuesta al llamado de Dios en su vida.

Desafortunadamente, la vocación es uno de los conceptos más incomprendidos en nuestro mundo hoy en día, principalmente porque la mayoría de las personas desconocen que en

realidad hay tres niveles en nuestra vocación que deben integrarse en nuestras vidas. Estas tres capas son: el llamado universal a la santidad; estado de vida; y misión personal.

La primera capa, el llamado universal a la santidad es el llamado a "ser perfecto como nuestro Padre Celestial es perfecto" que discutimos en el último capítulo. Siempre debemos recordar que cada uno de nosotros recibió la vida del amor perfecto abundante y desbordante de Dios. Y es a este amor perfecto al que estamos invitados a regresar, y para hacer eso, debemos convertirnos y estar en unión con el amor perfecto y santo al que estamos regresando.

La segunda capa se basa en la realidad de que cada uno de nosotros está diseñado para retratar la imagen y semejanza de Dios de una manera distinta de acuerdo con los dones y talentos particulares con los que nos ha dotado durante nuestra vida aquí en la tierra.

El padre Jacques Philippe, un maestro de retiros de renombre mundial y autor sobre la vida espiritual, escribió en su libro, *In the School of the Holy Spirit*:

> *"Dios ama a todos con un amor único; Él quiere guiarlos a todos a la perfección, pero al mismo tiempo tiene caminos muy **diferentes para diferentes personas**. Esto significa que la frecuencia y las características de las inspiraciones de la gracia diferirán de una persona a otra. No podemos forzar al Espíritu, Dios es el dueño de sus dones. Dicho esto, no se puede dudar de que Dios otorgará a cada persona al menos las inspiraciones que necesita para su propia santificación".[6]*

Estos "caminos diferentes" a los que se refiere el padre Philippe son los estados de vida: consagrados o matrimoniales. Muchas personas a veces se confunden porque hay muchas formas de consagración entre nosotros: sacerdotales, religiosos y solteros. Sin embargo, sea cual sea el camino que Dios llama

a una persona a seguir, Dios nos da las gracias para seguirlo. Es esta segunda capa de vocación a la que la mayoría de las personas se refieren cuando hablan de alguien que "discierne una vocación".

Finalmente, cada hombre y mujer tiene una misión única e irrepetible que fluye de su diseño inherente. Un diseño colocado allí por Dios desde el momento de la concepción para garantizar que cada uno de nosotros sea capaz de convertirse en un hombre o una mujer santos de nuestra manera particular. Y Dios nos dará, y seguirá dándonos, cualquier característica, ya sea un talento, un rasgo de personalidad o una habilidad, junto con las gracias necesarias para que podamos convertirnos y cumplir nuestra vocación única e irrepetible. Esta es la tercera capa, nuestra misión personal.

Cada uno de nosotros debe emprender la gran tarea de esforzarse por convertirse en lo que somos creados para ser, hacer lo que hemos sido creados para hacer, en el lugar donde Dios ha colocado a cada uno de nosotros para hacerlo. Uno de mis pastores anteriores expresó sucintamente la esencia de la misión personal de esta manera: "Sé quién eres, qué eres y dónde estás".

Estas son las tres capas de vocación: quién (un santo), qué (estado de vida) y dónde (misión personal), y las tres deben coincidir y convertirse en un todo integrado para que podamos cumplir la misión única e irrepetible para que Dios nos diseñó para ser signos y testigos de su amor en el mundo.

Porque la verdad es que *nadie más* en la historia de la creación puede ser quien eres, o hacer lo que solo tú puedes hacer, y hacerlo en cualquier parte del mundo en este momento particular de la historia.

Ahora, esta idea puede ser bastante desalentadora.

¿La realidad de que soy una creación única e irrepetible destinada a hacer lo que nadie más en el mundo ahora, o en toda la historia, ha hecho antes?

¡Wow! ¡Espera un minuto! ¡No soy Abraham Lincoln ni George Washington! Solo soy la pequeño yo. No tengo ninguna

"superpotencia" de la que hablar. Simplemente me levanto y paseo al perro, voy a trabajar, mantengo la casa en orden, llevo a los niños a la práctica de fútbol y veo un espectáculo ocasional de Netflix o veo la última película de Marvel.

¿Cómo podría ser único e irrepetible?

Bueno, Dios nos dice en Jeremías 1: 5: *"Antes de formarte en el útero, te conocía"*.

Usted ES importante. USTED tienes un propósito. Y USTED tiene una misión.

El mundo puede ver que usted y su vida son insignificantes, pero para Dios, es el papel de toda una vida.

El poema del cardenal John Henry Newman, "Propósito", nos da una mayor comprensión de esta idea:

Estoy creado para hacer algo o para ser algo para lo que nadie más ha sido creado; Tengo un lugar en los consejos de Dios, en el mundo de Dios, que nadie más tiene; Ya sea que sea rico o pobre, despreciado o estimado por el hombre, Dios me conoce y me llama por mi nombre.

Dios me ha creado para hacerle algún servicio definitivo; Me ha encomendado un trabajo que no se ha comprometido a otro. Tengo una misión: nunca lo sabré en esta vida, pero me lo contarán en la próxima .... Participo en un gran trabajo; Soy un eslabón en una cadena, un vínculo de conexión entre personas. No me ha creado para nada. Haré el bien, haré su obra; Seré un ángel de paz, un predicador de la verdad en mi propio lugar, aunque no lo intente, si lo hago, pero guardo Sus mandamientos y le sirvo en mi llamado.

Por lo tanto, confiaré en él. Lo que sea, donde quiera que esté, nunca me pueden echar de lado. Si estoy enfermo, mi enfermedad puede servirle; en perplejidad, mi perplejidad puede servirle; Si estoy triste, mi pena puede servirle. Mi

enfermedad, mi perplejidad o mi tristeza pueden ser causas necesarias de algún gran final, que está más allá de nosotros. No hace nada en vano; Puede prolongar mi vida, puede acortarla; Él sabe de qué se trata. Puede quitarme a mis amigos, puede arrojarme entre extraños, puede hacerme sentir desolado, hacer que mi espíritu se hunda, esconderme el futuro. Todavía sabe de qué se trata. Pido no ver, pido no saber, pido simplemente ser utilizado.

Déjeme decirlo de nuevo, USTED tiene un propósito. USTED tiene una misión.

Sin embargo, en nuestro mundo actual, la mayoría de las personas dudan en aceptar su propósito y misión.

¿Por qué? Porque nuestra sociedad actualmente está experimentando una "crisis de propósito".

La Dra. Holly Ordway, profesora de inglés y apologética en la Universidad Bautista de Houston, describe esta "crisis de propósito" como una consecuencia directa de la cultura en la que hay una distracción continua. Una cultura prácticamente sin silencio, sin reflexión, sin sentido de "hogar", y donde tanto la historia como la herencia cultural han sido negadas por tener poca o ninguna consecuencia en la vida de hombres y mujeres.

El resultado es que ahora tenemos generaciones de personas que tienen poco o ningún conocimiento verdadero de nosotros mismos, lo que resulta en una incapacidad para vivir vidas ordenadas correctamente, con un propósito o llenas de significado. En consecuencia, a pesar de la preponderancia de actividades orientadas a buscar y obtener la felicidad, esta "crisis de propósito" prácticamente garantiza que la felicidad se eludirá continuamente.

Esta incapacidad para experimentar la verdadera felicidad ha creado un ciclo interminable en el que las personas ahora dudan en tomar *cualquier* decisión, o seguir *cualquier* camino por miedo a que luego, de forma irrevocable, impidan encontrar la felicidad en algún momento debido a decisiones anteriores.

Sin embargo, como somos hijos e hijas de Dios amados, ¡no debemos temer a tomar decisiones!

¿Por qué? Porque Dios está usando todo en nuestras vidas para ayudarnos a cumplir nuestro propósito y misión.

Dios nos comunica esto a través de San Pablo en Romanos 8:28: *"Sabemos que todas las cosas funcionan para bien para los que aman a Dios, que son llamados según su propósito"*.

Sí, *todas*.

> *"Su trabajo, ya sea una tarea doméstica, una tarea, una práctica deportiva o un trabajo con una oficina y un sueldo, no es solo un medio para un fin económico. Tampoco es algo con lo que deba "terminar" a tiempo para el fin de semana. Es una parte esencial de su santificación, una participación en la fraternidad divina de Cristo y un medio para descubrir su verdadero yo".*[7]

Christopher Wesley, ministro de juventud de la parroquia y autor de varios libros, incluido *Rebuilding Conformation*, comparte la idea de que cada persona necesita descubrir su "GPS". Similar a un GPS (Sistema de Posicionamiento Global) que nos dirige a un lugar geográfico en particular, el GPS de un individuo puede hacer lo mismo para dirigirlos a su misión particular.

El GPS de un individuo se compone de sus **Regalos**, **Pasiones** y de **Sí mismo**. Los dones están en correlación con los talentos / habilidades, las pasiones son con respecto a intereses / motivaciones y el yo está en relación con la personalidad / temperamento / motivaciones de uno.

Por supuesto, cada uno de nosotros tenemos nuestras propias personalidades distintivas. Por ejemplo, algunos de nosotros somos mariposas sociales y nos encanta ir a todas las fiestas en la ciudad, mientras que otros prefieren una vida más tranquila, tal vez pasar tiempo paseando a su perro o reuniéndose con amigos para tomar un café.

También es evidente que cada uno de nosotros tiene habilidades, intereses, talentos y motivaciones únicos. Pero debemos esforzarnos por ponerlos en uso de manera ordenada y dirigida por Dios, para que puedan guiarnos por el camino que debemos caminar para convertirnos en los santos que Dios nos creó para ser.

Además, debemos esforzarnos por descubrir nuestra exclusiva "superpotencia". Nuestra superpotencia es lo único que haces mejor que casi cualquier persona que conozcas. Esto es lo que más le gusta hacer y también le encanta aprender continuamente. Probablemente también sea algo en lo que sobresalga naturalmente, pero eso no significa necesariamente que no tendrá que trabajar para continuar desarrollándolo.

Afortunadamente, en el mundo de hoy hay algunas maneras muy fáciles, prácticas y probadas en el tiempo para identificar sus dones, habilidades y talentos, lo que podría motivarlo e inspirarlo, y puede darle una idea de sus fortalezas, debilidades y otras características generales de tanto su personalidad, temperamento como motivaciones.

Hay numerosas evaluaciones y evaluaciones que se pueden hacer para identificar con mayor precisión nuestros dones, pasiones y personalidad y composición de temperamento, y le recomiendo que los use, como Myers-Briggs, Clifton StrengthFinders, Bennett Spiritual Temperament Assessment y el Inventario de dones espirituales (carismas) del Instituto Siena.

Pero la evaluación más precisa que he encontrado en las últimas tres décadas es el MCORE.

El MCORE (Motivational Core) es diferente a la mayoría de las evaluaciones en el sentido de que usa historias de logros personales (cosas que las personas determinan que hicieron bien, disfrutaron y encontraron satisfacción profunda mientras las realizaban) como la herramienta narrativa para facilitar el autodescubrimiento.

MCORE se deriva del SIMA® (Sistema para identificar habilidades motivadas), que es profundamente poderoso para

identificar su patrón único de comportamiento motivado, y está respaldado por más de medio siglo de investigación empírica.

En pocas palabras, el MCORE revela el equivalente de su "huella digital" espiritual al revelar las motivaciones centrales que lo motivan fundamentalmente. Esto le proporciona una visión significativa de lo que, naturalmente, puede brindarle una gran satisfacción, y / o la perspectiva que pueda necesitar al participar en actividades o circunstancias particulares para experimentar la mayor satisfacción personal cuando se dedica a esas actividades o circunstancias.

Sin embargo, lo que más me gusta de MCORE es que puede darle rápidamente una declaración de misión personal muy clara que se basa en sus tres motivaciones principales. Para mí, mis tres motivaciones principales son: Servir, explorar y cumplir el desafío. Por lo tanto, mi declaración de misión integrada es: "Estoy fundamentalmente motivado para servir a los demás mientras exploro y enfrento desafíos".

Una declaración de misión personal puede ayudarlo a aclarar sus prioridades y enfocarse en su propósito y misión única e irrepetible.

Los cuatro componentes de cualquier buena declaración de misión son: 1) debe ser algo que lo motive; 2) es algo que hace (o puede hacer); 3) tiene un objetivo, persona o grupo al que está ayudando; y 4) describe el impacto positivo que busca a través de su acción.

Algunas declaraciones de misión personal de algunas personas con las que puede estar familiarizado son:

"Cuento historias para ayudar a las personas a crecer" -Steven Spielberg

"Servir a Dios y a mi prójimo siendo un ejemplo de una vida comprometida con el servicio" -Tony Robbins

"Para ser un testimonio de esperanza". San Juan Pablo II

"Para calmar la sed de Jesús sirviendo a los más pobres de los pobres" -Santa Madre Teresa de Calcuta

Mi declaración de misión integrada MCORE hace lo mismo para mí de manera concisa, simple y directa. Proporciona claridad y enfoque sobre quién soy y qué y dónde hago esas cosas que me brindan una profunda satisfacción al cumplir mi misión personal.

Ahora, una nota rápida de precaución. Todas las evaluaciones y una declaración de misión personal solo deben usarse como las *herramientas* para las que fueron diseñadas para ayudarlo a aumentar su autoconocimiento.

Cualquier resultado que reciba debe ponerse al servicio de obtener una idea de cuáles son sus dones, talentos, carismas, personalidad, temperamento y motivaciones únicos para descubrir, desarrollar e integrar las tres capas de su vocación, y darse cuenta con mayor precisión de quién, qué y dónde *Dios* quiere que esté mientras cumple con su misión personal única e irrepetible.

Toda esta tarea de descubrir su verdadero ser debe hacerse a la luz del plan de Dios para usted. Porque es solo cuando buscamos la voluntad de Dios a lo largo de este proceso que descubriremos lo que realmente está en armonía con la esencia más profunda de nuestro ser, y esto es lo que crea una verdadera claridad y propósito.

Cuando esta claridad y propósito orienta todos los aspectos de nuestras vidas, se traduce en una autenticidad y sencillez auténticas acerca de la vida que encarna toda la existencia, y esto tiende a atraer a otros hacia ellas como las polillas a una llama.

Mire a cualquier gran líder a lo largo de la historia: Alejandro Magno, Julio César, Napoleón, George Washington, Abraham Lincoln, Mahatma Gandhi, Winston Churchill, Nelson Mandela e incluso Adolfo Hitler, inspiraron a otros a seguirlos debido a su claridad y propósito.

Pero, ¿cómo encontrar esa claridad y propósito en su vida? ¿Cómo podría descubrir su misión única e irrepetible?

El padre Jude Winkler, O.F.M, nos da un buen lugar para comenzar:

"Es esencial discernir lo que el Espíritu quiere cuando tomamos decisiones importantes en nuestras vidas. A través de la oración, el ayuno, la lectura espiritual, el consejo espiritual, el discernimiento de los signos, la clasificación de nuestras motivaciones ocultas, etc., desarrollamos un sentido de lo que Dios quiere de nosotros".[8]

Dios está revelando continuamente su voluntad para con nosotros, ya sea a través de su propia Palabra, a través de su Iglesia y a través de otros.

Es por eso que sumergirnos en las Escrituras mientras le pedimos a Dios que revele nuestra misión única e irrepetible para la cual Él nos creó y que es tan poderosa. San Agustín, Antonio de Egipto y muchos otros santos han llegado a conocer la voluntad de Dios para ellos a través de la meditación en la Sagrada Escritura.

Incluso otros han adquirido conocimiento a través del estudio de las enseñanzas de la Iglesia, o al sumergirse en obras de misericordia corporales y espirituales como lo hicieron los santos Francisco de Asís o la Madre Teresa de Calcuta.

La comprensión de nuestra misión personal también viene al hacernos preguntas a nosotros mismos y a otros, como: ¿En qué soy bueno? ¿A quién haría algo para ayudar? ¿Para quién desearía poder hacer más? ¿Para quién se rompe mi corazón? ¿A quién ha puesto Dios en mi camino que necesita mi ayuda en este momento? ¿Qué me hace cobrar más vida? ¿O cuándo me he sentido más vivo ayudando a alguien más? ¿Qué puedo empezar a hacer hoy? ¿Qué puedo aprender hoy? ¿A quién puedo contactar para ayudarme de una manera que me intriga?

A medida que haga estas preguntas y otras similares, comenzará a surgir claridad sobre su propósito, y luego, a medida que

tome medidas para alcanzar ese propósito, obtendrá aún más información sobre su misión personal.

Necesitamos tomar el tiempo, todos los días, para perseguir nuestro propósito y esforzarnos por cumplir nuestra misión personal. Porque su propósito, misión y felicidad están todos interrelacionados. Todos están atados a usted sabiendo quién es usted (un hijo o una hija de Dios); por qué fue creado (el llamado a la santidad y su destino eterno para convertirte en santo); y para lo que fue creado (su misión personal de amar a Dios y a los demás de una manera única e irrepetible en el lugar donde Dios le ha colocado); *si* tiene alguna posibilidad de encontrar satisfacción (felicidad).

La única forma de que esto sea posible es orientarse hacia Dios, esforzarse por santificarse al ser "ordenado" y buscar continuamente lo que *Él* desea para usted y su vida.

La búsqueda continua de su voluntad es el proceso de discernimiento, y se han escrito libros completos sobre cómo hacerlo. Pero el discernimiento puede ser una palabra especialmente desalentadora en los círculos católicos donde la mayoría de la gente cree que solo tiende a suceder cuando hay una decisión trascendental ante nosotros.

Pero tenemos que cambiar esta mentalidad. El discernimiento no es solo para "grandes decisiones". Más bien, debe hacerse de forma continua. No es uno, dos o incluso tres, y hemos terminado con discernimiento. Más bien, el discernimiento se trata de aprender a *percibir*, de poder ver o escuchar algo. Probablemente una de las definiciones más bellas que escuché para describir el discernimiento fue compartida por una hermana religiosa de los Apóstoles de la Vida Interior que dijo: *"El discernimiento es que Dios revela para ti su voluntad para tu vida"*.

Y esa es la parte más hermosa del hecho de que cada uno de nosotros ha sido creado por amor; por amor real, auténtico y de pacto; y destinado a vivir en amor con Cristo por toda la eternidad. El mismo Jesucristo en quien vivimos, nos movemos y tenemos nuestro ser.

Nuestro Dios no es un capataz duro que nos da una lista de verificación de las cosas que tenemos que hacer para que nuestras vidas sean miserables e ingobernables. Ese no es el propósito o la misión para la cual nos creó.

No, Dios nos invita a aceptar su invitación a abrir nuestros corazones a Él para que pueda HACER el trabajo de transformación dentro de nosotros.

Esta transformación no ocurre de la noche a la mañana. Es un trabajo lento y duro. A veces es con botas de cemento puestas mientras tratamos de subir una colina fangosa y terminamos deslizándonos hacia atrás más de lo que avanzamos. Entonces, a veces, puede ser doloroso, desalentador y agotador.

Pero a pesar de todo, Dios nos ama sin medida. Somos sus hijos que Él ha creado para amarlo a Él y a los demás a medida que cumplimos nuestra misión única e irrepetible.

Mientras nos derramamos como signos del amor de Dios en el mundo de la manera única e irrepetible que solo somos nosotros, y de la forma en que solo nosotros podemos hacerlo, y en el lugar donde Dios nos ha colocado, cumplimos nuestra misión personal. Y al igual que Jesús, podremos dar testimonio del magnífico y maravilloso amor que Dios tiene por todas y cada una de las personas en los mundos.

Santa Catalina de Siena dijo: *"Sé quien Dios quiso que fueras y prenderás fuego al mundo Es hora de encender una cerilla y comenzar a quemar"*.

Ya es hora de encender el fósforo y comenzar a quemar.

DIGA SÍ a su misión única e irrepetible.

Ahora, pase esta página para comenzar a ver.

CAPÍTULO 5
VEN A VER

Hasta este punto, nos hemos centrado en asegurarnos de tener claras las respuestas a las preguntas fundamentales de nuestras vidas.

Quiénes somos, por qué estamos aquí y cuál es el propósito de nuestras vidas.

Las respuestas a estas preguntas son los cimientos sobre los cuales descubrimos nuestro profundo propósito y nos ayudan a prepararnos para comenzar nuestro viaje espiritual en serio. Debemos decidir si aceptaremos la invitación ofrecida por Dios para que comencemos a participar en la vida de la Trinidad aquí y ahora, a fin de prepararnos para vivir en unión con Él por toda la eternidad.

Esta es la decisión clave que Jesús coloca ante cada uno de sus discípulos. Lo vemos hacer esto en los Evangelios, y podemos ver cómo cada persona que Jesús encuentra responde de manera diferente.

En Juan, Capítulo 1, versículos 35-51, vemos a Jesús reuniendo a Sus primeros discípulos:

El siguiente día otra vez estaba Juan, y dos de sus discípulos. Y mirando a Jesús que andaba por allí, dijo: He aquí el Cordero de Dios. Le oyeron hablar los dos discípulos, y siguieron a Jesús. Y volviéndose Jesús, y viendo que le

seguían, les dijo: ¿Qué buscáis? Ellos le dijeron: Rabí (que traducido es, Maestro), ¿dónde moras? Les dijo: Venid y ved. Fueron, y vieron donde moraba, y se quedaron con él aquel día; porque era como la hora décima. Andrés, hermano de Simón Pedro, era uno de los dos que habían oído a Juan, y habían seguido a Jesús. Este halló primero a su hermano Simón, y le dijo: Hemos hallado al Mesías (que traducido es, el Cristo). Y le trajo a Jesús. Y mirándole Jesús, dijo: Tú eres Simón, hijo de Jonás; tú serás llamado Cefas (que quiere decir, Pedro).

El siguiente día quiso Jesús ir a Galilea, y halló a Felipe, y le dijo: Sígueme. Y Felipe era de Betsaida, la ciudad de Andrés y Pedro. Felipe halló a Natanael, y le dijo: Hemos hallado a aquél de quien escribió Moisés en la ley, así como los profetas: a Jesús, el hijo de José, de Nazaret. Natanael le dijo: ¿De Nazaret puede salir algo de bueno? Le dijo Felipe: Ven y ve. Cuando Jesús vio a Natanael que se le acercaba, dijo de él: He aquí un verdadero israelita, en quien no hay engaño. Le dijo Natanael: ¿De dónde me conoces? Respondió Jesús y le dijo: Antes que Felipe te llamara, cuando estabas debajo de la higuera, te vi. Respondió Natanael y le dijo: Rabí, tú eres el Hijo de Dios; tú eres el Rey de Israel. Respondió Jesús y le dijo: ¿Porque te dije: Te vi debajo de la higuera, crees? Cosas mayores que estas verás. Y le dijo: De cierto, de cierto os digo: De aquí adelante veréis el cielo abierto, y a los ángeles de Dios que suben y descienden sobre el Hijo del Hombre."9

En estos dieciséis versículos, vemos las diversas formas en que los discípulos vinieron a Jesús. Primero, Andrés y Juan, el Discípulo Amado, fueron a buscarlo, y cuando Jesús les preguntó qué estaban buscando, respondió con una invitación para que *"Vengan y vean"*.

Andrés fue y trajo a su hermano, Simón, quien se convertiría en Pedro, a Jesús. En este caso, vemos a Pedro siendo presentado por otro a Jesús. Sin embargo, cuando Pedro mismo vino antes que Jesús, tuvo que decidir si aceptaba su nuevo nombre y si iba a quedarse con Jesús junto a su hermano y Juan.

Entonces Jesús busca un discípulo al día siguiente. Este es Felipe. Felipe no solo decide seguir a Jesús, sino que también va a buscar a su amigo, Natanael. Cuando Natanael expresa dudas sobre la verdad de quién podría ser Jesús, Jesús le revela a Natanael cómo ya lo ha visto parado debajo de la higuera. En resumen, Jesús revela que ya conocía a Natanael, y es esta revelación la que convence a Natanael de profesar que Jesús es el Hijo de Dios y el Rey de Israel.

En la reunión de los discípulos iniciales, vemos muchas de las diferentes formas en que las personas pueden llegar a ser seguidores de Jesús. Algunos buscan, como Andrés y Juan, mientras que otros son traídos a Jesús por un miembro de la familia, como Pedro. Jesús busca a otros, Felipe, y luego otros no solo necesitan ser presentados por un amigo, sino que también requieren una revelación de la verdad sobre la realidad de quién es Jesús antes de estar dispuesto a seguir a Natanael.

Este no fue solo el caso en Palestina hace más de dos mil años, sino que continúa siendo el camino de Dios a lo largo de los siglos desde entonces, y nada ha cambiado hasta nuestros días.

Cada uno de nosotros recibe una invitación similar porque Jesús no dejará de encontrarse con todas y cada una de las personas en el mundo en cualquier lugar, forma o manera que puedan necesitar para llegar a conocerlo.

Independientemente de la forma en que nos encontremos, y luego nos paremos ante Jesús, cada uno tiene que tomar una decisión.

¿Vamos a seguir?

¿Diremos que SÍ y aceptaremos la invitación de *"venir a ver"* el gran amor que Él tiene por cada uno de sus hijos e hijas?

¿Experimentaremos la realidad de cómo nos ha conocido desde *"Antes de formarte en el útero ya te conocía"*?[10]

¿Confiaremos en su promesa *"Porque conozco bien los planes que tengo en mente para ti, planes para tu bienestar y no para la desgracia, para darte un futuro de esperanza"*?[11]

¿DIREMOS QUE SÍ?

Desafortunadamente, la mayoría de las personas en nuestra Iglesia hoy ni siquiera se dan cuenta de que hay *una* opción.

Los pensamientos tienden a seguir estas líneas, o muy similares, (al menos lo hicieron por mí)... "He sido católico toda mi vida, y estoy haciendo lo que se supone que debo hacer. Vengo a misa cuando puedo. Recibo la comunión y me confieso si he hecho algo realmente serio. Dono a la parroquia. Soy un buen esposo / esposa y padre / madre. No soy perfecto, pero lo hago bastante bien la mayor parte del tiempo. Dios es misericordioso, así que lo entenderá. No es que haya matado a nadie, así que debería ser bueno entrar al purgatorio al menos..."

Sin embargo, la realidad es que el viaje espiritual es mucho más que simplemente sobrevivir.

Porque si realmente respondemos a la invitación de Jesús de "venir y ver", entonces emprendemos el viaje más grande de nuestras vidas. Y la Iglesia enseña que, durante ese viaje, nos movemos a través de los caminos purgativo, iluminativo y unitivo. Cada una de estas "formas" representa una etapa a través de la cual progresamos a medida que crecemos en intimidad con Dios.

Usando las descripciones de San Francisco de Sales, el Camino Purgativo es la etapa del viaje espiritual cuando comenzamos a "purgarnos" de nuestro egoísmo a través de un compromiso serio de crecer en nuestra relación con Dios a través de la oración regular y alejarnos de todo pecado grave. El Camino Iluminativo es un tiempo para continuar profundizando nuestra vida de oración mientras crece en humildad, virtud y obediencia y un amor creciente al prójimo. El camino unitivo es un momento en que estamos gobernados por el amor, cuando nuestra voluntad está en perfecta unión con Dios, estamos siguiendo las

inspiraciones y consejos del Espíritu Santo, y Jesús está viviendo en nosotros y a través de nosotros.

Esta es la esencia completa de lo que significa establecer y seguir al Maestro. Pero la mayoría de las personas apenas llegan a la línea de inicio del Camino Purgativo.

Pero incluso si llegamos a esa línea de partida, y nos damos cuenta de que hay que tomar una decisión seria ante nosotros, normalmente todavía tenemos que superar algunos conflictos internos y / o externos, o no ser víctimas de algunos errores mentales muy comunes.

Esos conflictos internos tienden a ser cosas como creer que no somos amables, que somos un pecador demasiado grande o que no somos dignos del amor de Dios. Los obstáculos externos son como si mi familia estuviera molesta, o no tengo tiempo, o tengo demasiadas responsabilidades, o no estoy dispuesto a arriesgarme a perder lo que sea que sea más importante para mí.

Invariablemente, casi todos estos conflictos tienen su origen en una comprensión errónea de lo que significará decir sí a Jesús para nuestras vidas, y aquí es donde tendemos a caer presas de errores mentales comunes.

Estos errores mentales se denominan sesgo de supervivencia, aversión a la pérdida, heurística de disponibilidad y sesgo de confirmación, pero si aguanta conmigo un minuto, le daré ejemplos para que pueda ver si están funcionando en su vida.

El sesgo de supervivencia es la idea de que nos centramos solo en las personas que tienen éxito y lo que sea que hicieron para tener éxito, y suponemos (aquí está el error mental) que cualquiera que use una estrategia similar también encontrará el éxito.

Entonces, cuando consideramos si DECIR SÍ y seguir a Jesús, nos enfocaremos en los muchos ejemplos de personas que son personas exitosas, satisfechas y felices que *no* son personas de fe. Nuestro sesgo de supervivencia nos hace centrarnos en esos ejemplos, y luego concluimos que para ser exitoso, realizado o feliz no es necesario ser un seguidor de Cristo.

La aversión a la pérdida se refiere a nuestra tendencia a querer evitar cualquier tipo de pérdida en nuestras vidas. Esto parece tener un sentido lógico total porque ¿quién quiere perder algo o a alguien? Hasta que vea el hecho de que somos muy protectores de las cosas que tenemos y, a menudo, haremos cosas *ridículas* para mantener lo que ya tenemos.

Estoy seguro de que todos podemos pensar en un ejemplo de cuando hemos hecho algo ilógico para no tener la oportunidad de perder a alguien o algo así, tal vez seguir siendo amigos de alguien que fue una mala influencia para nosotros, o tal vez mantener demasiadas chaquetas (o lo que sea) "por si acaso" podríamos necesitarlas.

Cuando elegimos seguir a Cristo, esta idea de aversión a la pérdida se ejemplifica en el joven rico que viene y le pregunta a Jesús qué debe hacer para encontrar la vida eterna. Jesús le dijo al joven que necesitaba guardar los mandamientos, y cuando el joven les dijo que había hecho esto desde que era un niño, Jesús respondió con la invitación: *"Si deseas ser completo, ve y vende tus posesiones y da a los pobres, y tendrás un tesoro en el cielo; y ven, sígueme"*. El joven respondió alejándose triste porque tiene muchas posesiones.[12]

El error mental común de la aversión a la pérdida es pensar que, si seguimos a Jesús, entonces podríamos perder a alguien importante para nosotros, o podríamos tener que renunciar a todo lo bueno, como divertirnos o ser dueños de cosas hermosas, o ir de vacaciones agradables, pero este no es el caso en absoluto. Pero la aversión a la pérdida nos hace dudar al hacernos pensar que ese es el caso.

La disponibilidad heurística es cuando suponemos que cualquier información que se nos ocurra más fácilmente debe significar que son las cosas más importantes para recordar. Este error mental nos hace sobrevalorar el impacto de las cosas que podemos recordar, al tiempo que subestimamos las cosas que no escuchamos.

Un ejemplo de esto es que debido a que no escuchamos o no podemos recordar numerosas instancias de personas que se están convirtiendo en santos, creemos que muchas personas NO se están convirtiendo en santos o que no es posible convertirse en un santo, y hacemos de esto una "verdad" que luego aplicamos a nuestras vidas.

Matthew Kelly, menciona esta idea de que usted, yo mismo o cualquier otra persona en el mundo es incapaz de convertirse en un santo, como *"la mentira más grande jamás contada en la historia del cristianismo"*. [13] Pero todo es solo el resultado de un error mental común.

Finalmente, hay un sesgo de confirmación. Esto es cuando inconscientemente estamos buscando información que confirme nuestras creencias preexistentes mientras ignoramos o devaluamos cualquier información que contradiga lo que ya creemos.

Cuando esto se aplica a si elegimos seguir y poner a Cristo primero en nuestras vidas, significa que tendemos a encontrar solo información que respalde lo que ya creemos que es verdad para NO hacer un cambio. Como "No tengo tiempo", "No es posible" o "Es demasiado difícil". Por lo tanto, justificamos nuestra "decisión" de no tomar una decisión. Para no hacer un cambio.

Entonces, ¿estamos condenados a nunca poder tomar una decisión que no sea defectuosa de alguna manera?

De ningún modo.

Pero la clave es reconocer cuándo pueden estar en juego estos errores mentales y compensarlos a través de la autoconciencia. Pero la autoconciencia debe basarse en una comprensión sólida de las tres preguntas que discutimos anteriormente: quiénes somos, por qué estoy aquí y qué estoy llamado a hacer.

Y es por eso que debemos comenzar con esas preguntas y las tres verdades fundamentales de las respuestas a esas preguntas *primero*. Debido a que nuestra comprensión de estas preguntas y las respuestas a ellas influirán si somos capaces o no de *considerar* responder a la invitación de Dios.

Si no tengo esas respuestas sólidas en mi mente, entonces probablemente ni siquiera vea el punto de responder con un sí o un no. Porque todavía estoy demasiado atrapado en todo lo que el MUNDO dice que es importante.

Pero una vez que esté al tanto de las respuestas, y luego de la realidad de la invitación de Dios, y luego se mueva a través de todas las "cosas" internas o externas que pueda tener, todavía nos quedamos frente al elefante REAL en la habitación.

Nuestro miedo

Ahora, la mayoría de las personas no se dan cuenta de que nuestro miedo está intrínsecamente ligado a lo que realmente amamos.

Santo Tomás escribe en su *Summa Theologica*: *"El miedo nace del amor"*. [14]

Por lo tanto, sea lo que sea lo que más tememos perder, esa es la misma cosa (o persona) que más amamos, y eso tiende a ser lo que más apretamos y resistimos a todo lo que creemos que podría amenazar lo que amamos.

Entonces, al considerar la gran invitación que tenemos ante nosotros, *tenemos* que controlar nuestro miedo.

Pero luego, después de controlar nuestro miedo, debemos responder con valentía.

Pero, ¿qué es exactamente el coraje?

Brene Brown, autor de *Daring Greatly*, define el coraje como "actuar en presencia de vulnerabilidad". Y la vulnerabilidad es "cada vez que hay incertidumbre, riesgo y / o exposición emocional".

Entonces, el coraje es la voluntad de ser vulnerable.

En el libro infantil que hice de ficción histórica, *March to Canada*, Abraham Hollister, le dice a su hijo de once años de edad, Mateo, *"Hacer lo correcto cuando tienes miedo es de lo que se trata el coraje."* [15]

Pero hacer lo correcto cuando tienes miedo de perder algo (o alguien) que amas es francamente difícil, *si no amas lo suficiente.*

Y así es como el miedo nos paraliza cuando elegimos seguir a Jesús.

Amamos las cosas que poseemos y tenemos miedo de perderlas más de lo que amamos a Dios, por lo que descubrimos que nos falta el coraje para dejar de lado esas cosas y hacer lo necesario para acercarnos a Dios.

En particular, encontramos que rara vez tenemos el coraje de responder a la invitación de Dios para participar en la plenitud de la vida de la Trinidad en el aquí y ahora.

Porque creemos que *nuestros* planes, *nuestro* pensamiento y *nuestras* cómodas formas de vida son más importantes, y no encontramos el coraje para responder a la maravillosa invitación de Dios.

No respondemos la invitación a *"venir y ver"* cómo Jesús puede transformarnos y ayudarnos a vivir vidas con propósito y significado. Simplemente porque no estamos dispuestos a actuar con coraje en presencia de vulnerabilidad.

O aceptar la incertidumbre sobre lo que puede suceder si ponemos a Dios primero en nuestras vidas. O estar dispuesto a arriesgarse a fracasar mientras luchamos por desarrollar los hábitos necesarios para permitir que Dios nos transforme verdaderamente. O para exponernos emocionalmente a los demás al admitir que necesitamos un Salvador.

Para mí, esta oración de la Santa Madre Teresa de Calcuta resume mi respuesta a la invitación de Jesús:

"Él es la vida que quiero vivir.
Él es la vida que quiero vivir.
Él es la luz que quiero irradiar.
Él es el camino al Padre.
Él es el amor con el que quiero amar.
Él es la alegría que quiero compartir.
Él es la paz que quiero sembrar.
Jesús es todo para mí.
Sin Él, no puedo hacer nada".

Pero primero, cada uno de nosotros debe decidir: ¿lo seguiré? ¿O me alejaré como el joven rico?

Es hora de que responda con valentía.

Es hora de que deje de lado todos sus miedos y venga a ver los grandes planes que Dios tiene para usted: planes de esperanza, propósito, paz y abundancia.

Pero Él necesita que confíe en sus promesas.

Él le necesita para abrir la puerta y pasar.

Él necesita que salga con Él en el viaje y que *"No tenga miedo"*.

DIGA SÍ y *"Ven a ver"*.

Ahora, pase la página. Su Amado le está esperando.

PARTE 2

ENCONTRANDO LA PAZ AUTÉNTICA

Capítulo 6
LOS CUATRO PASOS
HACIA LA SANTIDAD

Nuestro viaje hasta ahora se ha centrado en las verdades que deben ser sólidas en nuestras mentes para que podamos descubrir y vivir nuestro profundo propósito.

Los fundamentos sobre los que construimos son: la claridad absoluta y el enfoque de quienes somos; saber sin lugar a dudas que nuestras vidas tienen dignidad y estamos llamados a la santidad; comprendemos que nuestras vidas tienen sentido porque tenemos una misión única e irrepetible que solo nosotros podemos hacer en el mundo; y, finalmente, que debemos DECIR SÍ al viaje y prepararnos para abrazar y perseguir el propósito de nuestra vida a través del cual encontraremos nuestra máxima felicidad y satisfacción.

Todo esto es crítico porque es solo después de haber aceptado las respuestas a estas preguntas de nuestra vida que tendremos una base lo suficientemente sólida como para intentar que el viaje se convierta plenamente en lo que hemos sido creados para ser, signos únicos de El amor y la misericordia del padre en el mundo.

Pero, ¿*qué podríamos* hacer para convertirnos en esos signos únicos e irrepetibles de amor y misericordia en el mundo?

Pasé décadas buscando las respuestas.

Pero San Gerard Majella cristaliza la esencia de cuál es la clave de qué y cómo necesitamos convertirnos en lo que somos

creados para ser cuando escribió: *"¿Quién, excepto Dios, puede darte paz? ¿Ha sido alguna vez el mundo capaz de satisfacer el corazón?*

Es vital saber y comprender que es nuestro núcleo espiritual, nuestra vida interior, lo que despierta nuestra imaginación, inspira nuestros corazones, da vida a su belleza y nos ayuda a dar forma al mundo en el que vivimos. Como discípulos de Cristo, la realidad espiritual que profesamos es lo que es moldear nuestros pensamientos, palabras y acciones, ya que es "de Él en quien vivimos, nos movemos y somos".[16]

Todos los libros y programas de autoayuda del mundo contienen un tema común. La idea es que es a partir de los pensamientos y creencias sobre uno mismo que las realidades físicas que nos rodean se ven afectadas, y esto no solo determina nuestras capacidades, sino también si tendremos éxito en el ejercicio de esas capacidades.

Dentro de la vida interior, esto significa que debemos sumergirnos en el desarrollo de una relación con Aquel que debe moldear nuestras mentes, inspirar nuestros corazones y, en última instancia, transformarnos en imágenes de Sí mismo en el mundo: vivir, respirar, hacer maravillas. santos

Pero, ¿qué nos motiva exactamente a hacer algún cambio en nuestras vidas? La gente debate esto, pero la mayoría de las veces, un cambio verdaderamente *duradero* está enraizado en el amor.

Santa Clara de Asís dijo: *"Nos convertimos en lo que amamos"*, y esto es absolutamente cierto. Pero la *totalidad* de su observación nos da una idea de por qué es tan vitalmente importante elegir lo que amamos con cuidado:

"Nos convertimos en lo que amamos y a quienes amamos da forma a lo que nos convertimos.
Si amamos las cosas, nos convertimos en una cosa.
Si no amamos nada, nos convertimos en nada.

La imitación no es una imitación literal de Cristo, sino que significa convertirse en la imagen del Amado, una imagen revelada a través de la transformación.
Esto significa que debemos convertirnos en vasos del amor compasivo de Dios por los demás.

¿Entonces como hacemos esto? ¿Cómo nos convertimos en un santo? ¿Cómo nos volvemos santos, o para "llegar a ser perfectos como nuestro padre celestial es perfecto"?

Al emprender cuatro prácticas, o pasos.

Estos "Cuatro pasos para la santidad" son: oración diaria y meditación; Vivir una vida de gracia frecuentando los sacramentos; Creciendo diariamente en una vida de virtud; y Abandonarte a la Voluntad de Dios.

Estos parecen ser pasos muy simples, y lo son. Pero el hecho de que sean simples no significa que sean fáciles, y aquí es donde es clave contar con nuestra firma de fundaciones.

Porque todo lo que hacemos debe estar motivado por nuestro amor por Jesús. Nuestro enfoque debe estar en hacer los cambios que sean necesarios para ser transformados por Aquel a quien amamos.

Thomas Merton observó acerca de su propia vida que una vez que llegó a comprender que no se suponía que debía tratar de aclarar sus ideas, sino más bien de aclarar su vida, entonces fue liberado para perseguir realmente una relación íntima con Dios. Un buen amigo mío, John Granger, llama a este proceso de enderezar nuestras vidas, como "estar bien ordenado".

Y eso es realmente por lo que estamos aquí. Nos esforzamos por poner a Dios primero en nuestras vidas para que podamos ser ordenados y transformarnos completamente a su imagen en el mundo.

La Iglesia Católica ha enseñado estas prácticas fundamentales durante más de dos milenios, y las vidas de todos los innumerables santos también nos instruyen. *Cada* práctica espiritualmente fructífera de la vida interior cae en uno u otro de

estos cuatro pasos. Y sin uno u otro de los pasos, es inevitable que te detengas, o incluso te detengas por completo, en tu viaje espiritual.

Todo lo que debemos hacer y cómo debemos llevar a cabo estas prácticas en nuestra vida interior es para que podamos convertirnos en la creación que Dios nos hizo ser: hombres y mujeres santos.

DIGA SÍ a los cuatro pasos de la santidad.

Ahora, pase la página. Es hora de empezar.

Capítulo 7
PASO UNO: ORACIÓN DIARIA Y MEDITACIÓN

"De todas las actividades humanas, el hombre que escucha a Dios es el acto supremo de su razonamiento y voluntad".

— Santo Papa Pablo VI

Como acabo de comentar en el capítulo anterior, todo lo que debemos ser y cómo debemos hacerlo en nuestra vida espiritual recae en la práctica de los 4 Pasos.

Es la primera, oración diaria y meditación, la cual abordaré ahora.

Para mí, la oración es cómo yo me recargo y me reenfoco todas las mañanas. Para usar una analogía tecnológica, así es como me estoy "conectando para recargar y reiniciar". Todos necesitamos recargarnos, y muy a menudo, debido a las responsabilidades que tenemos en nuestra vida diaria, es vital que tomemos un descanso y reiniciemos para que podamos tener una perspectiva de por qué estamos haciendo todo lo que se trata. Pero es absolutamente imposible que se recargue o reinicie sin que nos conectemos.

Okay. Sé que existen plataformas de carga inalámbricas, pero aún tiene que colocar su dispositivo en ese cargador inalámbrico para que se realice la recarga, y el reinicio solo es posible si, según Apple, ¡"Su dispositivo está enchufado y conectado a una red inalámbrica"!

Entonces, ¿alguno de nosotros hace que su dispositivo pierda una actualización clave porque no hizo una u otra de esas 2 cosas con su dispositivo? Sé que sí, y los resultados fueron catastróficos, ¡al menos tecnológicamente!

En el lenguaje espiritual, el proceso de conectarse a la red inalámbrica se llama oración. El hecho es que debemos estar presentes ante Dios, orar, todos los días porque es a través de la oración que somos "recargados" y Dios tiene la oportunidad de darnos un "reinicio": su perspectiva sobre todos los problemas y eventos pasando en nuestras vidas.

"La oración no es una cuestión de lo que dices o sientes, sino del amor. Y amas cuando tratas de decirle algo al Señor, aunque en realidad no digas nada". [17]

Santa Teresa de Lisieux se hizo eco de esta comprensión de simplemente estar presente cuando escribió: *"Para mí, la oración es un latido del corazón; es una simple mirada hacia el cielo, es un grito de reconocimiento y de amor, que abarca tanto la prueba como la alegría".* [18]

Y habrá pruebas y alegrías en su oración, pero de todas las prácticas espirituales por las que debe luchar, es esta. Vale la pena cada minuto. Vale la pena cada lucha y desafío para formar el hábito de la oración diaria y la meditación.

Ahora, hay tres tipos diferentes de oración sobre los que la Iglesia nos instruye: estos son la oración vocal, la meditación y la contemplación. Los primeros dos tipos de oración están sobre nosotros en que tenemos que comenzar a hacer la mayor parte del trabajo. Tenemos que aparecer.

Las oraciones vocales con las que la mayoría de nosotros tendemos a estar muy familiarizados, por ejemplo, el Padre Nuestro, el Ave María, las oraciones de novena, las coronillas, etc. Hay

muchas, muchas oraciones vocales diferentes: las palabras de otra persona. Por lo tanto, el nombre de la oración vocal.

La meditación es donde se sumerge en la Palabra de Dios y pasa tiempo en una reflexión tranquila hablando con Dios. La forma más común de entrar en meditación es usar la Sagrada Escritura, especialmente los Evangelios.

La razón de esto es que la Escritura es la *Palabra Viviente*.

La Iglesia enseña cómo se experimenta esto al discutir los cuatro sentidos de la Escritura.

Los eruditos bíblicos se refieren a cuatro sentidos distintos de la Escritura: el literal, el alegórico, el anagógico y el moral. Un poema latino de la Edad Media resume muy bien de qué se trata cada sentido. [19] En español, se lee de esta manera:

El sentido literal enseña lo que sucedió,
Lo alegórico de lo que debes creer,
La moraleja de lo que debes hacer,
El anagógico a donde vas.

Y el Catecismo enseña bellamente que, "La profunda concordancia de los cuatro sentidos garantiza toda su riqueza a la lectura viva de las Escrituras en la Iglesia". [20]

Es en esta riqueza que nos sumergimos en la meditación diaria. Es por eso que el mismo pasaje de las Escrituras nunca nos hablará de la misma manera que antes. (¡Y si descubrimos que este es el caso, entonces probablemente necesitemos regresar y escuchar la voz de Dios un poco más fuerte!).

Por eso la meditación es *inmersiva*. Nos sumergimos en la riqueza y la belleza de la voz viva de Dios que nos llega en su Palabra, y debemos estar callados y pasar tiempo en silencio con la Palabra para escuchar sus susurros. Porque Dios *siempre* nos susurra.

Ahora, toda nuestra meditación nos prepara para el tercer tipo de oración: la contemplación.

Pero solo *si* Dios lo quiere.

Porque la contemplación es todo según la gracia de Dios. Hacemos el trabajo, preparamos nuestros corazones y nuestras mentes y nos presentamos para tener esa conversación con Dios, y luego, si Él lo desea, entraremos en tiempos de contemplación. Momentos en que realmente estamos en unión con Dios. Pero nuevamente, la contemplación no es algo que *hacemos*, sino que es la gracia de Dios obrando en nosotros.

Y eso es lo que debemos tener siempre en mente. Que ser amigo de Dios solo significa tener una conversación con él. Santa Teresa de Ávila, que es la Doctora de la Iglesia de Oración, nos dice exactamente que la oración es simplemente una conversación con Dios. Entonces, en lugar de quedar atrapado, ¿cómo puedo rezar? Solo recuerde que es realmente bastante simple. Se trata de sentarse y tener una conversación.

Entonces, ábrase para encontrar la encarnación de la paz en la persona de Jesús.

Comprométase a tener conversaciones íntimas y amorosas con la persona que es su mejor amigo.

Entre en *la* amistad amorosa que le transformará a usted y a su vida ahora y por toda la eternidad.

DIGA SÍ a la oración y meditación diarias.

Y es hora de pasar la página. su teléfono está timbrando.

Capítulo 8
CONTESTANDO EL TELÉFONO

Entonces, usted quiere practicar el paso de la oración diaria y la meditación. Está preparado para tener conversaciones con Dios y crecer en amistad con él.

¿Pero exactamente *cómo* lo haría?

Como mencioné brevemente en el último capítulo, la Iglesia enseña que hay tres tipos de oración: vocal, meditación y contemplación.

Las oraciones vocales son solo eso, todo lo que decimos en voz alta por nosotros mismos o con otros. Hay un *montón* de oraciones y novenas para el Espíritu Santo, los ángeles y cada uno de los santos, o por una intención particular, etc. Lo que sea, y hay una oración por ello.

No faltan las oraciones vocales que uno puede ofrecer, y puede volverse abrumador rápidamente. Entiendo totalmente la lucha porque es difícil elegir en quién enfocarme. Pero lo importante no es que hagamos todas las oraciones, sino que nos esforzamos por ofrecer oraciones que tengan un significado para nosotros.

Por ejemplo, si nosotros, o alguien que conocemos, está luchando contra el cáncer, tal vez rezamos una novena a Saint Peregrine, la santa patrona de aquellos que luchan contra el cáncer. O si estamos buscando misericordia o consuelo para alguien que está muriendo, podemos ofrecer una Coronilla

de la Divina Misericordia. O si estamos ofreciendo oraciones por la protección de alguien espiritualmente, podemos ofrecer una oración de San Miguel o Ángel de la Guarda, o tal vez la Coronilla de San Miguel.

Las opciones son casi innumerables, así que esté atento a cómo el Espíritu Santo le está llamando a interceder en su nombre, pero especialmente para otros que Dios se ha cruzado en su camino y adapte sus oraciones vocales en respuesta a las necesidades que encuentre en su propia vida y en la vida de los demás.

Ahora, uno de los grandes desafíos para mantener y perseverar en la oración diaria es que puede ser desafiante o simplemente difícil, porque parece que la otra persona en la conversación no está respondiendo. Como si Dios no hubiera levantado el teléfono de su lado.

Pero eso no es verdad. Dios *siempre* nos susurra.

Dios siempre está en la línea. El siempre está hablando. Pero tenemos que aprender a escuchar.

Y este es el propósito de la meditación, el segundo tipo de oración. Es necesario que trabajemos duro para que podamos aprender a escuchar y a identificar la voz de Dios más fácilmente. Para hacer eso, tenemos que pasar tiempo teniendo una conversación para empezar, porque si no nos presentamos, entonces es bastante difícil tener una conversación.

Es el mismo concepto que si no contesta una llamada telefónica. Es imposible hablar con alguien más si no está en la línea. Y ese es el propósito de la oración diaria y la meditación. Se trata de nosotros contestando el teléfono.

Y una de las mejores maneras de contestar el teléfono y tener una conversación con Dios, es abriendo las Escrituras y encontrándonos y sumergiéndonos en la Palabra misma.

LECTIO DIVINA Y LAS CUATRO R

La forma más común de hacerlo es a través de una práctica conocida en la Iglesia como Lectio Divina. Lectio Divina es

una antigua forma de oración de abrir la Palabra de Dios y luego sumergirnos en oración y meditar sobre ella. No voy a entrar en detalles sobre la Lectio Divina aquí, sino que le voy a dar un tipo de acrónimo un poco diferente y más simple para tener en cuenta si recién está comenzando a meditar.

Porque hay TONELADAS por ahí. Pero quiero compartir con ustedes esta que compartieron conmigo los Apóstoles de la Vida Interior, una comunidad religiosa de hermanos y hermanas consagrados. He tenido el beneficio y el privilegio de conocerlos y estar en comunidad con ellos, ya que soy un prometido miembro de la familia de los apóstoles. Parte de mis promesas como miembro de la Familia es vivir esta práctica de oración y meditación diaria, y el acrónimo de los Apóstoles sobre cómo participar en la oración meditativa es mediante el uso de las "cuatro R".

Las cuatro "R" son: Repasar, Reflexionar, Relacionar y Resolver.

Entonces, comienzas con *Repasar*. Cada vez que viene ante nuestro Señor en oración, le pide al Espíritu Santo que le ayude a abrirte a sumergirse en Su Palabra, y luego lee y repasa.

Lo siguiente es *Reflexionar*. Entonces, a medida que lea, intenta usar todos sus sentidos y comprometer su mente dirigiendo sus pensamientos a Aquel que es la Palabra Viviente. Esto es similar a una forma de oración imaginativa, llamada oración ignaciana, durante la cual buscas usar todos sus sentidos para ubicarse junto al Señor durante una escena del Evangelio.

Y luego *Relaciona*. Esto significa que relaciona lo que hay en su corazón con Dios. Comparte lo que está sintiendo, viendo, oyendo y saboreando, tal vez incluso oliendo, a medida que profundiza en las Escrituras. La parte más importante de la relación es recordar que es una conversación. Entonces, mientras se relaciona con nuestro Señor todo lo que está pensando y sintiendo, debe permitirle que le hable sobre lo que sea que desee compartir con usted. Esto significa que necesitamos practicar el silencio.

Esto definitivamente requiere tiempo y práctica. Y a veces usted está sentado, y piensa: "No tengo nada". Pero si persevera, eventualmente comenzará a escuchar el susurro de su voz. Y una vez que escuche su susurro, el timbre, el ritmo y la cadencia del mismo, será mejor escuchar su voz más fácilmente. Cuanto más practique, mejor lo hará. Es por eso que es TAN importante que luche tan fuerte como pueda para sacar tiempo para meditar todos los días.

Y la R final es la *Resolución*. Una resolución es una acción pequeña y concreta que hace durante el día que le ayuda a tomar lo que sea que nuestro Señor le haya dicho durante su meditación y hacer que forme parte de su vida durante todo el día. Aquí es donde el caucho se encuentra con el camino, ya que es a través de su resolución que el poder de la Palabra de Dios realmente puede revelarse y estar presente en su vida. Es a través de una resolución que estarás más abierto a permitir que su palabra arraigue en tu corazón y te pida que te veas como Él te ve, y que puedas identificar esos momentos en los que no está en buenas relaciones con Él. Podrá preguntarse: "¿Cómo no soy santo?" y luego escucha su respuesta. O "¿Cómo voy a tratar de responder a lo que has compartido conmigo hoy, Señor?" Su resolución surge al responder estas preguntas.

Entonces esas son las cuatro R. Son una de las formas más fáciles en que puede comenzar a practicar la oración meditativa usando las Escrituras.

EL ROSARIO

Una de las oraciones más hermosas que puedes usar para meditar es el Rosario. Mucha gente piensa que es simplemente una oración vocal repetitiva, pero esto no es del todo exacto. El rosario puede ser de gran valor, porque, aunque tiene elementos de oración vocal, puede llevarle fácilmente a la meditación. Esto se debe a la oportunidad de meditar en los misterios de la fe. Esto se hace más comúnmente usando los diferentes Misterios del

Rosario, que son escenas de la vida de Jesús y María. Pero también se pueden usar otros extractos de las Escrituras, o cualquier enseñanza de la Iglesia, o escritos de un santo. Cualquier cosa que le haga leer, reflexionar, relacionarse y resolver reflexionar más profundamente sobre la verdad, la bondad y la belleza de las Buenas Nuevas.

San Juan Pablo II elogió la fecundidad de la práctica de rezar el Rosario por los creyentes cuando dijo: "Rezar el Rosario es sentarse al pie de María. Y cuando nos sentamos en la escuela de María, aprendes a sus pies sobre la vida de su Hijo". [21]

El Rosario es tan efectivo que puede servir como el instrumento perfecto para ayudarnos a prepararnos para entrar en el tercer tipo de oración, la contemplación. Al presentarse y hacer el trabajo dentro de nuestros corazones, mentes y almas a través de oraciones vocales y meditación, Dios puede compartir más fácilmente las gracias necesarias para que alguien entre en la contemplación. Y la contemplación son aquellos momentos en los que se acerca a Él y entra en una conversación verdaderamente transformadora con Él en la que no se necesitan palabras. Donde solo lo mira y Él lo mira a usted, y es una unión perfecta.

CONSISTENCIA

Aunque hay muchas maneras diferentes en las que puede elegir orar, no se obsesione con la oración que debe hacer, o si está haciéndolo perfectamente. Por el contrario, asegúrese de elegir un momento y un lugar, y luego ORAR. Bloquee el tiempo, incluso si solo son diez minutos, pero asegúrese de elegirlo y comprométase con él. Así es como comienza a cultivar el hábito de la oración y la meditación diarias.

Sin embargo, la consistencia es la clave.

Durante mucho tiempo, aunque *sabía* que la clave para estar más cerca de Jesús era pasar tiempo con Él en oración, luché por establecer una vida de oración diaria. Primero, tuve la excusa de "No tengo tiempo para rezar, estoy ocupado haciendo otras

cosas". Entonces, después fue "rezaré cuando tenga tiempo durante el día".

Pasé por una gran variedad de excusas diferentes durante años, pero no fue hasta que finalmente admití que realmente no *quería* tomarme el tiempo para sentarme y rezar que realmente comencé a avanzar de manera fiel pasar tiempo todos los días en oración.

Y se trataba simplemente de aparecer fielmente y contestar el teléfono.

Jesús quiere ser nuestro refugio. Él quiere ayudarnos a no distraernos por el millón de cosas que suceden a nuestro alrededor, sino más bien enfocarse en Aquel que es la paz en medio de las tormentas de la vida. Él sabe que solo en Él los infinitos anhelos de nuestros corazones encontrarán una respuesta infinita, y solo en Él encontraremos una paz verdadera y duradera.

El Dr. Allen Hunt, en su libro, *Dreams for Your Grandchild*, escribe: "Diez minutos al día pueden marcar la diferencia en el mundo. Mientras más tiempo pases en el aula de silencio, más claramente oirás la voz de Dios en tu vida... Una rutina diaria de oración es lo que cambia las reglas del juego. A medida que comiences a orar constantemente, notarás que otras partes de tu vida se abren de una manera saludable que nunca anticipaste". [22]

Toda oración es una comunicación de amor por el otro. Cómo, dónde y cuándo rezamos no es tan importante como el hecho *de que lo hagamos*. No por obligación, sino por amor. Nace de nuestro deseo de pasar tiempo con nuestro mejor amigo, nuestro amante, nuestro Amado, Aquel en quien descubrimos nuestro propósito, significado y destino. O: "Aquel en quien vivimos, nos movemos y tenemos nuestro ser".

Pero en realidad, pasar tiempo con Jesús en oración y meditación *todos* los días es la clave.

Es el conducto primario a través del cual nuestra relación con Dios se establece y mantiene a lo largo de nuestras vidas —minuto a minuto, hora a hora, día a día, semana a semana, mes a mes, año a año— y hacia la eternidad.

Y se convertirá en el medio a través del cual Dios te transformará en el signo único de Su amor y misericordia en el mundo para el que Él lo creó a usted.

DIGA SÍ a tomarse el tiempo todos los días y entablar una conversación para asegurarse de tener el amor y la visión de *Dios* para su vida.

Pregunte y *recibirá*.

Dios está en la línea.

DIGA SÍ y conteste el teléfono.

Ahora, pase la página para dar el siguiente paso y vivir la vida de la gracia.

Capítulo 9

PASO DOS: VIVIR LA VIDA DE GRACIA

"Pocas almas entienden lo que Dios lograría en ellos si se abandonasen sin reservas a él y si permitieran que su gracia los moldeara en consecuencia".

— San Ignacio de Loyola[23]

Paso dos: Vivir la vida de gracia es un componente crítico en nuestro viaje hacia la santidad. Debido a su importancia, debemos asegurarnos de que estamos recibiendo las gracias de Dios que están disponibles para nosotros y permitir que esas gracias nos moldeen en consecuencia.

Para lograr esto, debemos estar atentos a tres aspectos diferentes para vivir la vida de la gracia. Estos aspectos son: 1) asegurar que estamos viviendo la vida de la gracia de acuerdo con las enseñanzas de la Iglesia; 2) buscando aumentar el flujo de la gracia; y 3) haciendo el trabajo necesario para mantener la vida de gracia fluyendo sin parar.

La vida de gracia comienza con un encuentro en los sacramentos de la Iglesia. Y digo *encuentro* intencionalmente, porque es a través de los sacramentos que podemos encontrarnos

personalmente con la persona de Jesucristo de manera real y tangible.

El Catecismo de la Iglesia Católica, párrafo 1131 establece:

> *"Los sacramentos son signos eficaces de la gracia, instituidos por Cristo y confiados a la Iglesia, por los cuales se nos entrega la vida divina. Los ritos visibles por los cuales se celebran los sacramentos, significan y hacen presentes las gracias propias de cada sacramento.* **Dan fruto en aquellos que los reciben con las disposiciones requeridas".** [24] **(Lo que está en negrita enfatiza lo mío)**

El propósito de este capítulo no es entrar en una discusión sobre qué *son* los sacramentos, sino cómo podemos garantizar que sean más efectivos en nuestra vida interior.

En los últimos dos capítulos, nos enfocamos en el primer paso de la santidad: pasar tiempo en oración y meditación diarias.

El primer paso es *la clave* para asegurar que estará abierto a recibir el amor y la visión de Dios para su vida. Y es por eso que es necesario comprometerse a hacer de la oración una práctica *diaria*.

Lo siguiente en el viaje es vivir la vida de la gracia. Vivir la vida de la gracia se logra principalmente frecuentando los sacramentos de la Sagrada Eucaristía y la Reconciliación. "Frecuentar" simplemente significa que estamos buscando recibir las gracias de Dios en estos dos sacramentos repetibles con más frecuencia de lo que la Iglesia exige en sus Preceptos.

Si no lo sabe, los Preceptos son la guía de la Iglesia en cuanto a las responsabilidades de los fieles en cuanto a cuáles son los mínimos necesarios para vivir la fe.

Los siete preceptos son:

1. Asistir a misa todos los domingos y días santos de obligación.

2. Confesar nuestros pecados al menos una vez al año.

3. Recibir la Sagrada Comunión al menos una vez al año, durante la temporada de Pascua.

4. Observar los días prescritos de ayuno y abstinencia de carne.

5. Proveer para las necesidades materiales de la Iglesia, cada una de acuerdo con sus habilidades.

6. Observar las leyes matrimoniales de la Iglesia.

7. Participar en la misión de evangelización de las almas de la Iglesia.

Entonces, si está cumpliendo los Preceptos, entonces asistirá a Misa todos los domingos y el Día Santo de la Obligación, y muy probablemente recibirá la Sagrada Eucaristía más de una vez al año.

Sin embargo, para vivir la vida de la gracia y *frecuentar* verdaderamente los sacramentos, tendrá que comprometerse a ir a misa en algo más que domingos y días santos. Para la reconciliación, esto significa recibir el sacramento más de una vez al año.

¿Por qué? El P. Jacques Philippe nos dice en su libro, *In the School of the Holy Spirit*:

> *"Sin importar cuán grandes sean nuestros esfuerzos, no podemos cambiarnos a nosotros mismos. Solo Dios puede llegar al fondo de nuestros defectos y nuestras limitaciones en el campo del amor; solo Él tiene suficiente dominio sobre nuestros corazones para eso. Si nos damos cuenta de que nos salvaremos a nosotros mismos. una gran cantidad de desánimo y lucha infructuosa. No tenemos que convertirnos en santos por nuestro propio poder; tenemos que aprender a dejar que Dios nos convierta en santos. Eso no significa, por supuesto, que no tenemos que hacer cualquier esfuerzo... Debemos luchar, no para alcanzar la santidad como resultado de nuestros propios esfuerzos, sino para dejar que Dios*

*actúe en nosotros sin que presentemos ninguna resistencia contra Él; **debemos luchar para abrirnos lo más plenamente posible a Su gracia,** lo que nos santifica". [25] **(Lo que está en negrita enfatiza lo mío)***

Para esforzarnos por abrirnos lo más posible a las gracias de Dios, tenemos que estar trabajando para asegurarnos de que realmente los estamos recibiendo en primer lugar. Esto significa que debemos estar atentos a vivir nuestra fe, vivir la vida de la gracia, de acuerdo con las leyes de la Iglesia.

El P. Joseph Langford, en su libro, *I Thirst:40 Days with Mother Teresa*, explica esto:

"Esto significa que no es suficiente que recibamos la Eucaristía diariamente o que reflexionemos sobre la palabra de Dios diariamente. El problema es que nuestra propia fe débil puede tener el efecto de apagar el Espíritu. Aunque es cierto que los sacramentos son fuentes de infinito poder y santidad, solo hacemos sonar sus profundidades de acuerdo con el grado de nuestra fe. El ejercicio de la fe nos cambia de 2 maneras. Primero, despierta e intensifica nuestra conciencia de la presencia y sed de Jesús en nuestras vidas. Y, en segundo lugar, aumenta nuestra disposición para recibirlo ... Para beneficiarnos plenamente de nuestro contacto diario con el Señor, debemos estar seguros de que estamos tocando a Jesús en la fe". [26]

Como aprendí en mi propio viaje, estamos absolutamente bendecidos por la realidad de que como católicos tenemos acceso a todo lo que Jesús quiere darnos para ayudarnos a ser santos en esta vida. Él nos ha dado Su Palabra en las Escrituras, Su propio ser en los sacramentos de la Iglesia y Su Espíritu presente en Su Iglesia para guiarnos, alentarnos y apoyarnos.

Esto se debe a que Jesús sabía por experiencia que la vida puede ser difícil y llena de desafíos, con muchos altibajos, alegrías

y tristezas. Y Jesús sabía que, sin Él, no podríamos lograrlo. Sabía que no podríamos hacer lo que nos pide que hagamos, que es seguirlo y llegar a ser "perfecto como nuestro Padre Celestial es perfecto".

Sin Jesús, no podemos convertirnos realmente en los santos que Dios nos creó para ser. Jesús sabía que no podríamos compartir el amor y la misericordia que Dios desea derramar sobre el mundo si no estuviéramos llenos de Su amor y misericordia.

Entonces, cuando comenzamos a considerar la cuestión de "¿Cómo vivo una vida de gracia?" Nuestra respuesta es directa. Además de la oración diaria, debemos venir y recibir a Jesús en sus sacramentos. Para hacer esto, vamos a Misa, recibimos la Sagrada Eucaristía y vamos a la Reconciliación frecuente.

Pero la realidad es que primero debemos comenzar asegurándonos de ser fieles al asistir a misa. El padre Roman Guardini nos instruye que *todo* lo que hacemos en la misa debe tener una sola intención: servir a Dios.

> *"No venimos a la iglesia para asistir al servicio como espectadores, sino para, junto con el sacerdote, servir a Dios. Todo lo que hacemos: nuestra entrada, estar presentes, arrodillarnos, sentarnos y estar de pie, nuestra recepción de lo sagrado alimento: debe ser un servicio divino. Esto es así solo cuando todo lo que hacemos se desborda de la conciencia de un corazón recogido y la atención de la mente".*[27]

Entonces, ¿qué tan bien estamos sirviendo? ¿Qué tan presentes estamos al entrar en la presencia de Dios? ¿Cuándo nos arrodillamos, cuándo nos sentamos, cuándo nos paramos? Pero, ¿qué tan atentos estamos cuando recibimos nuestro alimento sagrado?

¿Y vamos a misa con tanta frecuencia como deberíamos? ¿*Todos* los domingos (o sábados por la noche) *y* todos los días santos de obligación?

Ahora obligación puede ser una palabra difícil en nuestra sociedad hoy. Pensamos, oh Dios, tengo que hacer algo, así que no queremos hacerlo. Es como cualquier niño de dos años a quien se le dice que tiene que hacer algo y, por supuesto, ¡la primera palabra es no! Jajaja

Aunque podamos ser mayores, somos de la misma manera. Parte de la razón de un hábito de oración y meditación diaria es para que se nos enseñe y aprenda a ser como un niño: humilde y confiado, para que podamos confiar en la Iglesia que Jesús fundó a través de la venida de Su Espíritu Santo hace 2000 años porque es en Su Iglesia, que Sus gracias más abundantes nos llegan, particularmente en los sacramentos.

En nuestro bautismo, cada uno de nosotros es bautizado en la vida de la Trinidad, y es a partir de nuestro bautismo que estamos llamados a ser sacerdotes, profetas y reyes. Donde estamos llamados a entrar en la obra que Dios nos está dando a cada uno de nosotros para poder ayudarlo a lograr la redención del mundo.

Sin embargo, Jesús sabía que nos cansaríamos. Sabía que lucharíamos. Que tendríamos hambre. Que lo necesitaríamos para poder cumplir con nuestras obligaciones. Para poder responder con amor a todo lo que Él nos llama. Y esto nos lleva de vuelta al hábito de frecuentar los sacramentos, de vivir la vida de la gracia.

Para los dos sacramentos que nos van a dar la gracia que necesitamos de manera consistente es la Sagrada Eucaristía y la Reconciliación.

Ahora, *todos* los sacramentos son encuentros con Cristo y la oportunidad de recibir Su gracia para el viaje. Pero la Eucaristía es la fuente y la cumbre de nuestra fe. Santo Tomás de Aquino lo resume maravillosamente: *"La Eucaristía es el sacramento del amor; Significa amor, produce amor. La Eucaristía es la consumación de toda la vida espiritual".* [28]

Necesitamos crecer en el amor y la gracia de Dios, y para hacerlo debemos seguir los preceptos de la Iglesia y cumplir con nuestras obligaciones. Necesitamos observar los días prescritos

de ayuno y abstinencia de la carne, satisfacer las necesidades materiales de la Iglesia como somos capaces, observar las leyes matrimoniales de la Iglesia y participar en la misión de evangelización de la Iglesia.

Pero lo más importante, debemos ir a misa *todos* los domingos y *todos* los días santos de obligación y recibir los sacramentos de la Sagrada Eucaristía y la Reconciliación más que el mínimo de una vez al año.

Este es el primer aspecto de vivir la vida de la gracia. Para asegurarnos de que lo estamos viviendo de acuerdo con la enseñanza de la Iglesia.

Así que ponga a Dios primero en su vida y haga que sea una prioridad ir y recibir las gracias que Dios desea darte de acuerdo con las enseñanzas de la Iglesia.

DIGA SÍ a vivir la vida de gracia.

Ahora, pase la página para comenzar a recibir la plenitud de Sus gracias.

Capítulo 10

VIVIENDO LA PLENITUD
DE LA VIDA DE GRACIA

El segundo aspecto de vivir la vida de gracia es buscar aumentar el flujo de gracia.

¿Por qué?

¿No está haciendo lo que la Iglesia enseña en los Preceptos lo suficiente como para vivir nuestra fe?

No, no es.

Vivir nuestra fe de acuerdo con los Preceptos es lo *mínimo* para garantizar que nuestra vida espiritual no muera. Los preceptos son el equivalente a estar en soporte vital. Nuestras almas apenas respiran si intentamos vivir nuestra fe simplemente al nivel de los Preceptos.

Si nos tomamos en serio la lucha por la santidad, la búsqueda del propósito, la paz y la abundancia que Dios desea para nosotros, entonces debemos hacer todo lo posible para obtener toda la gracia que podamos, y luego algunos para que nos sea posible vivir en la plenitud de la vida de la gracia.

Esto significa que debemos estar buscando recibir con *frecuencia* los sacramentos.

Ahora, lo hermoso de nuestra fe es que hay muchas maneras en que podemos sumergirnos más profundamente en la vida de la gracia, especialmente con respecto al misterio que es la Eucaristía. Podemos utilizar fácilmente numerosos métodos para

aumentar nuestra devoción y continuar creciendo en las disposiciones correctas necesarias para recibir la plenitud de las gracias presentes en la Eucaristía.

Sin embargo, los tres que estoy a punto de compartir con ustedes aquí, no solo son muy simples y fáciles de implementar, sino que también han demostrado ser *extremadamente* efectivos para crecer rápidamente en la vida de gracia.

EN PRIMER LUGAR, IR A MISA MÁS DE UNA VEZ A LA SEMANA.

Piénselo. Si solo comemos alimentos una vez a la semana, nuestros cuerpos físicos disminuirán bastante rápido. Nuestra alma interior también necesita alimento, y venir a misa más de una vez por semana nos permite recibir más alimento para nuestra vida espiritual.

La Iglesia nos da la obligación de venir al menos una vez a la semana principalmente porque necesitamos nuestro alimento espiritual, la Eucaristía al menos una vez a la semana, pero cuanto más frecuentemente podamos recibir la Eucaristía, más estamos llenos de la gracia de Dios.

Vamos a misa para recordar el amor de Jesús por nosotros y lo amables que somos. TAN amables que Jesús no solo murió por nosotros, sino que se convierte en alimento para nosotros. Entonces, cuando recibimos la Eucaristía, nos ponemos en contacto con DIOS: Cuerpo, Sangre, Alma y Divinidad.

San Juan Vianney nos dice: *"Al recibir la Sagrada Comunión, la Adorable Sangre de Jesucristo realmente fluye por nuestras venas y Su Carne realmente se mezcla con la nuestra".* [29]

Porque la Sagrada Eucaristía no es una comida ordinaria. El beato Pier Giorgio Frassati dijo: *"Le insto con toda la fuerza de mi alma a acercarse a la Mesa Eucarística con la mayor frecuencia posible. Aliméntese de este Pan de los Ángeles del cual extraerá la fuerza para luchar en las luchas internas".* [30]

¿Cómo podríamos decir no a eso?

LA SEGUNDA PRÁCTICA ES IR ANTE NUESTRO SEÑOR EN ADORACIÓN.

Esta es nuestra oportunidad de simplemente "pasar el rato" y pasar un momento tranquilo con Él. Donde continuamos siendo transformados simplemente por estar en Su presencia.

Muchas personas cuestionan, o incluso, dudan del valor de esta práctica porque puede ser difícil ver cómo pasar tiempo haciendo lo que el mundo considera "nada", podría tener un impacto tan profundo en nosotros. Para ilustrar, permítanme compartir la analogía de cómo la Adoración es como ir a la playa a tomar el sol.

A mucha gente le encanta ir a la playa y simplemente tumbarse al sol. El calor mientras literalmente se "hornea" al sol, y la paz que experimentan cuando no hacen nada más que tumbarse en su toalla de playa. Ahora, si usa protector solar y hace esto varios días, termina con un bronceado (en comparación con si olvida usar protector solar, ¡y luego se puede quemar bastante rápido! jajaja).

Pero esta es una hermosa manera de pensar sobre el tiempo que pasa ante nuestro Señor en la Adoración. Porque cuando disfruta del resplandor de su amor por usted, descansa en su presencia. Y, a medida que pasamos tiempo en la Adoración, también terminamos recibiendo un bronceado. Pero este es un "bronceado", donde en lugar de que nuestra piel se oscurezca, Jesús nos transforma gradualmente interiormente para que nos parezcamos cada vez más a Él a cualquier persona que nos encuentre.

Incluso, la simple práctica de venir ante Jesús cuando el Santísimo Sacramento descansa en el Tabernáculo puede tener un impacto positivo. Entonces, incluso si no hay Adoración disponible en su área local, desarrollar la práctica de pasar por la iglesia para una "visita corta" para saludar también tendrá un impacto de largo alcance en su vida espiritual.

La tercera práctica es pasar tiempo en Acción de Gracias después de la Sagrada Comunión.

En muchas parroquias hay un momento de música tranquila o suave que suena mientras recibimos la Sagrada Comunión. Esto está diseñado para ayudarnos a reflexionar sobre el hecho de que acabamos de recibir al Señor de los Lores, y para recordarnos que cuando recibamos la Sagrada Eucaristía, esto es lo más cerca que estaremos de Jesús en este mundo.

Pero parte de la razón para pasar tiempo intencionalmente en Acción de Gracias es aumentar el tiempo que podemos dar gracias. Esto es para asegurar que, independientemente de lo que las diferentes parroquias puedan hacer o no, aún podamos mantener la gratitud a la vanguardia de recibir a Jesús en la Sagrada Eucaristía.

Entonces, en lugar de darse la vuelta y hablar con sus vecinos en el banco después de la bendición final, o apurarse para llegar al estacionamiento, tómese un momento y arrodíllese o siéntese en silencio y pase un poco de tiempo dando gracias a nuestro Señor por la gran gracia que le acaban de dar. Intente pasar al menos 3-5 minutos sumergiéndose en el amor de Jesús por usted.

Ahora, mientras busca incorporar esta práctica en su propia vida espiritual, puede que se pregunte qué o cómo debería orar. Sin embargo, sugiero que una forma aún mejor de pasar este tiempo es no orar usando palabras particulares, sino simplemente compartir lo que hay en su corazón e intentar permanecer lo más cerca posible de Jesús.

Sin embargo, si todavía encuentra que esto es difícil, una imagen maravillosa para usar es de la Última Cena. Para imaginar cómo el Amado Discípulo, Juan, apoyó la cabeza sobre el pecho de Jesús después de la primera Eucaristía durante la Última Cena. Y para que seamos conscientes de esta imagen mientras nos esforzamos por estar cerca de Jesús de una manera similar.

Sé que, si aprovechamos la oportunidad para aumentar la conciencia y la acción de gracias por este gran regalo, y nos

esforzamos por estar tan íntimamente conectados con Jesús como sea posible durante el tiempo que damos gracias, entonces realmente nos abrimos para crecer en nuestra apreciación de La Sagrada Eucaristía.

El padre Jacques Philippe escribe:

"Lo que nos impide recibir gracias más abundantes de Dios puede ser simplemente que no estemos lo suficientemente agradecidos y no le agradezcamos por las gracias que ya nos ha dado. No hay duda de que, si agradecemos a Dios con todo nuestro corazón por cada gracia recibida, especialmente por las inspiraciones [del Espíritu Santo], Él nos otorgará más".[31]

Entonces, al practicar el Día de Acción de Gracias después de la Comunión, permitimos que Jesús nos transforme y ayude a aumentar dentro de nosotros las "disposiciones correctas" mencionadas en el Catecismo para que podamos realmente abrirnos a recibir la plenitud de la gracia de los sacramentos.

El Papa Juan Pablo II nos recuerda que *"De la Eucaristía proviene la fuerza para vivir la vida cristiana y el celo para poder vivir la vida con los demás".* [32] Esto es absolutamente cierto, por lo que debemos esforzarnos por crecer en nuestra capacidad de recibir e incorporar prácticas en nuestra vida diaria que nos ayuden a crecer en la apreciación de la Sagrada Eucaristía.

Procure vivir la vida de la gracia lo más plenamente posible para que Dios pueda moldearlo en la imagen perfecta e irrepetible de sí mismo que Él creó para usted. Porque si lo hacemos, seremos transformados de formas que ni siquiera podemos comenzar a imaginar.

¿Y cómo podríamos decir no a eso?

DIGA SÍ a vivir la plenitud de la vida de gracia.

Ahora, pase la página para que la vida de gracia fluya sin parar.

Capítulo 11

LA VIDA DE GRACIA QUE FLUYE SIN PARAR

E ntonces, ¿por qué decimos no a vivir la vida de gracia en su plenitud?

Porque amamos nuestro pecado más que a Jesús.

¡Ay!

Duro, pero cierto, ¿no? Porque la verdad es que, si no estamos dispuestos a hacer *lo que sea* necesario para recibir a Jesús con más frecuencia en sus sacramentos, especialmente su cuerpo, sangre, alma y divinidad en la Santísima Eucaristía, entonces estamos *mintiendo* cuando decimos queremos que Jesús sea el Señor de nuestras vidas.

¿Por qué estoy siendo tan directo? Porque, de nuevo, somos maestros en el autoengaño. Particularmente cuando se trata de nuestra pecaminosidad.

> *"Muchos cristianos consideran la confesión a la luz de un acto de piedad sin importancia, si no una mera ceremonia. . . muchos van incluso con frecuencia a la confesión, pero muy pocos corrigen, y consecuentemente obtienen poco o ningún beneficio del sacramento. ... Sea, entonces, completamente convencido de la inmensa importancia de este sacramento, y esté lleno de un ferviente deseo de acercarse a él dignamente, otorgando el mayor cuidado y atención*

a su preparación para este gran deber, si desea obtener la eterna salvación.

La confesión es uno de los siete sacramentos instituidos por Cristo; se le llama el Sacramento de la Penitencia, y solo por él puede el que ha cometido pecado mortal, después del Bautismo, esperar salvar su alma; por eso es llamado por el santo Concilio de Trento: el segundo tablón después del naufragio. En este sacramento, Jesucristo ha depositado Su Preciosa Sangre, para que sea para nuestras almas como un baño saludable en el que puedan ser limpiados de todas las manchas del pecado, sus heridas cerradas, sus enferme-dades curadas, su debilidad fortalecida y la gracia para la salvación importado a ellos. Esta Sangre Divina nos la dispensa el sacerdote en la santa absolución, y se derrama **abundantemente sobre todas las almas que se acer-can al tribunal de confesión con las disposiciones apropiadas ".** [33] **(lo que está en negrita es mío)**

Es por eso que necesitamos recibir con frecuencia el sacra-mento de la Reconciliación (también conocido como Confesión o Penitencia). Se trata de cultivar esas "disposiciones correctas" en medio de este sacramento más hermoso del perdón y la cu-ración de nuestro Señor, el cual tendemos a descuidar y olvidar.

¿Y por qué podría ser eso? Como dije antes, ¿tal vez es porque amamos nuestro pecado más que a Jesús? Puede ser una reali-dad difícil de enfrentar, pero si no estamos dispuestos a ajustar nuestros horarios, hacer que el tiempo con nuestro Señor en Adoración sea una prioridad, o asegurarnos de venir a encon-trarlo regularmente en confesión, entonces ¿cómo podemos real-mente afirmar que realmente amamos a Dios "con todo nuestro corazón, toda nuestra fuerza y toda nuestra alma"? [34]

El Catecismo explica esta dicotomía maravillosamente:

"A través de los sacramentos de la iniciación cristiana, el hombre recibe la nueva vida de Cristo. Ahora llevamos esta vida "en vasijas de barro", y permanece "oculta con Cristo en Dios". Todavía estamos en nuestra "tienda terrenal", sujetos a sufrimiento, enfermedad y muerte. Esta nueva vida como hijo de Dios puede debilitarse e incluso perderse por el pecado. El Señor Jesucristo, médico de nuestras almas y cuerpos, que perdonó los pecados del paralítico y lo devolvió a la salud corporal, ha querido que su Iglesia continúe, en el poder del Espíritu Santo, su obra de curación y salvación, incluso entre sus propios miembros. Este es el propósito de los dos sacramentos de la curación: el sacramento de la Penitencia y el sacramento de la Unción de los Enfermos".[35]

Porque cada vez que llegamos a la confesión, no solo estamos siendo perdonados por nuestra pecaminosidad. También estamos siendo *sanados*.

La confesión se trata de encontrar la hermosa misericordia de Dios y permitirle que nos dé las gracias que necesitamos para poder luchar contra lo que estamos confesando. Ese es el *verdadero* propósito de la reconciliación. Para sanarnos no solo de nuestro pecado, sino para sanarnos de esos pecados que estamos confesando. Como nuestro Señor le explicó a San Pablo: *"Mi gracia es suficiente para ti, porque mi fortaleza se perfecciona en la debilidad".[36]*

El sacramento de la reconciliación también puede ayudarnos a aumentar nuestra conciencia de cuáles son exactamente las cosas que podría necesitar confesar. Sé que una de las cosas con las que luché al principio cuando comenzaba a tratar de llegar al sacramento de la Reconciliación con más frecuencia fue, bueno, ¿qué confieso? No he cometido ningún pecado mortal que yo sepa, entonces, ¿qué es lo que debo confesar?

El venerable arzobispo, Fulton Sheen, nos da una hermosa visión de cómo debemos mirar nuestras vidas con respecto al pecado. Él dice:

"Nadie que piense que es solo el incumplimiento de una ley realmente comprende el mal del pecado. Cuando tenemos el Espíritu de Cristo, entendemos que el pecado está haciendo daño a alguien que amamos... Nada más que el Espíritu Santo realmente puede convencernos del pecado... nuestra conciencia está sofocada por el mal repetido. Racionalizamos nuestras malas acciones. La opinión pública a veces incluso aprueba el pecado". [37]

Entonces, en un mundo que a menudo aprueba nuestro pecado, e incluso adormece nuestra conciencia de ese pecado, ¿cómo podemos desarrollar la conciencia que necesitamos para que el Espíritu Santo pueda ayudarnos a identificar esos momentos en los que dañamos intencionalmente o no ¿A quién decimos amar por encima de todas las cosas?

El Examen Diario

Integrado en un hábito de oración y meditación diaria, la práctica de un Examen diario puede ser una herramienta hermosa. Nos ayuda a permitir que el Espíritu Santo nos guíe y transforme nuestra conciencia en una que sea sensible sobre cómo y cuándo dañamos a Dios y a los demás.

El Examen es una herramienta que nos dio San Ignacio de Loyola. San Ignacio fue el fundador de la Compañía de Jesús, los jesuitas, y alentó a sus hermanos sacerdotes jesuitas a realizar un Examen al menos una vez al día. Así como los ayudó, también puede ayudarnos a nosotros.

El Examen está diseñado para ser *breve* y nos pide que nos centremos primero en las bendiciones de Dios. Esto comienza con lo que escuchamos en algunos círculos hoy como "una actitud de gratitud". A partir de ahí, luego tratamos de tratar de ver el movimiento del Espíritu Santo en medio de los eventos, las personas y las actividades de nuestro día, e identificamos los momentos en los que hemos fallado en amar y servir a Dios como Él nos ha llamado. Una vez que vemos cómo hemos fallado, pedimos el perdón de Dios y luego pedimos que Su gracia comience nuevamente. A través de la práctica del Examen, gradualmente crecemos en nuestra conciencia y en nuestra capacidad para

identificar nuestros pecados. Finalmente, también nos ayuda a comenzar a identificar cualquiera que sea nuestro pecado predominante.

¿Qué es un pecado predominante? Simplemente, un pecado predominante es el pecado que tendemos a confesar siempre. Probablemente sabes de lo que estoy hablando. Es aquel que cuando llegamos a confesarnos, es el pecado que parecemos estar confesando, *nuevamente*.

Para mí, mis pecados predominantes son el orgullo y la ira. He luchado continuamente con ellos a lo largo de mi vida, y aunque he mejorado (y definitivamente puedo ver algo de crecimiento en estas áreas de mi vida), todavía lucho. Puede ser extremadamente frustrante y desalentador enfrentarse una y otra vez con lo que parece ser el mismo pecado, especialmente si nos esforzamos por profundizar nuestras vidas interiores y acudir con más frecuencia al sacramento de la Reconciliación.

Pero esa es exactamente *la razón* por la que necesitamos ir con más frecuencia al sacramento de la Reconciliación.

Porque como dije antes, la confesión no se trata solo del hecho de que somos perdonados, también es la oportunidad de ser sanados de nuestras heridas. Esas heridas que tendemos a ver como debilidades, pero que en realidad pueden convertirse en lugares de fortaleza que nuestro Señor puede superar, si lo dejamos. Y si frecuentamos el sacramento de la reconciliación.

Todo viene junto

De esta manera, Jesús puede hacernos vasos de Su gracia, amor y misericordia para todas las personas que nos encuentran en medio de nuestra vida diaria. Porque entonces la gente no solo se encontrará con nosotros, sino que también se encontrará con Jesús, especialmente si estamos siendo llenos con frecuencia de sus gracias en los sacramentos de la Sagrada Eucaristía y la Reconciliación.

Es solo entonces que somos capaces de ser su presencia de amor y misericordia para los demás. Y de esto se trata la vida de gracia. Donde nos permitimos ser llenos de la gracia de Dios, y

luego salimos al mundo como signos irrepetibles de su amor y misericordia.

"Como un hombre debe nacer antes de que pueda comenzar a llevar su vida física, debe nacer para llevar una Vida Divina. Ese nacimiento ocurre en el Sacramento del Bautismo. Para sobrevivir, debe ser alimentado por la Vida Divina; eso es hecho en el sacramento de la Sagrada Eucaristía".[38]

No hay otra forma auténtica de luchar por la perfección.

"Todo en el orden religioso - sacramentos, devociones, enseñanza, escritura, disciplina moral, predicación, etc. - está destinado a llevarnos a este estado más profundo del ser, a esta Conexión Divina. Jesús lo llama "permanecer" (Jn 15: 4). El latín para esto es maneo, que significa "permanecer" o "quedarse" o "soportar" (o como el Semper Fi del Cuerpo de Marines). Esta conexión divina, esta conformidad con el amor, esta participación en la vida divina de Dios es el poder mismo del Espíritu Santo y se conoce como estar en un estado de gracia".[39]

Es por eso que la recepción frecuente de la Sagrada Eucaristía y la Reconciliación son instrumentos tan fenomenalmente efectivos para lograr la santidad. Porque simplemente NO es posible recibir con frecuencia a nuestro Señor: Cuerpo, Sangre, Alma y Divinidad, y permanecer igual.

Así que deje de lado esas cosas que cierran su corazón, mente y alma para recibir las gracias que necesita para ser sostenido en la búsqueda de la santidad. Porque vivir la vida de la gracia se trata de cómo permitimos que la gracia de Dios nos transforme en los santos que Él nos creó para ser.

Porque a través, con y en Su gracia todas las cosas SON posibles.

DIGA SÍ a las gracias de Dios que fluyen en su vida sin parar.

Dele vuelta a esta página. Es hora de dar el siguiente paso en el viaje hacia la santidad.

CAPÍTULO 12

PASO TRES: CRECER DIARIAMENTE EN VIRTUD

"Piensa bien. Habla bien. Haz el bien. Estas tres cosas, por la misericordia de Dios, harán que un hombre vaya al Cielo."

— San Camilo

Si bien podemos pasar tiempo con Dios cada día en oración y esforzarnos por recibir sus gracias con frecuencia, aún debemos hacer nuestra parte para sentar las bases sobre las cuales podamos construir una vida dirigida hacia la búsqueda de la santidad. De esto se trata el tercer paso: se trata del crecimiento diario en la virtud.

Entonces, ¿qué es exactamente la virtud? Simplemente, la virtud es la disposición habitual de hacer el bien con facilidad, rapidez y alegría. Cuando alguien es virtuoso, no tiene que pensarlo, simplemente lo hace. Y es por eso que esta es una actividad que debe practicarse a diario. Para que seamos capaces de hacer el bien de manera fácil, rápida y alegre.

Es imposible enfatizar lo suficiente lo importante que es intentar cada día crecer en virtud como nuestro Señor nos llama a hacerlo. Pero muchas veces dudamos en hacer esto porque

creemos que el crecimiento diario en la virtud es algo teórico que está sucediendo "allá afuera", en lugar de algo que es intrínsecamente una parte de cada evento que ocurre en nuestras vidas.

El crecimiento diario de la virtud es, en esencia, nuestra capacidad de reconocer y ver que Dios está trabajando en, a través y con todo, todas las personas, cosas y eventos de nuestra vida, para ayudarnos a ser más como Él.

La Madre Angélica, fallecida fundadora de la comunidad de las Clarisas de la Adoración Perpetua en Irondale, Alabama, pero que es más conocida como la fundadora de Eternal Word Television Network (EWTN), dijo una vez: *"Toda la vida es una escuela de santidad. Todo lo que te sucede, el mal tiempo en una uña encarnada, es una oportunidad para que seamos como Jesús"*.

Si tenemos esto en mente, nos damos cuenta de que crecer en virtud cada día no es algo etéreo "allá afuera", sino que es una parte normal y natural de nuestras vidas. Esta realidad es evidente por cómo la Iglesia comienza a determinar si alguien debe ser declarado santo. El proceso de canonización comienza examinando si esa persona vivió una vida de virtud heroica. En otras palabras, si vivieron vidas santas. Entonces, la virtud vivida *es* santidad.

Pero como cualquier cosa en la vida, la virtud tiene que ser practicada. No solo somos virtuosos. Tenemos que trabajar en eso. Es por eso que muchas prácticas y devociones para ayudarnos a crecer en virtud se han desarrollado a lo largo de los siglos. Todos estos métodos se centran en ayudarnos a invitar a Dios a lo que sea que estemos haciendo a lo largo del día, independientemente de nuestro estado de vida, ocupación o ubicación.

Ahora, ninguna de estas prácticas o devociones se trata de otra "cosa que hacer". Más bien, estas devociones se tratan de proporcionar oportunidades para que nos demos cuenta de la presencia de Dios, y luego para permitirle intencionalmente estar más presente en cada aspecto de nuestras vidas, hasta cada pensamiento, cada palabra y cada acción.

Esta es la razón principal por la cual el primer paso que debemos tomar en el camino hacia la santidad es la oración y la meditación diarias. Porque es solo en medio de sumergirnos en conversaciones con la Palabra Viviente, que podemos ser transformados como San Pablo escribe en Romanos 12: 2, *"Y no se conforme con este mundo, sino que sea transformado por la renovación de su recuerda que puedes probar cuál es la voluntad de Dios, lo que es bueno, aceptable y perfecto".*

A medida que nuestros pensamientos se transforman, también lo serán nuestras palabras y acciones. Realmente es justo como Jesús nos dice en Marcos 7:15: *"No es lo que entra en un hombre lo que lo contamina; pero qué cosas salen de un hombre que lo contamina".*

Luego, a medida que nos transformamos lentamente, estamos en mejores condiciones para luchar contra nuestras tendencias desordenadas y nuestra pecaminosidad. Nos alineamos cada vez más correctamente y señalamos hacia "lo que es bueno, aceptable y perfecto". Nos convertimos en lo que se conoce como "bien ordenado".

Cuando la gente me pregunta qué es ser "correcto", me encanta usar una analogía de un buen amigo mío, John Granger. Es un "muñeco de nieve al revés".

Simplemente piense en un muñeco de nieve. Tienes la bola de nieve más grande en la parte inferior, una bola de nieve mediana en el medio y una bola de nieve más pequeña en la parte superior. Todo está en proporción y equilibrado, por lo que el muñeco de nieve se pone de pie sin problemas.

Ahora, en el mundo clásico, se pensaba que una persona estaba compuesta de tres partes: cuerpo, mente y alma. Ahora, correlacione cada parte de la persona clásica con una bola del muñeco de nieve: el Cuerpo es la bola de nieve grande en la parte inferior, la Mente es la bola de nieve mediana en el medio y el Alma es la bola de nieve pequeña en la parte superior. Una persona "bien ordenada" es aquella en la que la mente, o la voluntad,

dirige el cuerpo, y luego el alma, o el corazón de la persona, dirige la mente y el cuerpo hacia una meta o propósito superior.

Ahora, piense en nuestro mundo hoy. Casi todo se trata de las necesidades corporales primero. Lo que se siente bien y sabe bien tiene prioridad sobre cualquier otra cosa. A veces escuchará sobre el uso de "mente sobre la materia" o "fuerza de voluntad" para hacer que nuestros cuerpos actúen como lo deseamos, al imponer programas de entrenamiento o autodisciplina para lograr un "cuerpo de playa" o perder peso no deseado, o comer alimentos más saludables para evitar enfermedades o dolencias. O tal vez deseamos un trabajo en particular, o queremos un ascenso, por lo que estamos dispuestos a sacrificar el sueño y otras actividades recreativas para recibir la capacitación o tomar los cursos necesarios para obtener un título en particular y así poder solicitar un trabajo diferente.

¿Pero para que alguien se esfuerce por un propósito mayor fuera de las cosas que aquellos asociados con el Cuerpo o la Mente? Extremadamente raro.

Entonces, si toma esto y lo aplica a la analogía del muñeco de nieve, verá que en nuestro mundo de hoy, la pequeña bola de nieve del Alma está en la parte inferior, la bola de nieve central de la Mente está en el medio y la bola de nieve grande del cuerpo está en la parte superior. Esto nos hace "muñecos de nieve al revés".

Y como resultado de ser "muñecos de nieve al revés", pocos de nosotros estamos "bien ordenados" en nuestras vidas espirituales porque estamos siendo distraídos por todos los bienes menores asociados con nuestros cuerpos y mentes.

Llegar a ser "correcto" es la gran lucha y el objetivo de la vida espiritual. Donde luchamos y nos esforzamos al máximo de nuestras habilidades junto con la gracia de Dios, para transformar cada pensamiento, palabra y acción para reflejar lo que es bueno, aceptable y perfecto.

Cuando nos volvemos completamente correctos, al poner las primeras cosas primero en nuestra vida, luego cada pensamiento,

palabra y acción demuestra ser lo que es bueno, aceptable y perfecto, y nos hemos convertido en "perfectos como nuestro Padre Celestial es perfecto". Viviremos virtuosamente, eligiendo hacer lo que es bueno fácilmente, con prontitud y con alegría.

Habremos sido transformados en santos.

Para reiterar, esta es la razón por la cual el primer paso hacia la santidad es practicar la oración y la meditación diarias. La conversación con Dios debe estar sucediendo, para permitir que comience la transformación. Luego, a través del segundo paso, viviendo la vida de la gracia y frecuentando los sacramentos, recibimos la ayuda de Dios en la lucha, junto con la gracia de perseverar en el viaje.

Pero nuestros esfuerzos son necesarios en esta batalla.

Dios puede hacer lo que quiera, por lo que, si desea que seamos santos, puede hacerlo, con o sin nuestra ayuda. Pero no es así como Dios generalmente trabaja. Dios desea que lo *elijamos*.

Pero no solo eso. Dios también desea que DIGAMOS SÍ y que lo ayudemos a lograr no solo la santificación de nosotros mismos, sino también a todos y a todo en el mundo.

Dios hace esto haciendo posible que cada palabra y acción *tenga significado*.

En su infinito amor y gracia, Dios ha creado cada una de sus creaciones, pero particularmente aquellas que han sido bautizadas en el nombre del Padre, el Hijo y el Espíritu Santo, para convertirse en Sus hijos e hijas adoptivos. Y son estos hijos e hijas quienes tienen la oportunidad de ayudar a santificar el mundo en el que viven a través de sus pensamientos, palabras y acciones.

Pero solo si esos pensamientos, palabras y acciones se ofrecen a través de, y en unión con Él.

Así es como nuestras vidas tienen un propósito y un significado. No hay accidentes en cuanto a quiénes somos, qué somos o dónde estamos. Dios nos ha hecho únicamente para ser y hacer exactamente lo que Él nos creó para ser, exactamente donde estamos, para hacer exactamente lo que solo nosotros podemos hacer.

¿Por qué? Entonces, para ayudar a santificar y "hacer santo", todo lo que nos rodea a través de nuestros pensamientos, palabras y acciones.

Pero tenemos que *elegirlo*.

Hay una relación entre nuestra oración diaria, la vida de gracia y nuestro crecimiento diario en virtud. Porque cuando pasamos tiempo conversando con Dios y le permitimos transformar nuestras mentes y corazones, entonces Sus sacramentos nos darán la gracia y la dirección que necesitamos para que podamos crecer en virtud *de la manera particular que Dios nos pide que hagamos en nuestra vida en ese momento en particular.*

Este NO es un programa de mejora de autoayuda. No, este es Dios, nuestro amoroso Creador y Padre, quien nos invita a entrar en la obra de nuestra propia redención. No como esclavos, sino como *amigos* junto a Él.

Y a medida que continuamos creciendo en nuestra relación con Él mientras continuamos recibiendo Sus gracias, lo que sucede es que aumentamos nuestra capacidad de percibir Su Mano en el trabajo en todas las cosas, y perseverar en nuestra vida diaria, sea lo que sea que venga, sea un mal clima o una uña encarnada.

Y esto nos permite ayudar a pelear la buena batalla. La buena lucha para ser ordenados y vencer el pecado con la ayuda de Dios, y convertirnos en lo que Dios originalmente nos creó para ser. Así es como el crecimiento diario en la virtud se convierte en una pieza vital para progresar en la vida espiritual.

Porque cuando peleamos la buena batalla y luchamos para vencer el pecado en nuestras vidas con la ayuda de Dios, nos convertimos en un poco más de lo que Dios nos creó para ser. Comenzamos o continuamos perfeccionando las virtudes en nuestra vida.

¿Cómo es eso? Nos volvemos un poco más pacientes. Nos volvemos un poco más amables. Nos volvemos un poco más pacíficos y menos ansiosos a medida que respondemos a los

eventos que ocurren en nuestra vida. Estamos llenos de alegría, incluso cuando suceden cosas difíciles y desafiantes.

Y la gente comienza a ver eso. Esa es la diferencia. Es una transformación lenta y gradual de nuestros pensamientos, palabras y acciones que se vuelven correctas al dirigirnos solo hacia lo que es bueno, verdadero y bello. Esta transformación eventualmente se convierte en virtud perfeccionada, o "virtud heroica", cuando se ve expresada en las vidas y ejemplos de los santos.

La virtud heroica es una señal clara de que Dios está presente y trabajando en la vida de una persona, particularmente cuando responde rápidamente a los desafíos y situaciones en sus vidas con un amor o misericordia o bondad que no puede explicarse racionalmente, excepto que debe ser la gracia de Dios.

Esto es lo que debemos esforzarnos por cada día.

DIGA SÍ a crecer diariamente en virtud.

Ahora pase la página para seguir avanzando, paso a paso y día a día.

Capítulo 13

PASO A PASO, DÍA A DÍA

Hemos dicho que sí a crecer diariamente en virtud, pero ¿cómo podríamos hacerlo?

Hay una gran cantidad de actividades dentro de la Tradición de la Iglesia que pueden ayudar en nuestra búsqueda. Cosas como: una ofrenda matutina; pidiendo la ayuda de nuestro Ángel Guardián; haciendo un "minuto heroico", donde al despertar, inmediatamente te levantas de la cama y comienzas tu día; rezando el Ángelus; ayunar, ofrecer sacrificios de todo lo que no nos gusta, no elegimos, no podemos cambiar o no podemos entender.

Honestamente, hay tantas maneras de crecer en nuestra conciencia de la presencia de Dios y cómo invitarlo a participar activamente en nuestras vidas como personas en el mundo.

Esto no es para evitar responder la pregunta de cómo uno puede crecer diariamente en virtud. Más bien, es para enfatizar el punto de que hay una *multitud* de prácticas, métodos y actividades que uno puede realizar para ayudar a lograr el crecimiento de la virtud en la vida de uno, por lo tanto, no hay *una* manera de hacerlo.

¿Que quiero decir? Simplemente, lo que funciona para su vida y los hábitos que necesita cultivar para crecer en virtud serán diferentes de lo que serán la vida y los hábitos de otra persona para crecer en virtud.

Entonces, ¿eso significa que tenemos que tropezar en la oscuridad hasta que encontremos los mejores que funcionen para nosotros?

De ningún modo. La vida de los santos es nuestro mayor recurso para ayudar a determinar qué prácticas son más efectivas. En los últimos dos milenios, han surgido algunos puntos en común, y es evidente que hay algunas prácticas que deberían ser parte del viaje de *todos* hacia la santidad.

Pero para usar en este paso de crecimiento diario en virtud, centrémonos en cuatro: resolución diaria, lectura espiritual, obras de misericordia y el nombre de Jesús.

RESOLUCIÓN DIARIA

La clave para crecer y seguir creciendo en virtud es intentar *hacer algo* todos los días. No tiene que ser un logro importante. Más bien, una resolución diaria debería ser algo pequeño. Algo concreto. Algo *factible*

Muy a menudo, la pregunta que la gente me hará es: "¿Cómo se me ocurre una resolución?"

Primero, señalo en broma que no se trata de cómo llegar a una resolución, sino de cómo discernir con mayor precisión lo que *Dios* quiere que hagamos hoy. Y esto nos lleva de vuelta a nuestro primer paso: la práctica de la oración diaria y la meditación.

¿Qué compartió Dios contigo durante tu conversación con Él ese día? ¿Qué mensaje de Su Palabra Viviente en las Escrituras te habló o conmovió tu corazón? ¿O qué cosa en particular le señaló Dios acerca de una actitud, comportamiento o hábito en particular que debería estar atento a ajustar? Todos estos se convierten en fuentes para una resolución diaria.

Por ejemplo, de las Escrituras, Jesús nos dice que "... a menos que un grano de trigo caiga al suelo y muera, solo queda un grano de trigo; pero si muere, produce mucha fruta. Quien ama su vida la pierde, y quien odia su vida en este mundo la preservará para la vida eterna"[40]. A partir de esta Escritura, mi reflexión y posterior

conversación con mi Señor podrían llevarme a reconocer cómo me aferro a la vida tal como la imagino, en lugar de aceptar la vida que tengo delante. Tal vez una mayor conversación y reflexión revele que me falta gratitud por las muchas bendiciones que Dios me ha dado, y que debería trabajar para cultivar una mayor actitud de gratitud, por lo que una buena resolución diaria para mí ese día podría ser buscar bendiciones en mi vida a lo largo del día, y cada vez que reconozco uno, para detenerme intencionalmente y decir "Gracias, Señor".

Entonces, durante el día, me esfuerzo por implementar esa resolución. Al final del día, puedo usar un Examen diario para ver cómo respondí, o no, al responder a la gracia de Dios ese día. Hago esto enfocándome en lo bien (o mal) que hice para implementar mi resolución para ese día.

Algunos días, cuando miro hacia atrás, me va muy bien respondiendo a la gracia de Dios e implementando mi resolución diaria. Sin embargo, ¡otros días, soy malísima en eso! Jajaja

Pero la mayoría de las veces, lo hago bien. Me parece que respondo algunas veces a la gracia de Dios, y en otras ocasiones, no lo hago. Esto puede ser desalentador, especialmente si estamos tratando de cambiar un hábito, como abstenerme de tener la última palabra en una conversación, y veo que durante el transcurso del día que solo me abstuve de este hábito en dos de las 20 conversaciones que tuve, pero en la vida de crecimiento en la virtud, no puedo enfatizar lo importante que es tratar de ser un tipo de persona medio lleno. Esto se debe a que estamos buscando *progreso*. (Este es un proceso, no un programa, ¡recuerda!)

Debemos centrarnos en el hecho de que pudimos hacer *algo* un poco mejor. Nos abstuvimos de una acción poco caritativa. O nos detuvimos antes de hablar con criterio sobre el desempeño de alguien en el trabajo. O pensamos en una persona que nos lastima con misericordia. Estos parecen ser sucesos pequeños e insignificantes, pero en la vida espiritual, *todo importa*.

Porque la gracia de Dios puede tomar incluso las cosas más pequeñas y hacerlas grandiosas. Solo tenemos que hacer lo que

podamos, y Dios hará el resto. San Francisco de Sales ilumina brillantemente el proceso de implementación de resoluciones diarias: *"… ¿qué puedes hacer para fortalecer tus resoluciones y hacer que tengan éxito? No hay mejores medios que ponerlos en práctica".* [41]

Entonces, independientemente de lo que pueda considerar el "éxito" de sus resoluciones diarias, si simplemente las pone en práctica, crecerá en virtud.

LECTURA ESPIRITUAL

En nuestro mundo de videos y medios dominados por imágenes, la idea de leer puede parecer un poco "pasada de moda", pero el poder de la palabra escrita no puede ser sobrestimado.

En el mundo de los negocios y el liderazgo, es un hecho que, si una persona quiere convertirse en una persona de alto rendimiento y tener éxito, debe leer. Y no estoy hablando del libro ocasional, sino de un hábito en el que una persona lee constantemente.

Estudios recientes muestran que el 85% de las personas exitosas leen dos o más libros de superación personal o educativos por mes, por lo que la lección aquí es que, si queremos tener éxito en la vida espiritual, también debemos estar leyendo. [42]

Cuando leemos, nos estamos involucrando activamente en el proceso. No podemos "sentarnos" y ver cómo se presentan las ideas. Tenemos que encontrarnos activamente con ellos y comprometernos con ellos, y luego esas mismas ideas nos acompañan a medida que luchamos con lo que pensamos sobre ellos hasta que determinamos si vamos a aceptar o dejar de lado lo que se ha propuesto, y luego decidir cómo va a impactar nuestros pensamientos, palabras o acciones. El resultado final es que la lectura, especialmente la lectura espiritual, es fundamentalmente *transformadora*. (¿Debería sorprendernos esto teniendo en cuenta el hecho de que nuestro Señor es el Logos? ¿La Palabra Viviente descendió del Cielo? Pero estoy divagando)

Entonces, si deberíamos estar leyendo, ¿qué deberíamos leer? En un mundo en el que se publican más de un millón de libros al año, encontrar un libro para leer no es demasiado difícil, pero encontrar libros que puedan servir como lectura espiritual buena, profunda, rica y fiel puede serlo, por lo que necesitamos ser un poco juicioso en nuestras elecciones.

El mejor lugar para comenzar es comenzar leyendo algo que amas, o crees que amarás, y luego seguir adelante. La lista de buenos autores católicos está creciendo exponencialmente día a día, así que visite editoriales como Ignatius Press, Augustine Institute, Dynamic Catholic, Ascension Press, St Mary's Press y Sophia Press, por nombrar solo algunos. O lea los "clásicos". *An Introduction to the Devout Life*, *The Interior Castle* de Santa Teresa de Ávila o *Confessions* de San Agustín son excelentes (aunque tengo una inclinación personal por la Ciudad de Dios de Agustín).

O otra forma de abordar el proceso es considerar la pregunta: "¿Cómo deseamos ser transformados?" ¿Deseamos ser más misericordiosos? Luego, lea el libro de Santa Faustina Kowalska, *Diary of Divine Mercy*. ¿Deseamos desarrollar una devoción a María? Entonces echa un vistazo a *True Devotion to Mary* de San Luis de Montfort. ¿O qué tal crecer en confianza? Luego lea *Abandonment to Divine Providence* de Jean-Pierre De Caussade. Sea lo que sea, hay una persona, pero la mayoría de las veces, un santo, que ya ha escrito sobre eso y puede ayudarlo en su viaje.

Pero el punto final que debemos recordar cuando buscamos una buena lectura espiritual es tener en cuenta que un libro realmente bueno también sirve como guía, y no hay mejores guías para la vida espiritual que los santos. Entonces, lea sobre sus vidas. Lea sobre sus luchas y desafíos. Sus éxitos y alegrías. Sus tentaciones y fracasos. Deje que aquellos que han recorrido el camino de la santidad antes de ayudarlo lo guíen hasta el cielo.

Ahora, una vez que tenga un libro, tiene que leerlo. Un libro no le sirve de nada en su estante o en su mesita de noche. Necesita abrirlo y leerlo. Cada día si es posible.

Pero aquí es donde la lectura espiritual difiere *enormemente* de otros tipos de lectura. La lectura espiritual debe hacerse por un período de tiempo establecido durante un día en lugar de tratar de leer un número determinado de páginas (o incluso párrafos). Esto es para permitirnos leer tan rápido (o tan lentamente) como el Espíritu Santo lo desee para nosotros.

Esto significa que, mientras leemos, deberíamos hacer una pausa y reflexionar mientras las ideas nos "golpean". De esta manera, debemos reflejar nuestro tiempo diario de oración y meditación, donde nos detenemos a reflexionar antes de continuar. Nuestra lectura espiritual no necesariamente nos lleva a relacionarnos, a tener una conversación profunda con Dios, pero podría serlo. Pero ese no es el objetivo principal de la lectura espiritual.

Aunque esperamos leer con la ayuda del Espíritu Santo, especialmente para poder tener "ojos que vean y oídos que escuchen", el objetivo durante la lectura espiritual es proporcionar alimentos buenos, verdaderos y hermosos para nuestras mentes. A través de la lectura espiritual, buscamos intencionalmente transformar nuestras mentes, y eso nos ayudará a transformar nuestros pensamientos, palabras y acciones. Es por eso y cómo la lectura espiritual es un medio tan efectivo para crecer en virtud en nuestra vida diaria.

Obras de Misericordia

Las obras de misericordia son la forma más fácil para nosotros de crecer diariamente en virtud. Esto se debe a que cada vez que hacemos un trabajo de misericordia, estamos pensando o haciendo el bien de los demás. Y la mayoría de las veces, estamos pensando o haciendo por amor a los demás, por lo que las obras de misericordia nos hacen más amorosos; más como Cristo

La Iglesia Católica tiene dos categorías de misericordia: corporal y espiritual. Los trabajos corporales: alimentar a los hambrientos, dar de beber a los sedientos, vestir a los desnudos,

refugiar a las personas sin hogar, visitar a los encarcelados, cuidar a los enfermos y enterrar a los muertos: todos los trabajos corporales se centran en las necesidades físicas de una persona. Las obras espirituales: instruir al ignorante, aconsejar al dudoso, amonestar al pecador, consolar al afligido, soportar los errores con paciencia, perdonar las ofensas o heridas, y orar por los vivos y los muertos, todos pertenecen a la vida espiritual de una persona.

Es fácil ver cómo realizar cualquiera de las obras de misericordia puede generar un aumento de la virtud, y Santa Faustina ilustra cómo la misericordia se puede expresar en nuestras palabras, acciones y pensamientos:

"Porque hay tres formas de realizar un acto de misericordia: la palabra misericordiosa, perdonando y consolando; en segundo lugar, si no puedes ofrecer una palabra, reza, eso también es misericordia; y tercero, hechos de misericordia".

Santa Faustina es la santa de la Divina Misericordia, y su diario completo es un recuento de las visitas y conversaciones posteriores que Jesús tuvo con ella durante su vida sobre Su Divina Misericordia por las almas. Sin embargo, este extracto nos da una visión sucinta de por qué la Iglesia Católica ha enfatizado la necesidad de que los cristianos se esfuercen por realizar obras de misericordia en medio de su vida diaria. La misericordia es una expresión del amor de Dios, por lo que hacer, decir o rezar cualquier acto de misericordia traerá el amor de Dios a los demás, y esa es la esencia de la evangelización.

Pero, ¿cómo puedo vivir misericordia en mi vida diaria cuando no tengo tiempo para alimentar al hambriento o salir y consolar a alguien que está triste?

"No pierdas ni una sola oportunidad de hacer un pequeño sacrificio, aquí con una mirada sonriente, allí con una palabra amable; siempre haciendo lo más mínimo y todo por amor".

Este consejo es de Santa Teresa de Lisieux, también llamada la "Pequeña Flor". Ella nos da la clave no solo para vivir una vida de misericordia y amor, sino también para crecer diariamente en

virtud. El "Pequeño Camino" de Santa Teresa nos guía sobre el crecimiento en la virtud al decirnos que hagamos uso de todo, la más pequeña de las acciones, palabras y pensamientos, y que lo hagamos todo, con y por amor.

Al igual que practicar una resolución diaria y hacer lecturas espirituales constantes y continuas, realizar obras de misericordia puede ayudarnos a crecer en virtud y asegurar la transformación gradual de nuestras mentes, corazones y almas hasta que cada uno de nosotros se convierta en una luz brillante del amor y la misericordia de Dios en el mundo.

El nombre de Jesús

La idea de usar el nombre de Jesús para crecer en virtud fue algo que me presentaron recientemente, pero he descubierto que es especialmente eficaz con mis hábitos más perniciosos y tercos. (¡¿Debería sorprenderme considerando el poder del nombre de Jesús?!)

De todos modos, la práctica es nombrar cualquier espíritu de tentación que enfrente durante su día, como soledad, ira, amargura, resentimiento, falta de perdón, lujuria, codicia, orgullo, pereza, tristeza, envidia, intemperancia, baja autoestima, duda, desesperación, etc., y luego confrontarlo pidiéndole a Jesús que le dé la virtud o la gracia: espíritu de paciencia, bondad, alegría, confianza, coraje, perseverancia, generosidad, pureza, humildad, templanza, filiación divina o filiación, fe, esperanza, amor, etc., que combate la tentación que está enfrentando.

Entonces, se vería así:

ESPÍRITU DE (nombre de la tentación), EN EL NOMBRE DE JESÚS, RENUNCIO Y TE RECHAZO.

ESPÍRITU DE (nombre de la virtud opuesta), EN EL NOMBRE DE JESÚS, ENTRA EN MI CORAZÓN.

PERSEVERAR

Al concluir nuestra discusión sobre el tercer paso hacia la santidad, solo una breve palabra sobre la perseverancia. Porque el crecimiento diario en la virtud se trata casi por completo de perseverancia. Sí, se trata de ofrecer nuestros mejores esfuerzos, pero se trata más de ofrecer nuestros mejores esfuerzos de manera constante y continua. Santa Teresa de Ávila aborda esto bien:

"... esforcémonos por progresar constantemente: deberíamos sentirnos muy alarmados si no nos encontramos avanzando, porque sin duda el maligno debe estar planeando herirnos de alguna manera; es imposible para un alma que ha llegado a este estado no ir más lejos, porque el amor nunca está inactivo. Por lo tanto, es una muy mala señal cuando uno se detiene en la virtud". [43]

Por lo tanto, reconocer que nunca debemos detenernos en el crecimiento de la virtud es extremadamente importante.

La paciencia es otro aspecto de la perseverancia. San Francisco de Sales nos dice:

"Tenga paciencia con todas las cosas, pero principalmente tenga paciencia consigo mismo. No pierda el coraje al considerar sus propias imperfecciones, sino que de inmediato procure remediarlas, comience la tarea de nuevo todos los días".

Debemos ser pacientes en este viaje. Es un maratón, no un sprint, por lo que sea paciente y perseverante.

Por último, debemos recordar que es una batalla. Thomas a 'Kempis escribe:

"Un hombre debe atravesar un largo y gran conflicto en sí mismo antes de que pueda aprender a superarse por completo y atraer todo su afecto hacia Dios. Cuando un hombre se para sobre sí mismo, es fácilmente apartado de las comodidades humanas. Pero un verdadero amante de Cristo, y un diligente perseguidor de la virtud, no busca comodidades, ni busca dulzuras tan sensibles, sino que está dispuesto a soportar pruebas y trabajos forzados para Cristo". [44]

Y elegimos hacer esto al comienzo de cada día. Tenemos que confiar en Dios y comenzar una y otra vez. Todos los días, como si no se hubiera hecho nada, recordamos que es solo a través de

Su poder y gracia que podemos hacer algo de esto, pero que Él nos dará las gracias que necesitamos para hacer exactamente lo que Él desea para nosotros: ser santos

Hacer y esforzarse por ser fiel a una resolución diaria. Haga una lectura espiritual que fortalezca su mente y su corazón para la batalla contra nuestra propia naturaleza desordenada y contra el Maligno. Haga obras de misericordia de acuerdo con su vocación personal, su estado de vida y los impulsos del Espíritu Santo en su metro cuadrado móvil. Use el poder del nombre de Jesús para conquistar todas las tentaciones.

DIGA SÍ para crecer diariamente en virtud. Paso a paso y día a día.

Ahora, pase la página y abandónese a la voluntad de Dios.

CAPÍTULO 14

PASO CUATRO: ABANDONARNOS A LA VOLUNTAD DE DIOS

"La vida se llena de alegría y paz como resultado de nuestro completo abandono a la Voluntad de Dios, para ser probada diariamente"

— El P. Francisco Fernández[45]

Ahora dirigimos nuestra atención a completar los cimientos necesarios para nuestro viaje espiritual. Esto se hace enfocándose en el paso cuatro: abandonándonos a la voluntad de Dios.

La práctica de abandonarnos a la voluntad de Dios es donde realmente integramos los primeros tres pasos: oración diaria y meditación, frecuentar los sacramentos y crecer diariamente en virtud; porque es en este cuarto paso que nos volvemos más obedientes y desapegados de cómo deseamos que progresen nuestras vidas, y cada vez más abiertos a cómo *Dios* desea que progresen nuestras vidas.

Hacemos esto simplemente aceptando las circunstancias ordinarias y las experiencias diarias de nuestra vida como la mano de Dios moviendo y moldeando nuestras vidas. No es que cuando

sucede algo malo, pensamos que Dios nos está castigando, sino al ver que incluso en esas circunstancias y experiencias difíciles y dolorosas, Dios todavía está trabajando. Creyendo que Él realmente usará todas las cosas para "el bien de los que lo aman".[46]

Y es por eso que, si realmente deseamos crecer en la vida espiritual, *debemos* comenzar con la oración y la meditación diarias. Porque es allí, durante nuestro tiempo a solas con el Creador del universo que nos ama sin medida, que crecemos en nuestro amor por Él y somos alentados e inspirados para creer verdaderamente en Sus promesas.

Y a medida que continuamos infundidos con las gracias de amor, fe y esperanza de Dios, nuestros corazones se vuelven más receptivos *a todas* las gracias que Él desea darnos a través de Sus sacramentos. Y luego, con su amor y gracia, tenemos la fuerza y el coraje para intentar tratar de crecer en virtud mientras caminamos junto a Él cada día.

Si nos abandonamos a la voluntad de Dios, si aceptamos poco a poco sin quejarnos de las circunstancias y experiencias ordinarias de nuestra vida diaria, lo que sucede es que podemos morir a nosotros mismos, y luego podemos morir a nosotros mismos. poco a poco, también.

A medida que nos confiamos cada vez más a Dios, comenzamos a encarnar lo que San Juan Bautista habló cuando dijo: *"Él debe aumentar, y yo debo disminuir"*,[47] y también cuando San Pablo, quien escribió en su carta a los Gálatas, *"Ya no soy yo quien vive, sino Cristo quien vive en mí"*.[48]

¡Este es el objetivo de la vida cristiana! Para llegar a ser como Aquel que nos ama. Esto es santidad.

Es realmente así de simple.

Entonces, ¿por qué no hacemos esto? Bueno, como todas las cosas en la vida, no es una respuesta en blanco y negro, sino un montón de gris.

Debido a que la realidad es que para que podamos entrar efectivamente a vivir este cuarto paso en nuestra vida diaria, necesitaremos luchar y llegar a un acuerdo con algunas de las

más grandes cuestiones filosóficas y teológicas de la existencia humana, principalmente, la realidad del mal y el sufrimiento humano y la bondad y la providencia de Dios.

Porque uno de los mayores desafíos para la vida espiritual es que el mundo le propone todo tipo de cosas que *parecen* ser razones muy lógicas con respecto a por qué ni siquiera deberíamos comenzar a intentar este viaje, y esa es la existencia del mal y Sufrimiento humano.

Las preguntas normalmente son algo así como: "¿Cómo puede Dios ser realmente bueno si niños inocentes sufren y mueren de cáncer?" o "El hermano pequeño de mi amigo murió en un accidente automovilístico, ¿cómo puede ser parte de un plan amoroso de Dios?" o "Si Dios realmente amó al mundo, ¿por qué hay tantas guerras, o tanto dolor y sufrimiento?"

A primera vista, parecen objeciones lógicas y racionales a la creencia en la bondad y la providencia de Dios. Pero Dios es todo bueno e infinito. Y el Catecismo de la Iglesia Católica nos dice que Dios no es, de ninguna manera, directa o indirectamente, la causa del mal. Más bien, el mal fue desatado por el abuso del libre albedrío angelical y humano, y esto es lo que trajo el mal al mundo con el Pecado Original, lo que causó una falta de armonía dentro de la creación. [49]

Pero, ¿por qué Dios permite que permanezca el mal?

Dios permite el mal debido a nuestro libre albedrío.

El libre albedrío es el poder de elegir actuar para bien o para mal. Y es nuestro libre albedrío lo que hace posible el verdadero amor.

Desafortunadamente, el libre albedrío también hace posible el pecado y el mal. Por lo tanto, si Dios previniera todo pecado y maldad, tendría que quitar nuestro libre albedrío, pero esto significaría que no podríamos amar de verdad. Entonces, para asegurarnos de que somos libres de amar y hacer el bien, también somos libres de hacer el mal.

Pero otra razón por la que Dios permite que el mal permanezca es porque Él es capaz de extraer grandes bienes de él.

¿Cuáles son algunos de esos bienes? El Papa Juan Pablo II nos dice que hay varios: formación y / o corrección, un aumento en el amor, acercarse a Dios y desatar un mayor amor en nombre de los demás, como el buen samaritano. [50]

San Agustín describió magníficamente la naturaleza providencial de la bondad de Dios cuando escribió: *"Porque el Dios todopoderoso, porque es supremamente bueno, nunca permitiría que existiera ningún mal en sus obras si no fuera tan poderoso y bueno como para* **causar el bien. emerger del mal mismo"**. *(lo que está en negrita enfatiza lo mío)*

Solo piense en ello por un momento.

Para mí, ¡eso me detiene en seco y me hace caer de rodillas maravillada y asombrada!

Aunque en realidad *he visto* este tipo de milagro, (uno que me viene a la mente es la madre de una de las víctimas del tiroteo en la escuela Sandy Hook que públicamente perdonó al tirador), y aunque actos de amor misericordioso como este pueden resultar en una completa transformación de la persona perdonada para que ya no se parezca a su yo anterior; tiendo a ignorar estos milagros, o me olvido de la realidad de lo que el poder de Dios realmente puede hacer.

Nuestro mayor fracaso en esta área (al menos para mí) es olvidar constantemente que Dios ha tomado el mayor mal y sufrimiento *de todos los tiempos*, la muerte de su Hijo, y ha hecho que el mayor bien imaginable emerja de él, la salvación del mundo entero. [51]

Dios trabaja de manera similar en nuestras propias vidas cuando permite que nuestras vidas sean tocadas por el mal o el sufrimiento, pero nos rebelamos contra él. Tendemos a olvidar la sabiduría de Santa Catalina de Siena que nos dijo: "Todo proviene del amor; todo está ordenado para la salvación del hombre, Dios no hace nada sin este objetivo en mente".

Y eso, creo que es el quid. El problema subyacente que podemos tener con el mal, el dolor y el sufrimiento en el mundo es *en realidad* más un reflejo o una pregunta que *tenemos* sobre la

bondad y la providencia de Dios que sobre la presencia del mal y el sufrimiento.

Porque frente al mal, luchamos para confiar en que Dios es todopoderoso y todo bien. Que Él es nuestro Salvador y que está trabajando a través de todos los eventos y circunstancias para nuestra salvación eterna (en comparación con nuestra dicha terrenal).

Ahora, no me malentiendan. No es que las realidades del mal, el dolor, el sufrimiento, la enfermedad y la muerte no sean cuestiones importantes que abordar. Sin embargo, estas preguntas son importantes solo en cómo nuestras *respuestas* informan nuestra respuesta a la presencia de estas cosas en el mundo, dentro de nuestras vidas y en las vidas de quienes nos rodean.

¿Y cuál debería ser nuestra respuesta? Lo mismo que los discípulos, "Señor, ¡aumenta nuestra fe!"[52] Muy a menudo, nuestras dudas surgen debido a la falta de fe suficiente en la bondad y la providencia de Dios cuando nos enfrentamos al mal, al dolor o al sufrimiento.

¿Y qué *es* la fe? Tener plena confianza en alguien o algo.[53]

Ahora, permítanme ser clara. Tener fe y confianza en Dios no es tan simple como decir que tengo fe o que confío en Dios. Se trata de *vivirlo*. Se trata de tener fe y confiar en la voluntad de nuestro Amoroso Padre Celestial y permitirle que le llene de Su paz en medio de cualquier tormenta que esté presente en su vida.

Y es por eso que abandonarnos a la voluntad de Dios es el cuarto paso en el camino hacia la santidad. Es el agente integrador para los pasos uno a tres.

Abandonarnos a la voluntad de Dios integra y fortalece nuestra oración diaria, las gracias de Dios recibidas en sus sacramentos y nuestras luchas para crecer en virtud todos juntos en los hábitos necesarios para luchar por la santidad en nuestras vidas.

DIGA SÍ a abandonarse a la voluntad de Dios.

Pase la página y veamos cómo estamos golpeando la voluntad de Dios en el punto.

Capítulo 15

ACERTAR LA VOLUNTAD DE DIOS EN EL "BLANCO"

"Dios nos da a cada uno de nosotros la gracia suficiente para conocer su santa voluntad y hacerlo plenamente"

— San Ignacio de Loyola

Una vez que DIGAMOS SÍ al Paso Cuatro: Abandonarnos a la voluntad de Dios, debemos responder a la pregunta de cómo vivimos esta idea. ¿Cómo nos volvemos tan buenos en eso que vivimos *Su* voluntad para nosotros cada día?

Hacemos esto intentando acertar en el "BLANCO" a través de las prácticas de desapego, obediencia y confianza.

DESAPEGO

San Ignacio de Loyola nos dice que *"Dios nos da a cada uno de nosotros la gracia suficiente para conocer su santa voluntad y hacerlo plenamente"*. Esto es absolutamente cierto, pero para vivir la santa voluntad de Dios y hacerlo plenamente, necesitamos practicar el desapego.

La idea principal del desapego es aceptar el sufrimiento en cualquier forma que pueda surgir. Además, también debemos estar "separándonos" simultáneamente de cualquier cosa que pueda interponerse en el camino de saber y luego hacer eso.

Durante más de veinte siglos, la Iglesia ha enfatizado el concepto de dejar de lado las "cosas del mundo" para seguir a Cristo y el camino del discipulado. Sin embargo, fue San Ignacio, durante once meses que pasó en una cueva en las afueras de la ciudad de Manresa, España en 1522, le había revelado, por la gracia de Dios y el Espíritu Santo, la verdad fundamental de que son nuestros *apegos* a bienes creados — cosas como dinero, poder, honor, placer — que se interponen en nuestro camino para poder responder plenamente a la voluntad de Dios en nuestras vidas.

Pero, quizás se pregunte, ¿cómo puede algo como el placer interponerse en la voluntad de Dios?

Aquí hay un ejemplo realmente simple. Digamos que le gusta animar a su equipo deportivo favorito. Realmente disfruta viendo el juego, particularmente porque también puede pasar el rato con su familia y amigos mientras lo hace. Y tal vez, incluso, tenga algo de comida y algunas bebidas mientras anima a su equipo a la victoria también. Todas estas cosas le traen mucho placer.

Ahora, en este ejemplo, no pasa nada *malo*. Ser fanático de los deportes no es algo malo. Tampoco pasar tiempo con familiares o amigos. Y tener algo de comida y algunas bebidas tampoco es algo malo. De hecho, todas estas son cosas *buenas* en sí mismas.

Entonces, ¿cómo es posible que el placer pueda obstaculizar la voluntad de Dios?

Bueno, dependiendo de cuán grande sea un fanático, es muy probable que sus actividades placenteras entren en conflicto con la posibilidad de asistir a misa el fin de semana. Entonces, para llegar a la misa dominical (la voluntad revelada de Dios para cada uno de nosotros), tendrá que elegir entre disfrutar de actividades buenas y placenteras o hacer la voluntad de Dios.

Con suerte, tendremos nuestras prioridades correctamente en orden, y seremos virtuosos, por lo que haremos la voluntad de Dios con facilidad, rapidez y alegría antes de elegir actividades placenteras. Si no elegimos la voluntad de Dios, entonces tenemos un apego que nos impide hacer su voluntad.

Es por eso que debemos practicar el desapego para realmente abandonarnos a la voluntad de Dios.

¿Pero cómo lo practicamos? Nuevamente, comience con el primer paso: oración diaria y meditación.

¿Por qué? Porque es solo a la luz del amor de Dios por nosotros que podemos llegar a conocernos y vernos más claramente. Y cuanto más claramente nos vemos a nosotros mismos, más capaces somos de identificar los apegos, esas mismas cosas que nos impiden conocer y hacer la voluntad de Dios, y buscar dejarlos de lado a través de la práctica del desapego.

Pero el desapego no se trata simplemente de cosas del mundo. El desapego también se trata de nuestras disposiciones interiores, cosas como nuestro orgullo y deseo de control. El desapego también se trata de dejar de lado nuestras ideas sobre cómo deberían ser o ser nuestras vidas. El padre Jacques Philippe, en su libro, *In the School of the Holy Spirit*, escribe:

> *"Para llegar a ser santos, para convertirnos en santos, debemos, por supuesto, esforzarnos tanto como podamos para hacer la voluntad de Dios de una manera general que sea válida para todos: a través de las Escrituras, los Mandamientos, etc. También es indispensable, como se acaba de decir, ir más allá: aspirar a saber no solo lo que Dios exige de todos en general, sino también* **lo que quiere más específicamente de nosotros individualmente"**.[54] **(Lo que está en negrita enfatiza lo mío)**

La gente me ha dicho que si Dios fuera más claro acerca de lo que quería que hicieran, como si pusiera un mensaje en una valla publicitaria en la carretera, lo harían.

Bueno, el hecho es que Dios *nos dice* cuál es su voluntad.

Dios nos revela su voluntad a través de su voluntad absoluta y permisiva. La voluntad absoluta de Dios se revela de muchas maneras: haciendo lo que es bueno y evitando el mal; siguiendo la ley moral que es evidente y conocible a través del sentido común; por el uso de la razón y las enseñanzas de Cristo que vienen a través de la Iglesia; a través de los deberes y responsabilidades de nuestro estado en la vida: religiosos casados, solteros o jurados; a través de nuestros compromisos de amar, honrar, cuidar y ser fieles a nuestro cónyuge; cuidando a nuestros hijos, haciendo nuestro trabajo como si trabajáramos para Dios, cumpliendo con nuestras responsabilidades; y a través de las inspiraciones que Dios da. En pocas palabras, la Voluntad Absoluta de Dios se revela cuando haces lo que sabes que se supone que debes hacer.

La voluntad permisiva de Dios se revela a través de los eventos y circunstancias que Dios permite o permite que sucedan en nuestras vidas. En pocas palabras, la voluntad de Dios se encuentra en aquellas cosas que no podemos cambiar. [55]

Ahora, puedo oírle decir, ¿qué? ¿Dios *me permite* perder mi trabajo? ¿O para que tenga un accidente donde pierda el uso de mi ojo derecho? ¿O para que mi cónyuge abandone a su familia? ¿O para que tenga una enfermedad que me hace imposible pasar un día sin tomar descansos frecuentes en medio de cualquier actividad física?

¿Cómo puede alguna de estas cosas ser la voluntad de Dios?

"Incluso cuando la voluntad de Dios no se corresponde con tus propios deseos, siempre es beneficioso para ti". [56]

Esta comprensión y nivel de aceptación de confianza expresada en esta cita de Saint Arnold Janssen es el epítome del desapego. ¿Por qué? Porque nos muestra la actitud por la que debemos luchar. Una actitud de aceptar, confiar y vivir la realidad de que Dios es un Padre amoroso que se preocupa por todos y cada uno de Sus hijos, *incluso cuando no lo parece para el resto del mundo.*

Como puede ver, nos esforzamos incluso por separarnos de nuestras propias ideas y expectativas de cómo debería ser nuestra vida. Es solo cuando dejamos de lado nuestras propias ideas y expectativas sobre lo que debería ser la vida, y DIGAMOS SÍ a las ideas de Dios, que Dios es libre de moldearnos en lo que Él sabe que podemos ser. Porque Él es quien nos creó para ser así en primer lugar.

Entonces, ¿por qué es tan difícil el desapego? Por el temor.

El padre Jacques Philippe describe esta realidad y las consecuencias del miedo perfectamente:

> *"Lo que realmente duele no es tanto el sufrimiento como el miedo al sufrimiento. Si nos acogen con confianza y paz, el sufrimiento nos hace crecer. Nos madura y nos entrena, nos purifica, nos enseña a amar desinteresadamente, nos hace pobres de corazón, humildes, gentiles y compasivos con nuestro prójimo. El miedo al sufrimiento, por otro lado, nos endurece en actitudes defensivas y de autoprotección, y a menudo nos lleva a tomar decisiones irracionales con consecuencias desastrosas".*[57]

Entonces, ¿cómo podríamos superar nuestros apegos y nuestras actitudes autoprotectoras, defensivas y endurecidas?

A través de la oración y sumergiéndonos en el poder de la Palabra.

La misma Palabra que nos habla una y otra vez acerca de dejar de lado nuestro miedo y confiar en Él. Como en el Salmo 27: 1 *"El SEÑOR es mi luz y mi salvación; ¿A quien temeré? El SEÑOR es la fortaleza de mi vida; ¿De quién tendré miedo?*

O en 2 Timoteo 1: 7, *"Porque Dios no nos ha dado un espíritu de temor y timidez, sino de poder, amor y autodisciplina".*

Y en 1 Juan 4:18, *"No hay miedo en el amor. Pero el amor perfecto expulsa el miedo, porque el miedo tiene que ver con el castigo. El que teme no se hace perfecto en el amor".*

Pero especialmente en Romanos 8:28, *"Porque todas las cosas funcionan para bien para los que aman a Dios"*.

Sumérjase en la Palabra y pase tiempo en oración y meditación con Él, y el desapego de las cosas de este mundo y nuestra capacidad de conocer y hacer la voluntad de Dios puede aumentar con cada día que pasa.

OBEDIENCIA

La segunda práctica es la obediencia. La esencia de la obediencia se encuentra en la frase en latín, *"In verbo autem tuo"*, que significa *"A tu palabra"*. Ser obediente es estar listo "en tu palabra" para hacer lo que me mandes.

Es por eso que Santa Catalina de Bolonia dijo que, *"Sin duda, la obediencia es más meritoria que cualquier otra penitencia. ¿Y qué mayor penitencia puede haber que mantener la voluntad continuamente sumisa y obediente?"*

¡Aquí solo puedo hablar por mí mismo, pero ser continuamente sumiso y obediente es *definitivamente* penitencial para mí! Jajaja

Sin embargo, cada vez que luchamos por ser obedientes, podemos mirar la vida de Cristo y su ejemplo.

"¿Cuál fue la primera regla de la vida de nuestro querido Salvador? Sabes que era hacer la voluntad de su Padre. Bueno, entonces, el primer fin que propongo en nuestro trabajo diario es hacer la voluntad de Dios; en segundo lugar, hacerlo de la manera Él quiere; y en tercer lugar, hacerlo porque es su voluntad".[58]

Jesús les dice a sus discípulos (¡nosotros!) Que el discipulado genuino, seguirlo, implica sufrimiento e incluso la muerte. Él comparte este mensaje con sus discípulos en los Evangelios una y otra vez.

Por ejemplo, en el capítulo 16:21 de Mateo: *"Desde ese momento, Jesús comenzó a explicar a sus discípulos que debía ir a Jerusalén y sufrir muchas cosas a manos de los ancianos, los principales sacerdotes y maestros de la ley, y que debe ser asesinado y al tercer día resucitado"*.

Solo en el Evangelio de Marcos, Jesús predice su muerte tres veces diferentes. La instancia más memorable es Marcos 8: 31-33 cuando Jesús hace su pronunciamiento sobre Su próximo sufrimiento y muerte, y luego Pedro trata de discutir, pero Jesús lo reprende diciendo: *"¡Quítate de delante de mí, Satanás! ¡No tienes en mente las cosas de Dios, sino las cosas de los hombres!"*

Y luego, en Lucas 9:43, *"Presta atención a lo que te estoy diciendo. El Hijo del Hombre debe ser entregado a los hombres..."*

¿Por qué el sufrimiento, la muerte y la cruz? Porque la resurrección *solo* se logra con la cruz.

Las Escrituras no son la única fuente de esta enseñanza. La Iglesia y todos sus santos a lo largo de los siglos se hacen eco del mandato de Cristo de que la verdadera vida solo puede lograrse a través del sufrimiento y la muerte.

En el párrafo 2015 del Catecismo, *"El camino de la perfección pasa por la Cruz. No hay santidad sin renuncia y batalla espiritual. El progreso espiritual implica la ascesis y la mortificación que gradualmente conducen a vivir en la paz y la alegría de las Bienaventuranzas"*.

Santa María de Mattias nos exhorta a *"...amar mucho la cruz, porque es allí donde descubrimos nuestra vida, nuestro verdadero amor y nuestra fuerza en nuestras mayores dificultades"*, y luego Santa Katherine Drexel nos dice: *"El paciente y la humilde resistencia de la cruz, sea cual sea su naturaleza, es el trabajo más importante que tenemos que hacer"*.

Pero, ¿cómo podemos lograr este tipo de obediencia? No podemos. Al menos no por nuestra cuenta.

Aquí es donde el segundo paso, vivir la vida de gracia, es crítico.

Antes de sanar a las personas, Jesús siempre le preguntaba a la persona si creía que podía hacerlo. Y luego, cuando expresaban fe en su poder, Jesús usaba signos físicos (imposición de manos, saliva, barro, etc.) para lograr la curación. Jesús continúa haciendo esto hoy a través de sus sacramentos.

Al igual que aquellos a quienes Jesús curó en Palestina, cuando expresamos nuestra fe en su poder que se encuentra en los sacramentos, Jesús puede usarlos para tocarnos y sanarnos de nuestro pecado, sufrimiento y muerte. Cristo puede conformarnos cada vez más plenamente para ser instrumentos obedientes y dispuestos. Esto se debe a que el poder de los sacramentos mismos fluye del sufrimiento y la muerte de Jesús a través de los cuales Jesús dio un nuevo significado al sufrimiento, e hizo posible que cada uno de nosotros ayudemos a lograr la redención del mundo.[59]

Pero la razón final para luchar por la obediencia está directamente vinculada a una enseñanza de San Juan de la Cruz en la que declaró: "... *la forma de sufrimiento es más segura y también más rentable que la de regocijarse y actuar. En el sufrimiento, Dios da fuerza, pero en acción y alegría, el alma no muestra sino sus propias debilidades e imperfecciones. Y en el sufrimiento, el alma practica y adquiere virtud, y se vuelve pura, más sabia y más cautelosa*".

En pocas palabras, vaciarnos y ser obedientes, especialmente en medio del sufrimiento, es cómo practicamos y adquirimos la virtud y nos volvemos más santos. ¿Necesito decir mas?

CONFIAR

La práctica final que debemos cultivar para llegar al BLANCO y abandonarnos a la voluntad de Dios en nuestras vidas es la confianza.

La confianza es el acto de seguir el camino, incluso cuando no tiene sentido, siempre y cuando no nos lleve al pecado. Y se trata de encontrar la fuerza y el coraje para creer y confiar en las promesas de Dios para nosotros. Sus promesas de que Él es

un Padre bueno y amoroso, que todas las cosas funcionan para aquellos que lo aman, y que Él es verdaderamente capaz de sacar el bien de cualquier cosa.

San Francisco de Sales nos asegura: *"Conduciremos con seguridad a través de cada tormenta, siempre y cuando nuestro corazón sea correcto, nuestra intención ferviente, nuestro coraje firme y nuestra confianza puesta en Dios".*

El Padre Pío lo dice aún más simplemente: *"Ora, espera y no te preocupes".*

Este es el tipo de confianza que debemos cultivar en nuestros corazones y mentes para que podamos experimentar de lo que San Pablo estaba hablando cuando escribió: *"Que el Dios de la esperanza te llene de alegría y paz mientras confías en él, para que puedas puede desbordarse de esperanza por el poder del Espíritu Santo".*[60]

Sin embargo, a menudo dudamos en confiar en sus promesas o en seguir el camino que nos ha presentado. O al menos sé que lo hago.

Sin embargo, aquí hay una gran analogía que da perspectiva a lo que estamos haciendo cuando no confiamos en Dios:

> *"Confiamos en nosotros mismos ante un médico porque suponemos que él conoce su negocio. Él ordena una operación que implica cortar parte de nuestro cuerpo y lo aceptamos. Le estamos agradecidos y le pagamos una gran tarifa porque juzgamos que no actuaría como lo hace a menos que el remedio fuera necesario, y debemos confiar en su habilidad. ¡Sin embargo, no estamos dispuestos a tratar a Dios de la misma manera! Parece que no confiamos en su sabiduría y tenemos miedo de que no pueda hacer su trabajo correctamente. Nos permitimos ser operados por un hombre que fácilmente puede cometer un error, un error que nos puede costar la vida, y protestar cuando Dios se pone a trabajar en nosotros. Si pudiéramos ver todo lo que Él ve, sin vacilar desearíamos todo lo que Él desea".*[61]

Nuestro miedo, nuestra falta de confianza, está impidiendo que Dios, el Médico Divino mismo, ¡nos opere de la manera que Él cree que es lo mejor! ¿Qué tan orgulloso y arrogante es eso?

Porque la verdad es que no hay *nada* que Dios haga que sea en vano. *Todo* tiene un propósito: todo el sufrimiento, el dolor, las angustias, las frustraciones, los desalientos, los fracasos. Todo tiene un propósito y un significado, incluso si no podemos ver ni entender.

Pero, ¿abandonarte a Dios te parecerá demasiado?

¿Tal vez tienes miedo? ¿Miedo de que el dolor y el sufrimiento sean demasiado?

¿O tal vez solo parece una franca imposibilidad?

Yo solía pensar todas esas cosas también. Hasta que leí esto:

> *"Me doy cuenta como nunca antes de que el Señor es gentil y misericordioso; no me envió esta pesada cruz hasta que pudiera soportarla. Si la hubiera enviado antes, estoy seguro de que me habría desanimado... No deseo nada en absoluto ahora, excepto amar hasta que muera de amor. Soy libre, no tengo miedo de nada, ni siquiera de lo que solía temer sobre todo... una larga enfermedad que me haría una carga para la comunidad. Estoy perfectamente contento de seguir sufriendo en cuerpo y alma durante años, si eso le agrada a Dios. No tengo el menor miedo de vivir durante mucho tiempo; estoy listo para seguir luchando".*[62]

Eso fue escrito por Santa Teresa de Lisieux. Una simple campesina francesa que se convirtió en una monja carmelita que ahora es reconocida como una santa y fue nombrada Doctora de la Iglesia por su "Pequeño Camino".

Teresa también tenía miedo, pero superó ese miedo poco a poco a través del amor y la gracia de Dios, y abandonándose a la voluntad de Dios. Ella nos mostró que también podemos hacerlo, si confiamos.

CONCLUSIÓN

Sin embargo, para confiar debemos aprender a amar y ser amados.

Y así es como nos encontramos volviendo al primer paso, pasando tiempo en oración y meditación diarias.

Porque solo confiamos en aquellos que realmente nos conocen y nos aman. Es por eso que se produce un colapso de cualquier relación cuando se rompe la confianza. Entonces, para crecer en confianza, debemos esforzarnos por crecer en amor. ¡Y la única forma de crecer en el amor es pasar tiempo con Aquel a quien buscamos amar!

Santa Madre Teresa de Calcuta una vez compartió: *"El fruto del silencio es la oración, el fruto de la oración es la fe, el fruto de la fe es el amor, el fruto del amor es el servicio, el fruto del servicio es la paz"*.

Es por eso que perseveramos en la oración y la meditación, incluso cuando no podemos ni sentir esa devoción o amor. Confiamos en que Dios está trabajando en nuestros corazones y mentes para darnos su paz, pero tenemos que aparecer.

Y luego, cuando nos presentamos, debemos hacer un acto de fe y entregarnos a Dios. Cuando decimos SÍ, Dios usa nuestro SÍ y hace que algo bueno salga de él.

Simplemente, nos convierte en los santos para los que nos creó.

Cuando decimos SÍ a abandonarnos a la voluntad de Dios, nos abrimos completamente a la posibilidad de transformar la unión con Dios.

Esto es santidad. De eso se trata ser un santo.

Se trata de…

…luchar por el desapego y poner su vida en conformidad con la voluntad de Dios para su vida, en lugar de la suya.

… luchando por la obediencia y tomando su cruz sabiendo que el yugo de nuestro Señor es fácil y su carga ligera.

... confiando en que todas las cosas importan, y en la promesa de que Dios compartió en Su Palabra *"que todas las cosas funcionan para bien para los que lo aman".[63]*

DIGA SÍ a acertar la voluntad de Dios en el "BLANCO".

Expresemos nuestro ferviente deseo de abandonarnos a la voluntad de Dios orando:

¡Oh Jesús, me entrego a ti, hazte cargo de todo![64]

Ahora, pase la página y comencemos a vivir una vida de abundancia.

PARTE 3

ABRAZAR LA ABUNDANCIA PERMANENTE

Capítulo 16
EL MITO DEL LLANERO SOLITARIO

P ara aquellos de ustedes de cierta edad, probablemente recuerden haber visto, o al menos haber escuchado, las aventuras del Llanero Solitario. Para aquellos de ustedes que pueden no estar familiarizados con la serie de televisión occidental, la premisa básica era que el Llanero Solitario iba a diferentes ciudades y otras situaciones sin ley a petición de personas inocentes que estaban en peligro o que se estaban aprovechando de ellas, y el Llanero Solitario trabajaría para descubrir quiénes eran los malos, y luego lucharía para lograr justicia, antes de cabalgar en su gran caballo blanco, Silver.

Al final de cada episodio, habría una escena en la que una de las personas que habían sido ayudadas por el Llanero Solitario descubriría una bala de plata (el símbolo del Llanero Solitario), y al darse cuenta de quién las había ayudado, miraría hacia arriba y vería al Llanero Solitario en Silver encaramándose sobre sus patas traseras en victoria antes de emprender su próxima aventura y tratar de lograr justicia para otra persona.

Esta idea resume la mentalidad de muchas personas cuando se trata del viaje espiritual. La idea de que, al igual que el Llanero Solitario, tenemos que entrar en situaciones tentadoras y luchar por la justicia y ayudar a los demás, y luego nos vamos para hacerlo todo de nuevo, por nuestra cuenta.

Todo el problema con esto, por supuesto, es el hecho de que todo es un mito.

Porque el Llanero Solitario TENÍA ayuda.

Tenía a Tonto, su fiel amigo nativo americano, para acompañarlo y ayudarlo a superar a los malos y las situaciones sin ley y lograr la justicia.

Entonces, el Llanero Solitario no estaba *realmente* solo. Y tampoco deberíamos estar en el viaje espiritual.

Una vez que DIGAMOS SÍ al deseo de Dios de derramar Sus abundantes bendiciones sobre nosotros, podemos comenzar a reconocer y utilizar plenamente todas estas bendiciones que están presentes en nuestra vida diaria, y realmente podemos experimentar una vida de abundancia permanente.

El Llanero Solitario ilustra una de las primeras claves para esta vida de abundancia que está presente en nuestra vida diaria. Necesitaba un asesor y un amigo que lo acompañara, y nosotros también tenemos asesores y amigos a nuestro alrededor.

De hecho, el acompañamiento es una NECESIDAD fundamental que tenemos en la vida. Fuimos creados para la relación en general, pero estamos *especialmente* diseñados para acompañarnos durante el viaje espiritual. El Papa Francisco ha hablado repetidamente sobre la necesidad de encontrar y acompañar a nuestros hermanos y hermanas en Cristo, especialmente aquellos que están en las periferias.

Desafortunadamente, en muchas culturas occidentales, pero particularmente en los Estados Unidos, tenemos este sentimiento generalizado de individualismo, la idea de que los individuos son tan buenos como personas fuertes, asertivas, autosuficientes e independientes que "lo hacen solos". " Esto se traduce en la idea cultural adicional de que es una debilidad incluso pedir ayuda, o que eres defectuoso si *necesitas* amigos y tener una relación vivida con los demás.

En el viaje espiritual, esto es anatema. Literalmente es la muerte para nosotros mismos si negamos nuestra necesidad de relación. Pero este imperativo cultural es *extremadamente* difícil

de superar, por lo que hay muchas personas que intentan luchar por la santidad por su cuenta. Lamentablemente, dado que han aceptado la idea de que es debilidad pedir ayuda, o que deberían hacerlo solos, están perpetuando "el mito del Llanero Solitario".

Pero Dios nos ha dado todo el Depósito de Fe: la Sagrada Escritura, la Sagrada Tradición y la autoridad de enseñanza de la Iglesia, el Magisterio, para asegurarnos de que nos acompañen en nuestros viajes individuales hacia la santidad.

Sagrada Escritura y Sagrada Tradición, toda la sabiduría y el conocimiento que se salvaguarda y comparte a través del Magisterio de la misma Iglesia que Jesús fundó sobre Sus Apóstoles.

Las Escrituras y la Tradición son los medios de comunicación sobrenaturales más comunes de Dios.

¿Por qué sobrenatural? Quiero decir, ¿no son las Escrituras y las enseñanzas de la Iglesia simplemente fabricaciones humanas de lo que Dios nos dice acerca de sí mismo y nos dice cómo vivir?

En una palabra, no.

¿Por qué? Porque el Espíritu Santo es la fuente de ambos.

Sí, los seres humanos escribieron las Escrituras, pero *fue* por inspiración del Espíritu Santo que fueron escritas para asegurar que las Escrituras siempre sean verdaderas y sin errores, cuando, como a un ex pastor mío le gustaba decir, "están hablando de lo que están hablando".

¿Y de qué están hablando las Escrituras? Dios y su amor por su pueblo. De su deseo apasionado y sed de cada uno de nosotros, sus hijos e hijas. Y cuando las Escrituras hablan de estas cosas, *no hay duda* de que son verdaderas y sin error.

¿Pero esto se aplica también a la Sagrada Tradición? ¿Es esto cierto para toda la sabiduría contenida en las enseñanzas de la Iglesia y compartida por el Magisterio de la Iglesia?

En una palabra, otra vez, sí.

Y a través de las inspiraciones del Espíritu Santo, la Tradición Sagrada ahora contiene todo el conocimiento de todas las mentes más grandes de los últimos dos milenios.

El obispo Robert Barron utiliza una analogía maravillosa para mostrar la obra del Espíritu Santo mientras explica el desarrollo de la enseñanza católica:

"En un sentido muy real, el Padre habla todo lo que puede hablar en Su Hijo, llamado correctamente el Logos. No hay más que revelar, ni más que decir, que lo que se expresa en Jesús. Sin embargo, la plenitud de esa revelación se desarrolla solo en el espacio y el tiempo, de manera muy parecida a como una semilla se desarrolla gradualmente en un poderoso roble".

Una mente viva toma una idea, le da vuelta, la considera, la mira desde varios puntos de vista, la cuestiona. Luego, en una conversación animada, esa mente arroja la idea a otra mente, que realiza un conjunto similar de operaciones.

Este "juego de mentes vivas" ha continuado a lo largo de los siglos. San Juan lanzó la idea de la Encarnación a San Policarpo, quien se la lanzó a San Ireneo, quien se la lanzó a Orígenes, quien se la lanzó a Agustín, quien se la pasó a Tomás de Aquino, quien la compartió con Robert Bellarmine, quien se lo habló a John Henry Newman y a otros, que luego nos lo dieron.

Ahora, ¿quién garantiza que este proceso avance? La respuesta es el Espíritu Santo, a quien Jesús prometió a la Iglesia".

El venerable arzobispo Fulton Sheen se hace eco de la realidad de cómo la Iglesia es una extensión de la presencia de Cristo en el mundo cuando dijo:

"... el Espíritu Santo como era importante en el cuerpo físico de Cristo, también es importante en su cuerpo eclesial. La Iglesia, es la manifestación histórica del Cristo

suprahistórico, gracias a Su Espíritu ... Por eso obedecemos
a la Iglesia: ella es Cristo y el Espíritu está en ella". [65]

Entonces, cuando el Magisterio enseña y comparte las verdades de la fe, es Cristo hablando, es el Espíritu Santo que se hace visible en medio de nosotros.

Sin embargo, a pesar de saber esto, ¿por qué tanta gente descuenta la Iglesia y trata de ir sola en el mundo?

Debido a que muchas veces, tendemos a quedar atrapados en lo que podemos ver ante nosotros, que desafortunadamente, la mayoría de las veces, tienden a ser seres humanos defectuosos que abusan de su poder, están limitados por sus propios prejuicios y preconceptos, vicios y temores. que la asombrosa majestad de las almas llenas del Espíritu Santo y en llamas con el amor de Dios y su pueblo.

En mi propio viaje personal a la Iglesia, esta idea de que la Iglesia es una extensión de la presencia de Cristo en el mundo fue en realidad una de las principales razones por las que me convertí en católica. Mientras estudiaba historia, se me hizo evidente que no hay otra manera de explicar la supervivencia de la Iglesia a lo largo de los siglos con todas las personas defectuosas y quebrantadas que han estado a su cargo periódicamente, *excepto* que el origen y la fuente de la Iglesia de poder fluye del Espíritu Santo.

Es lo que celebramos en Pentecostés. El nacimiento de la Iglesia a través de la venida del Espíritu Santo sobre los apóstoles de Jesús. Y luego de los Apóstoles vino la predicación, las conversiones y los bautismos hasta nuestro propio tiempo y lugar.

Entonces, si no son las fallas humanas de aquellos que se esfuerzan por servir como instrumentos de Cristo en la tierra, ¿cuál es la *verdadera* razón por la que decidimos perpetuar el mito del Llanero Solitario y descartar la realidad de la presencia del Espíritu Santo en Su Iglesia ahora?

Obediencia.

La obediencia proviene de la palabra latina "obedere", "escuchar". Desafortunadamente, en nuestro mundo de hoy, la

gente ya no escucha mucho. Pero en el viaje espiritual, la obediencia es necesaria para preparar nuestros corazones para una conversación, para un diálogo interno con Dios mientras escuchamos profundamente su verdad.

Y capitalicé la verdad por una razón, porque Jesús ES la Verdad. Él es el camino, la verdad y la vida que estamos buscando. Y Él es a quien buscamos escuchar. No para mí, sino para Aquel que sabe lo que es mejor para mí y desea compartirlo conmigo, pero solo si lo escucho.

Pero no queremos escuchar, o ignoramos, o modificamos lo que escuchamos. Sin embargo, Dios lo *sabía*, y es por eso que no solo nos dio la Sagrada Escritura y la Sagrada Tradición, sino también Su Magisterio dentro de la Iglesia para guiarnos y acompañarnos durante todo el viaje.

Porque Dios desea que aprovechemos estos tres medios en el viaje de regreso a Él. Sin embargo, la mayoría de las veces, la mayoría de las personas solo usan uno o dos de estos, y esto lleva a más luchas en el viaje espiritual que las que nuestro Señor tuvo en mente para nosotros.

¿Qué quiero decir? Bueno, nuestro Señor *sabía* lo difícil que es la vida. Lo *vivió* con nosotros. Experimentó lo bueno, lo malo y lo feo. Quiero decir, ¿qué podría ser más feo que ser traicionado por un amigo, abandonado por todos menos su madre y algunos discípulos mientras experimenta una muerte cruel y tortuosa?

O la realidad de vivir en el exilio cuando era un niño; la muerte de su padre adoptivo, José; ser incomprendido y perseguido por líderes religiosos y seculares; ¿e incluso sobrevivir a un intento de asesinato por parte de sus propios vecinos en su ciudad natal cuando comenzó su ministerio?

Diría que Jesús sabía bastante sobre los desafíos y las penas de la vida humana. Y sabiendo esto, nos dio las herramientas que necesitamos para asegurarnos de que podamos encontrar nuestro camino a casa.

Pero nuestro Señor no es un Dios de necesidades básicas. El es un Dios de *abundancia*.

Debido a que no solo nos dejó lo mínimo de lo que sabía que necesitaríamos para recorrer esta vida humana, más bien, nos dio una *abundancia* de gracias y asistencia. Nos ha dado su creación y otros seres humanos; Su Palabra en la Sagrada Escritura; Él mismo y el Espíritu Santo en los sacramentos; la sabiduría del Espíritu Santo encontrada en su iglesia a través del magisterio y la sagrada tradición; y para colmo, ¡se pone a nuestra disposición cada vez que buscamos conversar con Él en oración!

Cuando alguien solo usa una o dos de las herramientas que Él ha provisto (como usar las Escrituras solo, o solo recibir los sacramentos), pueden (y a veces lo hacen) acercarse a Él y pueden crecer en santidad, pero el viaje no es tan fácil para ellos como nuestro Señor desea que sea.

Sabemos esto porque se hace evidente cada vez que nos encontramos con una persona que está haciendo pleno uso de todos los medios que Dios nos ha dado para el viaje espiritual. Es posible entonces ver los límites impuestos por una vida humana normal desechada, y vemos a una persona viviendo con propósito, paz, alegría y abundancia en sus vidas, y naturalmente compartirán esa realidad con otros.

Esto es lo que estamos llamados a ser y hacer en el viaje espiritual. Jesús les dijo a sus discípulos que dejaran todo atrás para el viaje, pero Jesús no los envió sin nada. Él envió su Espíritu con ellos, de modo que cuando los discípulos regresaron y preguntó: *"Cuando te envié sin bolso, bolso o sandalias, ¿te faltaba algo?"* Y ellos respondieron: *"Nada"*. (Lucas 22:35)

Nuestros problemas en esta vida tienden a provenir simplemente de la falta de escucha de lo que Jesús nos dijo que necesitamos, y de tratar de hacer este viaje por nuestra cuenta.

Debemos dejar a un lado el mito del llanero solitario.

DIGA SÍ a ser obediente a lo que Dios ha revelado a través de Su Magisterio.

Ahora, pase la página para descubrir el poder de un amigo del alma.

Capítulo 17
EL PODER DE UN
AMIGO DEL ALMA

"Cuántas almas pueden alcanzar un alto grado de santidad si se las dirige adecuadamente desde el principio. Sé que Dios puede santificar las almas sin ayuda, pero, así como le da al jardinero la habilidad de cuidar plantas raras y delicadas mientras las fertiliza, así lo desea usar a otros en su cultivo de almas".[66]

— St Teresa de Lisieux

El concepto de tener un mentor o director espiritual es una idea que ha estado presente en la Tradición de la Iglesia desde el principio. Jesús lo modeló para sus discípulos, y envió a sus discípulos en parejas para asegurarse de que fueran alentados y sostenidos en el trabajo que les envió a hacer. Jesús continúa alentándonos a hacer esto a través de Su Iglesia, quien enseña que, para progresar en el viaje espiritual, debemos buscar y confiar nuestras almas al cuidado de otro que tenga habilidad en el acompañamiento.

Santa Teresa compara esta habilidad de acompañamiento con la de un jardinero. Pero este tipo de jardinero es uno que busca activamente ser un instrumento del Espíritu Santo en el

proceso de ayudar a crear un hermoso jardín dentro de las almas de aquellos a quienes se les ha confiado. Estos "jardineros de almas" también han sido llamados maestros espirituales, guías, magos, directores, mentores y amigos del alma. Pero independientemente del nombre, su importancia para el viaje espiritual no puede subestimarse.

Se citó a St. Brigid of Ireland diciendo: *"Sal y no comas nada hasta que tengas un amigo del alma, porque cualquiera sin un amigo del alma es como un cuerpo sin cabeza; es como el agua de un lago contaminado, no es bueno para beber ni para lavarse".*

La tradición celta era tal que se esperaba que *todos*, ya sean laicos o clérigos, hombres o mujeres, tuvieran un mentor espiritual y un compañero en el viaje del alma. Una persona en quien podrían confiar todas sus luchas internas, que les ayudaría a encontrar su camino y que podría ayudarlos en el discernimiento. Una genuina calidez e intimidad en esta relación y un profundo respeto por la sabiduría del otro fueron vistos como una fuente de bendición, y las diferencias de edad o género importaban. [67]

Un amigo del alma, un mentor espiritual o un guía espiritual, es una de las claves para nuestro continuo crecimiento espiritual. Esto se debe a que pueden ayudarnos a ver lo que tendemos a no ver, simplemente porque estamos demasiado cerca para ver con precisión lo que sucede dentro de nuestras propias vidas interiores.

Como seres humanos, tenemos una capacidad infinita de autoengaño porque nos cegamos muy fácilmente por nuestras ideas, sentimientos, miedos y vicios. Esto se muestra cada vez que nos evaluamos a nosotros mismos, ya que tendemos a evaluarnos a nosotros mismos de acuerdo con lo que aspiramos frente a la realidad de dónde estamos realmente, y también tendemos a no juzgarnos con dureza, sino a darnos crédito por nuestras buenas intenciones. Todo esto apunta a nuestra necesidad de que alguien nos acompañe y esté fuera de nuestra lucha y pueda darnos una perspectiva.

La provisión de esta perspectiva se puede comparar a una persona en su cuerda de aseguramiento. Una persona que sirve en su amarre es la persona que asegura su cuerda y lo mantiene atado a la montaña de manera segura. Para cualquier persona que haya escalado una montaña o haya descendido por un acantilado, tener a una persona en su amarre es una necesidad fundamental para su seguridad porque usted puede ver lo que no puede ver, ayudarlo a buscar su próximo asidero y evitar puntos peligrosos en la montaña. Pero la característica más fundamental en esta relación es de confianza. Debes confiar en que tu aseguramiento no te dejará caer, al mismo tiempo que tienes fe en que te están guiando en la dirección correcta.

De la misma manera, un mentor o director espiritual está allí en la montaña con usted, acompañándole, ayudándole y guiándole. Sin embargo, al igual que al escalar una montaña, USTED todavía tiene que hacer el trabajo de escalar. Un mentor camina CON, no PARA usted en la vida interior.

Los beneficios y el poder de tener un mentor para el alma no tiene precio. Es de conocimiento común que si quiere ser excelente en algo, obtiene un entrenador. Entonces, si usted quiere llegar a ser grandioso en la vida espiritual, también encontrará un entrenador. Un mentor o director que puede desafiarlo, alentarlo y acompañarlo mientras se esfuerza por escalar la montaña de Dios.

Pero uno de los mayores beneficios de tener un entrenador es la responsabilidad.

Estudio tras estudio muestra que es solo cuando se nos hace responsables que realmente progresamos en cualquier esfuerzo, y la vida espiritual si no es diferente. Por ejemplo, el simple hecho de saber que alguien va a preguntar cómo va mi vida diaria de oración, ¡es una motivación para que realmente esté orando a diario!

Además de la responsabilidad, los beneficios de un mentor espiritual son tener una persona que escuche profundamente y sirva como caja de resonancia para crecer en santidad en la vida

diaria; puede brindarle aliento y apoyo cuando enfrente desafíos y cuando se involucre en un discernimiento continuo en cuanto a su misión personal dentro de su estado de vida; ser un recurso de orientación sobre por qué, qué y cómo continuar creciendo en su vida interior; y finalmente, alguien a quien puedes mirar como un modelo a seguir para vivir la fe.

Se ha escrito mucho más sobre los beneficios de un mentor espiritual, pero lo más fundamental que debemos hacer en el viaje espiritual *es encontrar uno.*

Ahora, créame cuando le digo que conozco los desafíos de encontrar un director o mentor espiritual. Durante varios años, conduje cada seis semanas durante más de tres horas y media de UNA SOLA MANERA para reunirme con mi director espiritual durante una hora antes de pasar por la unidad para almorzar en mi automóvil mientras regresaba a tiempo para recoger a mi hijo cuando salía de la escuela.

¿Fue esto difícil? Absolutamente. ¿Valió la pena? Sí.

¿Siempre he tenido un director espiritual o mentor? No, pero incluso en esos momentos, *nunca* dejé de buscar a una persona que estuviera abierta a acompañarme en el viaje espiritual. Y con el tiempo, Dios me revelaría a esas personas a través de la oración y las circunstancias. Algunos funcionaron, mientras que otros no, pero *todos* esos hombres y mujeres que me han acompañado a lo largo de los años me han proporcionado sabiduría y perspicacia que me han ayudado a continuar mi viaje para acercarme a Dios y ser más como Jesús.

Entonces, la clave es perseverar siempre en la búsqueda. Dios desea que usted tenga un mentor o director espiritual. Él no quiere que lo haga solo. Él quiere que tenga a alguien a su disposición que pueda señalarle el próximo asidero para que considere alcanzarlo mientras intenta escalar Su montaña sagrada.

Por lo tanto, *no* se rinda nunca en la búsqueda y haga lo que sea necesario para permitirle participar en lo que podría ser una relación extremadamente llena de gracia.

Y eso me lleva a hacer un breve comentario sobre las dificultades de la vida interior. Cosas como la sequedad espiritual, el desánimo o las tentaciones. Porque los encontraremos en el viaje espiritual.

¿Pero por qué? La mayoría de las veces, es simplemente debido a algún tipo de alineación inadecuada, o un desorden, en nuestras vidas en relación con lo que Dios nos creó y desea para nosotros. Este desorden se revelará en nuestras tendencias humanas, como cuando estamos completamente enfocados en hacer lo que queremos, cuándo queremos y cómo queremos, y esto generalmente puede resultar en que no estemos en completa unión con la voluntad de Dios para nuestras vidas, y luego nos encontramos con desafíos.

Ralph Martin en su libro, *The Fulfillment of All Desire*, escribe:

> *"Es posible que nos hayamos descuidado al ser fieles a nuestros compromisos espirituales, como la asistencia a la misa diaria, nuestro tiempo diario de oración, lectura espiritual, etc. O puede que nos hayamos descuidado al valorar los dones que Dios nos da, o al rechazar o perder el tiempo con la tentación. O puede que hayamos comenzado a permitir distracciones, entretenimientos y participación en actividades mundanas para calmar nuestra hambre de Dios. . .*
> *La sequedad experimentada como resultado de negligencia, tibieza e infidelidad, y cualquiera que sea la etapa de la espiral descendente a la que haya llevado, solo tiene una solución: el arrepentimiento. Esta sequedad es autoinducida; La solución es volver a la fidelidad en nuestras prácticas espirituales".*[68]

Pero, ¿qué pasa con esos momentos en nuestras vidas cuando no se trata de nuestros fracasos o de nuestro desorden? ¿Qué pasa cuando simplemente estamos experimentando la vida con sus penas, luchas y tragedias?

Es especialmente durante esos momentos que necesitamos perseverar y recurrir cada vez más firmemente a las herramientas que nuestro Padre Celestial amoroso y fiel nos ha brindado para ayudarnos: Su Palabra, Su Iglesia y aquellas personas que Él ha puesto en nuestras vidas, mientras siempre recordando POR QUÉ estamos haciendo esto, para convertirnos en santos en el cielo.

Como comentó una vez Santa Catalina de Siena, *"Nunca se logra nada grandioso sin mucho perdurar"*.

Entonces, así como tenemos que estar dispuestos a seguir buscando una persona de confianza que pueda servir como nuestro mentor o director espiritual, debemos perseverar en medio de las pruebas, penas y tragedias.

Porque nuestro Señor no nos ha dejado soportar y luchar solos.

Él nos ama demasiado para hacer eso, y es por eso que nos dejó las herramientas que necesitamos para ayudarnos a perseverar durante este viaje de toda la vida. Pero debemos estar dispuestos a utilizar la guía que Dios nos brinda a través de otros, y buscar poner la guía que recibimos al servicio de crecer en santidad.

Comience a buscar a su amigo del alma hoy.

DIGA SÍ a ser acompañado en el viaje.

Es hora de pasar la página para descubrir cómo los santos vienen en grupos.

CAPÍTULO 18

LOS SANTOS VIENEN
EN RACIMOS

"Necesitamos una comunidad que nos ayude a alcanzar nuestra meta. La fe no es un viaje individual; Es un deporte de equipo. Nos necesitamos el uno al otro. Estamos en el viaje juntos"

— Matthew Kelly

La segunda herramienta, la próxima joya escondida para nuestra eventual corona de gloria en el cielo que Dios nos ha dado para ser alentados, inspirados y capaces de perseverar en la vida espiritual es la amistad.

Ahora, usted se puedes estar diciendo a sí mismo ahora mismo, espera un minuto, tengo muchos amigos, ¿por qué necesito pasar tiempo leyendo un capítulo que se centra en la amistad? Porque diría que, aunque muchos de nosotros tenemos "amigos", la mayoría de nosotros probablemente no tengamos *amistades* verdaderas y auténticas.

Distingo aquí porque en nuestro mundo de hoy, especialmente en las redes sociales, tenemos una comprensión extremadamente extraña de quién es un "amigo". El estado de "amigo" se otorga a cualquiera a quien le guste, comparta o interactúe

con nuestras publicaciones e imágenes, y aunque hay un nivel de compromiso, esta no es una amistad verdadera y auténtica.

¿Por qué? Porque la amistad auténtica consiste, como escribe Scott Galloway, *"en hacer una inversión visible en otra persona con su recurso más preciado, usted"*.[69]

Si no estamos invirtiendo todos nosotros (tiempo, talento, tesoro) en una relación con otro, entonces no es realmente auténtico. Y dado que nuestro tiempo es limitado, en quién (y en qué) nos invertimos es en lo que se vuelve real. Se vuelve auténtico. Es por eso que las amistades verdaderas y auténticas son pocas y distantes entre sí, y por qué, si has encontrado una, entonces realmente has encontrado un tesoro invaluable.

Porque dice en Sirach 6: 14-17

"Un amigo fiel es un refugio resistente; el que encuentra uno encuentra un tesoro. Un amigo fiel no tiene precio, ninguna suma puede equilibrar su valor. Un amigo fiel es un remedio que salva vidas, como el que teme que Dios encuentre; Porque el que teme a Dios se comporta en consecuencia, y su amigo será como él".

Cuando la gente habla de lo que debería ser la amistad, estos versículos del libro de Sirach en las Escrituras a menudo se mencionan como un manual de "cómo hacerlo" para determinar quién es un verdadero amigo, pero particularmente la importancia de que un amigo ayude a determinar cómo Dios como eventualmente nos convertiremos.

Los viejos adagios de *"Muéstrame a tus amigos y te mostraré quién eres" y "Te conviertes en las 5 personas con las que pasas más tiempo". Elija con cuidado",* ambos están enraizados en la idea que San Pablo expresa en 1 Corintios 15:33 <u>*"La mala compañía corrompe el buen carácter"*.</u>

Entonces, si *realmente* estamos buscando el cielo y buscando la santidad, ¿por qué vamos a pasar tiempo con aquellos que no nos ayudan en esa búsqueda? Si nuestro objetivo número uno

es ser santos, y dado que la vida es corta (e incierta), entonces es una razón más por la que deberíamos buscar amigos verdaderos y auténticos que teman a Dios y se comporten en consecuencia, porque esto solo ayudará a garantizar la posibilidad que haremos lo mismo.

De hecho, James Clear, autor del libro, *Atomic Habits*, y la principal autoridad sobre cómo lograr el fomento de cualquier tipo de cambio en la vida de uno, enfatiza este punto cuando discute el valor de los demás durante la búsqueda de cambiar sus hábitos. Él escribió: *"Una de las cosas más efectivas que puede hacer para desarrollar mejores hábitos es unirse a una cultura donde su comportamiento deseado es el comportamiento normal"*.

Esta es una de las razones *clave* por las cuales la amistad es tan vital en la búsqueda de la santidad cuando buscamos convertirnos en lo que Dios nos creó para ser.

Pero un beneficio igualmente importante de la amistad buena y auténtica es que realmente no hay nada más motivador, alentador e inspirador que estar entre personas de ideas afines que se esfuerzan por lograr un objetivo que es más grande que ellos.

Estoy seguro de que todos hemos escuchado al menos una historia de cómo se ganó una guerra, un equipo ganó un campeonato, una empresa logró ganancias o resultados increíbles, cómo una comunidad se reconstruyó después de un desastre o tragedia, o cómo un grupo de las personas pudieron superar una adversidad increíble mediante el simple proceso de elegir unirse, creyeron y se apoyaron mutuamente mientras perseguían implacablemente su objetivo compartido y luego lograron la grandeza juntos.

Es este tipo de esfuerzos para los que fuimos diseñados desde el principio. Hemos sido hechos para el amor. Hemos sido hechos para la relación. Hemos sido creados para la comunidad. Y la vida espiritual no es diferente.

Y es por eso que los santos tienden a venir en grupos.

Todos los grandes santos de los últimos veinte siglos: Benedicto, Francisco de Asís, Domingo, Ignacio de Loyola, Teresa de Ávila, Madre Teresa de Calcuta, y así sucesivamente, comenzaron su camino particular hacia la santidad, y luego su claridad acerca de lo que había que hacer para acercarse a Dios y volverse más como Jesús atrajo a otras personas de ideas afines hacia ellos, y luego juntos, lucharon por la santidad.

Pero ninguna familia o grupo de amigos ejemplifica mejor esta realidad de amor y relaciones entrelazadas centradas en la búsqueda de la santidad que la que encabezaron Basilio y el élder Emmelia en una pequeña comunidad en Capadocia a principios del siglo IV. De los nueve niños, cuatro, Macrina, Gregory, Basil y Peter, son todos santos canonizados, así como dos amigos de la familia: Gregory de Nazianzus y Eustathius de Sebaste.

Este grupo de santos hizo más para avanzar en la difusión del cristianismo y garantizar su ortodoxia que cualquier otro grupo de hombres y mujeres en todo el siglo IV. Sus escritos influyeron, solo en su propio siglo, en los grandes santos de Jerónimo, Ambrosio y Agustín, pero continúan siendo solicitados incluso dentro de la Iglesia hoy.

Dios trabajó poderosamente y milagrosamente a través de todos ellos. Y hay muchos más santos que están eternamente entrelazados con el nombre de sus amigos, como los santos Ignacio y Policarpo, Felicity y Perpetua, Basilio y Gregorio, Ambrosio y Agustín, Benedicto y Escolástica, Gregorio y Martín de Tours, Francisco y Clara de Asís, Teresa de Ávila y Juan de la Cruz, Madre Teresa y el Papa Juan Pablo II.

La lista podría seguir y seguir, pero lo que quiero destacar es que, para convertirnos en los santos que Dios nos ha creado para ser, *necesitamos* buenas y auténticas amistades para desafiarnos, inspirarnos, alentarnos y sostenernos.

Entonces, ¿cómo hacemos para encontrar tales amistades?

Bueno, primero, necesitamos saber qué estamos buscando realmente. Necesitamos entender la naturaleza de la amistad misma. Y además del amor, probablemente no haya nada más

incomprendido en nuestro mundo hoy que lo que realmente es la amistad, o lo que parece.

Muchos en nuestro mundo de hoy hablan de diferentes "tipos" de amigos, o las características que debemos buscar en un amigo. Esta comprensión de tener "tipos" de amigos se basa realmente en la comprensión griega antigua de los tres "tipos" de amistad que fue enseñada por Aristóteles. Esos tres tipos eran amistad agradable, amistad útil y amistad virtuosa.

La amistad agradable se puede describir más fácilmente como alguien con quien disfrutarías pasar el rato, tomar una cerveza, ir a ver una película o tal vez ver un evento deportivo. En pocas palabras, la amistad agradable es donde cada persona se divierte y pasa un buen rato juntos, pero no hay nada más en la relación que no sea el tiempo agradable que pasa.

La amistad útil surge cuando perseguimos juntos un objetivo común. Suelen ser personas con las que trabajamos, son parte de una organización o grupo del que formamos parte, o tal vez personas con las que vamos de excursión, en bicicleta o corriendo. Cada uno de nosotros ganamos valor con la presencia del otro porque tenemos algo que compartir, ya sea experiencia, habilidades, apoyo o aliento, pero aún existe una falta de profundidad en la relación, ya que no es necesario conocer realmente a la otra persona. Con el fin de perseguir el objetivo común, y cuando se elimina el objetivo común, la relación tenderá a desviarse también porque el objetivo es el unificador, no la relación entre las personas. Estos son "amigos por las circunstancias".

Ahora la amistad virtuosa es donde queremos lo mejor para el otro. Es una amistad que está enraizada en el amor porque conozco, acepto y aprecio tu *verdadero* yo, tal como eres sin otro motivo que el de buscar tu felicidad. Y si la verdadera felicidad solo surge de la unión transformadora con Dios, entonces un amigo virtuoso naturalmente buscará ayudar a otro amigo a descubrir este propósito, encontrar esta paz e invitarlos a una relación cada vez más profunda con Aquel que da vida en abundancia.

San Francisco de Sales escribe acerca de la amistad cristiana virtuosa, como una que se enfoca en buscar lo mejor para la otra, *"¡Si el vínculo de tu mutuo gusto es la caridad, la devoción y la perfección cristiana, Dios sabe cuán preciosa es una amistad! Precioso porque proviene de Dios, porque tiende a Dios, porque Dios es el vínculo que te une, porque durará para siempre en él".*

Podemos ver que esta es la forma más alta y perfecta de amistad. Es el tipo de amistad que Jesús modeló para sus discípulos, y el mismo tipo de amistad a la que nos invita con su Padre Celestial y el Espíritu Santo. Y este es el tipo de amistad que debemos esforzarnos para rodearnos aquí en la tierra.

Los santos de Capadocia ejemplifican esta idea de amistad cristiana virtuosa. Por lo tanto, debemos estudiar sus formas. Debemos preguntarnos: ¿Cómo permanecieron tan bien conectados, en una amistad tan fuerte con Dios, para que su río de gracia sobrenatural pudiera fluir tan libremente a través de ellos? ¿Qué pueden enseñarnos sobre las disciplinas espirituales ideales, el último régimen diario de oración, de crecer en virtud cada día y de abandonarnos a la voluntad de Dios?

Estas son las preguntas que debemos tratar de responder mientras trabajamos para crear un grupo de amigos en nuestras vidas. Amigos que se esfuerzan y animan, inspiran y apoyan a otros en el camino hacia la santidad. Cuando podemos llegar a ser nosotros mismos como los santos de Capadocia, y estar rodeados de otros que luchan de manera similar por la santidad, ¿quién sabe qué planes tiene Dios en mente para nosotros y su Iglesia cuando somos fieles al utilizar este gran regalo de la abundancia de Dios en nuestras vidas?

Ahora no hay nada "malo" con los otros tipos de amistad, o con tener diferentes "tipos" de amigos. Como aquellos en los que confiamos, o personas que nos guían, u otros que nos entienden y aceptan, u otros que son divertidos, o que nos desafían, u otros que son presencias leales y fieles en nuestras vidas sin importar lo que pase.[70]

Pero mi pregunta para usted es esta, si la realidad es que nos volvemos como aquellos con los que pasamos más tiempo, y realmente comprende quién es usted, y tiene claro en qué quiere enfocarse y ha dicho que sí para perseguirlo, combinado con el hecho de que el tiempo es corto, ¿por qué no está haciendo *todo* lo que está a su alcance para convertirse, y también exige a todos los que le rodean, el objetivo de ser amigos verdaderos y auténticos?

El obispo Robert Barron dijo una vez: *"No te metas con la amistad; no lo conviertes en algo abstracto; no te comprometes con eso. Entras completamente en él"*.

Esta es la única forma en que podemos llegar a ser, y la única forma en que podemos encontrar una amistad auténtica en nuestra vida. Al entrar en él por completo. Pero tendemos a contenernos. Por supuesto, debemos ejercer prudencia y no simplemente confiar en alguien completamente desde el primer día. Pero aún queremos "cubrir nuestras apuestas" en caso de que nos equivoquemos acerca de con quién hemos decidido entablar amistad. Pero esa "contención" garantiza que la relación nunca será verdaderamente auténtica.

Porque donde no hay riesgo, hay una falta de amor. Y donde hay una falta de amor, hay una falta de autenticidad. Y esto es realmente triste porque *"la amistad es la fuente de los mayores placeres, y sin amigos, incluso las actividades más agradables se vuelven tediosas"*.[71]

Por lo tanto, debemos estar decididos a buscar a cada uno de los verdaderos y auténticos amigos que Dios ha puesto en nuestras vidas. Y debemos estar dispuestos a conformarnos con nada menos que rodearnos lo más posible con la *plenitud* de la amistad auténtica y amorosa.

No se venda barato cuando se trata de amistad.

No solo debemos buscar ser una fuente de aliento, inspiración y apoyo para quienes nos rodean como un amigo auténtico y amoroso, sino que debemos asegurarnos de que nosotros

también recibamos el aliento, la inspiración y el apoyo necesarios para luchar por santidad todos los días.

Es hora de que surja un nuevo grupo de santos en la Iglesia hoy.

DIGA SÍ a la amistad verdadera y auténtica.

Ahora, pase la página para descubrir la amistad escondida a simple vista.

CAPÍTULO 19

AMISTAD OCULTA A
SIMPLE VISTA

Uno de los problemas más comunes sobre la amistad en nuestro mundo de hoy, del que hablé brevemente en el último capítulo, es el de encontrar una amistad auténtica. Muchas veces, nuestro fracaso en encontrar amigos con quienes compartir el viaje hacia la santidad provoca dudas en nosotros mismos para entrar plenamente en una relación por temor a ser rechazados o heridos.

Entonces, ¿cómo podríamos aprender a superar esta vacilación? ¿Cómo podemos superar este miedo a ser auténticos unos con otros mientras luchamos por la santidad?

Diríjase intencionalmente a la Comunión de los Santos.

LA COMUNIÓN DE LOS SANTOS

Como parte del Cuerpo de Cristo, estamos en unión con todo el pueblo santo de Dios, vivo y muerto. La Comunión de los Santos se compone de tres partes: la Iglesia Militante, el Sufrimiento de la Iglesia y la Iglesia Triunfante. La Iglesia Militante son aquellos que están vivos en la tierra, el Sufrimiento de la Iglesia son esas almas en el purgatorio, y la Iglesia Triunfante son todos los que son santos en el Cielo.

La Comunión de los Santos es una idea que muchas personas malinterpretan o no abrazan por completo, y por eso, muchas personas no utilizan las amistades que están ocultas a simple vista.

IGLESIA MILITANTE

La Iglesia Militante en particular se trata de luchar activamente por la santidad a través de cada uno de nuestros pensamientos, palabras y acciones porque nuestra salvación y santidad están intrínsecamente ligadas al bien de los demás. Por lo tanto, todo en la vida es importante y puede tener valor para ayudar a alguien a acercarse a Dios y ser más como Jesús.

Esto es especialmente importante de recordar cuando vivimos en la comunidad cristiana. Esta idea se ilustra en esta reflexión sobre confiar en los dones de los demás en una comunidad:

"Los apóstoles eran un grupo cercano (en realidad, todo el cuerpo de discípulos lo era). Ciertamente, tenían sus argumentos, pero tenían algunas amistades muy profundas. Podemos recoger esto de los Evangelios y verlo explícitamente en los Hechos de los Apóstoles.

La amistad de Peter y John es particularmente grande. Son personajes principales en los Evangelios, y su relación se revela en particular, aquí, al final del Evangelio de Juan y en el Libro de los Hechos. Hechos incluso habla del tiempo específico que pasaron juntos. Ninguno de ellos poseía todos los dones cristianos necesarios. Pero combinados, deben haber sido un equipo increíble. Peter tenía gran pasión, audacia y liderazgo. John tenía gran profundidad, fidelidad y amor.

Del mismo modo, ninguno de nosotros tiene todo lo que necesitamos en la vida cristiana. Necesitamos confiar en

otros para obtener fortalezas y regalos que no poseemos. Y otros necesitan confiar en nosotros para los regalos que les faltan. Los matrimonios y las familias también son así. Todos somos partes necesarias del único Cuerpo de Cristo. Deberíamos desarrollar nuestras cualidades, intereses y talentos únicos. Además, debemos alentarlos en otros".[72]

CS Lewis, uno de los más grandes escritores y apologistas cristianos del siglo veinte lo explica de esta manera:

"Es algo muy serio vivir en una sociedad de posibles dioses y diosas, recordar que la persona más aburrida y menos interesante con la que hables algún día puede ser una criatura que, si la vieras ahora, estarías fuertemente tentado a adorar, o de lo contrario, un horror y una corrupción como la que ahora se encuentra, en todo caso, en una pesadilla. Durante todo el día, en cierto grado, nos estamos ayudando mutuamente a uno u otro de estos destinos. A la luz de estas posibilidades abrumadoras, es con el asombro y la circunspección propia de ellos, que debemos llevar a cabo todos nuestros tratos entre nosotros, todas las amistades, todos los amores, todos los juegos, todas las políticas. No hay gente común. Nunca has hablado con un simple mortal... Pero es a los inmortales con quienes bromeamos, trabajamos, nos casamos, nos despreciamos y explotamos: horrores inmortales o esplendores eternos".

Sin embargo, en un mundo donde las personas son descartadas, no amadas y aparentemente reemplazables, ¿dónde vamos a experimentar ser apreciados?

Dentro de nuestras familias y con nuestros amigos. Se supone que la familia cristiana es un lugar de amor, tanto humano como divino, con relaciones entrelazadas entre amigos, pobres, enfermos y otros cristianos, todos unidos en la adoración a Dios. Y nuestras amistades deberían esforzarse por lo mismo.

Como compartí en el último capítulo, los santos de Capadocia que surgieron en el siglo IV en los alrededores de la casa de Basilio y el élder Emmelia son el modelo que estamos buscando. Familias y amigos que se reúnen en torno al propósito compartido de luchar por la santidad en una atmósfera de aceptación amorosa.

De todas las lecciones de los santos de Capadocia, la lección más importante que tienen para nosotros es el amor. Porque fue solo por amor a su hermana, Macrina, después de su fallecimiento, que Gregory de Nyssa escribió su biografía titulada "Vita Macrinae Junioris", y es por eso que conocemos a esta familia y su grupo interconectado de amigos.

Tal es el poder del amor en la Iglesia Militante dentro de la Comunión de los Santos.

Ahora sé que muchos de nosotros podríamos no tener la bendición de experimentar este tipo de amor dentro de nuestras familias o amigos. De hecho, en un artículo reciente, Charles McKinney hizo la siguiente observación:

"Muchos han perdido su fe en Dios, porque han perdido, por falta de fe, su fe en el hombre. La duda de la realidad del amor se convierte en la duda de la realidad de la vida espiritual. No poder ver lo divino en el hombre es tener los ojos cegados a lo divino en cualquier lugar. El engaño en la esfera del amor sacude los cimientos de la religión. Su resultado es el ateísmo, quizás no como un sistema de pensamiento consciente especulativo, sino como una sutil influencia práctica en la conducta. Corrompe la fuente de la vida y contamina toda la corriente. La desesperación del amor, si es final y completa, sería la desesperación de Dios, porque Dios es amor. Por lo tanto, la ruina de la amistad a menudo significa una ruina de fe temporal. No debería ser así, pero existe el peligro de que nos impresione con un sentido más profundo de la responsabilidad asociada a nuestras amistades. Nuestra vida sigue la fortuna de nuestro amor".[73]

Y aquí es donde se supone que el Cuerpo de Cristo en la forma de nuestras iglesias parroquiales llena el vacío. El Papa Francisco nos dice que una parroquia debe ser *"una familia entre familias, abierta a dar testimonio en el mundo de hoy... abierta a la fe, la esperanza y el amor por el Señor y por aquellos a quienes Él tiene un amor preferencial. Una casa con puertas abiertas"*.

¿A que podría parecerse?

Sería una comunidad en la que cada persona ayuda a otra a llegar a una conversión cada vez más profunda de muchas maneras: una sonrisa, o una disposición al perdón, o al esforzarse por comprender y estar presentes el uno al otro. El uso caritativo de dones y talentos para el beneficio de cada persona que encontramos al compartir las cargas de la vida junto con amor y alegría.

Es en un lugar como este donde reside la Iglesia Militante. Un lugar donde los que están aquí en la tierra se esfuerzan por crecer en santidad mientras ayudan a otros a hacer lo mismo. Donde enseñamos y ayudamos a otros a ver cómo ve Dios, para que todos podamos ver y sentir la forma en que Jesús se ve y siente, y experimentar y aprender a dejar que nuestros corazones laten con amor como lo hace Jesús.

Pero si nuestras iglesias no son tales lugares, ¿entonces qué?

Aquí es donde la Comunión de los Santos tiene la capacidad de sostenernos hasta la eternidad.

Debido a que la Comunión de los Santos no se trata solo de aquí y ahora, también se trata de todos los que han venido antes y de todos los que ya están en el Cielo. Y solo porque nuestros amigos pueden haberse alejado de esta vida, nunca se han ido ni han sido olvidados, ni su influencia cesa.

Santa Elizabeth Ann Seton escribió: *"Los accidentes de la vida nos separan de nuestros amigos más queridos, pero no nos desesperemos. Dios es como un espejo en el que las almas se ven. Cuanto más nos unimos a Él por el amor, más cerca estamos de quienes le pertenecen"*.

EL SUFRIMIENTO DE LA IGLESIA, LOS DEL PURGATORIO

Nuestros hermanos y hermanas en el purgatorio experimentan una gran alegría y un gran dolor. Gran alegría porque saben con certeza que algún día estarán con Dios en el cielo, pero gran pena porque se les ha dado una visión clara de sí mismos, y ahora se dan cuenta de cuán lejos están aún de ese eterno momento de unión transformadora con Dios.

Es por eso que la Iglesia nos pide que recemos por las almas del purgatorio. Porque los lazos de la comunidad cristiana no cesan con la muerte, sino que estos lazos pueden ser perfeccionados por el poder del Espíritu Santo cuando estamos en unión con Cristo en la oración.

El Sr. Schmaus en su libro, *Dogmatic Theology*, explica:

> *"El amor y la fidelidad de la Iglesia en la tierra gana alegría y alivio para aquellas almas que anhelan entrar en la dicha eterna. Esta corriente de caridad se eleva en beneficio de las almas del Purgatorio, incluso cuando estamos distraídos. Sin embargo, cuando nos aseguramos de dirigir estas oraciones para esta intención, podemos trabajar por un bien aún mayor".*[74]

El Papa Benedicto XVI describe el resultado de esta "corriente de caridad" maravillosamente:

> *"Debemos recordar que ningún hombre es una isla en sí misma. Nuestras vidas están involucradas entre sí, a través de innumerables interacciones están vinculadas entre sí. Nadie vive solo. Nadie peca solo. Nadie se salva solo. Las vidas de otros continuamente se derraman sobre los míos: en lo que pienso, digo, hago y logro. Y, por el contrario, mi vida se derrama en la de los demás: para bien o para mal. Así que mi oración por otro no es algo ajeno a esa persona, algo externo, ni siquiera después de la muerte".*

Tan cierto, la amistad auténtica nunca muere. Se acaba de transformar. Todavía podemos hacer el bien del otro al ofrecer amorosamente oración y sacrificio por nuestros familiares y amigos. Cada día, se nos da la oportunidad de continuar amando a través de las muchas obras de misericordia; o al recibir los sacramentos; u ofreciendo nuestro sufrimiento físico o los desafíos que enfrentamos en nuestra vida diaria.

Y a medida que amamos, continuamos transformándonos y purificándonos a nosotros mismos, lo que nos hace aún más capaces de ser un amigo verdadero y auténtico, pero también nos prepara cada vez más para la relación de amor con Jesús por toda la eternidad en el Cielo.

LA IGLESIA TRIUNFANTE

Convertirse en santos simplemente significa cumplir completamente lo que ya somos como hijos e hijas adoptados de Dios. *"Nada puede acercarnos más a la belleza de Cristo mismo que el mundo de la belleza creado por la fe y la luz que brota de los rostros de los santos, a través de los cuales su propia luz se hace visible".*[75]

San Antonio de Padua nos dice que *"Cada santo en el cielo se regocija por la glorificación del otro, y su amor se desborda hacia él... la misma alegría llenará a todos los bendecidos, porque me alegraré por su bienestar como si fuera mi propia, y te regocijarás por la mía como si fuera tuya... Así será en la vida eterna: mi gloria será tu consuelo y alegría, y la tuya será mía".*

Ser parte de la Iglesia Triunfante de la Comunión de los Santos es experimentar exactamente eso, pero incluso aquellos en el Cielo están llamados a amar aún.

"Los santos nos enseñan, nos alientan, nos desafían e inspiran... Dios está constantemente tratando de abrir nuestros ojos a las increíbles posibilidades que Él ha envuelto en nuestro ser. Los santos continúan este trabajo, animándonos a explorar todo nuestro potencial dado por Dios, no con discursos, sino con el ejemplo de sus vidas".[76]

El cielo no es la jubilación. No, el cielo es donde tendremos la mayor cantidad de oportunidades para amar a través de la intercesión y orar por los demás, particularmente por aquellos que luchan por la santidad como parte de la Iglesia Militante.

Es por eso que los santos patronos son tan importantes.

Aunque lo mismo es cierto para todos los santos, nuestros santos patrones están *particularmente* interesados en ayudarnos. Hay un santo patrón para cada profesión y pasatiempo que se le ocurra, e invocamos su patrocinio cuando elegimos y tomamos su nombre en la Confirmación.

Para mí, mi santo patrón oficial es San Miguel Arcángel. Él era mi santo de la Confirmación, y siendo un ex oficial militar, ¡puedo dar fe de que recurrí a su ayuda y protección MUCHO!

Además de nuestros santos patronos, cualquier santo que nos inspire a través de sus escritos o con el ejemplo de su vida tiene una conexión con nosotros, y en realidad desea que les pidamos ayuda en cualquier momento, de día o de noche.

Personalmente, tengo todo un *panteón* de santos a los que llamo regularmente. Con los años, lo que ha surgido para mí en mi vida espiritual es tener un santo para cada día de la semana. Santos como John Vianney, patrón de los párrocos, a quien le pido su intercesión cuando ofrezco oraciones por los sacerdotes actuales y por las futuras vocaciones sacerdotales y religiosas.

O Francis Xavier que me inspira a evangelizar y compartir las Buenas Nuevas. O mi "otro" Francis - Francis de Sales, que es el mecenas de los escritores. Maximillian Kolbe me inspira a vivir más plenamente mi consagración mariana cada día. La Madre Teresa de Calcuta y Teresa de Lisieux y Faustina me enseñan lo que es llevar una vida de amor misericordioso. Y luego mi precioso Ignacio de Loyola, que, como yo, dejó de lado una profesión militar para perseguir ser un mejor discípulo de Jesús, y que me inspira a acercarme a Dios y llegar a ser más como Jesús todos los días.

Si por alguna razón todavía no ha conocido a los santos, le animo a que comience. Como mínimo, busque al santo

patrón para su profesión, o tal vez redescubra a su santo de la Confirmación. Pero conozca a los santos que ya están presentes en su vida, independientemente de si los conoce o no.

Ahora, estos son solo algunos ejemplos de cómo los santos pueden ayudarnos, inspirarnos e interceder por nosotros. Pero lo más importante es pedir e invocar su ayuda. ¡Asegúrese de pedir su ayuda! Porque vendrán en su ayuda. Ellos intercederán por usted. Ellos le ayudarán.

ASISTENCIA ANGELICAL

San Francisco de Sales escribió: *"Haz amigos con los ángeles, que, aunque invisibles siempre están contigo. A menudo invócalos, elogia constantemente y aprovecha su ayuda y asistencia en todos tus asuntos temporales y espirituales".*

Ya mencioné a San Miguel, ya que él es mi Santo de la Confirmación, pero San Miguel y los otros Arcángeles que conocemos de las Escrituras, Rafael y Gabriel, son totalmente rockeros.

Y, sin embargo, Dios nos ha dado un regalo aún más precioso: nuestro propio ángel guardián personal.

Con demasiada frecuencia, olvidamos que hay un ayudante angelical que está allí para protegernos, guiarnos y ayudarnos en cada momento de cada día. Se nos recuerda esto cada vez que rezamos la oración del Ángel Guardián: *"Ángel de Dios, mi guardián querido, a quien el amor de Dios me confía aquí. Siempre este día, quédate a mi lado, para encender, proteger, gobernar y guiar".*

¡Que bendición! ¡Un ángel que está presente cada minuto de cada día únicamente para ayudarnos e interceder por nosotros!

Pero incluso más que eso, debemos tratar de imitar a nuestro ángel guardián. Por ejemplo de cómo debemos reverenciar ante la presencia de Dios en el Tabernáculo; de cómo debemos recordar y desear estar en unión con Dios en todas las actividades de nuestro día, desde nuestro primer aliento hasta nuestros últimos

pensamientos antes de quedarnos dormidos; de cómo enfrentarse a las tentaciones y luchar contra el diablo; pero especialmente en cómo ejemplificar y practicar las virtudes, especialmente las virtudes de caridad, paciencia, gentileza, generosidad, pureza y rectitud de corazón.

¡Hable sobre el amigo perfecto!

Ahora, cada uno de nosotros tiene un ángel guardián. Entonces, incluso si falta nuestra familia o parroquia, incluso si está teniendo dificultades para encontrar amigos verdaderos y auténticos a su alrededor, incluso si no conoce el panteón de los santos listos para interceder por usted, Dios *todavía* le ha dado a todos y cada uno de nosotros acceso a un amigo verdadero y auténtico.

Pero solo si estamos dispuestos a pedirles ayuda e invocar su ayuda.

Del mismo modo, debemos estar dispuestos a buscar todas las fuentes de amistad que están ocultas a la vista. Buscar amistades entre toda la Comunión de los Santos, los que viven, los que nos han precedido y los que ya nos esperan en el Cielo.

Manténgase en amistad aquí en la tierra y hasta la eternidad.

DIGA SÍ a la amistad escondida a plena vista.

Y ahora, pase la página y descubra el poder de la historia.

CAPÍTULO 20
EL PODER DE LA HISTORIA

"Nos convertimos en las historias que escuchamos".

— Mateo Kelly[77]

O tra herramienta, y la tercera joya escondida para nuestra eventual corona de gloria en el Cielo, es la historia.

Dios nos diseñó desde el principio en cómo nos formó para que seamos alentados, inspirados y apoyados de manera única en nuestras vidas a través del poder de la historia.

Las historias son el lenguaje que la humanidad usa para comunicarse.

Sin embargo, numerosos estudios muestran que después de graduarse de la escuela, la mayoría de las personas ya no leen nada más que lo que podría ser necesario para algún propósito práctico, como su trabajo. Esto es realmente triste, porque las historias pueden ser la puerta a través de la cual podemos embarcarnos en el viaje de la transformación, y las estadísticas confirman esta realidad una y otra vez y muestran cómo las personas que se sumergen en la historia son más imaginativas y curiosas, más empáticas, la experiencia reduce el estrés y aumenta la capacidad de comunicación y habilidades sociales.

Para mí, las historias siempre han sido una gran parte de mi vida. Fui bendecido con un amor por la lectura, y eso nunca se ha desvanecido, ya que todavía soy un ávido lector, así como también me encantan las películas y la televisión. Con los años, sin embargo, me he dado cuenta de que tiendo a gravitar hacia esos programas de libros, cine y televisión que todos cuentan una historia realmente fenomenal. Lo hacen a través de la trama en sí o al tener personajes que tienen una gran profundidad y complejidad. Si una u otra de esas cosas no están presentes, entonces tiendo a perder interés con bastante rapidez.

Uno de mis libros favoritos es el de J.R.R. Tolkien, *La trilogía de El señor de los anillos.* Debido a la magnífica adaptación cinematográfica de Peter Jackson de la trilogía, la mayoría de las personas ahora están familiarizadas con la historia de Frodo el Hobbit, una de las criaturas más pequeñas que reside en la Tierra Media, a la que se le asigna la gran tarea de llevar el gran Anillo de Poder al Monte del Destino a que se destruya y, al hacerlo, salva a toda la Tierra Media del gran mal de Sauron. Otro de mis favoritos es el personaje de George Bailey en la película clásica *It's a Wonderful Life*, donde el ángel, Clarence, le muestra a George cuán profundamente importante ha sido su vida, incluso si el propio George no puede verla.

Uno que no es tan conocido es el personaje de Lewis Gillies en la trilogía *Song of Albion* de Stephen Lawhead. Lewis, un flaco estudiante graduado de una familia sin importancia en nuestro mundo, es transportado a la tierra de Albion. Y mientras lucha por defender la esencia de lo que es bueno, verdadero y bello durante la Guerra del Paraíso, Lewis se ve transformado a través de sus muchas batallas y pruebas, y finalmente se convierte en el gran Rey Supremo, Llew Silver Hand. Como Llew, no solo es el defensor del reino de Albion, sino que también sirve como el protector de todo lo que es bueno, verdadero y hermoso en todos los reinos de todos los mundos, incluido el nuestro.

Más recientemente, las historias en la película *Avengers: End Game* y en la serie de televisión *Game of Thrones* (GOT) han

sido inspiradoras en su representación del amor y el sacrificio. En ambas historias, que tomaron *años* para compartir, todos los personajes tuvieron que recurrir y confiar el uno en el otro para tratar de derrotar la mayor amenaza que cualquiera de ellos haya enfrentado. Al final, es solo a través del *sacrificio y el amor* que incluso existe la posibilidad de ganar el día. Pero fueron las *historias* de redención en medio de los sacrificios que se hicieron y el amor que se mostró, lo que posteriormente inspiró, se llenó de lágrimas y les dio a los otros personajes el coraje necesario para continuar su propio viaje.

Y es lo mismo para nosotros.

La razón por la cual estas y otras grandes historias son tan fenomenalmente populares es porque *anhelamos* inspirarnos en las historias de otros que se sacrifican por amor a otro, porque entonces estamos inspirados y tenemos el coraje de tratar de hacer lo mismo en nuestra propia vida.

Edward C. Sellner, autor del libro, *Stories of Celtic Soul Friends*, señala que todas las grandes tradiciones espirituales, incluido el judaísmo, el islam, el budismo y el hinduismo, relacionan su comprensión de Dios y el destino de la humanidad a través de las historias que cuentan de sus fundadores, héroes y santos. Este es el resultado del impulso primordial de la humanidad de expresar lo que la gente ha visto, escuchado y experimentado que ha suscitado preguntas, asombro y asombro.[78]

Otro autor, Russell W. Dalton, explica que la humanidad ha construido mitos y leyendas a lo largo de la historia en un intento de proporcionar explicaciones para la naturaleza y, al igual que Sellner, afirma de manera similar que las historias deben ser un medio para explorar las últimas preguntas de la vida.

Esta afirmación de ambos autores es firmemente evidente si uno se toma el tiempo de mirar mitos y leyendas de todo el mundo. A pesar de los muchos lugares y culturas diferentes, todos comparten temas y motivos similares. Pero el motivo principal es la idea del viaje del héroe.

El viaje del héroe comienza con "el héroe" llamado a una aventura por un extraño misterioso, que luego se asegura de que el héroe reciba regalos especiales para su búsqueda. Además, el héroe se encuentra o se reúne con un grupo de compañeros que se convierten en sus amigos, y luego juntos deben encontrar el camino a través de algún tipo de bosque oscuro o cueva donde el héroe debe descender a las profundidades para enfrentar un gran mal, y finalmente, después de hacer un gran sacrificio, el héroe finalmente sale victorioso. [79]

Dalton sostiene que estos temas y motivos aparecen porque expresan verdades profundamente entendidas sobre la experiencia humana, junto con visiones humanas de lo que es divino. Por lo tanto, dado que todos los humanos comparten un anhelo de encontrar un propósito y un significado en sus vidas y conocer a Dios, estos "anhelos" espirituales se encuentran detrás de las similitudes en los mitos y leyendas antiguos. [80]

Las historias poderosas son evidentes en la forma en que pueden comunicar varios significados diferentes dentro de la misma historia. Estos significados diferentes, o los cuatro sentidos de la literatura, son: literal, moral, alegórico y anagógico.

El literal es la historia en sí misma; la moraleja es la lección que comunica la historia; lo alegórico es cómo la historia representa y señala algo más (esto se hace con mayor frecuencia presagiando); y lo anagógico (a menudo llamado escatológico) revela el significado de esta historia con respecto a la vida y la muerte misma.

Puedes tener una idea rápida de cómo los diferentes sentidos pueden estar trabajando después de una misa, cuando la gente está discutiendo la homilía. Algunos comparten el hecho que los impactó, mientras que otros comparten sobre la lección que aprendieron, mientras que otros hablan sobre lo que los motiva a actuar.

Dando un paso más allá, el p. Thomas Dubay, en su libro, *The Fire Within*, utiliza esta ilustración para describir lo que está ocurriendo:

"De la misma manera, quinientas personas en una iglesia parroquial escuchan las mismas ondas sonoras durante la homilía, pero se benefician de ella exactamente como están o no dispuestas para el mensaje. Jesús enseñó la misma verdad en su parábola del sembrador: de la palabra de Dios algunos oyentes no dan nada en absoluto, mientras que otros dan treinta o sesenta o cien veces".[81]

Sinceramente, esto no debería sorprendernos, ya que hay muchos ejemplos de este hecho en un nivel natural todo el tiempo, donde las personas van a escuchar a un orador motivador y todos "escuchan" algo diferente que los inspira a la acción. O cuando la gente va y ve una película, y alguien llora durante una escena, pero luego otra persona llora durante otra y otra persona no llora en absoluto. Este es el poder de la historia y sus diversos significados en el trabajo en los corazones, las almas y las mentes de las personas.

Pero no solo la historia tiene poder, sino también las palabras mismas.

Esto fue ilustrado más recientemente por un experimento realizado por la empresa de muebles, IKEA.

Tomaron dos plantas, construyeron contenedores alrededor de cada una, y luego hicieron que la gente registrara mensajes positivos y negativos. Luego enviaron los mensajes a los contenedores de la planta. Todo positivo para uno y todo negativo para el otro. En un mes, era físicamente evidente el poder de las palabras en cada una de las plantas, ya que la planta que no había escuchado nada más que negativo estaba muriendo: sus hojas estaban marchitas, su crecimiento estaba atrofiado y tenía mucho color marrón y amarillo. entre su crecimiento; mientras que la planta que había recibido mensajes positivos era vibrante, exuberante, llena de hojas verdes y crecimiento fresco, estaba prosperando.[82]

Existen muchos otros estudios que se han realizado con otros artículos físicos, como el arroz o uno con agua. Cada

experimento revela el poder de las palabras en nuestro entorno físico, y señala la realidad de que las palabras mismas tienen un gran significado y poder.

Este hecho se evidencia en las Escrituras al comienzo del Génesis con el uso del motivo de "Y Dios dijo" y "entonces fue" que se utiliza a lo largo de toda la historia de la creación. De hecho, la palabra "abracadabra" significa literalmente en hebreo, "creo mientras hablo".

Incluso a nivel natural podemos reconocer el poder de los nombres, ya que es algo especial cuando alguien nos llama por nuestro nombre. Si escuchamos que alguien dice nuestro nombre, nos detiene en seco y sentimos un deseo de responder. Cuando escuchamos nuestro nombre, nos llama la atención. Este es el poder que reside en nuestro nombre.

Y esto recuerda a Dios dando nuevos nombres a aquellos con quienes se relaciona, como Abram convirtiéndose en Abraham, o más tarde las palabras de Jesús cuando proclama: *"Lo que pidas en mi nombre, lo haré".*[83]

En el Evangelio de Juan, se nos da una idea de quién es exactamente la Segunda Persona de la Trinidad cuando se nos dice: *"Al principio era la Palabra; y la Palabra estaba con Dios; y la Palabra era Dios".*[84] Y más adelante en ese mismo Evangelio, escuchamos cómo la Palabra se hizo carne y habitó entre nosotros, y luego esa misma Palabra, Jesús, nos habló; *"Yo soy el camino, y la verdad y la vida".*

Jesús es la "Palabra" definitiva hablada por Dios y toda la Revelación Divina se resume en Él.

La palabra ES la vida misma.

Entonces, ¿qué tiene esto que ver con el poder de la historia en nuestra vida espiritual?

Todo.

La clave para entender el poder de la historia en nuestras vidas espirituales es darse cuenta de que la historia es en realidad Su historia, y que *todas* nuestras historias son parte de Su historia. Cuando vemos nuestras historias como intrincadamente

conectadas e integrales a *la* Historia, somos capaces de ver cómo todas las historias, especialmente la nuestra, son ecos de *la* Historia.

La historia del sacrificio amoroso de Jesús. Una historia arraigada *en su amor completo, total e interminable* por cada uno de nosotros. Estas son las Buenas Nuevas, y por qué los hombres y las mujeres durante más de dos milenios se han inspirado al sacrificio y al amor como Jesús.

Y ahora llamamos a estos hombres y mujeres santos.

A lo largo de la Sagrada Escritura y la historia de la historia de la salvación, podemos ver que la historia de *todos* importa porque Dios siempre usa a las personas más improbables una y otra vez para lograr su plan para la salvación de toda la humanidad.

Cuanto más nos sumergimos en grandes historias, más podremos cumplir nuestra triple vocación. Cuanto más escuchemos y compartamos las historias de los demás, más nos inspiraremos y alentaremos a seguir el llamado a la santidad y a vivir nuestra misión personal de quiénes somos, qué somos y dónde estamos en nuestro estado particular de la vida, y así escribimos nuestros respectivos capítulos en Su historia.

Sumérjase en grandes historias. Historias que lo inspiren y alienten a hacer el bien, buscar la verdad y abrazar lo bello.

Historias que le den el coraje de luchar cada día de su vida a medida que se transforma en el héroe que Dios le ha creado para estar dentro de su propia vida y la de los demás.

Conviértase en un envalentonado guerrero de Cristo.

DIGA SÍ al poder de la historia.

Ahora, pase la página para comenzar a compartir la vida divina de hoy.

Capítulo 21
COMPARTIENDO LA VIDA DIVINA

"Lo que sucede es de poca importancia en comparación con las historias que nos contamos sobre lo que sucede. Los eventos importan poco, solo las historias de eventos nos afectan".

— Rabih Alameddine, El contador de historias

Otro aspecto de la historia es la necesidad de *compartir* nuestra historia con otros. Es solo a través del intercambio de nuestras historias sobre nuestra relación con Dios, y cómo esa relación ha marcado la diferencia en el mundo dentro de nuestras vidas, que los demás se sienten motivados a considerar la posibilidad por sí mismos, y también se sienten alentados por su relación con Él.

Sin embargo, dudamos en hablar. Nos convencemos de que "mi historia no importa" o "¿Quién soy yo para hablar de esas cosas? No soy nadie importante".

Pero estas son mentiras que nos dice el mundo. La historia de *todos* importa.

A menudo, cuando escuchamos la genealogía de Jesús, o cualquiera de las genealogías en las Escrituras, podemos

"desconectarnos" o distraernos para pensar que estos son solo un montón de nombres que no tienen significado. Pero trate de pensar en ellos un poco diferente.

Esos nombres son en realidad *nosotros*.

Enos, Thara, Esrom, Menan, Addi, Joanna y Melchi tuvieron un papel integral que desempeñar (estas personas son todos antepasados de Jesús), y nos dice que nosotros también tenemos un "papel" en LA gran historia. Pero nuevamente, creemos que no somos importantes, y que nuestras vidas no importan y, por lo tanto, nuestras historias tampoco importan.

Pero nuestras historias son importantes. Desesperadamente.

Porque hay un aspecto aún más vital en la importancia de compartir nuestra historia con otros, y me tomó años antes de que realmente obtuviera claridad sobre este punto. Lo que he aprendido es que, *si no compartimos nuestra historia, estamos matando la vida divina que reside dentro de nosotros.*

Porque es solo compartiendo nuestra historia (evangelizando) que nosotros mismos somos evangelizados.

"... *encontramos la salvación para nosotros precisamente en la medida en que llevamos la vida de Dios a los demás",*[85] *por lo tanto, "cada uno de nosotros debería preguntarse a sí mismo: ¿He hecho todo lo que pude en el transcurso de este año por la Inmaculada, por la salvación y la santificación de mi alma y la de mi prójimo? ¿O mi conciencia me reprocha mi pereza, la apatía, mi pobre fervor... o mi falta de auto-sacrificio?"*[86]

Y así como es cierto que alguien que enseña llega a conocer su material más profundamente en el proceso de preparación para presentarlo a otro, lo mismo es cierto para nosotros en el proceso de compartir nuestra historia con otros.

Porque cuando no compartimos cómo Dios está trabajando en nuestras vidas, nuestra propia fe se debilita. Negamos la esencia misma de quiénes somos, nuestra historia, cuando no compartimos nuestra historia.

Es por eso que Dios ha hecho de la historia la forma más fundamental en la que nos comunicamos unos con otros.

¿Por qué digo esto? Porque es EXACTAMENTE cómo lo hizo Dios en forma humana, con Jesús.

Jesús compartió *historias* con los que lo rodeaban en la antigua Palestina, y continúa compartiendo su historia con cada uno de nosotros todos los días, mientras escribe los detalles de nuestras vidas al confiarnos sueños, para que puedan volverse realidad. con Él, en Él y a través de Él para los demás.

Una vez que nos damos cuenta de que nuestras *historias* importan, queda muy claro que *debemos* compartir nuestra historia y escuchar las historias de los demás si queremos asegurarnos de que la vida divina que reside dentro de nosotros arda brillantemente y pueda encender, alentar y sostener la vida divina de otros.

LA NECESIDAD

Jean-Baptiste Chautard relata en su libro *The Soul of the Apostolate*, el Papa San Pío X estaba conversando con un grupo de sus cardenales un día. El papa les preguntó:

—¿Qué es lo que más necesitamos hoy para salvar a la sociedad?

—Construir escuelas católicas —dijo uno.

—No.

—Más iglesias —dijo otro.

—Aún no.

—Acelerar el reclutamiento de sacerdotes —dijo un tercero.

—No, no —dijo el Papa—, lo más necesario de todo, en este momento, es que cada parroquia posea un grupo de laicos que sean al mismo tiempo virtuosos, iluminados, resueltos y verdaderamente apostólicos.

Chautard continúa: "Más detalles nos permiten afirmar que este santo Papa al final de su vida no vio esperanza para la salvación del mundo a menos que el clero pudiera usar su fervor para formar cristianos fieles llenos de ardor apostólico, predicando con palabras y ejemplos, pero especialmente con

el ejemplo. En la diócesis donde sirvió antes de ser elevado al papado, le dio menos importancia al (recuento) de feligreses que a la lista *de cristianos capaces de irradiar un apostolado"*. *(enfatiza lo mío)*

Si observamos el testimonio de todos los santos a lo largo de los últimos dos milenios, ser capaces de "irradiar un apostolado" significa que debemos ser obedientes a hacer la voluntad de Dios mientras cumplimos la Gran Comisión de "salir y proclamar las Buenas Nuevas y bautizar todas las naciones".

¿Y cómo proclamamos las Buenas Nuevas? Al compartir nuestras historias.

Compartimos nuestra historia de cómo las Buenas Nuevas han transformado nuestras vidas y han marcado la diferencia en la vida. De cómo, como ya no somos prisioneros de pecado y muerte, podemos vivir vidas llenas de propósito, paz y abundancia.

Es *por eso* que son las "¡Buenas noticias!"

Sin embargo, en nuestro mundo científico, tendemos a negar que la historia tenga algún poder para ayudarnos. Tendemos a pensar que las historias son solo para niños, que, si somos adultos maduros, habremos dejado de lado todo lo que huele a "cuentos de hadas" y abracemos cosas "reales" que podemos ver, oír, oler, saborear y toque. Pero cuando dejamos de lado la historia, dejamos de lado el misterio, y cuando lo hacemos, comenzamos a sofocarnos y matar a nuestro verdadero ser, nuestra alma espiritual.

El Dr. Tod Warner describe bellamente de lo que estoy hablando en su artículo, "Misterio, modales y redescubrimiento de la gran literatura":

"La ciencia puede explicar, pero nunca en total. ¿Cómo vamos a sondear las profundidades del amor? ¿Con un artículo sobre neurotransmisores? ¿Cómo podremos comprender plenamente las comodidades de la lealtad y la angustia de la traición? ¿Con coloridos escaneos PET de nuestros cerebros? Durante la Ilustración, ciertos pensadores

nos aseguraron que la moralidad pronto se definiría y predeciría por completo utilizando ecuaciones matemáticas. Para tomar prestado de una cita mal hecha pero brillante, "Algunas ideas son tan absurdas que solo un intelectual las creería".

Debemos leer y experimentar. Debemos abrirnos al misterio que no se explicará completamente a este lado de la tumba. Debemos dar la bienvenida a las contribuciones de la ciencia sin estar limitados por ellas. Después de todo, no somos simplemente seres materiales; **somos almas de una profundidad inefable mayor que nuestras partes constituyentes".**[87] **(Lo que está en negrita enfatiza lo mío)**

Somos almas de profundidad inefable que son mayores que nuestras partes constituyentes. Para ninguno de nosotros es simplemente lo que podemos hacer o haber hecho. Tampoco somos simplemente un conglomerado de nuestras emociones e ideas. Somos *mucho* mas

Nuestra historia es la vida divina intrincadamente entrelazada y que reside dentro de cada uno de nosotros. Pero esa realidad solo se hace evidente en el contexto de compartir nuestras historias entre nosotros.

Santa Rosa de Lima observó: *"Sepa que el mayor servicio que el hombre puede ofrecer a Dios es ayudar a convertir las almas".* Por lo tanto, nadie es insignificante y todos estamos interconectados para lograr el "final feliz", cuando el Rey regrese y todo estará bien nuevamente, cuando el dolor, el sufrimiento y la muerte ya no existan.

Y, sin embargo, tenemos miedo de compartir nuestra historia. ¿Por qué?

A menudo, es simplemente porque tenemos miedo de cómo podemos mirar o temer la incomodidad de una situación en particular. Pero no podemos dejar que nuestro orgullo y miedo nos impidan hacer lo que sea necesario para ayudar a la otra persona

a acercarse a Dios. Como cristianos, tenemos el deber de vivir como Cristo, y eso significa amar lo mejor que podamos, incluso si eso significa que fracasamos o somos rechazados.

"Todos fallan en ser quienes se supone que son. Un héroe está determinado por lo bien que es quien debe ser, en lugar de ser quien se supone que debe ser ".[88]

Y buscar lo que estamos destinados a ser es la esencia del llamado a la santidad. Es a través de nuestros esfuerzos de cooperar con la gracia de Dios para convertirnos en santos que realmente nos convertimos en los "personajes" en la Gran Historia que estamos destinados a ser.

Pero "¿Qué historia estoy contando actualmente con mi vida?"[89] ¿Es tu historia una historia que inspirará y alentará a otros a la grandeza?

Porque no solo nuestra historia es parte de *la* historia, nuestra historia es el vehículo exacto que Dios quiere que usemos para compartirlo con los demás.

Y Él te creó específicamente para hacer exactamente eso.

Entonces, *"considere el entorno de uno, los miembros de la familia, conocidos, compañeros de trabajo y lugares de residencia, como el lugar de su misión, para ganarse a estas personas..."*[90]

Esta es la esencia de evangelizar. Simplemente participar en el acto de compartir su historia con otra persona.

Hacemos esto porque *"Hemos sido llamados a sanar heridas, a unir lo que se ha derrumbado y a traer a casa a los que han perdido el rumbo".*[91] Y debemos *"Descartar toda ira y mirarnos un poco a nosotros mismos. Recuerde que él, de quien estás hablando, es tu hermano, y como él está en el camino de la salvación, Dios puede hacerlo santo, a pesar de su debilidad actual".*[92]

Por eso es tan importante compartir nuestra historia. Al ser vulnerables, invitamos a otros a hacer lo mismo y luego podemos cumplir verdaderamente el mandato que Cristo nos dio de "ir a hacer discípulos".

Y si realmente amamos a Jesús, entonces estaremos dispuestos a ser "incomodados" por otras personas que tienen sed de

escuchar nuestra historia (de Dios). Debemos estar dispuestos a dejar ir nuestra comodidad y abrazar nuestra grandeza.

Hacemos esto amando a los demás de manera pequeña para que ellos también se inspiren a hacer lo mismo, y luego juntos, podremos ayudar a derrotar a un ejército aún más poderoso que cualquier ejército dirigido por un villano ficticio o un ejército de los no muertos. Al hacer sacrificios, amar a los demás y compartir nuestras historias, podemos ayudar a ganar la victoria en la gran batalla espiritual para el mundo y para aquellos que lo eligen, ¡la vida eterna!

Pero debemos comenzar llamándonos por su nombre en una cultura que languidece por la conexión y la relación. Jesús nos llama a cada uno por su nombre, y debemos modelar eso a los demás.

Santo Tomás de Aquino una vez instruyó que, si deseamos *"Convertir a alguien, ve y tómalo de la mano y guíalo"*. Porque *"... no hay un camino directo para ser verdaderamente conocido si no permitimos que nos veamos completamente, porque mejor o peor. Pero este tipo de vida siempre requerirá vulnerabilidad"*.[93]

Y la vulnerabilidad es absolutamente necesaria si deseamos construir un puente de confianza con otra persona. Brene Brown, un investigador de renombre mundial sobre lo que es necesario para las relaciones profundas y permanentes, dijo: *"La confianza se gana prestando atención, escuchando y con gestos de afecto genuino"*.

La observación de Brown está integralmente ligada al dicho: "A nadie le importa cuánto sabes, hasta que sepan cuánto te importa".

Esto significa que debemos tratar de entablar relaciones de confianza entre nosotros, por lo que es posible que nuestras historias sean vivificantes. Y precisamente por eso Dios nos hizo exactamente quiénes somos, qué somos y dónde estamos.

"El talento viene a todas partes. Todos son talentosos... Pero tener algo que decir, y una forma de decirlo para que la gente lo escuche, es otra bolsa. A menos que salgas y trates de hacerlo, nunca

lo sabrás... Si hay una razón por la que se supone que debemos estar aquí, es para decir algo para que la gente quiera escucharlo..."[94]

Y es inherente a nosotros superar nuestro miedo. Como compartí en el último capítulo, la práctica de sumergirnos en grandes historias puede ayudarnos a alentarnos e inspirarnos a superar nuestro miedo.

Y cuando nos compartimos con otros, ellos, a su vez, compartirán su historia con nosotros, y luego nos convertiremos en vida el uno para el otro porque las palabras dan vida.

Porque la Palabra ES vida.

Y la Palabra misma es Amor Encarnado.

Es a través de nuestras palabras de vida el uno al otro que la vida divina en el interior se fortalece para ayudar a transformarnos con, y a través del Amor mismo en vida y amor mutuo.

¿Pero está prestando atención? ¿Está escuchando? ¿Está escribiendo su historia? ¿Está compartiendo palabras de vida con otra persona en medio de tus conversaciones?

Esfuércese por irradiar un apostolado y comparta las Buenas Nuevas de que Dios ama a todas y cada una de las personas y desea pasar la eternidad con ellas.

Busque superar su miedo y comparte la vida divina dentro de usted y comparta su historia con los demás.

Su historia *importa*.

DIGA SÍ para compartir su historia hoy.

Ahora, pase la página y descubra la joya de la corona para su corona celestial.

Capítulo 22
La joya de la corona

"Nunca tengas miedo de amar demasiado a la Santísima Virgen.
Nunca puedes amarla más que Jesús".

— San Maximiliano Kolbe

Era abril de 2008. Casi dos décadas después de haber sido recibida en la Iglesia. Fue entonces cuando encontré lo que posteriormente transformó por completo mi viaje espiritual.

Estaba aprendiendo el hecho de que María es *la* joya de la corona en nuestra corona celestial que estamos diseñando aquí en la tierra a través de la gracia de Dios mientras vivimos nuestra vida de fe.

Primeros sábados y la Legión de María

En ese momento, estaba trabajando en el ministerio parroquial, y nuestro pastor fue fiel al asegurar que hubiera oportunidades para que la parroquia experimentara las misas del primer sábado y las horas santas. Hasta ese momento, a pesar de todos mis estudios teológicos, nunca había encontrado Devoción al Inmaculado

Corazón (Primer sábado), así que me intrigó escuchar y aprender sobre los mensajes de María a los fieles a lo largo de los siglos, particularmente en Fátima.

Como aprendí y entré más profundamente en la práctica de los Primeros Viernes[95] y Primeros Sábados en mi propia vida espiritual, también me encontré con el apostolado de la Legión de María por primera vez. En nuestra parroquia, la Legión se dedicó a visitar a los enfermos y confinados en su hogar, pero una de las principales intenciones del fundador, Frank Duff, fue inspirar a los laicos a vivir una espiritualidad mariana en medio de la evangelización de los demás, y se organizó el apostolado usando terminología militar de la antigua Roma.[96]

Debido a mi propia experiencia militar, este lenguaje era cómodo para mí, pero más aún fue el término que escuché usado en referencia a María, el de "Nuestra Señora". La idea de convertirme en un legionario, un caballero, en nombre de una Reina celestial en la lucha contra el mal resonó profundamente en mi corazón, y me encontré deseando saber más.

Los miembros de la Legión, particularmente su Asesor Espiritual en ese momento, el Diácono Skip Graffagnini, siempre estuvieron presentes en la Misa del Primer Sábado ya que se reunieron inmediatamente después. Esto dio lugar a que mantuviera numerosas conversaciones con el Diácono Skip sobre María y su papel en la vida espiritual. Nuestras conversaciones fueron de largo alcance y muy esclarecedoras, pero siempre estaré eternamente agradecida con él por presentarme la idea de la consagración mariana, así como los escritos de San Luis de Montfort.

SAN LUIS DE MONTFORT

Cuando el Diácono Skip mencionó por primera vez la Consagración Mariana, estaba un poco desconcertado, pero en lugar de tratar de explicármelo él mismo, simplemente me señaló al principal defensor de la Consagración Mariana, St Louis de Montfort.

Yo, siendo la que sobresalía del grupo, fui a buscar el mejor libro que había sobre San Luis de Montfort, María y la Consagración Mariana, y terminé con un libro del Padre Helmuts Libietis titulado, *St Louis de Montfort's True Devotion Consecration to Mary* y se describía en la contraportada como una "forma corta, fácil y perfecta de hacer esa Consagración".

¡Poco sabía que este libro en realidad contenía extractos de los diez libros que St Louis recomendó que formaran parte de la preparación de consagración de 33 días! Y también contenía extractos de todos los escritos principales de San Luis de Monfort para incluir *El amor de la sabiduría eterna, El secreto del rosario, El secreto de María y Carta a los Amigos de la Cruz.* Huelga decir que me sumergí en el fondo de lo que se trataba la consagración mariana y la espiritualidad mariana, y al final de mi tiempo de preparación de consagración, estaba, en una palabra: asombrada.

¿Qué me sorprendió?

Primero, que San Luis de Montfort se mantuvo firme en su afirmación de que la consagración a María es "la manera fácil, segura y perfecta de alcanzar el cielo". También me presentó por primera vez la idea de que María es la "Nueva Eva", así como Jesús es el "Nuevo Adán". En otras palabras, Dios libremente quiere a María como excepcionalmente necesaria en el orden actual de salvación debido al pecado original de Adán y Eva. Para llevar a cabo el plan para la salvación de la humanidad, Dios decide invitar a María a convertirse en su Madre y, posteriormente, de toda su Iglesia.

Esto significa que, por la aceptación de María de la invitación de Dios de la Divina Maternidad, una relación permanente ha resultado entre María y las Personas de la Trinidad. En otras palabras, ella es *siempre* la Esposa del Espíritu Santo, porque ella consiente en fe a la Encarnación de la Sabiduría Eterna dentro de ella.

San Luis de Montfort resume esta idea brillantemente: *"Es a través de la Santísima Virgen María que Jesús vino al mundo y también es a través de ella que tiene que reinar en el mundo".*[97]

Todas estas ideas me sorprendieron y humillaron. Los escritos de San Luis me mostraron cuán completamente carente estaba en mi comprensión de lo que era la vida espiritual, o la misión para la cual yo, y cada persona bautizada, estaba llamada. La misión de ser verdaderamente como Cristo, también debemos ser hijos de María, por lo que, al igual que Jesús, podemos ser formados por el poder del Espíritu Santo en representantes profundos y poderosos del amor y la misericordia de Dios en el mundo.

Ahora, sé que algunas personas han recibido la comprensión y la comprensión de la importancia de María al principio de sus vidas espirituales, junto con el conocimiento de que María es una parte integral de su viaje para acercarse a Dios y llegar a ser más como Jesús. Pero estas ideas eran casi extrañas para mí.

Y como posteriormente he compartido estas verdades con otros, me he encontrado con más personas que eran como yo, que no necesariamente tenían ningún problema con María, pero que invariablemente la mantenían a distancia de una manera u otra, y al hacerlo, nos habíamos estado negando las gracias que necesitábamos para convertirnos en los santos que Dios nos creó para ser.

Ahora, hasta este punto, mi experiencia con María había sido todo conocimiento de la cabeza. Sabía *de* ella y, sinceramente, no tuve ningún problema con ninguno de los dogmas asociados con ella: las realidades de su Inmaculada Concepción y Asunción, así como de que era la Madre de Dios y siempre Virgen. Honestamente, estos dogmas tenían sentido lógico para mí desde el principio cuando estaba llegando a la fe católica, especialmente cuando se combina con mi experiencia de quién es Dios, y a través de mi lectura de los escritos de los primeros Padres de la Iglesia, especialmente de los Concilios de Nicea y Efeso.

Pero mi *experiencia* sobre María fue algo diferente. La idea de necesitar una madre que pudiera llevarme con su Hijo no era algo que creía que necesitaba (¡qué poco sabía!) Porque pensaba

que ya estaba bastante unido a Jesús. Entonces, mi pregunta siempre fue "¿Por qué necesito que María me traiga a Jesús?" Esta actitud fue probablemente un vestigio de mi educación protestante, así como el hecho de que siempre tuve una madre amorosa en mi vida, por lo que nunca sentí que realmente necesitaba otra madre en mi vida.

Pero aún más, una parte fue probablemente porque nunca había sido una gran admiradora de rezar el rosario. Mirando hacia atrás, puedo ver que mi experiencia vino más de mi exposición a una recitación de memoria, un método no meditativo de rezar el rosario, combinado con la ignorancia de por qué, qué y cómo se debe rezar el rosario.

Alabado sea Dios, aunque en su sabiduría infinita, siempre nos abrirá los ojos y revelará las verdades de sus caminos, si no tenemos más que ojos para ver y oídos para oír. Para mí, esta revelación del papel siempre presente de María en la vida espiritual, y por ayudarme a ser santa fue un momento transformador para mí. Pero lo que realmente perjudicó a este hogar fue descubrir que todos los santos han tenido una relación especial con María.

Descubrí esto mientras me preparaba para mi Consagración Mariana durante la cual también descubrí los escritos de los Santos Maximiliano Kolbe y el Papa Juan Pablo II.

Tanto Kolbe como el papa Juan Pablo se basaron en las enseñanzas de Montfort. Mientras Montfort instó a la consagración mariana porque "es el medio seguro, el camino directo e inmaculado a Jesús y la guía perfecta para él", Kolbe enfatiza cómo recurrir a María hace que nuestros actos sean más eficaces, mientras que John Paul agrega que la consagración a María es expresamente La voluntad de Cristo.

A su manera, tanto Kolbe como Juan Pablo II enfatizan el papel necesario de María en la vida espiritual de uno para verdaderamente abrirse a los trabajos del Espíritu Santo. Y los tres sostienen que es solo a través de una espiritualidad arraigada en María que podemos estar más perfectamente unidos con la

voluntad de Dios para nosotros. Esto se debe a que María fue quien hizo exactamente eso durante toda su existencia.

San Maximiliano Kolbe escribe:

> *"La Inmaculada: aquí está nuestro ideal. Acercarse a ella, volverse como ella, permitirle tomar posesión de nuestro corazón y de todo nuestro ser, para que pueda vivir y actuar en nosotros y a través de nosotros, para que pueda amar a Dios con nuestro corazón, para que podamos pertenecer a ella sin ninguna restricción: este es nuestro ideal".*[98]

Además, si realmente queremos ser seguidores de Cristo, entonces debemos imitar a Cristo. ¿Y qué hizo Jesús? Desde su primer momento de convertirse en el Verbo hecho carne en la Encarnación, Jesús se entregó al cuidado de María. Él pertenecía por completo a ella, y dependía completamente de ella, por lo que, si realmente deseamos ser como Jesús, debemos imitarlo confiándonos también a María.

CONSAGRACIÓN MARIANA

Al prepararse para su consagración mariana, una de las primeras cosas que debe hacer es seleccionar la fiesta mariana en la que hará su consagración, ya que esto determina la fecha en que comenzará su preparación. Y es entonces cuando descubrí algo de lo que no me había dado cuenta en cuanto a la fecha de mi recepción en la Iglesia Católica.

Cuando me estaba preparando para ser católica, estaba completamente enfocada en el domingo de Pascua, 26 de marzo de 1989. Sin embargo, poco sabía en ese momento que debido a que la Iglesia celebra el Triduo Sagrado, en realidad iba a ser bautizada y recibida en la Iglesia el Sábado Santo en la Vigilia Pascual el 25 de marzo.

Ahora, tradicionalmente, el 25 de marzo se celebra como la Fiesta de la Anunciación. Es considerado por muchos como la

mayor fiesta mariana del año litúrgico porque es la celebración del momento del "sí" de María y de la cual la salvación de la humanidad está asegurada porque este es el momento de la Encarnación.

Sin embargo, cuando esta fiesta cae durante el Triduo Sagrado, se transfiere y celebra en otra fecha. Y eso fue lo que sucedió el año en que fui recibida en la Iglesia.

Pero imagínense mi sorpresa cuando me di cuenta de que la fecha en que María había dicho que sí, y la fecha en que dije mi propio sí y fui recibida en la Iglesia, ¡eran exactamente las mismas! Sin que yo lo supiera, María había estado presente y a mi lado todo el tiempo.

No me había dado cuenta de que María, en su forma hermosa y tranquila, ya había estado trabajando completando mi "sí" y ayudándome en el viaje para continuar trabajando para perfeccionar mi creencia, deseo y voluntad de convertirme en una santa. Todo para que yo pudiera llegar a ser más como su Hijo.

Pero ella no hace esto solo por mí. Al igual que su Hijo, María comparte estas gracias que su Hijo le ha confiado a *todos*. En unión con el Espíritu Santo, María nos ayuda a cada uno de nosotros a esforzarnos por perfeccionar nuestras creencias, deseos y voluntades para que podamos acercarnos cada vez más a Dios y ser más como su hijo, Jesús.

Así es como María es la joya de la corona entre las gemas ocultas de asistencia que Dios nos da para el viaje espiritual.

San Maximiliano lo resumió bien cuando escribió:

"Cuando examinamos a fondo nuestra alma, vemos cuán extensa ha sido la acción de la Inmaculada desde el comienzo de la vida de cada uno de nosotros hasta el momento presente. Vemos cuán grande es su promesa de los beneficios que tiene para el futuro... Baste recordar que cualquier gracia que recibimos todos los días, cada hora y

cada momento de nuestra existencia es su gracia, que fluye
de su corazón maternal que nos ama tanto".[99]

Ahora sé que todo lo que he descrito hasta ahora, especialmente sobre la Consagración, puede ser un poco desagradable para muchas personas. Tal vez piense como yo solía hacerlo, ¿no estoy disminuyendo mi amor y obediencia a Jesús, que es mi Señor y Salvador al consagrarme a María?

San Bernardo de Claraval respondió bellamente a esta objeción cuando escribió: *"No debemos imaginar que oscurecemos la gloria del Hijo con la gran alabanza que le prodigamos a la madre; porque cuanto más se honra, mayor es la gloria de su Hijo".*

O tal vez usted está diciendo: "¡Espera un minuto! No tengo un mes para leer y meditar. Ahora, puedo ver cómo podría ser algo realmente grandioso y todo eso, ¡pero no tengo tiempo para eso!"

Pero déjeme asegurarle. La consagración mariana es en realidad bastante simple. Simplemente puede pedirle que sea su madre espiritual y luego comenzar a vivir como uno de sus hijos.

La oración de consagración de San Luis de Montfort es: *"Renuncio y me entrego enteramente a ti, María".*

Entonces, ¿qué le impide reclamar la joya de la corona por la corona eterna que le espera en el Cielo?

DIGA SÍ a consagrarse a María.

Ahora, pase la página para comenzar a vivir esa consagración.

CAPÍTULO 23
VIVIENDO LA CONSAGRACIÓN

"Toda nuestra perfección consiste en ser conformados, unidos y consagrados a Jesucristo; y, por lo tanto, la más perfecta de todas las devociones es, sin ninguna duda, la que más perfectamente se conforma, nos une y consagra a Jesucristo. Ahora, como María es la criatura más conformada de Jesucristo, se deduce que, de todas las devociones, lo que más consagra y conforma el alma a Nuestro Señor es la devoción a Su santa Madre, y cuanto más un alma está consagrada a María cuanto más se consagra a Jesús".

— San Luis de Montfort[100]

Desde que hice mi primera Consagración Mariana en enero de 2009, he practicado la preparación para la renovación de mi Consagración al menos una vez al año. Además, he caminado con otros mientras se preparan para su propia consagración, y puedo dar fe de que cada vez que me abro al poder de la consagración, otro nivel de gratitud por las gracias que María comparte a través de la consagración en nombre de Su Hijo, Jesús, y su Cónyuge, el Espíritu Santo, han resultado en mi corazón, mente y alma.

Pero la parte *realmente* importante de la consagración mariana es vivir su consagración viviendo como uno de sus hijos.

Entonces, ¿por dónde empezar a hacer eso?

Comience rezando el rosario.

¿Por qué? Porque es a través de rezar el rosario que nos convertimos más efectivamente en esos niños pequeños sentados en lo que el Papa Juan Pablo II llama, la "escuela de María".

LA ESCUELA DE MARÍA

Ahora, la idea de rezar el rosario para mí fue muy difícil. Para empezar, soy una aprendiz visual y cinética, y aunque tiene alguna actividad cinética con rosarios, las imágenes definitivamente me parecieron insuficientes. Pero esto se remonta a que no sé ni entiendo por qué, qué y cómo rezar el rosario es tan importante para la vida espiritual.

En primer lugar, permítanme aclarar rápidamente un par de ideas erróneas.

Rezar el rosario, NO se trata de recitar un montón de oraciones lo más rápido posible para "terminarlo", o rezar todas las oraciones de la manera más perfecta posible para asegurarse de que esas oraciones sean "aceptables".

Ambas actitudes reflejan un malentendido de lo que es el rosario. En su núcleo fundamental, el rosario se trata de meditar sobre la vida de Jesús junto a María.

Esta idea tuvo mucho más sentido para mí una vez que estuve casada y mi suegra y yo comenzamos a compartir historias sobre mi esposo cuando era pequeño. A través de los ojos de mi suegra, pude ver a mi esposo bajo una luz completamente diferente, y luego pude apreciarlo, y quién es él, de una nueva manera.

Y María hace lo mismo por nosotros con Jesús. Al meditar en la vida de su Hijo a través de los misterios, se nos da una nueva perspectiva, o una comprensión diferente, y podemos apreciar más profundamente a Jesús por quién y qué es Él: el Camino, la Verdad y la Vida.

El padre Reginald Garrigou-Lagrange, O.P., un teólogo dominicano que se desempeñó como asesor doctoral en teología para el Papa Juan Pablo II, escribió esto sobre el Rosario:

> *"Después de la Santa Misa, el Rosario es una de las formas de oración más bellas y eficaces. ... Los misterios recuerdan toda la vida de Jesús y María en su gloria en el cielo. Los misterios del Rosario, así divididos en grupos, no son más que aspectos diferentes de los grandes misterios de nuestra salvación: la Encarnación, la Redención, la vida eterna ... Por lo tanto, el Rosario es un Credo; no uno abstracto, sino uno concretado en la vida de Jesús ... es todo el dogma cristiano en todo su esplendor y elevación, traído a nosotros para que podamos llenar nuestras mentes con él, para que podamos saborearlo y alimentar nuestras almas con eso. Esto hace del rosario una verdadera escuela de contemplación. Nos eleva gradualmente por encima de la oración vocal e incluso por encima de la meditación razonada o discursiva... El Rosario bien entendido es, por lo tanto, una forma de oración muy elevada que hace que todo el dogma sea accesible para todos".*

Entonces, cuando rezamos el rosario, se trata de tomarse el tiempo suficiente para permitir que María nos muestre un aspecto de su Hijo que quizás no hayamos notado antes, o para profundizar nuestra apreciación de algo que no necesariamente nos hemos tomado el tiempo para apreciar realmente.

Por otro lado, rezar el rosario tampoco se trata de hacerlo "bien". Hay muchas, muchas oraciones hermosas asociadas con el rosario, y todas ellas tienen un énfasis un poco diferente. Pero la Iglesia enseña que, para rezar una década del rosario, solo necesitas rezar un Padre Nuestro, diez Ave Marías y un Gloria. Nada más es necesario.

Ahora, María nos pidió en sus apariciones en Fátima que agreguemos la oración: *"Oh Jesús mío, perdónanos nuestros pecados,*

sálvanos del fuego del infierno, lleva a todas las almas al Cielo, especialmente a las que más necesitan tu misericordia". Deberíamos intentar agregar eso, pero de lo contrario, no deberíamos hacer que rezar el rosario sea complicado. Manténgalo simple.

Pero la parte más importante de rezar el rosario es *rezar* el rosario.

Esto puede ser difícil en nuestro mundo obsesionado con el tiempo, pero a menudo desafío a las personas que tienen problemas para encontrar tiempo para rezar el rosario para comenzar rezando un Ave María cada vez que se encuentran esperando en algún lugar, ya sea en un semáforo o en la oficina del doctor o en la tienda de comestibles.

Y cuando se encuentre en estas situaciones, solo rece por el número de Ave María para las que tenga tiempo, y luego observe cuán rápido obtiene hasta cinco de Padre Nuestro, cincuenta de Ave María y cinco Glorias. Al igual que ellos, le sorprenderá lo fácil que es, pero no solo eso, entonces tendrá que trabajar en su nombre, el arma más fuerte y poderosa que Dios nos ha dado en toda la historia: su propia Madre.

Porque no se puede negar la eficacia de la intercesión de María a lo largo de la historia. Existen numerosos ejemplos de la ayuda de María que se está alistando, y cómo su apariencia ha provocado la conversión de pueblos enteros. Desde eventos como las Batallas de Lepanto, Viena y Varsovia, hasta el Milagro del Sol en Fátima, a su imagen milagrosa en la tilma de Juan Diego como Nuestra Señora de Guadalupe y cómo eso provocó la posterior caída del imperio azteca, a las aguas curativas en Lourdes, Francia, y los muchos, muchos milagros atribuido a la Medalla Milagrosa, una medalla creada y distribuida en la dirección de María a Santa Catalina Laboure en la que María ha intercedido y respondido a las fervientes oraciones de creyentes y no creyentes por igual.

San Maximiliano Kolbe escribió sobre la intercesión de María:

"[La Inmaculada] quiere lo mejor para mí, más de lo que podría desear, y puede ayudarme, porque el Creador no puede rechazarle nada. Por lo tanto, es mejor confiarle mis preocupaciones y mis problemas, ella pondrá ellos correctos más rápido y más fácil de lo que puedo".[101]

Así es como podemos vivir como hijos de María. Rezamos el rosario y confiamos en su intercesión en nuestro nombre.

Entonces, cuando DECIMOS SÍ y nos consagramos a María, le damos permiso a María y al Espíritu Santo para que nos transformen activamente formando a Jesús en nuestras mentes, corazones y almas.

Pero aún más importante que permitirnos transformarnos, es enlistar la ayuda de María en la conversión de los demás.

San Maximiliano Kolbe nuevamente escribe:

"Cada conversión y cada paso en el camino hacia la santificación son obra de la gracia, y el dispensador de todas las gracias que fluyen del Sagrado Corazón de Jesús no es otro que Su Madre, la Inmaculada. Por lo tanto, cuanto más se acerca un alma a ella, más abundantemente puede recurrir a estas gracias. Como resultado, nuestra misión clave es acercar las almas a ella, conducirla a las almas".[102]

María nos acerca a Jesús porque sigue cumpliendo la voluntad de Dios y es nuestra Madre, la Madre de la Iglesia.

Al pie de la Cruz, en el Evangelio de Juan se nos dice que Jesús dice: *"Al ver a su madre y al discípulo que amaba estar cerca de ella, Jesús le dijo a su madre: 'Mujer, mira a tu hijo'. Luego al discípulo, Él dijo: "He aquí a tu madre". Y desde ese momento, el discípulo la llevó a su casa".*[103]

Fue en este momento que María, en unión con la voluntad de Dios, aceptó su papel como madre espiritual de la Iglesia, y ha seguido sirviendo como Madre para toda la Iglesia a lo largo de los siglos.

El Papa Juan Pablo II describe bellamente cómo María cumple el papel de Madre de la Iglesia:

"Después de los eventos de la resurrección y la ascensión, María entró en el aposento alto junto con los apóstoles para esperar a Pentecostés, y estuvo presente allí como la Madre del Señor glorificado. ...Así comenzó a desarrollar un vínculo especial entre esta Madre y la Iglesia. Porque la Iglesia infantil era el fruto de la Cruz y la Resurrección de su Hijo. María, que desde el principio se había entregado sin reservas a la persona y la obra de su Hijo, no podía sino derramar sobre la Iglesia, del desde el principio, su entrega materna. Después de la partida de su Hijo, su maternidad permanece en la Iglesia como mediación materna: intercediendo por todos sus hijos, la Madre coopera en la obra salvífica de su Hijo, el Redentor del mundo. De hecho, el Concilio enseña que "la maternidad de María en el orden de la gracia ... durará sin interrupción hasta el cumplimiento eterno de todos los elegidos". Con la muerte redentora de su Hijo, la mediación materna de la sierva de los Lo rd adquirió una dimensión universal, porque el trabajo de redención abarca a toda la humanidad".[104]

María, eclipsada por el Espíritu Santo, concibió y dio a luz a Jesús, y luego lo alimentó, protegió y educó junto a San José, ayudó a iniciar y apoyar su ministerio público, permaneció a su lado durante toda su pasión y muerte, y luego estuvo presente para Su resurrección antes de que ella continuara entregándose a la obra de su Hijo al convertirse en madre de su iglesia.

Aquí es donde la frase "A Jesús a través de María" suena permanentemente verdadera. Porque a través de María, nos transformamos en los apóstoles para los que fuimos creados, y el Espíritu Santo nos autoriza a cumplir y encarnar nuestros votos bautismales para llevar nuestra cruz e inspirarnos en todo

lo que hacemos en esta vida hasta que entremos vida con su hijo en el próximo.

VIVIENDO SU CONSAGRACIÓN

Entonces, ¿cómo son los fieles hijos e hijas de María?
San Antonio María Claret nos dice que se ven así:

"Porque un Hijo del Inmaculado Corazón de María es un hombre en llamas con amor, que extiende sus llamas donde quiera que vaya. Él desea poderosamente y se esfuerza por todos los medios posibles para prender fuego al mundo entero con el amor de Dios. Nada lo intimida; se deleita en las privaciones, acoge con beneplácito el trabajo, abraza los sacrificios, sonríe a la calumnia y se regocija en el sufrimiento. Su única preocupación es cómo puede seguir mejor a Jesucristo e imitarlo en su trabajo, sufrimiento y lucha constante y decidida por la mayor gloria de Dios y la salvación de las almas".

San Luis de Montfort describe a los fieles hijos e hijas de María de esta manera:

"La verdadera devoción a Nuestra Señora es constante. Confirma el alma en el bien y no le permite abandonar fácilmente sus ejercicios espirituales. Lo hace valiente al oponerse al mundo en sus modas y máximas, la carne en su cansancio y pasiones, y el diablo en sus tentaciones; para que una persona verdaderamente devota de nuestra Bendita Señora no sea cambiante, irritable, escrupulosa ni tímida. No es que una persona así no se caiga, o cambie a veces en el sentimiento sensible de la devoción. Pero cuando cae, vuelve a levantarse estirando la mano hacia su buena madre. Cuando pierde el gusto y el gusto de las devociones, no se molesta por eso; porque el cliente justo y fiel de María vive

por la fe (Heb. 10:38) de Jesús y María, y no por un sen-
timiento natural".[105]

Pero en términos más prácticos, ¿cómo sería vivir la consagración de uno en María en su vida diaria?
Hay cinco principios:

1. Renuncie a su propia voluntad. Acepte cosas que no le
   gustan, que no eligió, que no puede cambiar y que no
   entiende.

2. Encomiéndese a María todos los días. Comience cada
   mañana con una ofrenda matutina y rece el rosario.

3. Haga todas las cosas con María y Jesús, y busque recor-
   datorios de María durante todo el día para que tenga
   muchas oportunidades de confiar en ella.

4. Permítale a María dirigir cualquier transición, enfermedad o pérdida en su vida al pedirle que interceda por
   usted, especialmente para que se le dé el valor de sopor-
   tarla en unión con la voluntad de Dios.

5. Conduzca a otros a María para que ella pueda ayudarle
   a guiarlos a Jesús.

Los cinco principios también son consistentes con los mensajes que María ha compartido en sus apariciones en todo el
mundo a lo largo de los siglos. Por lo tanto, al hacer estas cosas,
no solo vive su consagración a María, sino que también le permite que le ayude a acercar a otros a su Hijo, Jesús.

Esto se debe a que María es nuestro mayor modelo de discipulado, ya que su voluntad siempre ha estado en unión con Dios.
También es porque María es nuestra Madre, y la Madre de la
Iglesia, y a través de ella, la Iglesia continúa atrayendo a otros
hacia su hijo, Jesús. Además, María es nuestra mayor intercesora,
ya que presenta ante nuestro Señor todas nuestras necesidades,

mientras hace cada ofrenda y sacrificio que hacemos aún más eficaces. Finalmente, como esposa del Espíritu Santo, María puede ayudar a que la imagen de su Hijo, Jesús, se haga presente cada vez más en nuestros corazones y mentes.

Así como el Papa Juan Pablo II nos dice: *"Es de María que aprendemos a rendirnos a la voluntad de Dios en todas las cosas. Es de María que aprendemos a confiar incluso cuando toda esperanza parece haberse ido. Y es de María que aprendemos a amar a Cristo".*

Así que no se preocupe y recurra a María. Al consagrarnos y vivir nuestra consagración, María nos verá a salvo en la casa del Cielo.

Entonces, ¿recuerda el poder de la Historia y la importancia de nuestro papel en ella? El obispo Robert Barron nos recuerda esto cuando compartió esto sobre el papel de María en la historia de Dios:

> *"El teatro dramático es la gran historia contada por Dios, la gran obra dirigida por Dios. Lo que hace que la vida sea emocionante es descubrir tu papel en ella. Esto es precisamente lo que le ha sucedido a María. Ella ha encontrado su papel —de hecho, un papel culminante— en el teatro dramático, y quiere conspirar con Isabel, quien también ha descubierto su papel en el mismo drama. Como María, tenemos que encontrar nuestro lugar en la historia de Dios".*

Esta es la forma final en que María nos ayuda en el viaje espiritual.

María ha estado allí. Ella sabe de las luchas que enfrentamos porque era completamente humana. Pero la diferencia entre María y nosotros es que María dijo SÍ, a cada momento e instancia de la gracia de Dios en su vida.

Ella *vivió* la frase, *Fiat Voluntas Tua* - Tu voluntad será hecha.

María nunca dijo que no, independientemente de los muchos desafíos, pruebas, tribulaciones y sacrificios que experimentó a lo largo de su vida aquí en la tierra, y esta es la forma preeminente

en que María nos modela el camino del discipulado. Ella nos muestra que nosotros también podemos decir SÍ a la gracia de Dios y ser transformados en los santos que Él nos creó para ser.

Entonces, comprométase a consagrarse a María y permite que el Espíritu Santo forme más activamente a Jesús en usted, tal como lo hizo el Espíritu Santo dentro de María.

Abrace a María como tu madre y deje que interceda por usted en todos los aspectos de su vida mientras le ayuda a hacer cada oración y sacrificio más eficaz.

Permítase convertirse en un soldado en el ejército de María y ayude a tantas almas como sea posible a conocer, amar y servir a su hijo, nuestro Señor y Salvador, Jesús.

DIGA SÍ a vivir su consagración mariana.

Ahora, pase la página y conviértase en Dios y Su plan para usted.

Capítulo 24

"En equipo"

En 2010, la Universidad de Auburn ganó el campeonato nacional de fútbol americano universitario de la División 1 de la NCAA. Aunque el equipo había dotado a atletas talentosos como el ganador del Trofeo Heisman, el mariscal de campo Cam Newton, la verdadera esencia de su éxito se resumió en el lema del equipo para ese año, "En equipo".

El entrenador en jefe de Auburn en ese momento, Gene Chizik, explicó que "En equipo" se convirtió en el criterio para juzgar la excelencia. Significaba que cada miembro del equipo estaba completamente y completamente comprometido a hacer todo lo necesario para mejorar, tanto dentro como fuera del campo a lo largo de la temporada, y el resultado de esa actitud "En equipo" fue un campeonato nacional.

Sin embargo, lo que mucha gente no sabe es que la frase "En equipo" surgió de una discusión entre los entrenadores y miembros del equipo de Auburn sobre el versículo de Colosenses 3:23, "Trabaja voluntariamente en lo que sea que hagas, como si estuvieras trabajando para el Señor en lugar de para las personas", y lo que surgió de esa discusión fue lo que era necesario para hacer ese tipo de trabajo y lo que significaba estar "En equipo".

Esa discusión dio como resultado el enfoque y la claridad necesarios sobre el por qué, qué y cómo cada miembro del equipo debía participar en el proceso que eventualmente llevó al equipo

de fútbol Auburn Tigers a convertirse en Campeones Nacionales 2010.

Y este es EXACTAMENTE el mismo tipo de actitud que debemos tener si queremos convertirnos en los santos para los que hemos sido creados.

Dios nos está llamando a ir "En equipo" para llegar a un orden correcto al poner primero lo primero y vivir la vida que Él nos ha diseñado para vivir, una vida llena de propósito, paz y abundancia.

Revisemos.

LLAMADO A UNA VIDA DE PROPÓSITO

San Buenaventura escribió: *"Si aprendes todo excepto a Cristo, no aprendes nada. Si no aprendes nada excepto a Cristo, lo aprendes todo".*

Este es el fundamento de vivir una vida de propósito. Porque vivir una vida con propósito comienza por saber *quiénes somos*: hijos e hijas de Dios. A partir de este conocimiento, también llegamos a saber que estamos llamados a ser más de lo que el mundo nos dice que somos, que estamos destinados a una vida con Dios por toda la eternidad, y estamos llamados a transformar la unión con Dios, para convertirnos en santos.

Pero no los santos cortadores de galletas donde todos son como los demás.

No, Dios nos ha hecho únicos para ser un tipo particular de santo en el que solo nosotros podemos llegar a ser, porque nunca ha habido, hay o habrá alguien como nosotros en el mundo.

Pero tenemos que *elegir* vivir esta vida de propósito para convertirnos en quienes somos, qué somos, dónde estamos.

Tenemos que DECIR SÍ a la gran invitación que Dios nos da para entrar en su vida divina aquí y ahora y vivir una vida de profundo propósito.

LLAMADO A UNA VIDA DE PAZ

Para entrar y participar en la vida divina de Dios, debemos esforzarnos por poner primero lo primero y ponernos en orden. Esto sucede siguiendo los cuatro pasos hacia la santidad: oración diaria y meditación, viviendo la vida de la gracia, creciendo diariamente en virtud y abandonándonos a la voluntad de Dios.

Pero la clave de *todos* nuestros esfuerzos para ponernos en orden es la oración diaria y la meditación.

¿Por qué?

Porque debemos enamorarnos apasionadamente de Dios para embarcarnos en la aventura más magnífica y maravillosa que es nuestra vida.

San Agustín nos dice: *"Enamorarse de Dios es el mayor romance; buscarle la mayor aventura; encontrarlo, el mayor logro humano".*

Porque *solo* por amor estaremos dispuestos (y podremos) intentar hacer lo que sea necesario para cambiar nuestros pensamientos, palabras y acciones, y abrir nuestras mentes, corazones y almas a la paz y la sabiduría que Dios desea. para darnos a través de una amistad íntima consigo mismo.

Y a partir de esta amistad íntima, nos llenamos de Su Palabra y tenemos sed de más. Es por eso que debemos vivir activamente la vida de gracia frecuentando los sacramentos. Debemos buscar activamente y hacer espacio en nuestras vidas para recibir regularmente la vida divina de Dios a través de la recepción de Jesús en los Sacramentos, particularmente la Sagrada Eucaristía y la Reconciliación.

A medida que pasamos tiempo en oración y estamos llenos de la Vida Divina a través de los Sacramentos, se nos da cada vez más la sabiduría y la fuerza para crecer en virtud cada día y abandonarnos a la voluntad de Dios más plenamente.

¿Cómo?

Muy a menudo, a través de nuestra resolución diaria. La resolución diaria es donde el caucho se encuentra con el camino en la vida espiritual. Debido a que la resolución diaria toma la

sabiduría y la percepción que Dios le dio en sus conversaciones con Él y usted puede aplicarla de maneras pequeñas y concretas en su vida diaria.

Así es como comenzamos a ver, y luego a sostener, el crecimiento en la virtud. El proceso durante el cual nuestros pensamientos, palabras y acciones se transforman para que reflejemos más perfectamente la Vida Divina que reside dentro de nosotros. Y ver este progreso es lo que nos anima a continuar la lucha cuando las cosas se ponen difíciles, ¡lo que será así!

Pero estos signos de crecimiento también nos animan a confiar y abandonarnos a la voluntad de Dios más plenamente. Porque a medida que vemos pequeños cambios, aprendemos a confiar en los planes de Dios para nosotros, y luego crecemos en confianza, y aprendemos a abandonarnos cada vez más a Su voluntad en *todos* los eventos de nuestras vidas. Nuestra confianza alimenta, vigoriza y sostiene nuestra oración y meditación, lo que a su vez, nos abre a la dirección de Dios para nuestras vidas a través de nuestras resoluciones diarias, y esto provoca pequeños cambios en nuestros pensamientos, palabras y acciones, y esto crea un ciclo de cada vez más profunda confianza y abandono que alimenta nuestra oración y meditación, y así sucesivamente. Y es por eso que tenemos que esforzarnos por golpear la voluntad de Dios para nosotros "en el punto" a través de nuestro desapego, obediencia y confianza.

Tenemos que decir SÍ para esforzarnos por seguir fielmente estos cuatro pasos cada día lo mejor que podamos mientras confiamos en la gracia de Dios para hacer el resto.

El Catecismo nos dice:

"El progreso espiritual tiende hacia una unión cada vez más íntima con Cristo. Esta unión se llama "mística" porque participa en el misterio de Cristo a través de los sacramentos - "los santos misterios" - y, en él, en el misterio de la Santísima Trinidad. Dios nos llama a todos a esta unión íntima con él".[106]

¡Unión íntima con él! Esta unión nos lleva directamente a la vida de abundancia.

LLAMADO A UNA VIDA DE ABUNDANCIA

Santa Gianna Molla dijo: *"El secreto de la felicidad es vivir momento a momento y agradecer a Dios por lo que nos envía todos los días en su bondad".*

Y esto es perfecto.

Cuanto más nos centramos en el momento presente, más encontramos la felicidad. Pero no solo en nosotros mismos, sino especialmente en nuestra relación con los demás.

Porque a medida que vivimos con una actitud de gratitud, nos volvemos más y más conscientes de todo lo que Dios está enviando en su bondad, y esto nos hace más abiertos no solo a todo, sino a *todos* los que nos rodean.

Porque una vida de abundancia está arraigada en la realidad de que el hecho de ser ordenado correctamente y vivir la vida divina no se trata simplemente de mí mismo, de mis elecciones y mis acciones.

Esto se debe a que, en la vida de abundancia, no existe la idea de que una elección o acción esté bien siempre que no afecte a nadie más.

Porque la verdadera realidad es que *todo* afecta a *todos*.

Cada palabra, cada acción, sí, incluso cada pensamiento, tiene un impacto en quienes nos rodean.

Porque todos estamos interconectados. Puede que no lo veamos, pero lo estamos.

Por eso la oración es tan poderosa. Saber que alguien más está pensando en mí, intercediendo por mí, está activamente dispuesto a que mi bien, en otras palabras, me esté *amando* me afecta. Y porque me afecta, ese conocimiento afecta a todos.

Fuimos *diseñados* para la relación. Fuimos creados para estar en relación unos con otros, y vivir una vida de abundancia se trata de rechazar lo que el mundo nos dice que hagamos:

aislarnos, confiar en usted mismo y no confiar en nadie, y en su lugar entablar relaciones profundas con los demás, abandone nuestra autosuficiencia y abrace con confianza todo lo que Dios ha provisto para que podamos prosperar en este mundo mientras nos preparamos para pasar la eternidad con Él en el próximo.

Es por eso que debemos sumergirnos en las enseñanzas del Magisterio de la Iglesia y buscar un mentor o director espiritual que nos ayude a guiarnos en el viaje. Es por eso que debemos buscar un grupo de amigos (como lo hizo Jesús) para caminar junto a nosotros en medio de todas las alegrías y penas de la vida mientras nos alentamos y desafiamos unos a otros para luchar por la santidad. Es por eso que debes compartir *tu* historia de cómo Jesús te transforma, permitiendo que la Vida Divina que habita dentro de ti respire y crezca dentro de ti. Y finalmente, es por eso que debemos confiar voluntariamente en María, nuestra Madre, para que ella pueda cuidarnos como lo hizo con Jesús, pero también para que podamos ser un recordatorio e inspiración para quienes nos rodean de que todas las cosas *son* posibles para aquellos que aman Dios.

Al abrazar la relación, encontramos que no estamos solos. Tampoco hemos estado nunca.

Pero tenemos que DECIR SÍ para vivir la vida en abundancia.

"MÁS ARRIBA, MÁS ADENTRO"

Todo el proceso de luchar por la santidad, de ser ordenado correctamente, está diseñado para prepararnos para nuestro regreso al Reino Eterno.

En el libro final de la serie Crónicas de Narnia, *The Last Battle*, el autor C.S. Lewis describe la experiencia que tuvieron todas las personas y criaturas de Narnia al final de los tiempos, y su entrada en la vida eterna. Cada una de las personas y animales tiene la experiencia de que las cosas son más reales y verdaderas y más bellas en esta "nueva" Narnia frente a lo que

habían experimentado antes en la "antigua" Narnia, y esto ocurrió cuando se movieron "más arriba y más adentro".

De hecho, "Más arriba, más adentro" se convirtió en el grito de todos los que estaban en la "nueva" Narnia mientras corrían hacia lo que se reveló como un gran Jardín amurallado en el centro donde cada persona y criatura que había sido parte integral de La historia de Narnia se reunió en una realidad, y aún más hermosa, Narnia.

Y esta verdadera Narnia estaba conectada con los otros países reales, incluidos los lugares de nuestro propio mundo, y todos estos lugares eran solo espuelas de las grandes montañas de Aslan, el Gran Rey.

Todas estas escenas representan una hermosa y magnífica visión de cómo será el Cielo para nosotros. De una gran reunión de todas las personas y criaturas, donde somos lo mejor de nosotros mismos: jóvenes, sanos y vigorosos, donde no experimentamos miedo ni tristeza, sino simplemente amor y alegría.

LA SANTIDAD ES POSIBLE

Esta vida de amor y gozo eternos es lo que Dios desea para cada uno de nosotros. No solo unos pocos elegidos.

El Catecismo nos asegura este hecho: *"Todos los cristianos en cualquier estado o camino de la vida están llamados a la plenitud de la vida cristiana y a la perfección de la caridad". Todos están llamados a la santidad: "Sé perfecto, como tu Padre celestial es perfecto".*[107]

Convertirse en un santo es para *todos*.

De hecho, si no nos convertimos en el santo que Dios nos creó para ser, entonces el Cielo será menos de lo que Dios había deseado que fuera, porque no estamos allí.

Con suerte, a través de lo que he compartido en este libro, puede ver que la santidad es posible. Que cada uno de nosotros puede convertirse en el santo Dios nos diseñó para ser desde el principio del mundo, de modo que podamos irradiar su amor

y misericordia a los demás de la manera única e irrepetible que solo nosotros podemos hacer.

Es por eso que *"la santidad consiste simplemente en hacer la voluntad de Dios y ser exactamente lo que Dios quiere que seamos".[108]*

Así que nunca se rinda a la desesperación. La santidad es posible.

Pero tiene que elegir seguirlo.

Y elegir perseguirlo es una decisión de vida o muerte.

ELIJA LA VIDA Y PERSEVERE

"Sé uno de los pocos que encuentran el camino a la vida y entra por la puerta angosta al cielo. Tenga cuidado de no seguir a la mayoría y al rebaño común, muchos de los cuales están perdidos. Que no te engañen; solo hay dos caminos: uno que conduce a la vida y es angosto; el otro que lleva a la muerte y es amplio. No hay un camino intermedio".

San Luis de Montfort no escribió estas palabras para asustar a la gente. Y no los estoy compartiendo ahora para reprenderle por no buscar seriamente la santidad, o que le van a pasar cosas malas si no se esfuerza y vive una vida ordenada correcta. Así no es como Dios trabaja.

Sin embargo, la verdad es que tenemos que tomar una decisión. Y como cualquier elección, tiene consecuencias.

Incluso la elección de seguir el Camino de la Vida y buscar la santidad será difícil. Todavía habrá lágrimas, desamor y tragedia en su vida, incluso si elige seguir el Camino.

De hecho, el Catecismo nos dice: *"El camino de la perfección pasa por la Cruz. No hay santidad sin renuncia y batalla espiritual. El progreso espiritual implica la ascesis y la mortificación que gradualmente conducen a vivir en la paz y la alegría de las Bienaventuranzas".* [109]

Esto es lo que debemos recordar. Simplemente eligiendo el estilo de vida, no lo absolverá ni significa que tendrá que pasar por tener que experimentar luchas, fracasos, enfermedades, penas, decepciones, traiciones o muerte. Pero elegir seguir el Camino de la Vida le permite saber que hay un propósito y un significado en todas sus luchas, fracasos, enfermedades, penas, decepciones, traiciones e incluso la muerte, incluso si no entiende qué ese propósito o significado podría ser.

LA FORMA DE VIDA ES UN PROCESO

A lo largo de este libro, lo que he compartido es *un proceso*, no un programa. No hay inicio ni parada. No hay primera clase ni última sesión. No hay graduación.

Es un proceso continuo que continúa todos los días de nuestras vidas.

El proceso a través del cual nos abrimos a ser transformados por la gracia de Dios en las mismas personas que Él nos creó para ser en primer lugar. Antes de que el pecado original y la concupiscencia se interpusieran en el camino y nos encontramos en la necesidad de un Salvador, y en la necesidad de que se nos muestre una Manera de volver a ser ordenado correctamente.

Este proceso de descubrir el propósito, la paz y la abundancia en su vida diaria está diseñado específicamente para ayudarlo a tomar los pasos necesarios *en este momento* para reordenar su vida para que, por la gracia de Dios, las relaciones que se rompieron originalmente en el Jardín del Edén, con uno mismo, Dios y otros, pueden ser sanados y renovados nuevamente.

Porque cuando estamos en una relación correcta con nosotros mismos, descubrimos nuestro verdadero propósito y vivimos como nosotros mismos. Y cuando estamos en una relación correcta con Dios, donde ponemos primero lo primero en nuestra vida, entonces descubrimos y encontramos la paz auténtica. Y cuando estamos en una relación correcta con los

demás, descubrimos y experimentamos una vida de abundancia que nunca podríamos imaginar.

¿ENTONCES, A QUÉ ESPERA?

Ahora, la única persona que puede evitar que viva una vida de propósito, paz y abundancia es USTED.

Es por eso que debe DECIR SÍ.

Pero tiene que ELEGIRLO.

Porque Dios no le va a forzar.

¿Por qué?

Porque le ama demasiado.

Le ama lo suficiente como para esperar que elija la vida, y no la muerte.

Él le ama lo suficiente como para esperar hasta que descubra y entienda su verdadero propósito y para llegar a creer cuán radical, profunda y profundamente es amado sin medida.

Él le ama lo suficiente como para esperar a que pruebe todas las formas que el mundo ofrece: placer, poder, fama, alcohol, drogas, posesiones para distraer, disminuir o mitigar sus preocupaciones y ansiedad antes de que finalmente esté dispuesto a confiar abandono a Él para proporcionarle la paz y la sabiduría que realmente anhela.

Él le ama lo suficiente como para esperar a que falle una y otra vez mientras trata de confiar en sí mismo y en sus propios recursos antes de que finalmente recurra a las herramientas que Él ya le ha proporcionado para que pueda perseverar y prosperar en este mundo como viaja a casa a Él.

DIGA SÍ a estar "En equipo".

Su verdadera vida le espera.

Él está esperando por usted.

DIGA SÍ.

DIGA SÍ LISTA DE VERIFICACIÓN

Introducción   DIGA SÍ a emprender el viaje para ser transformado.

Capítulo 1   DIGA SÍ al proceso.

Capítulo 2   DIGA SÍ a su dignidad y grandeza.

Capítulo 3   DIGA SÍ a la llamada a la santidad.

Capítulo 4   DIGA SÍ a su misión única e irrepetible.

Capítulo 5   DIGA SÍ y "Ven a ver".

Capítulo 6   DIGA SÍ a los Cuatro Pasos de Santidad.

Capítulo 7   DIGA SÍ a la oración y meditación diarias.

Capítulo 8   DIGA SÍ y conteste el teléfono.

Capítulo 9   DIGA SÍ a vivir la vida de la gracia.

Capítulo 10   DIGA SÍ a vivir la plenitud de la vida de la gracia.

Capítulo 11   DIGA SÍ a las gracias de Dios que fluyen sin parar en su vida.

Capítulo 12   DIGA SÍ a crecer diariamente en virtud.

Capítulo 13   DIGA SÍ para crecer diariamente en virtud. Paso a paso y día a día.

Capítulo 14   DIGA SÍ a abandonarse a la voluntad de Dios.

Capítulo 15   DIGA SÍ a golpear la voluntad de Dios en el "BLANCO".

Capítulo 16   DIGA SÍ a ser obediente a lo que Dios ha revelado a través de Su Magisterio.

Capítulo 17   DIGA SÍ a ser acompañado en el viaje.

Capítulo 18   DIGA SÍ a la amistad verdadera y auténtica.

Capítulo 19   DIGA SÍ a la amistad escondida a simple vista.

Capítulo 20   DIGA SÍ al poder de la historia.

Capítulo 21   DIGA SÍ al compartir su historia hoy.

Capítulo 22   DIGA SÍ a consagrarse a María.

Capítulo 23   DIGA SÍ a vivir su consagración mariana.

Capítulo 24   DIGA SÍ a estar "En equipo"

PRÓXIMOS PASOS Y RECURSOS

DESCARGUE LA GUÍA GRATUITA

Hay muchos recursos que pueden ayudarlo a tomar esta información y estas estrategias e implementarlas en su propia vida.

Para ayudarlo a hacer eso, preparé una guía de libros gratuita con preguntas de discusión y ejercicios adicionales que puede usar para decir SÍ.

Siga el Paso 1 y descargue esos recursos gratuitos visitando:

www.sayyestoholiness.com

ÚNETE AL MOVIMIENTO DE SÍ SÍ A LA SANTIDAD

¿Deseas aprender más? ¿O anhelas formar parte de una comunidad de personas de ideas afines que están ardiendo para salvar almas y con quienes puedes viajar mientras buscas la santidad? ¿O ambos?

Luego, tome el Paso 2 y vea las oportunidades para unirse al Movimiento Di Sí a la Santidad visitando:

www.sayyestoholiness.com

UNA ÚLTIMA COSA

Puedo pedirte un favor?

Si sacaste algo de este libro, ya sea que te inspiró o te enseñó algo, estaría siempre agradecido si hicieras algo pequeño por mí ...

¿Podría entregar una copia de este libro a un amigo, familiar o colega?

Pídales que lo lean.

Hágales saber lo que es posible para ellos si comienzan a buscar la santidad y hacen el trabajo necesario para abrazar la vida para la que Dios los creó.

Hágales saber que pueden decir SÍ.

Los necesitamos.

Te necesitamos.

Pasa la voz.

Gracias de nuevo,
Christina Semmens

NOTAS FINALES

1   *Catechism of the Catholic Church*, 1704.
2   Baltimore Catechism no.3, Question 6.
3   From the prayer "Prophets of a Future Not Our Own" written by Bishop Ken Untener. It was first presented by Cardinal Dearden in 1979 and quoted by Pope Francis in 2015. The poem was part of a homily written for Cardinal Dearden by then-Fr. Ken Untener on the occasion of the Mass for Deceased Priests, October 25, 1979. Pope Francis quoted Cardinal Dearden in his remarks to the Roman Curia on December 21, 2015. Fr. Untener was named bishop of Saginaw, Michigan, in 1980.
4   Father Bede Jarrett, *Catholic Meditations*, p. 51.
5   Fr. Jacques Philippe, *In the School of the Holy Spirit*, p. 26.
6   Father Augustine Wetta, OSB, *Humility Rules*.
7   Rev. Jude Winkler, O.F.M., *Daily Meditations with the Holy Spirit*, p.13.
8   John 1:35-51, New American Bible.
9   Jeremiah 1:4.
10 Jeremiah 29:11.
11 Matthew 19:16-22.
12 Matthew Kelly, *The Biggest Lie in the History of Christianity*.
13 Thomas Aquinas, *Summa Theologica*, II-II, q. 126, a.1.
14 Christina Semmens, *March to Canada*, p. 50.
15 Acts 17:28.
16 Josemaria Escriva, *The Way*, 368.
17 https://www.goodreads.com/quotes/166474-for-me-prayer-is-a-surge-of-the-heart-it
18 The Latin is: "Littera gesta docet, Quod credas allegoria. Moralia quod agas,Quo tendas anagogia."
19 Catechism of the Catholic Church
20 http://www.vatican.va/content/john-paul-ii/en/apost_letters/2002/documents/hf_jp-ii_apl_20021016_rosarium-virginis-mariae.html

21 https://images.app.goo.gl/mgb14oVWoAFZNSgK7
22 https://steubenvillefuel.com/2017/09/13/abandon-allow-grace-quote/
23 Catechism of the Catholic Church, paragraph 1131.
24 Fr. Jacques Philippe, *In the School of the Holy Spirit*, pp.14-15
25 Fr Joseph Langford, M.C., *I Thirst:40 Days with Mother Teresa*, pp.28-29.
26 Fr. Romano Guardini, *Meditations Before Mass*, p. 28.
27 https://www.knightsoftheholyeucharist.com/the-eucharist-is-the-sacrament-of-love/
28 https://www.azquotes.com/quote/1334078
29 https://www.frassatiusa.org/his-eucharistic-devotion
30 Fr. Jacques Philippe, *In the School of the Holy Spirit*, p. 28.
31 https://quotefancy.com/quote/891322/Pope-John-Paul-II-From-the-Eucharist-comes-strength-to-live-the-Christian-life-and-zeal
32 Fr. Ignatius of the Side of Jesus, *The School of Jesus Crucified*, pp.284-5.
33 Matthew 22:38.
34 Catechism of the Catholic Church, 1420-21.
35 2 Corinthians 12:10.
36 Daily Reflections with Fulton Sheen, p.103.
37 https://www.looktohimandberadiant.com/2013/05/sheen-and-sacraments.html
38 Church Militant Field Manual.
39 John 12:24-25.
40 Saint Francis de Sales, *The Art of Loving God*, p. 97.
41 Sandy Clarke, "How the Power of Reading Holds the Key to Success", https://leaderonomics.com/personal/power-of-reading-and-success
42 Teresa of Avila, *The Interior Castle*, p. 99.
43 Thomas a' Kempis, *Imitation of Christ*, p. 64.
44 Fr Francis Fernandez, *In Conversation with God*, Vol. 4, p. 419.
45 Romans 8:28
46 John 3:30
47 Galatians 2:20
48 Catechism of the Catholic Church, paragraph 311.
49 Pope John Paul II, *Salvifici Dolores*.
50 Catechism of the Catholic Church, paragraph 312.
51 Luke 17:5
52 Oxford Dictionary online.
53 Fr. Jacques Philippe, *In the School of the Holy Spirit*, p. 19.
54 Dr. Michael Scherschight, School of Faith Daily Rosary Reflection.
55 St. Arnold Janssen.
56 Fr. Jacques Philippe, libertad interior, p. 47.
57 Santa Elizabeth Ann Seton

58 CCC, 1504-5.

59 Romans 15:13

60 Fr. Jean Baptiste Saint-Jure, *Trustful Surrender to God's Providence*, p. 90.

61 St. Therese of Lisieux, *The Story is a Soul*, p. 122.

62 Romans 8:28

63 Father Don Dulindo Ruotolo, *Novena of Surrender to the Will of God*, 1882-1970.

64 Henry Dieterich, ed., *Through the Year with Fulton Sheen*, Ignatius Press, p. 108)

65 St. Therese of Lisieux, *The Story of a Soul*, p. 64.

66 Christine Valters Paintner, "12 Celtic Spiritual Practices that celebrate God in our world," *US Catholic.*

67 Ralph Martin, *The Fulfillment of All Desire*, p. 166.

68 Scott Galloway, "Humans Cannot Survive Alone" Medium, April 19, 2019.

69 Matthew Kelly, "The Six Kinds of Friends You Should Have in Your Life," dynamicctholic.com, November 27, 2018.

70 St Thomas Aquinas.

71 School of Love Daily Reflection.

72 Charles McKinney, "Faithlessness Is The Great Destroyer of Friendship," Feb 20, 2019

73 Cf M. Schmaus, *Dogmatic Theology*, II, p.503.

74 Pope Benedict XVI.

75 Matthew Kelly, *Rediscover the Saints.*

76 Matthew Kelly, *The Rhythm of Life.*

77 Edward C. Sellner, *Stories of the Celtic Soul Friends: Their Meaning for Today* (New York: Paulist Press, 2004), 4.

78 Russell W. Dalton, *Faith Journey Through Fantasy Lands: A Christian Dialogue with Harry Potter, Star Wars and the Lord of the Rings.* (Minneapolis: Augsburg Books, 2003), 8.

79 Ibid, 8.

80 Fr. Thomas Dubay, *The Fire Within*, p. 114.

81 If you want to see this experiment, simply Google, "IKEA Bullying Experiment."

82 John 14:13

83 John 1:1.

84 Bishop Robert Barron

85 Maximillian Kolbe, *Kolbe Writings,* 1079.

86 Dr Tod Warner, "Mystery, Manners, and the Rediscovery of Great Literature" May 20, 2019.

87 Frigga to Thor in *Avengers: End Game* movie

88 Matthew Kelly, *Building Better Families.*

89 Maximillian Kolbe, *Kolbe Writings*, 1127.

90 Saint Francis of Assisi.

91 Saint Thomas of Villanova.

92 Chip Gaines, "The Chip Chronicles" *Magnolia Journal*, p. 108.

93 Dialogue from Jack to Ally, *A Star is Born* movie, 2017.

94 The practice of First Fridays is focused upon Devotion to the Sacred Heart of Jesus.

95 Excerpt from the Legion of Mary Handbook: *"The Legion of Mary is an Association of Catholics who, with the sanction of the Church and under the powerful leadership of Mary Immaculate, Mediatrix of all Graces (who is fair as the moon, bright as the sun, and — to Satan and his legionaries — terrible as an army set in battle array), have formed themselves into a Legion for service in the warfare which is perpetually waged by the Church against the world and its evil powers. "The whole life of men, both individual and social, shows itself to be a struggle, and a dramatic one, between good and evil, between light and darkness." (Gaudium et Spes 13) The legionaries hope to render themselves worthy of their great heavenly Queen by their loyalty, their virtues, and their courage. The Legion of Mary is therefore organised on the model of an army, principally on that of the army of ancient Rome, the terminology of which is adopted also. But the army and the arms of legionaries of Mary are not of this world."*

96 St Louis de Montfort, *True Devotion to Mary*, p.1.

97 Maximilian Kolbe, *Kolbe Writings*, 1210.

98 Maximilian Kolbe, *Kolbe Writings*, 1322.

99 St. Louis De Montfort, *True Devotion to Mary*, p. 65

100 Maximilian Kolbe, *Kolbe Writings*, 1102.

101 Maximilian Kolbe, *Kolbe Writings*, 1277.

102 John, Chapter 19: 26-27

103 Pope St. John Paul II, *Mary: God's Yes to Man*, pp. 129-30.

104 St. Louis De Montfort, *True Devotion to Mary*, p.55.

105 Catholic Catechism of the Catholic Church, 2014.

106 CCC 2013.

107 St Therese of Lisieux

108 Catechism of the Catholic Church, paragraph 2015.